DRIVEN TO THE FIELD

THE AMERICAN SOUTH SERIES
Elizabeth R. Varon and Orville Vernon Burton, Editors

# Driven to the Field

*Sharecropping and Southern Literature*

DAVID A. DAVIS

UNIVERSITY OF VIRGINIA PRESS
*Charlottesville and London*

University of Virginia Press
© 2023 by the Rector and Visitors of the University of Virginia
All rights reserved
Printed in the United States of America on acid-free paper

*First published 2023*

9 8 7 6 5 4 3 2 1

Library of Congress Cataloging-in-Publication Data

Names: Davis, David A. (David Alexander), author.
Title: Driven to the field : sharecropping and Southern literature / David A. Davis.
Description: Charlottesville : University of Virginia Press, 2023. | Series: The American South series | Includes bibliographical references and index.
Identifiers: LCCN 2022025005 (print) | LCCN 2022025006 (ebook) | ISBN 9780813948645 (hardcover) | ISBN 9780813948652 (paperback) | ISBN 9780813948669 (ebook)
Subjects: LCSH: American literature—Southern States—History and criticism. | Literature and society—Southern States—History—19th century. | Literature and society—Southern States—History—20th century. | Sharecropping in literature. | African Americans in literature. | Race relations in literature. | Southern States—In literature. | Southern States—Historiography. | Sharecropping—Southern States—History. | Southern States—Economic conditions.
Classification: LCC PS261 D358 2023 (print) | LCC PS261 (ebook) | DDC 810.9/360975—dc23/eng/20221021
LC record available at https://lccn.loc.gov/2022025005
LC ebook record available at https://lccn.loc.gov/2022025006

*Cover image:* "Cotton sharecroppers. Greene County, Georgia. They produce little, sell little, buy little," Dorothea Lange (Library of Congress, Prints & Photographs Division, FSA/OWI Collection, LC-USF34-T01-017335-C)

*For Lucas and Ayden*

Just a herd of Negroes
Driven to the field,
Plowing, planting, hoeing,
To make the cotton yield.
—LANGSTON HUGHES, "SHARE-CROPPERS," 1935

## CONTENTS

Acknowledgments — xi

1. Sharecropping, Labor Exploitation, and Southern Literature — 1
2. Sharecropping, Reconstruction, and Postbellum Literature — 26
3. The New Slavery — 63
4. America's Number One Economic Problem — 98
5. The End of Sharecropping — 168
6. The Afterlife of Sharecropping — 213

Notes — 249
Bibliography — 287
Index — 309

→ ACKNOWLEDGMENTS ←

I would like to express my appreciation to the many friends, colleagues, and family members who have supported this project throughout its development.

I am grateful to have many friends within the vibrant academic community of southern studies. Among the many people who have encouraged and advised this project are William L. Andrews, Ted Atkinson, Michael Bibler, Gina Caison, Kate Cochran, Andy Crank, Pardis Dabashi, Sarah Gleeson-White, Trudier Harris, Lisa Hinrichsen, Fred Hobson, Sharon Holland, Minrose Gwin, Robert Jackson, Michael Kreyling, Barbara Ladd, Jennie Lightweis-Goff, Peter Lurie, John T. Matthews, Molly McGehee, Jarvis McInnis, Monica Miller, Tara Powell, and Jay Watson.

My colleagues at Mercer University have been a consistent pleasure and delight. I appreciate the support of Scott Davis, Jeff Denny, Penny Elkins, Chester Fontenot, Jonathan Glance, Anita Gustafson, Elizabeth Harper, Carmen Hicks, Gordon Johnston, Adam Kiefer, Kathy Kloepper, Cameron Kunzelman, Lake Lambert, James D. May, Mary Alice Morgan, Chelsea Rathburn, Gary Richardson, Andy Silver, Anya Silver, Deneen Senasi, Bobbie Shipley, and my colleagues in the Spencer K. King, Jr., Center for Southern Studies, Sarah Gardner and Doug Thompson. I also appreciate the work of Eric Brandt at University of Virginia Press, and I am grateful to Andy Edwards, Tammy Rastoder, and Bob Ellis for their assistance in producing this book. I am also thankful to Vernon Burton and Elizabeth Varon for including this book in their series.

A portion of chapter 3 appeared as "Faulkner's Stores: Microfinance and Economic Power in the Postbellum South" in *Faulkner and Money*, edited by Jay Watson and James G. Thomas Jr. The material is reprinted with permission of University Press of Mississippi.

    My family has been my greatest source of support in all ways and at all times. My gratitude will never be sufficient for my mother, Linda Smith, and my mother-in-law, Marilyn Margolis. All of my love goes to my sons, Lucas and Ayden, and my wife, Kris.

DRIVEN TO THE FIELD

→ 1 ←

# Sharecropping, Labor Exploitation, and Southern Literature

Two of the most important novels in southern literature, *Absalom, Absalom!* and *Gone with the Wind*, were published in 1936. Both books depict the rise and fall of plantation slavery, the Civil War's devastation, and the difficult process of Reconstruction. Both books are famous and notorious for the ways that they imagine the nineteenth-century South from their twentieth-century vantage points, romanticizing some elements of the past, revising others, and blatantly ignoring a few. Both books have generated cultlike followings, have become synecdoche for the complicated past they depict, and have been labeled "Great American Novels."[1] Both books reimagine the history of slavery in America, privileging the slave owners' perspectives, and their depictions of slavery have aroused considerable critical conversation.[2] The novels, however, are also interesting for the system of labor that they portray less clearly. Within the historical sweep of each novel, the end of slavery transitions into the emergence of sharecropping, the labor paradigm that dominated southern cash crop production from the end of the Civil War to the beginning of the civil rights movement, yet sharecropping plays only a minor role in the books. This is not an omission or oversight on the part of Faulkner or Mitchell. It is, instead, a result of the pervasive ideology of labor exploitation that perpetuated sharecropping in the South.

Sharecropping plays an important yet nearly invisible role in *Absalom, Absalom!* After the war, Thomas Sutpen returns to his plantation in Mississippi intending to rebuild, but the war's toll has been too great. Like all southern planters, he has lost his slaves, which represented an enormous percentage of his capital, and although his land has not been confiscated and redistributed, much of it is taken to pay taxes, reducing his plantation from Sutpen's Hundred to Sutpen's One, at least according to Quentin and Shreve's reconstructions of the story. They imagine Sutpen tending a store from which he sells cheap goods at inflated prices to the sharecroppers who work on what remains of his plantation. In the context of sharecropping, the store has an immense significance, which is not fully explained in the text. It signifies that Sutpen has transitioned from a slave owner into a landlord-merchant, the incarnation of plantation hegemony in the post-slavery South. Landlord-merchants contracted with laborers, allotting them plots of land to farm and placing a lien on the anticipated crop. From the store, the merchant provided furnish—tools, animals, seed, fertilizer, food, and other goods—on credit at a high rate of interest. At settlement time, after the crop is harvested and sold, the landlord-merchant takes most of the proceeds and the cost of furnish, plus interest, which often exceeded the laborer's entire profit. Sutpen's store, thus, replaces his plantation house as the seat of his power and authority, signaling a shift from the consolidated nearly absolute power of a slave owner to the complicated and fluid, yet highly coercive, authority of a landlord. In the context of sharecropping, the store also indicates that Sutpen, who once violated social norms by working alongside his slaves, has, much like the Tidewater planter in Virginia who inspired his design, become entirely dependent upon the labor of others. The closest the novel comes to discussing the power dynamics of sharecropping directly, however, is to mention that Charles Etienne St. Valery Bon, after marrying a dark Black woman, "farmed on shares a portion of the Sutpen plantation."[3]

*Gone With the Wind* also represents sharecropping obliquely. The book includes long, detailed accounts of postbellum politics and economics in Georgia, but it does not say anything specifically about sharecropping, in spite of Scarlett O'Hara's obsession with rebuilding Tara, her family's plantation, after the Civil War. Mitchell dwells at length on the taxes levied on the plantation, Scarlett's obsessive scheming to save the plantation, and her venture into a sawmill business operated with convict labor to subsidize the plantation. This focus on convict labor is in itself a curious point because the novel that romanticizes the conditions of slavery exposes the inhumane treatment of inmates in the South's postbellum penal system, which was still a highly controversial issue in the 1930s. Yet the book completely obscures the development of sharecropping even as it would have been used at Tara itself. Scarlett and Rhett are married in 1868, by which time Robert Brooks contends in *The Agrarian Revolution in Georgia, 1865–1912* (1971) that wage labor had been largely abandoned in the Georgia Piedmont and share arrangements had become the norm. Scarlett moves to Atlanta, becoming an absentee landlord, and on a visit back to Tara, her manager, Will Benteen, tells her, "Tara's the best farm in the County, thanks to you and me, Scarlett, but it's a two-mule farm, not a plantation."[4] This is the most overt comment in the book about the plantation's transition, and it suggests that Tara has been divided into sharecropping allotments, although the book is deliberately vague on this point. Ironically, Gerald O'Hara came to America because he killed "an English absentee landlord's rent agent" in Ireland, and his daughter becomes an absentee landlord herself.[5]

Why would two novels published in 1936 that depict southern plantations during the transition from slavery to sharecropping downplay the emergence of sharecropping? Raising this question leads to another good question. Considering the amount of scholarly attention devoted to the South in general and slavery in particular, why have scholars paid so little attention to sharecropping? Slavery existed in America from 1619 to 1866, but the era of cotton plantation slavery—the mythical Old South—lasted from roughly 1800, after the cotton gin came into production, to 1865, when slaves were emancipated. Sharecropping, the exploitative labor paradigm that replaced slavery, dominated the agricultural means of production in the South from Emancipation until after World War II, much longer than slavery, and forms of exploitive labor related to sharecropping still exist in southern agriculture. Along with segregation, lynching, single-party politics, and religious fundamentalism, sharecropping was one of the South's major social problems, and understanding the South as a regional construct requires understanding the social, political, economic, and cultural significance of sharecropping. One could speculate that Faulkner and Mitchell did not delve into the specifics of sharecropping because they would have been blatantly obvious to a reader in 1936, when sharecropping was widely practiced. Perhaps a reader, at least a southern reader, then would have immediately recognized the meaning of Sutpen's store without needing to have the contractual obligations of a crop lien explained. Maybe a reader in 1936 would have sensed the fundamental irony that the O'Hara family has progressed from tenant farmers in Ireland to absentee landlords in Georgia.

It is possible that in 1936 Faulkner and Mitchell, and the vast majority of southerners plus most Americans, would have been inculcated in the ideology of sharecropping. More contemporary readers and critics continue to overlook the significance of sharecropping.

Sharecropping waned in the latter half of the twentieth century as machines obviated the need for labor-intensive agricultural practices, but the social residue of sharecropping developed into other problems involving migrant labor, federal housing projects, segregation, the war on drugs, the academic achievement gap, and a host of other issues. By losing sight of sharecropping as a system of exploitative labor that defined the issues of race, regionalism, and cotton production for nearly a hundred years, a crucial link to understanding both the immensity of sharecropping as a social problem in itself and its continued resonance in contemporary America may be lost. Many of the issues of race and poverty in contemporary America can be traced to sharecropping, so understanding the history and dynamics of the system is vital to understanding modern America. This book focuses on sharecropping as an exploitative system of agricultural labor that was thoroughly imbricated with an elaborate ideological power structure and forms of cultural production in the South. Sharecropping defined southern culture for nearly a century.

The ideology of sharecropping rested on a complicated nexus of manufactured mutual dependency. Landowners depended on exploited labor to harvest cotton and other commodity crops, a circumstance that Emancipation did not change. To make laborers dependent on producing a crop, landowners developed a system of social, political, economic, and cultural controls that limited their mobility, forced them into debt, restricted their political agency, impeded their access to education, and sanctioned terroristic violence against them. While laborers had limited rights in this system of exploitation, they had some means of resistance and, unlike slaves, they owned their own bodies and their families could not be divided against their will, which was a categorical difference between slavery and sharecropping. Yet the practical difference between slavery and sharecropping was less great than one might want to imagine. In *Fictions of Labor* (1997), Richard Godden teases out the issue in *Absalom, Absalom!*, which he calls, "a novel of dependency both as a fact of labor and as a consequent mental fact for the owning class."[6] One of the few critics to analyze the role that sharecropping plays in the novel, Godden identifies a dynamic of dependency in

*Absalom, Absalom!* that runs through dozens of other novels and, indeed, through the foundations of southern culture. Many southerners on both sides of the labor equation fundamentally believed in the right to control and exploit labor and in rigid socioeconomic hierarchies of race and class.

In the 1930s, as the Great Depression wore on, sharecropping became a major economic crisis and the focus of federal programs and studies. In 1936, the same year that *Absalom, Absalom!* and *Gone with the Wind* were published, T. J. Woofter published *Landlord and Tenant on the Cotton Plantation*, a study of southern poverty commissioned by the Works Progress Administration to analyze the dynamics of sharecropping, which he describes as "based on an exploitive culture of a money crop with ignorant labor working under a paternalistic system."[7] His study uses exhaustive statistical data drawn from censuses and government records to document the extent of southern poverty, the effects of the Agricultural Adjustment Act on the South, and the persistent barriers that impeded government intervention, and it offers suggestions for constructive measures to ameliorate these problems. In the same year, Howard Odum published *Southern Regions of the United States*, an equally exhaustive catalog of the region's resources designed to support regional planning initiatives to combat the persistent economic problems sharecropping caused.[8] Meanwhile, Farm Security Administration photographs of destitute southerners, alongside images of long soup kitchen lines and unemployed factory workers in northern cities, proliferated in American print media, making the problem of sharecropping a prominent issue in the national consciousness in the 1930s.[9] One could reasonably conclude that most Americans—policymakers, scholars, and ordinary readers—were well aware of sharecropping as an obvious problem in the South with deleterious effects for the entire nation. Americans likely brought this awareness to their reading of southern literature, so Faulkner and Mitchell may not have needed to explain the nuances of sharecropping in their novels in 1936.

The relationships among the material history of sharecropping, the pervasive ideology of labor exploitation, and southern literature are complex and dynamic. During the hundred years that sharecropping dominated the South's labor paradigm, southern writers depicted a region rebuilding from the Civil War, wrestling with modernization, often different from and sometimes hostile toward the mainstream United States, and committed to racial segregation. While labor exploitation was, and still is, common across the nation—from workers in steel mills in Pennsylvania to migrant farm workers in California—sharecropping was a distinctive, pervasive, and prevalent form of exploitation predominantly endemic to the South. Sharecropping extended the transition from slavery to wage labor in the South, delayed the region's economic and social development, and greatly influenced the region's art, music, and literature. One of the best means to understand the South's culture between the Civil War and the civil rights movement is to read southern literature in context with economic history, which reveals the subtle, powerful forces of labor exploitation.

Sharecropping unavoidably figures, both implicitly and explicitly, in many works of southern literature. In *Absalom, Absalom!* and *Gone with the Wind*, its presence is obscured, which raises critical questions about how it operates in the background of the text, what it reveals about the characters' interactions, and what the authors and audience may have understood intuitively about labor exploitation. In many other works, however, sharecropping plays a primary role in the narrative tension, and it represents the region's labor structure, race and class hierarchy, social tensions, financial system, political dynamics, commodity production, education gap, and the multifarious interrelations among all these institutions. The culture of cotton production and labor exploitation defined the South, from the first crops of Sea Island cotton harvested along the Georgia and South Carolina coast in the 1780s to the acres of genetically modified cotton still harvested with enormous combines across the southeastern United States. In between, the region expanded its land by expelling Native Americans, instituted a political economy based on slavery, lost a brutal civil war, developed a system of sharecropping, witnessed the effects of mechanization and world wars, and experienced a transformative movement for civil rights. The literature of sharecropping illustrates an important period in the South's history and culture that explains the region's commitment to labor exploitation, its regional distinctiveness, and its persistent social problems.

Sharecropping endured for a century; it involved millions of laborers; it defined the South's economic system; it determined the region's political, racial, and social structure; it influenced every element of the South's culture; and it inspired dozens of works of literature. Surprisingly, however, scholars of southern literature and culture rarely discuss sharecropping or its effects. Consider, for example, the entries on "plantation" and "labor" in *Keywords for Southern Studies* (2016). In the entry for "plantation," Matthew

Pratt Guterl focuses primarily on the antebellum incarnation of the plantation and its continued, highly problematic, resonance in US culture as a synecdoche for the South.[10] He discusses the representation of plantations in the 1930s in *Absalom, Absalom!*, *Gone with the Wind*, and the photographs of Dorothea Lange, but his point of reference is slavery, and his attempts to complicate the term appeal to yeoman farmers, globalization, and legacies of violence. He does not mention the century-long history of sharecropping plantations that span the slow transition from slavery to the civil rights movement. Ted Atkinson's entry on "labor" does mention sharecropping, but he focuses more extensively on industrialization and labor activism, and he uses *River of Earth* (1940), James Still's novel about coal mining in Appalachia, as an illustration of labor issues in the South.[11] Both of these entries would be appropriate locations to discuss sharecropping as a persistent form of agricultural labor exploitation in southern culture and to assess the enormous impact of sharecropping on the region's economic, political, and intellectual history.

These entries are part of a much broader pattern of scholarly works about the South that minimize the role of sharecropping in the region's culture. Many of the most influential works of the theoretically informed approach known as the New Southern Studies, for example, also sidestep the significance of sharecropping, even when analyzing works that illustrate the system. When discussing novels that depict the emergence of sharecropping in her insightful work *Our South* (2010), Jennifer Rae Greeson concentrates on how the works represent the Reconstruction era as a form of domestic imperialism after the Civil War that parallels the development of imperialism in US foreign policy. In *Narrative Forms of Southern Community* (1999), Scott Romine analyzes William Alexander Percy's memoir *Lanterns on the Levee* (1941), which depicts the life of a plantation landowner in the Mississippi Delta. Romine conflates sharecropping and segregation with paternalism. He writes, "The intolerable nature of exploitation—in some ways, as intolerable for the exploiter as for the exploited—necessitated that brute economic necessity be translated into a rhetoric of interracial dependence and an image of a social order hierarchically divided by innate differences, yet bound together by common manners, codes, and mutual responsibilities."[12] Although he raises the issue of exploitation, he focuses primarily on the rhetorical practices of paternalism that he argues Percy uses to mask his complicity in the system. Leigh Anne Duck also raises the issue of sharecropping in *The Nation's Region* (2009), but she aligns it with Depression-era anxieties about fascism and collectivism. She asserts that some intellectuals found it "difficult to comprehend how the circumstances of southern laborers could exist in a modern nation," which made some liberals concerned about the potential for fascism in the South, while conservatives worried that New Deal social policies would lead to socialism.[13] These are insightful points, but they avoid many of the deeper issues about sharecropping as a problematic ideological system in its own right that impeded social progress in the US.

The precedent for avoiding examination of sharecropping extends back to the foundational works of southern literary studies. Louis Rubin, the most influential scholar of southern literature, rarely mentioned economic issues in his studies of southern writers. The connective theme in his work *A Gallery of Southerners* (1982), for example, is "the relationship of the literary work to the community, or more than that, the link between the writer, in and through the work, and the community."[14] Rubin's work inspired a generation of scholars who focused on issues such as community, tradition, and sense of place in southern literary studies. Lewis Simpson established another common theme in southern literary studies, namely, the resonance of the antebellum South in modern southern literature. In *The Fable of the Southern Writer* (1994), he states, "it is today a little startling to realize that although the actual slave society of the South ended almost a century and a half ago, the quest for the meaning of the society of the antebellum South has not ended," and he focuses most of his work on how writers of the twentieth century depict the antebellum period.[15] He does not turn his attention, however, to the ways in which sharecropping extends the culture of labor exploitation into the twentieth century. Rubin and Simpson share a tendency with many other scholars of their generation to disregard the presence of sharecroppers altogether and instead offer a version of southern culture based on small, independent farms.

The persistent, problematic fixation on so-called yeoman farmers in southern literary studies stems from the influence of the Nashville Agrarians.[16] John Crowe Ransom, Allen Tate, Donald Davidson, and Robert Penn Warren collaborated with some other southern intellectuals to publish a collection of essays that defended their notion of southern culture from the inevitable processes of modernization that were under way in the 1920s. The collection, *I'll Take My Stand* (1930), articulated a fundamentally flawed vision of the South as "an agrarian society . . . in which agriculture is the leading vocation, whether for wealth, for pleasure, or for prestige—a form of labor that is pursue with intelligence and leisure, and that becomes the model to which the other forms approach as they may."[17] Their idyllic notion of an agrarian society ignores the fact that millions of southern farmers did not own their own land. In many areas, in fact, the vast majority of farmers were sharecroppers, so the agrarian vision was a myth. Yet, because several of the contributors went on to become influential critics and writers, their vision of the white, rural South gained cultural currency, producing an inaccurate representation of the region's culture. Michael Kreyling accuses "the Agrarians of produc[ing] that South in the same way that all historically indigenous social elites produce ideological realities: out of strategies for seizing and retaining power (cultural, political, sexual, economic, and so on)."[18] Many of the intellectuals affiliated with the agrarian movement were also aligned with conservative politics, so Kreyling's accusation suggests that their depiction of the South served an ideological purpose that reifies white ruralism. Ted Ownby, similarly, observes that "southerners with power or close to those in power usually talked and wrote about farming, not tenancy and not sharecropping," and he calls *I'll Take My Stand* "the clearest restatement of traditional definitions of a South without poverty."[19] As a result of the agrarians' influence, southern studies continues to focus attention away from persistent issues of poverty and labor and to concentrate more often on mythical versions of the past than historically informed representations of the present.

Studies of sharecropping, meanwhile, have been largely limited to agricultural history and economic history. Gibert Fite's *Cotton Fields No More: Southern Agriculture, 1865–1980* (1984) offers the first comprehensive study of sharecropping, labor, and poverty in southern agriculture, and it thoroughly debunks the vision of the South offered by the Agrarians. Pete Daniel expands on Fite's work in *Breaking the Land: The Transformation of Cotton, Tobacco, and Rice Cultures since 1880* (1985). His book offers insights into the effects of government policy, technological developments, and market fluctuations on southern agriculture. In *The Cotton Plantation South since the Civil War* (1998), Charles Aiken charts the continuity of plantation agriculture after Emancipation. He argues that the plantation continued to be the foundational element of the southern economy after slavery ended and that it evolved to continue producing commodity crops. He makes the connection between the end of slavery and the emergence of sharecropping clear, and he explains that what the Agrarians mistook for a culture of small, independent farms was mostly a fragmented plantation system. Edward Royce dilates on the transition between slavery and sharecropping in *The Origins of Southern Sharecropping* (1993), demonstrating that what was initially an expedient system based on necessity developed quickly into a form of economic power and control. Sven Beckert's extensive study *Empire of Cotton: A Global History* (2014) demonstrates the globalized significance of commodity cotton and the textile industry as an economic and political force. His book explains that cotton powered the Industrial Revolution and influenced foreign policy and patterns of colonialization around the world, and it places southern laborers, who are usually marginalized, at the center of world history.

Economic histories have explored the function of sharecropping as a system of labor. In *The Roots of Black Poverty* (1978), Jay Mandle explains how the transition to sharecropping ensnared former slaves into an exploitative system of labor that prevented them from acquiring property and attaining wealth. He discusses the relationship between sharecropping and the laws known as black codes that prevented Black workers from competing fairly in the labor market, and he argues that the combination of labor-intensive agriculture and market manipulation is responsible for generational poverty among African Americans in the South. Roger Ransom and Richard Sutch's pathbreaking cliometric study of postbellum cotton markets *One Kind of Freedom* (1977) elucidates the nuances of microfinance used to coerce labor from sharecroppers. Landowners and merchants required sharecroppers to use their unharvested crops as collateral for furnish to produce the crops. Furnish includes all of the agricultural supplies, such as seeds and fertilizer, necessary to raise the crop, plus any tools or animals rented for the crop cycle, and all living expenses for the family, including clothing, food, and medicine. Their book explains that the crop lien transferred the risk for producing a crop to the laborers and allowed landowners to use debt to manipulate laborers by locking them into a planting cycle and limiting their ability to compete in an open market. *Old South, New South* (1997) by Gavin Wright argues that the South after the Civil War effectively operated on an alternate system of capital than the US. His analysis illustrates how sharecropping matured from an expedient transitional solution into an economic praxis that elevated the value of land and diminished the value of labor. This system limited investment in the South's infrastructure, deterred immigration into the region, delayed industrial growth, and insulated southerners from the national labor market until New Deal interventions opened the South to development. These studies help us to understand how sharecropping worked as an economic paradigm, why it emerged, and why it eventually ended.

All of these empirical historical studies of sharecropping are useful, but we do not yet have a cultural study of sharecropping that examines how the system of labor influenced the region's sociocultural development and how the region's culture reinforced and resisted the system of labor. This omission is partly to blame for the gaping lacuna in southern literary criticism regarding sharecropping. Dozens of works of literature directly depicted sharecropping, and they represent the attitudes, beliefs, and experiences of people enmeshed in all levels of the system over more than a century. These works also clearly reflect the relationship between sharecropping and social, political, and economic changes taking place in the United States, such as Jim Crow, the Progressive Era, World War I, the Great Migration, the Great Depression, the New Deal, World War II, and the civil rights movement. In the same way that sharecropping led to a distinctive economic structure in the South, it led to a distinctive system of cultural practices that reflect the pervasiveness of poverty and labor exploitation in the region. Focusing on sharecropping also demonstrates the complicated relationship between race and labor after Emancipation because the ideology of sharecropping allowed for the exploitation of labor regardless of race. Studying the culture of sharecropping represented in works of literature reveals how the system effected the region's development, how it influenced the lives of southerners, and how the region slowly progressed from slavery to the civil rights movement.

Sharecropping emerged out of a highly volatile socioeconomic environment, but it was based on some influential labor precedents. Before Emancipation, southerners often rented slaves on fixed contracts, paying a slave's owner for the slave's labor over a period of time, frequently for the duration of a crop cycle. While it is true that the majority of antebellum white southerners did not own slaves, many who did not own slaves rented them, so the practice of contract labor was a well-established precedent.[20] Southerners also were not the first people to practice sharecropping. Many semifeudal societies, from ancient Rome to contemporary India, compensate agricultural laborers with a share of the harvest, and these societies often develop paternalistic social hierarchies that impede mobility.[21] The emergence of sharecropping in the South, thus, was not unprecedented; neither was it intentional. Immediately after Emancipation, in fact, many former slaves worked on wage contracts often brokered by the Freedmen's Bureau, but in the cash-poor region, these arrangements quickly shifted from cash remuneration to commodity shares. Sharecropping developed organically across the region as a functional solution to a serious financial crisis, and it persisted because it replicated the hierarchal conditions of slavery.

The emergence of sharecropping was not inevitable.[22] At the end of the Civil War, some congressional Republicans advocated redistributing confiscated land to former slaves, which would have created thousands of farms under Black ownership and economically empowered African Americans in the first generation after slavery. But President Andrew Johnson followed through with Abraham Lincoln's plan to grant amnesty to former Confederates "with restoration of all rights of property, except as to slaves" in exchange for swearing an oath of allegiance to the United States.[23] The thrust of this order was to convert slave owners into landowners in need of labor and to convert slaves into laborers without resources. With the passage of the Thirteenth Amendment to the Constitution, the South lost the majority of its capital—the money invested in slaves—which left the entire region, whose infrastructure and financial system had been ruined by war, in a state of financial crisis with few assets other than land and a crop in danger of spoilage.

Immediately after the war, southerners employed different methods to fill the labor vacuum. One approach was to import a labor force, as French and British planters had done after their nations abolished slavery earlier in the nineteenth century, and "southern planters replicated efforts made in the Caribbean to augment the region's labor force through immigration, although their attempts were not as successful as those in the West Indies."[24] Southern states encouraged immigration and attempted to recruit Chinese laborers and European peasants, but the programs were expensive and not productive enough to make an impact. The most viable labor response and the approach sanctioned by the federal government through the Freedmen's Bureau was the employment of former slaves as wage laborers working for pay in the fields. This method, however, created several problems for both landowners and laborers. Landowners rarely had the liquid capital available to fund a payroll, and they worried about the reliable availability of workers during the time-sensitive and labor-intensive harvests. Laborers, meanwhile, resented working on gangs under an overseer exactly as they had in slavery, and they received no payment when the crop was laid by, leaving them destitute. With wage labor experiments failing, farms quickly turned to sharecropping contracts. "By 1868," Edward Royce writes in *The Origins of Southern Sharecropping*, "sharecropping was well on its way to becoming the principal replacement for slavery and the dominant economic arrangement in postbellum agriculture."[25]

Yet many former slaves, eager to achieve tangible freedom, aspired to own land, which would allow them to become productive, independent farmers and unrestrained economic agents. In a few instances, Black people were able to purchase small farms, using the depressed real estate values of Reconstruction to their advantage, but these were exceptional cases. More often, Blacks in the immediate aftermath of slavery lacked the resources to buy land, and whites refused to sell land even to Black people who did have money or collateral, which, as Leon Litwack explains in *Been in the Storm So Long* (1979), contributed to the development of sharecropping. "Unable to acquire ownership of land," he writes, "whether because he lacked funds or because local custom barred him, the Black laborer increasingly resolved on an alternative that would provide him with the feeling if not the status of a family farmer. He became a sharecropper."[26] In a typical sharecropping contract, a family worked as a unit on a specific plot of land, living separate from other laboring families and working outside the direct supervision of an overseer. In these respects, sharecropping families imitated the conditions of small farmers, but they depended upon the landowners for plots of land, homes, food, clothing, medicine, seed, fertilizer, tools, mules, and virtually every other material necessity.

Creating a system of manufactured dependency was crucial for landowners because it gave them control over laborers. Under slavery, a master owned a slave's body outright and had unmitigated control over the body's labor, but after Emancipation, controlling a labor force required more subtle forms of coercion. Wages, beyond being somewhat problematic in the fractured economic environment during Reconstruction, allowed the workers to decide when and where they would or would not work on a daily basis. A sharecropping contract, however, tied the laborers to a specific plot for the duration of a harvest cycle, investing months of their labor into the crop and deferring their payment until after the crop had been sold at market, which Gerald David Jaynes calls "the long pay."[27] The contract system made the landowners responsible for their laborers' welfare, at least insofar as it impacted the production of the crop, and this responsibility extended the legitimating ideology of paternalism that allowed slave owners to own and exploit human beings, mimicking for landowners the sense of domination of slaveholding.[28] Sharecropping, thus, allowed former slaves to act out a version of freedom with simulated economic agency, and it simultaneously allowed landowners to recreate a version of slavery with economic based social controls. This middle-ground dynamic between agency and exploitation best explains the reasons for sharecropping's emergence and for its persistence.[29]

The sharecropping dynamic was an inherently asymmetrical power relationship that allowed the landowner to exploit the laborer. This relationship was formalized in contracts that stipulated the responsibilities of both parties and the terms of the laborers' compensation. In most contracts, the laborer agreed to raise a specific crop on a plot of land from planting to harvest, and the landowner agreed to compensate the laborer in necessary agricultural material and living provisions during the crop cycle and a share of the proceeds from the crop. During the tenure of the Freedmen's Bureau, some landowners filed elaborate, formal contracts that specified the exact responsibilities of each part, including stipulating food provided for laborers, defining working hours, and detailing division of the crop.[30] Notably, to indicate the inequality of the contracts, the laborers often signed with an X, meaning that they were illiterate and relatively unable to participate in the formulation of responsibilities, so the contracts protected the landowners more than they protected the laborers. Over time, written contracts gave way to oral agreements that left the laborers with virtually no legally enforceable protections. Contracts varied according to the degree of support the landowner provided to the laborer. Laborers who provided only their own work and were paid with a fraction, usually one-fourth, of the crop were sharecroppers; laborers who provided some of their own materials, particularly a mule, and were paid with a larger percentage of the crop were tenants; and laborers who provided all of their own materials and provisions, paid rent for the use of the land, and kept all of the proceeds of the crop were renters. The most abject laborers were wage laborers, who worked without provisions during long stretches of the crop cycle. Each of these arrangements involved varying degrees of exploitation, and they were all part of the system of labor dependency.

Within a few years of Emancipation, the Freedmen's Bureau waned, and southern states passed laws that codified sharecropping contracts, enacting rules that defined issues of race, labor, and debt. The most powerful legal device in the sharecropping contract itself was the crop lien, a law that "stipulated that anyone who provided supplies, or money to purchase supplies, necessary to produce a crop received a lien on that crop when gathered."[31] By 1867, each southern state passed a crop lien law, and southern states allowed the practice of peonage, forcing a laborer to work until the balance of a crop advance is fully satisfied, which allowed many landowners to manipulate accounts and force laborers into involuntary servitude.[32] Southern states also passed laws known as black codes that further limited laborers' rights. These laws enforced labor contracts and plantation discipline by allowing landowners to punish laborers, prevented landowners from competing over laborers by forbidding enticement, prevented laborers under contract from negotiating contracts with other potential employers under "false pretenses," prohibited laborers from selling crops without the mediation of the landowner, and made it illegal for a person to be without a labor contract after January 1. This last law was a vagrancy statute, a notorious law with precedents in European feudalism that ensured a large labor pool by forbidding laborers from withdrawing themselves from entering a contract. The punishment for breaking these laws ranged from onerous fines to sentences of hard labor.[33] These laws institutionalized and ossified the system of sharecropping so that it was the standard labor arrangement across the South.

These laws and contracts indicate that the plantation system quickly regenerated in the South after Emancipation. The region remained the world's largest producer of cotton, although other international competitors developed during the Civil War, and its economic fortunes were directly tied to cotton and a small number of other commodity crops, including tobacco, rice, and sugar cane. Small farms dotted the landscape, but most of these operated as small-scale plantations, producing commodity cash crops and small amounts of subsistence crops, such as corn and vegetables, and employing small numbers of sharecroppers and tenants. The region's entire financial structure of banks, merchants, and services, moreover, was invested in and responsive to agricultural markets. All of these enterprises were utterly dependent on the international trading price of cotton and other commodity crops, which made the financial system inherently unstable, and the relative lack of economic diversification made the region highly vulnerable to a downturn when the prices of agricultural commodities fell. Within this system, with its rigid institutionalized structures and its unstable economic foundation, social mobility for laborers was difficult if not impossible.[34] In *Old South, New South,* Gavin Wright states, "even though the South moved toward the American mainstream in its economic behavior [after the Civil War], it emerged in the 1870s as a low-wage region in a high-wage country, a consideration that shaped its economic future for another century."[35] The region's economy depended upon commodities, which, in turn, depended upon easily exploitable labor; thus, the region's hegemonic structure had little incentive to change.

In fact, sharecropping expanded in the decades after the Civil War, both when the price of commodities rose and when it fell. Charles Aiken documents in *The Plantation South since the Civil War* that more than one million tenant laborers worked in the South in 1880, during a period when international commodity prices were relatively stable. Just before the spread of the boll weevil, in 1910, the first time the agricultural census distinguished among sharecroppers and tenant farmers, 2.4 million tenant farmers worked in the South, of whom more than 1.4 million worked on shares. In 1930, at the beginning of the Great Depression, the number of tenant farmers peaked at more than 2.6 million, although the census that year did not distinguish among classes of tenants. The numbers of tenants trailed off after World War II and tractors and mechanical cotton pickers obviated the need for a massive labor force, but as late as 1960 three-quarters of a million people were tenant farmers in the South.[36] The system was pervasive in the South, it involved a large segment of the nation's African American population with ever increasing numbers of the South's poor white population, especially during the Great Depression, and it disproportionately influenced the nation's political and economic development into the twentieth century.

Writing in 1951, anthropologist Morton Rubin described a southern plantation as a "total sociocultural system located in ecological space."[37] The southern economy depended upon farms large and small that produced commodity crops, and the entire sociocultural system of the region revolved around labor-intensive agriculture, so the object of the South as a hegemonic entity was to put hands on hoes, mules in fields, and croppers in cotton. The history, politics, and economics of sharecropping have been studied, but as a total sociocultural system, sharecropping also produced a distinctive ideology and culture, which is represented in the region's intellectual history, religion, art, music, and literature. The key issue in this book is the sharecropping imaginary, how writers represented the system in text. Because sharecropping was the nexus of a vast system of labor exploitation that spanned the progressive era in American political ideology and the emergence of modernism in American literature, it creates some unique forms of cultural tension within the nation, often antagonizing the American narrative of freedom and individualism. Sharecropping was not slavery nor was it freedom; it was exploitative dependency.

Sharecropping is different from both slavery and wage labor. In the economic history of the US South, it was an extended transition between the systems, but that does not mean that sharecropping was a necessary step in economic development. More likely, it hampered and delayed economic development in the region, but its ideological affinity with slavery made it perversely more attractive to the deposed planter class in the South than wage-labor capitalism. In sharecropping, the landowners retained both the means and production and the commodities produced, and they exerted nearly complete control over the laborers, more control than even the most exploitive versions of wage labor. Yet, as Jay Mandle explains, "However effective the denial of alternative employment opportunities was in binding Blacks to the estates, this mechanism did not provide planters with the same degree of authority which slavery had. Thus, although there was continuity, there was also change, and in some important ways the post-bellum plantation economy was a good deal weaker that the slave system of the old South."[38] Sharecropping differed from wage labor, but it was more compatible with capitalism than slavery.

Unlike sharecropping, slavery is an ontological state of being. In *Slavery and Social Death* (1982), Orlando Patterson argues that slaves are stripped of their individual identity and their social and familial bonds, held in almost total powerlessness by their masters, and subject to arbitrary physical and psychological violence. While slaves' bodies and labor belong to their masters, sharecroppers are workers whose bodies belong to themselves, who have some right to social and familial relationships, and who receive some degree of compensation for the work that they perform. Yet sharecroppers had significantly less power than the landowners for whom they worked, were often subject to violence, and were often not fully or fairly compensated for their labor. For these reasons, Marxist historians would likely note many points of correspondence between sharecropping and feudalism. According to the Marxist theory of history, feudalism was an intermediate stage between slavery and capitalism. Under feudalism, serfs, who had limited rights, worked small-scale agricultural plots for landowning nobles, receiving only a portion of their harvest as compensation. The feudal mode of production replicated a caste system that restricted social mobility, and it involved an elaborate system of ideology that reinforced the notion of labor exploitation as a right of the privileged landowners.[39]

Exploitation is a fundamental characteristic that sharecropping shares with feudalism, and exploitation has been the chief focus of a branch of economic theory called analytical Marxism. The pivotal text of this field is John Roemer's *General Theory of Exploitation and Class* (1982), which argues that differential ownership of productive resources determines economic exploitation. Roemer asserts that "an agent is exploited when the amount of labor embodied in any bundle of goods he could receive, in a feasible distribution of society's net product, is less than the labor he expended."[40] This definition applies in a wide range of instances, but in the sharecropping system, it was crucial to maintaining class division because the landowners' class depended upon the laborers' exploitation. Sociologist Erik Olin Wright develops this principle into a formula for the material interdependence of people. A situation is exploitive when (1) the well-being of the exploiting category causally depends on the deprivations of the exploited; (2) this causal link is based on some process of exclusion, which results in (3) the appropriation of effort of the exploited by the exploited.[41] Sharecropping met both of these definitions: laborers were compensated with a share of the crop that did not approximate their labor, and the well-being of landowners depended upon the deprivation of sharecroppers, who were excluded from legal and political agency.

Sharecropping differs from slavery and from wage labor in both the forms and the results of exploitation. In *Analytical Marxism* (1994), Tom Mayer outlines the differences. Slaves are directly coerced into labor, and the output of coercion is the labor itself. In a feudal system, laborers are exploited through a combination of coercion and ideology, and the results of their exploitation are the landowners' share of their production. Wage laborers are exploited through the labor market, and the result is the difference between the labor expended and the wages earned.[42] As a feudal mode of production, sharecropping involves both direct and indirect means of labor control, using coercion in the form of legal controls, economic restriction, and occasional violence, and using ideology in the form of an elaborate set of social, cultural, and religious traditions and practices to maintain and perpetuate the exploitation of laborers.

Texts that depict sharecropping depict the means of coercion, the ideology of exploitation, and the material interdependency of landowners and laborers. These works often portray the operations of legal, economic, and violent means of domination, and scenes of laborers' frustration with forces beyond their control, of landowners exercising privilege, of settlements swindled, and of beatings and lynchings are common. Coercion is obvious, but the workings of ideology are often more subtle, represented in attitudes and opinions that appear to follow tradition or common sense, in religious worship that emphasizes otherworldliness, in political offices that enforce the landowners' privileges, and in cultural products, including the texts themselves, that replicate the dominant ideology. T. J. Woofter articulates the effects of this ideology in *Landlord and Tenant on the Cotton Plantation* (1936): "Fundamental to the understanding of the living habits of tenants is the realization that they exercise a relatively limited choice in determining these habits, and they have been supervised for so long that if they did have a freer choice they would not have the knowledge of other ways of living essential to change."[43] Ideology conditions the sharecroppers into accepting their coercion and submitting to their own exploitation, and it conditions the landowners into participating in the exploitation.

Sharecropping texts demonstrate the dynamic interplay of ideological forces in American culture. Conventionally, Marxist critics who theorized about ideology, such as Antonio Gramsci and Louis Althusser, describe ideology as the abstract tool of hegemonic control, but the representations of ideology in sharecropping literature demonstrate that its hegemony responds to a vast array of social conditions.[44] In the immediate wake of Emancipation, a clash of ideological forces emerged, and representations of sharecropping vacillated between idealized memories of slavery that served the purpose of the landowning class and scathing critiques of deposed planters that reinforced northern attitudes toward the defeated South. As Jim Crow laws embedded segregation into southern culture, sharecropping literature reflected the tension between racists who defended the exploitive status quo and African American writers who gave voice to the exploited. By the Great Depression, the southern economy declined, drawing millions of white southerners into sharecropping, and making it a social problem to be addressed on a national scale while pitting nationalist ideologies of social progress against regional ideologies of traditionalism. After World War II, machines displaced sharecroppers, eroding the landowners' ideological commitment to labor exploitation and shifting the source of tension from labor to race, culminating with the civil rights movement. The legacy of labor exploitation remains in the South, contributing to numerous social problems involving entrenched racism and generational poverty that persist in the wake of sharecropping.

As a means of coercing labor, sharecropping proved to be highly resilient. The system remained entrenched in the South for a century, during which time the United States industrialized and urbanized, while the South remained agricultural and rural. Sharecropping endured through the Gilded Age, the Progressive Era, and the Great Depression. It continued through wars of American imperialism, through two world wars, and into the Cold War. Economic forces, market fluctuations, record droughts, and the boll weevil only made it stronger. It persisted until mass-produced machines made mechanization more cost-effective than labor exploitation. Meanwhile, the pervasiveness of labor exploitation in the South deterred economic innovation and development, discouraged in-migration and investment into the region, and slowed intellectual and cultural development. Today, largely as a legacy of sharecropping, the South remains the nation's poorest, most violent, least healthy, least educated, and least progressive region.

This book traces the culture of sharecropping from Emancipation to the twenty-first century. By reading works of literature in their historical context, it explains how sharecropping emerged from the end of slavery, initially as an expedient solution to an economic challenge but quickly evolving into a durable power structure that exploited the labor of Blacks and poor whites to produce agricultural commodities. Sharecropping was the economic linchpin in the South's social structure for a century, and the region's political system, race relations, and cultural practices intersected with the practice. This book analyzes literary depictions of sharecropping to focus attention on the system and explain how it defined the culture of the South, revealing multiple genres of literature about sharecropping, such as cotton romances, agricultural uplift novels, proletarian sharecropper fiction, and sharecropper autobiographies. Many of these texts are important works of southern literature that have not been discussed in their appropriate context to explain how they reflect and interrogate the culture of sharecropping. Because southern literary scholarship has avoided discussing sharecropping, dozens of works that depict the system have been marginalized, and this book recovers many of these texts to reveal a substantially broader range of works that reflect the sharecropping imaginary. This book reveals how the South progressed from Emancipation to the civil rights movement, how sharecropping continues to influence southern culture, and why labor exploitation defines southern culture.

Chapter 2 analyzes the literature of the Reconstruction and postbellum period from Emancipation to the end of the nineteenth century to explain the economic and political factors that led to the emergence of sharecropping and how writers depicted that process of development. Novels by Albion Tourgée, John W. De Forest, and George Washington Cable portray the efforts of the Freedmen's Bureau to broker wage labor contracts for former slaves to work for landowners and how pressures from freedmen, who preferred autonomy, and landowners, who demanded control of the laborers, led to sharecropping initially as an expedient means for production as a response to economic crisis. As the sections reunified, a genre of reconciliation novels appeared, and these works, such as Thomas Nelson Page's *Red Rock* (1898) and John W. De Forest's *The Bloody Chasm* (1881), portray interregional marriages as a metaphor for reunification. In these works, marriage is an economic arrangement that signifies the nation's financial dependence on cotton production, and these reconciliation novels illustrate the emergence of the ideology of exploitation that undergirded sharecropping as a labor paradigm. Postbellum works of local color fiction illustrate that economic growth superseded concerns about equality and human rights in the aftermath of a war to end slavery. Local color works, such as Thomas Nelson Page's story "Marse Chan" (1887) and Joel Chandler Harris's story "Free Joe and the Rest of the World" (1887), revise the history of slavery by portraying it as a benevolent institution and make the case for sharecropping as a paternalist form of labor control. Charles Chesnutt's novel *The Colonel's Dream* (1905), meanwhile, depicts the powerful forces that trapped African American laborers in a system of economic exploitation reinforced by repressive laws known as black codes and racial violence. The literature of this period represents the ideological shift from abolition in the wake of

Emancipation to sharecropping as a culture of labor exploitation that began as an expedient response to economic pressures and rapidly ossified into an enduring system of power and control.

Works set between the turn of the twentieth century and the Great Depression depict sharecropping as a fixed and inescapable system of labor exploitation, which is the focus of chapter 3. Novels by William Faulkner, John Faulkner, and T. S. Stribling portray landowner-merchants who use crop lien contracts to manipulate laborers and acquire capital. Their novels indicate that landowner-merchants are also subject to determinative economic forces that stem from the agricultural commodity monoculture, and these forces conditioned them to extract labor and debt from their tenants. Several novels by African American writers, including W. E. B. Du Bois, Welbourne Kelley, George Washington Lee, and George Wylie Henderson, illustrate the experience of Black sharecroppers ensnared in the repressive network of debt and Jim Crow that severely limited their social, political, and economic agency. Novels by white writers, meanwhile, show white sharecroppers similarly trapped within coercive economic forces that impede their social mobility and prevent their ascent up the agricultural ladder from sharecropping to landowning. These books include *The Cabin in the Cotton* (1931) by Harry Harrison Kroll, *This Body the Earth* (1935) by Paul Green, and *Cotton* (1928) by Jack Bethea. Millions of sharecroppers left the South in an effort to escape the repressive economic structures and find new opportunities, but sharecropper migration novels by Harriette Arnow, William Attaway, Carl Offord, and John Steinbeck portray sharecroppers as being reluctant to leave their communities, usually departing by force. These texts also depict labor exploitation as inevitable because migrants escaping sharecropping face abuse in factories and farms in the North and the West, usually leading to tragic endings. All of these works indicate that sharecropping was an intractable social problem that made the region's socioeconomic system highly precarious and resistant to change.

During the Great Depression, southern sharecropping became a national issue, which President Roosevelt called "the nation's number one economic problem." While the entire country grappled with massive unemployment, sharecroppers captivated the nation's attention as signifiers for poverty. During the 1930s, several genres of sharecropping narrative emerged, each co-opting the representation of sharecroppers to serve an agenda, and chapter 4 analyzes these Depression-era sharecropper narratives. The federal government commissioned several liberal southern intellectuals, such as T. J. Woofter and Will W. Alexander, to write reports that documented the need for federal intervention in southern agriculture, and the government-sponsored propaganda film *The River* (1938) by Pare Lorentz reinforced public perceptions of federal policies. John Faulkner's novel *Men Working* (1941), however, satirizes government intervention, suggesting that government relief is merely a replacement for manufactured dependency. Several social scientists, including anthropologists Hortense Powdermaker and John Dollard and sociologists Howard Odum and Charles Johnson, studied the South during the Depression, and they published works that analyze the region as a site of social problems. The most distinctive genre of sharecropper narrative to emerge during the Depression were photo documentaries that paired photographs of southern sharecroppers, usually taken by photographers working with the federal Farm Security Administration, with text by writers such as James Agee and Richard Wright that attempted to explain the plight of rural southerners living in poverty. These photo documentaries ventriloquized the experience of sharecroppers. Some sharecroppers, however, found ways to speak for themselves by forming labor unions and performing labor actions, and narratives of unionization reveal ideological conflict between Communist union leaders and union members who preferred land ownership to collectivization. Meanwhile, several proletarian sharecropper novels published during the Depression, such as *Land without Moses* (1938) by Charles Munz and *Hold Autumn in Your Hand* (1941) by George Sessions Perry, portray sharecroppers struggling against overwhelming economic forces. In these works, noble sharecroppers attempt to resist the existing power structure, which leads to tragic consequences. These different forms of sharecropper narrative revealed intense interest in the experiences of sharecroppers during the Depression, but that interest waned during World War II, and after the war, massive technological and social changes led to the end of sharecropping.

For decades, inventors struggled with designs for machines that could automate the labor-intensive elements of commodity agriculture. By the early twentieth century, many farms used tractors to replace labor for some tasks, but the delicate operation to remove cotton fiber from a boll was extremely difficult to mechanize until the Rust brothers developed a spindle picker. After World War II, mechanical cotton pickers and tractors went into mass production. Millions of sharecroppers were displaced from farms during the 1950s and 1960s, and sharecropping effectively ended by the early 1970s. Chapter 5 discusses works of literature that depict the end of sharecropping. Several works reflect the process of mechanization and sharecroppers leaving the farms, including *The Autobiography of Miss Jane Pittman* (1971) by Ernest Gaines, *The Third Life of Grange Copeland* (1970) by Alice Walker, and *And Their Children after Them* (1989) by Dale Maharidge and Michael Williamson. The process of mechanization contributed to the civil rights movement, and several novels, such as *'Sippi* (1967) by John Oliver Killens, portray the experiences of rural African Americans during the movement. Most of the greatest advances during the movement occurred in southern cities, partly because the displacement of sharecroppers increased the population density of urban African Americans. African Americans in rural areas were also engaged in the movement, but mechanization made them vulnerable to dispossession and violence. The autobiographies of southerners who came of age during the end of sharecropping describe the challenges of transitioning from generations of agricultural exploitation to displacement in an industrialized economy in the absence of a social safety net.

The end of sharecropping did not mean the end of labor exploitation in the South. Chapter 6 examines the afterlife of sharecropping, describing the ways in which the culture of sharecropping continues to affect the South in the twenty-first century. Globalization and mechanization have changed commodity agriculture in the South. Gerard Helferich's nonfiction work *High Cotton: Four Seasons in the Mississippi Delta* (2007) documents a year in the cycle of cotton production, and his narrative indicates how capital-intensive mechanized cotton production differs from labor-intensive sharecropping cotton production. He also discusses how global systems of finance put pressure on producers and how displaced workers have struggled to adapt to the post-sharecropping economy. Novels that depict agricultural labor in the generation since sharecropping ended reveal how exploitative systems of labor persist in the rural South. These works, such as *The Celestial Jukebox* (2005) by Cynthia Shearer, show how sharecropping plantations have transitioned into new forms of economic production and how new populations of workers, particularly Latino immigrants, continue to be exploited. For much of the rural South, the generation since the end of sharecropping has been a period of decline. Visual images of Hale County, Alabama, index the process of decline. For ninety years, the rural county has been the subject of documentarians including Walker Evans, William Christenberry, and RaMell Ross, and their collective works illustrate how population loss and generational poverty have affected the county, which functions as a synecdoche for the entire region.

For more than a century, sharecropping defined the South's socioeconomic structure. It was the region's dominant labor paradigm, it determined the conditions of daily life for millions of southerners, and it marked the South as different from the rest of the United States. To the extent that southern literature written during this period reflects material conditions in the region, it represents the experiences and consequences of sharecropping on an entire culture. At the same time, southern literature is a component of that culture, and it demonstrates how cultural products can alternately reinforce and challenge an economic system. The oblique references to sharecropping in *Absalom, Absalom!* and *Gone with the Wind* are part of a complex economic and cultural system that embedded issues of labor exploitation throughout southern literature, beginning almost as soon as the Civil War ended.

→ 2 ←

# Sharecropping, Reconstruction, and Postbellum Literature

A pair of images illustrate the regeneration of the southern system of labor after Emancipation. The first, a cartoon by Winslow Homer titled "The Great Labor Question from the Southern Point of View" published in *Harper's Weekly* on July 29, 1865, less than half a year after the Civil War ended, depicts a southern planter surrounded by his family leaning back in a wicker chair on a vine-covered portico of a columned mansion. In the background, Black laborers work in a field, and in the foreground, a Black man holding a pick and hoe stands on the ground at the step of the portico. The planter says to the Black man, "we've toiled and taken care of you long enough—now, you've got to work." Homer followed the Union Army during the war and painted several important works depicting slavery and soldiers, and Peter Wood argues in *Near Andersonville* (2010) that Homer had a deep understanding of freedom in the slaves' imagination. The cartoon clearly intends to ridicule the white planters' sense of entitlement and the persistence of labor exploitation.[1] It should not be read as humorous or ironic but, rather, as a plea for sympathy and support for the former slave, a handsome figure placed at the focal point of the image, forced to return to laboring in the cotton field. The sentiment that the planter in the image evokes, however, is an uncannily accurate depiction of postbellum labor ideology in the South.

The second image is a painting by William Aiken Walker titled "A Cotton Plantation on the Mississippi" (1883). In the foreground of the image, a white planter and his wife stand on a road with their industrious plantation unfolding behind them into the background. The planter points to his right

FIGURE 1. Winslow Homer, "The Great Labor Question from the Southern Point of View." (*Harper's Weekly*, July 29, 1865)

FIGURE 2. William Aiken Walker, "A Cotton Plantation on the Mississippi." (Gilcrease Museum, Tulsa, OK)

where a team of mules stands hitched to a wagon loaded with bales of cotton. Behind the road lies an immense field of cotton that stretches beyond the frame of the picture on both sides, and more than a dozen Black laborers busily pick cotton into large baskets and load the baskets into a wagon. Past the cotton field on one side grows a crop of corn, and on the other side stand outbuildings for processing and storing cotton. A steamboat on the Mississippi appears in the background, blowing coal smoke and steam into the clouds. Walker, a Confederate veteran, was a prolific painter of southern scenes, and this image was one of his most popular. Currier and Ives produced the image as a color lithograph in 1884.[2] The picture's layout and subject juxtapose postbellum southern agriculture signified by images of paternalist relations between the landowner and his laborers and northern industrialism with the orderly rows of the plantation, the representation of productivity, and juxtaposition of the capitalist landowner with his legion of laborers.

Together, these images construct a narrative about labor in the postbellum South. After Emancipation, working conditions for most laborers would not vary considerably from slavery, and freedom would not mean social equality among the races or an end to labor exploitation. With abolition accomplished, racial issues quickly took on a different tenor, one that reinforced white supremacy, in spite of political maneuvers by so-called Radical Republicans in Congress. For many Americans in both the North and the South, reestablishing the national economy, which depended substantially on the export of cotton, took precedence over issues of sectional animosity and racial equality. The decades after the war were highly dynamic politically with the complicated presidency of Andrew Johnson, the ascendency of the radical Republicans, the passage of the Thirteenth, Fourteenth, and Fifteenth Amendments, the Hayes/Tilden election, and the Bourbon Redemption. But this political volatility contrasts with a remarkable period of intractable ideological continuity as commitments to white supremacy and cotton production superseded elections, laws, and regimes. By the end of the nineteenth century, the New South was almost indistinguishable from the Old South.

Books set in the postbellum South by writers from both the North and the South depict the process of economic reconstruction and the normalization of labor exploitation in the region.[3] Those works that recognize the irony inherent in the process, similar to the message of Winslow Homer's cartoon, concede to the inevitability that economic production takes precedence over human rights in the US South. Many other works revise the history of slavery and of the South to create a mythical paternalism in order to legitimate exploitative labor practices, and this legitimating ideology guided labor, race, and political practices in the region for at least a century after Emancipation. The ideological Reconstruction represented in these texts illustrates how exploitive labor practices were embedded into Emancipation.

## Masters without Slaves/Slaves without Masters

The white planter on the portico in the Winslow Homer cartoon is a master without a slave, and the worker holding a pick and hoe is essentially a slave without a master. In spite of the planter's calm aspect and the look of dignified resignation on the face of the laborer, they illustrate a period of intense anxiety, when genuine questions about labor preoccupied everyone in the United States. Although the North had been relatively unaffected by combat, the loss of cotton exports damaged the nation's economy, and the British government, America's largest trading partner, put intense pressure on the United States to restart cotton trading immediately. The assassination of President Lincoln, meanwhile, greatly complicated plans for reunifying the nation, and an atmosphere of mistrust and lack of confidence shrouded the federal government with the antagonism between Congress and the president leading to Andrew Johnson's impeachment in 1868. Meanwhile, former slaves struggled anxiously to reunite their families, to find safe homes, and to find gainful employment. At the same time, former slave owners who now owned only land and debt worried about who would work their fields and how they would compensate these workers who now expected payment for their labor. Out of this desperate situation emerged the federal government's first clumsy attempt at a social welfare agency, the Freedmen's Bureau.

The Bureau of Freedmen, Refugees, and Abandoned Lands had a difficult and often contradictory set of tasks. In addition to developing a functional system of free labor, it was also responsible for establishing schools and hospitals for former slaves, adjudicating grievances between whites and Blacks, and securing political representation for Blacks before state governments. "In turn diplomat, marriage counselor, educator, supervisor of labor contracts, sheriff, judge, and jury," Eric Foner writes, "the local Bureau agent was expected to win the confidence of Blacks and whites alike in a situation where race and labor relations had been poisoned by mutual distrust and conflicting interests."[4] The enormity of the Bureau's tasks reflected the myriad problems with regenerating an elaborate social system in very short order, and the Bureau proved to be unequal to the task. Rather than ameliorating anxiety, the Bureau often intensified it through political maneuvering, incompetence, policy reversals, corruption, and systemic racism. Immediately after the war, for example, the Bureau began distributing plots of confiscated land to former slaves, but the policy was reversed the following year, so the Bureau removed the homesteaders from their land and returned it to its previous owners, the former Confederates.[5] When the Bureau evicted freedmen from their allotments, it essentially established the racial status quo in the United States since Emancipation: the government would consistently side with white supremacy and economic growth over equality and social justice. The Bureau, thus, functioned less as an agency for welfare and more as an entity of governmental power. Through the Bureau and the military occupation that lasted until the 1870s, the federal government asserted control over the South, unifying the nation through force.

Several writers who depicted Reconstruction in their work dwelled on the anxiety of the time and the false promise of Emancipation that dissolved into institutionalized labor exploitation. John W. De Forest, an officer in the Union Army, was attached to the Freedman's Bureau after the war to oversee three counties in Upstate South Carolina from his office located in Greenville. He served a fairly brief term, from October 1866 to January 1868, so he did not witness the agency's dissolution, but he published a series of accounts of his experience with the Bureau in national magazines, including *Harper's* and *The Atlantic*, between 1868 and 1869.[6] Albion Tourgée also witnessed Reconstruction firsthand. A Union veteran, he returned to the South after the war and served in the Republican government as a superior court judge in Greensboro, North Carolina, from 1868 to 1874. He wrote two novels that critique Reconstruction in the South, *A Fool's Errand* and *Bricks without Straw*, which were popular when they were published in 1879 and 1880, respectively. George Washington Cable, meanwhile, depicted Reconstruction from the perspective of a former slaveholder and Confederate soldier. Cable, however, did not represent the mainstream attitudes of most southerners. After publishing nonfiction works that made a case for racial equality and social justice, he left the South to settle permanently in the North, where he published the novel *John March, Southerner* in 1895. Cable was one of the most prominent southern writers at the time, but this novel, which severely criticized the course of Reconstruction, was not popular, even with northern readers.

Southern literature in the era of post-Emancipation anxiety was freighted with ideological baggage as writers used texts to substantiate various political agendas, revisions of the war, and visions of the future South. By the 1880s, as the Reconstruction era came to a political end, the South continued to captivate the nation's attention. In an 1888 essay, "The South as a Field for Fiction," Albion Tourgée asserted, "it cannot be denied that American fiction of today, whatever may be its origin is predominantly Southern in type and character."[7] National magazines, such as *Scribner's*, *Harper's*, and *The Atlantic* published popular local color stories frequently, creating an entire genre of fiction that memorialized and romanticized the South. Tourgée laments that southerners have grown self-absorbed and self-obsessed and that even when they have "no rush of business life" they continue to venerate "the past, present, and future of Southern life."[8] His biggest concern is that southern writers reduce Black characters to stereotypes, usually either the devoted slave or the destitute freedman, as they use the characters to idealize slavery. "The slave as a man," he writes, "with his hopes, his fears, his faith, has been touched, and only touched, by the pen of a novelist," and he predicts that the freedman as "a man with hopes and aspirations, quick to suffer, patient to endure, full of hot passion, fervid imagination, desirous of being equal to the best—is sure to be a character of enduring interest."[9] Tourgée's essay deliberately outlines his own efforts as an author to humanize Black characters and to press an ideological agenda that moves toward racial equality. Only a few years earlier, George Washington Cable, one of the most popular local color writers, advocated blurring the boundaries between the region and the nation. In a lecture on "Literature in the Southern States," he proposes relinquishing the obsession with regional defensiveness to embrace American nationalism. One of his reasons for this ideological shift is the persistent problems that plague the region, including the problem of sharecropping. "The plantation idea is a semi-barbarism," he writes. "It is the idea of the old South with merely the substitution of a Negro tenantry for Negro slaves. It is a pathetic and senile sentiment for the maintenance of a landed aristocracy in a country and in times that have outgrown that formidable error in political economy."[10] When these essays were written in the 1880s, the region's political economy had essentially regenerated along exactly the lines that Cable describes.

Tourgée and Cable bring their own ideological agendas to bear on their representations of Reconstruction in their novels. In *A Fool's Errand*, Tourgée dwells at length on the potential resolutions to the problem of Emancipation, listing four possibilities: first was Lincoln's plan to readmit the rebellious states, second was the Republican plan of Reconstruction with limitations and with Black franchise, and third was a plan to dissolve the former southern states and reorganize them into territories that would have to seek readmittance to the Union. The fourth plan, the one the narrator claims is adopted, is a rejection of all the others. It is a hasty and hostile opposition to any northern involvement in the South motivated by white anxiety over Black political power. "That a servile race," the fool explains, "isolated from the dominant one by the fact of color and the universally accepted dogma of inherent inferiority, to say nothing of a very general belief of its utter incapacity for the civilization to which the Caucasian has attained, should be looked on with distrust and aversion, if not with positive hatred, as a co-ordinate political power, by their former masters, would seem so natural, that one could hardly expect men of ordinary intelligence to overlook it."[11] Yet the other plans overlooked the inherent mutual racial animosity, and they were rejected through suppression and evasion, resulting in an extended period of confusion, turmoil, and violence.[12] The condition of former slaves compounded the problems, as the freedmen "had neither property, knowledge, right, or power," and so were without means to address their own needs.[13] Federal interventions could not forestall the inevitable outcome of Emancipation. Within a few years after the war, most former slaves found themselves "under a new bondage of wages instead of the old bondage of pure force."[14] Tourgée and Cable retrospectively revise the meaning of Reconstruction in these texts, recasting the promise of freedom as a difficult morass of social problems involving recalcitrant racism, political corruption, and immoral acts of economic expediency. The result is that freedom, for freedmen, is not dissimilar from slavery.

For landowners after Emancipation, now masters without slaves, a difficult ideological shift took place. They emerged from the Civil War "in a state of shock," according to Eric Foner, "their class had been devastated—physically, economically, and psychologically."[15] Out of necessity, planters accepted the practice of compensated free labor, but they feared that the system would eventually collapse into anarchy, or perhaps worse in their minds, Black domination. Eventually, however, relations between landowners and laborers in the post-Emancipation economy fell back into patterns of white domination.[16] Paying for labor changed the nature of the relationship between former masters and former slaves, but not in ways that inclined toward social equality; instead, wage labor ingrained racism, animosity, and exploitation. Tourgée compares the antebellum and postbellum attitudes toward labor between southerners and northerners in an elaborate chart. In the antebellum side, slavery is primarily a moral issue, pitting the northern sense of moral wrong against the southern sense of religious sanction. After the war, the issues are even more complicated and more political. He suggests that northerners expect Blacks to support the political party that won their freedom, and that southerners recognize that "the slave is now free, but he is not white. We have no ill will towards the colored man as such and in his place; but he is not our equal, cannot be made our equal, and we will not be ruled by him, or admit him as a co-ordinate with the white race in power. We have no objection to his voting, so long as he votes as his old master, or the man for whom he labors, advises him; but, when he chooses to vote differently, he must take the consequences."[17] Formers masters would only accept freedmen as former slaves, as people who could be controlled and dominated, and in the absence of slavery, new means for control were devised.

Tourgée dilates on the shifts in the former slaveholders' ideology in *Bricks without Straw*. "The state of mind of the Southern white man," he writes, "with reference to the freedman and his exaltation to the privilege of citizenship is one which cannot be too frequently analyzed or too closely kept in mind by one who desires fully to apprehend the events which have since occurred, and the social and political structure of the South at this time."[18] He argues that slaveholders were not often cruel to their slaves, but that the "real evils of the system" were the effects of dehumanizing slaves by depriving them of freedom and liberty while simultaneously developing a sense of "unimpeachable superiority" in the minds of the slave owners. Numerous accounts of cruelty contradict Tourgée's claim, but the pivotal issue for him is that Emancipation put whites and Blacks in an oppositional relationship: "The Southern mind had no antipathy to the negro in a menial or servile relation.... It was only *as a man* that the white regarded the black with aversion; and, in that point of view, the antipathy was all the more intensely bitter since he considered the claim to manhood an intrusion upon the sacred and exclusive rights of his own race."[19] Former slaveholders fundamentally resented the notion of equality with their former slaves, and they replaced slavery with a complicated set of social controls including racial ideology, terroristic violence, and radical political disenfranchisement. Sharecropping emerged as part of this context, and the ideological apparatus of racial domination and control suffused the system. Although predicated on the notion of economic cooperation, sharecropping as it was practiced in the South was explicitly a form of exploitation.

The freedmen's primary concern after the war was often much more personal—to reconstitute the families that had been sundered during slavery. "The first step in advance was taken neither by the nation nor by the freedmen," but by love and hope. Tourgée describes that common law marriages were recognized as Christian marriages: "All at once it was perceived to be a great enormity that four millions of Christian people, in a Christian land, should dwell together without marriage rite or family tie. While they were slaves, the fact that they might be bought and sold had hidden this evil from the eye of morality, which had looked unabashed upon the unlicensed freedom of the quarters and the enormities of the barracoon. Now all at once it was shocked beyond expression at the domestic relations of the freedmen."[20] Marriage recognized the rights of individuals to create their own permanent relationships and to solidify their intergenerational connections to their parents and their children. Heather Williams documents in *Help Me to Find My People* (2012) that separation was among the greatest sources of anguish among slaves and that reconnection was often the first priority for former slaves after freedom. Both former slaves and former slaveholders were looking after Emancipation to find something that had been lost: slaves for their families and slaveholders for their control. Sharecropping would allow them both to find what they sought—at a cost.

Realizing the vulnerability of former slaves and the necessity of regenerating economic systems after the war, Congress established the Freedman's Bureau. Part of their mission was to intervene on behalf of former slaves in labor disputes and to establish equitable contracts between landowners and laborers.[21] They also established schools for the former slaves, and, in some cases, they helped reunite families by paying transportation costs for one family member to travel to another. As an agent of the Freedmen's Bureau, John W. De Forest had a distinct insight into the anxiety of Reconstruction.[22] "Most of the difficulties between whites and Blacks resulted from the inevitable awkwardness of tyros in the mystery of free labor," he writes. "Many of the planters seemed to be unable to understand that work could be other than a form of slavery, or that it could be accomplished without some prodigious binding and obligating of the hireling to the employer."[23] While De Forest clearly understands the challenge of Reconstruction, he also embodies the fundamental problem preventing post-Emancipation equality. He goes on to assert that landowners believed that laborers would not be useful if they "were not bound body and soul," and he reveals his own racism when he replies, "with regard to many freedmen I was obliged to admit that this assumption was only too correct and to sympathize with the desire to limit their noxious liberty, at the same time that I knew such limitation to be impossible. When a darkey frolics all night and thus renders himself worthless for the next day's work; when he takes into his cabin a host of lazy relatives who eat him up, or of thievish ones who steal the neighboring pigs and chickens; when he gets high notions of freedom into his head and feels himself bound to answer his employers directions with an indifferent whistle, what can the latter do?"²⁴ Bureau officers probably held a range of social and racial positions, but De Forest published his own observations in *Harper's* in 1868, one of the nation's most prominent publications, while political Reconstruction was still in process, so his comments were influential and revealing. His article suggests that even the agency charged with establishing equality in the South sympathized with the racial ideology of the landowners, the same people who they had just defeated in a war to abolish slavery.

Inevitably, the southern economy reverted as far as possible to its antebellum outlines after Emancipation. In *Bricks without Straw*, Tourgée depicts a community of African Americans who attempt to live free and independent lives, but eventually white landowners undermine their community. With the help of the Freedmen's Bureau, a former slave buys a piece of land from his former master and establishes an autonomous community with several families and a school.²⁵ The story hinges on a case of enticement.²⁶ A white landowner accuses the leader of the community of enticing a laborer to break his contract, so the sheriff charges him with a crime. The man protests, "I t'ought dat when a man was free anudder could hire him widout axin' leave of his marster. Dat's what I t'ought freedom meant." But the sheriff responds, "Oh, not exactly; there's lots of freedom lyin' round loose, but it don't allow a man to hire another man's hands, nor give them aid and comfort by harboring and feeding them when they break their contracts and run away."²⁷ The crime of enticement was among the black codes, a set of laws southern states enacted after Emancipation to regain control over Black people. The laws defined Blackness and stipulated that certain laws would apply to Black people; enumerated the rights available to Black people, such as the right to marry, own property, and sue and be sued; and codified labor relations between white people and Black people by making sharecropping contracts unbreakable, outlawing enticement and false pretenses, and making vagrancy—not having a labor contract—illegal. Technically, the Fourteenth amendment made black codes unconstitutional, but they were tolerated at a federal level for decades, and the Supreme Court refused to overturn them in the case of *Plessy v. Ferguson*.²⁸ Beyond these legal forms of coercion, freedmen were subject to poll taxes that impeded their right to vote and wanton acts of violence and terrorism designed to intimidate and control them.²⁹ Eventually, the Black community in Tourgée's novel dissolves and relocates to Kansas, signaling that former slaves could not live free lives in the South.

Racial antipathy was the dominant social ideology among white southerners during Reconstruction, but George Washington Cable voiced a powerful dissenting opinion in "The Freedman's Case in Equity." He explains that, even after Emancipation, former slaves are still not free. "In these days of voluntary Reconstruction," he writes, "he is virtually freed by the consent of his master, but the master retaining the exclusive bounds of his freedom. Many everywhere have taken up the idea that this state of affairs is the end to be desired and the end actually sought in Reconstruction as handed over to the states."[30] Cable further argues that limited freedom has become the accepted outcome of Emancipation and that northerners have adopted the same ideology toward race as southerners. "The belief is all too common that the nation, having aimed as a wrong result and missed, has left us of the Southern states to get now such other result as we think best," he writes, suggesting that many Americans have concluded that abolition was a mistake.[31] He goes on to stipulate that not everyone in America shares that opinion, but the presumption that African Americans were not socially equal to white Americans clearly prevailed, if only because northerners allowed southerners to practice inequality. To illustrate how powerfully the racial ideology operated in the South, one need only look at Cable as an object lesson. At the time that he published "The Freedman's Case in Equity" in 1885, he was the most popular writer in the South, but the backlash against his position was so strong that he moved his family to Massachusetts out of concern for their safety.

In 1894, a generation after Emancipation, Cable published *John March, Southerner*, a novel that imagined an alternative history for the South. In the convoluted, romantic novel set in the town of Suez in the fictional state Dixie, John March attempts to convert his family's land into an industrial development with mills, mines, and factories after the war. At every side, however, forces conspire to undo his plan as ruthless industrialists, intolerant southerners, devious politicians, and misinformed Blacks work against him. His own mother even attempts to sell the property from under him. The plan eventually fails, and the ending is saved only because John's romantic interest warns him of a plot against him. The novel suggests that the South—Dixie—was incompatible with industrial development and that intractable forces would resist any deviation from the status quo. The novel, tellingly, was not a commercial or critical success, largely because it imagined a history for the South that did not reinforce the prevailing racial ideology.[32] Cable had made a career as a writer of historical novels that exposed the South's complicated racial past, such as *The Grandissimes*, but this version of the southern past did not fit with the prevailing narrative of regional reconciliation through racial exploitation.

Edward King captures a key element of the South's ideological redevelopment in his extensive 1874 travelogue, *The Great South*. King traveled throughout the region documenting the South's social, economic, and political reconstruction for the readers of *Scribner's* magazine.[33] In one revealing passage, he relates the comments of a southern planter who explains the difficulties of southern labor for northern readers. "What the planters are disposed to complain of is, that while they have lost their slaves, they have not got free laborers in any sense common either in the Northern States or in Europe," he quotes the planter as saying.[34] The planter goes into the details of the sharecropping contract, and he argues that planters are actually responsible for supporting their workers by extending them "privileges," such as seed, food, a cabin, and medicine. The planter apparently sees himself as supporting the laborers, not exploiting them, and this attitude was consistent with the prevailing representation of southern labor in the decades after Emancipation. Works of literature that critiqued Reconstruction were, in fact, unusual, even among the reading public in the North, as most Americans seemed to get on with the business of unifying a nation. In *Writing Reconstruction* (2015), Sharon D. Kennedy-Nolle explains that progressive writing about Reconstruction was ironically counterproductive because works "envisioning a radical change spurred conservative reaction, inadvertently helping to hasten the return of southern Democrats to office" and hastening the postbellum return to white supremacy.[35] The facts that former masters would resent their former slaves' freedom and actively work to reestablish the conditions of bondage, that former slaves would be vulnerable to exploitation, and that the federal government would be less than thoroughly committed to protecting formers slaves from exploitation are not surprising in retrospect. What is surprising is that the same attitudes that made the Civil War a moral campaign for abolition would quickly dissipate into an ideology that sanctioned racial antipathy. The explanation for that shift, however, is uncomfortably simple.

## Cotton: A Romance

After Emancipation, the regions reconciled, disquietly. Animosity and distrust lingered for generations, but the regions achieved a functional détente relatively quickly. While political tensions simmered, economic redevelopment took priority. Because the nation financially depended upon exports of southern cotton, reestablishing cotton production became the overriding factor in interregional relations after the war. The war depleted the entire nation's economy, and the most expedient means to redevelopment was through the sale of southern cotton in international markets, all of which craved raw materials after years of blockade. Factories in the North also demanded southern cotton to maintain their growth and to repay bonds used to finance the war. The destitute South, meanwhile, needed every cent of capital investment available, and cotton was the primary asset it had to offer. The common need for cotton formed a bond among the world's industrial powers, and with slavery abolished, the treatment and living conditions of the laborers were of little consequence.

Interregional romance novels provided a literary model for reconciliation. The genre emerged before the war with novels such as *The Planter's Northern Bride* (1854) by Caroline Lee Hentz in which the marriage between a northerner and a southerner becomes a metaphor for national unity. After the war, the plot contrivance became fairly common in the works of authors from both regions, including Tourgée's *A Fool's Errand* (1879), Julia Magruder's *Across the Chasm* (1885), several stories by Joel Chandler Harris, Constance Fenimore Woolson's "Old Gardiston" (1880), Charles King's *A War Time Wooing* (1888), Maud Howe Elliott's *Atalanta in the South* (1886), John W. De Forest's *Miss Ravenel's Conversion from Secession to Loyalty* (1867) and *The Bloody Chasm* (1881), Joseph A. Altshler's *The Last Rebel* (1898), and Thomas Nelson Page's *Red Rock* (1898). In addition to these works, reconciliation plays were popular after the war, as were poems using the reconciliation motif, and the ubiquity of the reconciliation romance trope suggests that Americans on both sides of the war craved reunion.[36] Suggesting that reunification followed the contours of a marriage, however, raises some interesting implications in the context of the patriarchal nineteenth century, where men assumed dominant positions within the marriage. Nina Silber comments in *The Romance of Reunion* (1993) that in many of these works the South plays a feminized role, and "the North, they suggested, had tamed and subdued and would now control the South in much the same way that husbands were assumed to take control in marriage."[37] The gender of the regions, however, tended to conform to the region of the writer, with northern writers often feminizing the South and southern writers often feminizing the North, indicating that the reconciliation might follow regionalized patterns of domination.

Who would dominate in these reconciliation romances played a crucial ideological role in the process of reunion. As the United States moved into Gilded Age prosperity, issues of economic and political equality between the regions became important, virtually obliterating the national importance of racial equality. Reconciliation romances reflected these developments with the male and female characters acting as metonyms for their regions, and the romantic relationships, thus, symbolize the terms and conditions of national reunification. Silber points out that "economic considerations, of course, were always linked with romantic ones," but she curiously asserts that these considerations underscore "the fact that the reunion was sealed by genuine emotion rather than insincere financial motives."[38] While many of these works appeal to sentiment and emotion to mask or complicate the underlying economic issues, their plots ultimately hinge on economic disparity between the prosperous North and the impoverished South, and the gendering of the regions illustrates how they use their resources to charm each other, either by the masculine northern capitalist using his wealth to entice the poor yet aristocratic southern woman or by the gallant Confederate veteran wooing the wealthy northern woman.

The real question is why would the prosperous North care to court or to be courted by the impoverished South? The answer to this question, and the answer even more troubling question about why the United States would abandon the issue of racial equality, is simple and transparent: money. The North's postwar prosperity depended directly upon southern cotton. In *Empire of Cotton* (2014), Sven Beckert describes the global interest in reestablishing southern cotton production, which was critical to the textile industries in the northern United States and Europe and the linchpin in the nineteenth-century global economy. Beckert writes, "The continued rapid growth of the industry over the next half century amplified this need: Global cotton consumption doubled from 1860 to 1890, and then by 1920 doubled once more."[39] During the war, British industrialists actively sought out new sources for cotton, leading to their expansion into India and Egypt, but the

South remained the world's largest producer of cotton well into the twentieth century.[40] Controlling this supply of cotton gave the United States a measure of financial independence and international economic and political leverage. Gilded Age prosperity, America's rapid postbellum industrialization, and the rise of America's imperial aspirations all depended to a significant extent on cotton production, so the United States had powerful financial motives to press for ideological reunification beyond military occupation. Reunion was a business proposition.

The romance of capitalist reconciliation allowed for the exploitation of labor without moral considerations. Wage laborers in the North worked long hours for low pay with little job security, so social protections for laborers in southern cotton fields were not a concern, and northern and southern capitalists largely ignored working conditions as long as a steady supply of cheap labor could be procured and coerced into work. An influx of immigrants into the North filled this need, and the conversion of former slaves into sharecroppers bound to their landowners filled it in the South. In most of the romances of reunion, labor issues are relegated to the background to draw the reader's focus to the interregional romantic relationship between aristocratic whites. In *Red Rock*, for example, Dr. Cary returns from the war and tells his slaves that they have been faithful servants, that they are free, and that they may leave, "but if they remained they would have to work and be subject to his authority."[41] Only one person talks back to the doctor, and "the next day there was a good force at work in the fields."[42] In most cases, laborers are represented in these works by retainers, former slaves who are loyal to their former masters to the point of refusing wages or accepting them reluctantly. In *The Bloody Chasm*, Virginia Beaufort, proud daughter of a ruined southern family, lives in a hovel with two former slaves, Aunt Chloe and Uncle Phil, and they are mutually dependent upon each other for subsistence. When labor problems do arise, it is usually a plot mechanism to bring the romantic protagonists together, such as an uprising among sharecroppers in "Old Gardiston" that brings a Union regiment led by a dashing young officer to protect a ruined plantation inhabited by a beautiful young woman, which leads to a predictable conclusion.

Reunion romances are about capital, not labor. All of these texts revolve either explicitly or implicitly around the investment of northern capital in the South. After the war, many northern investors sought to take advantage of postwar instability and low land prices to speculate in the potentially lucrative cotton market. Lawrence Powell writes that these investors regarded cotton planting as "a short road to wealth," which often proved to be untrue, but the possibility proved to be extremely attractive.[43] Luring northern investment was the crux of the New South creed, the campaign to redevelop the region economically, socially, and politically after the war.[44] The two most important reunion romances, Thomas Nelson Page's *Red Rock* and John W. De Forest's *The Bloody Chasm*, reflect both the ideological utility of the New South and the campaign for capital. A sycophantic character in *Red Rock* slavers over a northern capitalist, saying, "you've come to the right place for business, Major. . . . It's the garden spot of the world—the money's jest layin' round to waste on the ground, if the folks jist had brains to see it. All it wants is a little more capital."[45] This particular character proves to be a swindler, which critiques the New South creed, but the plot of the novel revolves around property rights to a plantation in which the capitalist invests. The premise of The *Bloody Chasm* makes the issues of capital even more evident.

A Gilded Age allegory of Reconstruction, *The Bloody Chasm* is the story of an arranged interregional marriage that leads to a romance of reconciliation. In the novel, a wealthy Bostonian, Silas Mather, whose late wife was a native southerner, stipulates in his will that his fortune will go to his northern nephew and his southern niece if they marry. This arrangement mirrors the forced marriage of Reconstruction, and De Forest describes the characters as "the North incarnate . . . and the South."[46] Although obstinately loyal to the vanquished Confederacy, the fiery southern woman, Virginia Beaufort, is utterly destitute, so she agrees to the arrangement, but she refuses to live with her husband, Nathan Underhill. She separates from him and moves to Paris with her aunt and two loyal former slaves. Her husband follows her to Paris, adopts a disguise and a fake name, and attempts to woo her. In a side plot, her rival for his affections is a poor Irish woman, who represents immigrants coming into the United States, but the book makes plain that the North and the South are destined to be together. Eventually, "time and distance and prosperity" weaken her allegiance to the South, and she yields to her husband's advances, reconciling to live together as man and wife.[47] De Forest's novel makes the reconciliation trope's economic and political ramifications explicit, illustrating that, in his opinion, the nation would not reunite through force but through the hearts and minds of the southern people.[48]

Page's *Red Rock* also employs the conventions of the reunion romance, but it inverts the dynamics to represent the southern perspective on reconciliation. The novel centers on the property title to the eponymous Red Rock plantation, which operates as a synecdoche for the South. A ruthless Freedmen's Bureau agent, Jonadab Leech, who symbolizes the federal government, uses his resources to seize the plantation and sell it under false pretenses to a well-intentioned northern investor, Major Welch. Steve Allen, a Confederate veteran and attorney, files a lawsuit against Leech and Welch challenging the title to the property. Against this background, Page tells a revisionist history of the postbellum South, depicting brave southerners suffering from the northern boot on their neck, loyal retainers who work faithfully for their former masters, bad Black men who threaten to rape white women, and the gallant Ku Klux Klan that restores order to the South. The book is heavily freighted with southern mythmaking and ideology, which play out in the relationship between Steve Allen and Major Welch's daughter, Ruth. Page, notably, masculinizes the South, and he resolves the property claim to the plantation by effecting a marriage between Allen and Welch. After their wedding, "Ruth received a deed which had been recorded, conveying to her the part of Red Rock" as a wedding gift and concluding the legal proceedings.[49]

Both of these novels are convoluted, nearly to the point of being preposterous, but they represent interpretations of complicated political and economic maneuvers that elapsed over a period of decades. The pivotal issue in both books is marriage and inheritance or property, directly yoking romantic issues with economic issues and eroding any pretense of genuine sentiment or emotion in the text. Reconciliation romances are actually political texts that illustrate an ideological roadmap to reunion, and marriage functions in the text as a metaphor for economic linkages. In the nineteenth century, issues of marriage and property were especially fraught in the South. Under English common law, all of a woman's property, including her debts, converted to her husband upon their marriage, a principle called coverture. Beginning in the 1840s, many states passed Married Women's Property Acts, which gave women the right to own property brought into the marriage and to acquire property while married.[50] In 1839, Mississippi was among the first states to pass an act, but southern states moved on the issue at varying rates, with South Carolina and Virginia among the last states to pass acts. These issues of how property would be shared, specifically the proceeds from cotton production, were highly relevant during Reconstruction. In *The Bloody Chasm*, both the northern man and the southern woman benefit from the provisions of Uncle Silas's [read, US] will, suggesting that De Forest saw reunion as mutually beneficial, but in *Red Rock*, Page makes a clear distinction between the villainous federal government, which defrauds southerners of their property, and good Yankees, who honor their contracts.

Romances of reunion provided an imaginary narrative for postwar reconciliation, but the reconciliations in these books are conspicuously white. As David Blight comments, "In the half century after the war, as the sections reconciled, by and large, the races divided. The intersectional wedding that became such a staple of mainstream popular culture, especially in the plantation school of literature, had no interracial counterpart in the popular imagination."[51] It is not coincidental that Black characters are marginalized in these texts because race remained the greatest impediment to reunion after the war. An exception to this marginalization would be Charles Chesnutt's story "Hot-Foot Hannibal," in which Uncle Julius uses a conjure tale to effect a rapprochement between an estranged interregional couple. Karen Keely argues that the story indicates the failure of Reconstruction, precisely because the couple has reconciled. "This unification," she states, "has been effected by the victors' yielding to the racial beliefs and ideology of the enemy they had apparently subjugated."[52] In other words, the North has become no better than the South or, rather, the South has become no worse than the North. If reunion romances did represent a marriage of equals motivated for financial reasons, then they were unified in their willingness to exploit the people whose labor brought them prosperity.

## Good Ole Times: Paternalism and Historical Revision

Postbellum writers frequently revised the history of the South and slavery, reimaging the past as an idyllic, prelapsarian time. In these reveries, the South is depicted frequently as a grand civilization populated almost exclusively with genteel and noble white people and their loyal servants, who are slaves of their own volition. According to David Blight, these revisionist depictions of the southern past influenced public perception of the region. "In an era of tremendous social change and anxiety," he writes, "a popular literature that embraced the romance of the Lost Cause, the idyll of the Old South's plantation world of orderly and happy race relations, and the mutuality of the 'soldier's faith' flowed from mass-market magazines as well as the nation's most prominent publishing houses. The age of machines, rapid urbanization, and labor unrest produced a huge audience for a literature of escape into a pre-Civil War, exotic South that, all but 'lost,' was now the object of enormous nostalgia."[53] With a receptive audience, southern writers could redefine the war's meaning and the history of slavery in America, and they could use the nation's sense of nostalgia for a bucolic past for ideological purposes. Many writers depicted paternalistic relations between slave owners and slaves in an imaginary historical past, in which the slave owners benevolently cared for their dependent and content slaves, to legitimate an exploitive and violent present.

Animosity between the regions after the war ran an unsteady course. Years of combat left deep scars, and the loss of hundreds of thousands of men left a nation in mourning, but by the end of the military occupation in the 1870s, the nation had largely returned to work, especially in the North, and the period of social change and anxiety softened some attitudes toward the South.[54] Constance Fenimore Woolson's short story "In the Cotton Country" (1876) is an example of sympathy for the defeated South. Raised in Cleveland and New York, Woolson wintered in Florida in the 1870s, and she found in the South a subject for her sentimental regionalism. "In the Cotton Country" is the story of a northerner visiting the South who encounters a pitiful widow working a farm alone with her orphaned child. She tells him her tale of anguish and woe about how all of her male relatives were killed in the war, leaving her destitute and bitter and facing an uncertain future. She offers her son to the northerner, telling him, "let him grow up under the regime; I have told him nothing of the old," suggesting that the South's past is dead and its future belongs to the North.[55] While this story projects northern sympathy for the South, it does not reflect the attitude of many southerners to the past or the North.

Among southerners, the cult of the Lost Cause emerged as soon as the war ended, signaled by the publication of Edward Pollard's revisionist history, *The Lost Cause: A New Southern History of the War of the Confederates*, in 1866, before the cannons cooled. Proponents of the Lost Cause defended the South's role in the war through a set of firm ideological positions. They contended that the antebellum South was a noble society based on principles of gentility and chivalry; they argued that slavery was a benign institution sanctioned by scripture; they held that the North defeated the South through superior industrial resources and population numbers, not through military prowess; and they believed the war was fought over states' rights, not the abolition of slavery.[56] The factual veracity of these tenets was not important to the vast campaign of historical revision that permeated all elements of southern culture in the decades after the war, becoming a civil religion in the South.[57] Memorial associations, veterans' reunions, history textbooks, monuments and markers, pageants and parades, memoirs and novels reinscribed the Lost Cause in southern memory, holding the region blameless for slavery, the war, and its own defeat. Postbellum plantation literature and the cult of the Lost Cause "worked to reinforce each other and to fashion a view of southern history quite helpful in changing outside opinion of the South."[58]

One of the most amazing and dangerous tenets of the Lost Cause was the contention that slavery was a benevolent institution. Considering that the cruelties and indignities of slavery were well documented and that the cause of Emancipation gave meaning to the war for the American people, the ideological maneuver to represent slavery as a social good seems outrageous, but it happened, and it substantially influenced American postbellum race relations. Thomas Nelson Page was possibly the most influential apologist for slavery and the southern planter aristocracy. The descendant of two first families of Virginia, Page grew up on a plantation in central Virginia during the war, and he internalized the ideals of the Old South. His story "Marse Chan" (1887) is a tour-de-force of southern mythmaking and historical revision, portraying slavery as not only benevolent but also enviable. In the story, a former slave tells a stranger the story of his late master, a heroic, chivalrous figure who courts Miss Anne in his youth, even carrying her on his shoulders across a flooded creek. When her father insults his father during a political campaign, he challenges her father to a duel, but refuses to shoot the old man when he has a chance, making a present of him to his family. Marse Chan's father risks his life to rescue a slave from a burning barn, losing his eyesight in the process. Marse Chan dies in the war, just before he is to marry Miss Anne. Page tells variations of the same story in the collection *In Ole Virginia*, crafting narratives of compassionate masters who are willing to risk their own lives for their slaves, such as Marse George, who dies rescuing his servant in "Unc Edinburgh's Drowndin,'" and of loyal slaves, such as Billy, who helps to protect his owners during the war in "Meh Lady."

In "Marse Chan," Page uses the slave character Sam to ventriloquize Lost Cause revision of slavery. He tells the stranger:

> Dem wuz good ole times, marster—de bes' Sam ever see! Dey wuz, in fac'! Niggers didn'hed nothin' 't all to do—jes' hed to 'ten' to de feedin' an' cleanin' de hosses, an' doin' what de marster tell 'em to do; an' when dey wuz sick, dey had things sont 'em out de house, an' de same doctor come to see 'em whar 'ten' to de white folks when dey wuz po'ly. Dyar warn 'ten' no trouble nor nothin'.[59]

Sam suggests that slavery was preferable to freedom. As a slave, he had direction and protection with no responsibilities for himself other than to follow his master's orders. The labor that the master requests of him is ludicrously light, only simple chores. Page idealizes slavery and glosses over the fundamental factor that slavery was an extractive labor arrangement that dehumanized enslaved people, utterly revising reality in the process. Nonetheless, his stories were extremely popular, and their message that slaves were dependent on their benevolent masters was highly influential.

Building on the popularity of his plantation stories and the novel *Red Rock*, Page published a definitive manual of postbellum paternalist ideology, *The Negro: The Southerner's Problem* (1904), that describes the mindset of many southern whites in fascinating detail. The precise inverse of W. E. B. Du Bois's *The Souls of Black Folks* (1903), the book's objective is to explain the race question to northerners from a southerner's point of view because he believes that northerners do not understand southern race relations until they see it for themselves. He writes:

> The chief trouble that arose between the two races in the South after the war grew out of the ignorance at the North of the actual conditions at the South, and the ignorance at the South of the temper and the power of the North. The North believed that the Negro was, or might be made, the actual equal of the White, and that the South not only rejected this dogma, but, further, did not accept emancipation with sincerity, and would do all in its power to nullify the work which had already been accomplished, and hold the Negroes in quasi-servitude. The South held that the Negro was not the equal of the White, and further held that, suddenly released from slavery, he must, to prevent

his becoming a burden and a menace, be controlled and compelled to work. In fact, as ignorance of each other brought about conditions which produced the war between the sections, so it has brought about most of the trouble since the war.[60]

Slavery, in his account, was a preferable condition for African Americans. He describes strong filial bonds that developed between slaves and their owners, and he asserts that slavery provided them with meaningful work and protection. Since Emancipation, their lives have regressed, he asserts, and they have become less productive and have "not advanced at all in morality."[61] According to Page, to control free Blacks, it is necessary to disfranchise them and to lynch those who commit "heinous offences."[62] Page contends that the postbellum condition of race relations is a direct outcome of Emancipation, which has led to black codes and sharecropping to force former slaves to work and acts of violence and coercion to maintain white supremacy. Tellingly, he immediately rejects the possibility of racial equality, and he takes on the responsibility of explaining the impossibility of equality to northern readers.

He justifies his arguments by appealing to his concept of "old-time negroes," which is his historical revision of race relations in slavery.[63] He tells several anecdotes of slaves who were completely devoted to their owners, and he writes that "no servants or retainers of any race ever identified themselves more fully with their masters."[64] Among his anecdotes are stories of house servants and mammies, slave overseers whose owners trusted them implicitly, and slaves who took up arms during the war to protect their owners' crops.[65] These anecdotes align with his stories of slaves, such as Sam in "Marse Chan," who look fondly on the days of slavery, and Page's racist assumptions about African Americans allow him to legitimate white supremacy and exploiting Black labor. In fact, after explaining his perception of the race question, he offers no solution "but to leave it to work itself out along the lines of economic laws."[66] His final objective, in other words, is to encourage northerners to accept the status quo. Racial uplift interventions, such as education, are doomed to failure, and former slaves are best suited to continue laboring for their former owners, just as they had before Emancipation. If Page's opinions were unique to him, they might be dismissed, but they unfortunately described the conventional wisdom on American race relations among white people by the end of the nineteenth century. The concurrent rise of American xenophobia and scientific racism made Progressive-era America less than fully interested in racial equality and willing to leave southerners undisturbed, culminating with the Supreme Court decision in *Plessy v. Ferguson* in 1896, which effectively made segregation the law of the land.

Page was not the only popular writer to revise southern race relations. Joel Chandler Harris, a newspaper writer from Georgia, became famous for his dialect folklore stories told through the character of Uncle Remus, a kindly slave who regales a young white boy on an antebellum plantation. Uncle Remus became well known as a version of the faithful retainer character, but Harris also published some stories about the antebellum South with a more ominous message. His story "Free Joe and the Rest of the World" (1884) suggests that slavery is preferable to freedom. In the story, a slave is freed after his master dies, but his wife remains a slave, so he stays near her, until she is sold away to Macon, and without the protection of an owner, he is left to die. Harris describes the paradox of freedom: "He realized the fact that though he was free he was more helpless than any slave. Having no owner, every man was his master."[67] If this story were published before Emancipation, one could dismiss the story as a shallow defense of slavery, but the story was originally published in 1884, nearly twenty years after Emancipation, so its message is somewhat more complicated. It suggests that the freedmen, without the protection of slave owners, were all vulnerable because, like Free Joe, "all [their] slender resources were devoted to winning, not kindness and appreciation, but toleration."[68] Harris's story supports the ideology that Page articulates that former slaves require direction and protection to be productive.[69]

Although much more sympathetic to African Americans than Page or Harris, Mark Twain communicates a similar message in *Adventures of Huckleberry Finn* (1884). The novel is also set before Emancipation, and in the story, both Huck Finn and Jim attempt to escape an uncertain fate. Jim fears being sold down the river, so he escapes his owner, and Huck takes on the awkward role of paternalist. Their mutual escape, ironically, takes them down the river, and at the Phelps' farm, Tom and Huck enact an elaborate plan that symbolically incarcerates Jim before helping him to escape. The point is moot because Jim has already been freed according to the conditions of his owner's will, but Tom Sawyer arbitrarily and disingenuously sets the conditions for Jim's freedom, and he represents a segment of society that used paternalism to subvert racial equality. "People who behaved like Tom Sawyer," Charles H. Nilon writes, "defined 'the Negro problem,' developed the concept of gradualism, and persuaded the nation to accept the 'separate but equal' principle as just. The Tom Sawyers of the South made the attempts of the Huckleberry Finns to free themselves and the Black people difficult and sometimes prevented or perverted those efforts."[70] Since *Adventures of Huckleberry Finn* was published in 1884, the same year as "Free Joe," the novel's readers would likely have recognized the similar outlines of historical revision, likely missing the more subtle transgressive elements of the plot.

Rewriting the past changed the meaning of Emancipation. These revisions of southern history cultivated sympathy for the South in the American imagination and made racial paternalism the national status quo in the later decades of the nineteenth century. This is an important point because these texts were not directed specifically to a southern audience; they were published in national magazines and mainstream presses, and their readership was nationwide, reaching many Americans who had no direct contact with the South. Jeremy Wells remarks in *Romances of the White Man's Burden* (2011) that "the plantation had become, in a word, national by the turn of the century."[71] Paternalist ideology extended beyond the South to normalize race relations throughout the country, allowing for the preservation of white supremacy and the exploitation of Black laborers, even to the extent of wanton violence. These stories about devoted slaves who remain with their owners after Emancipation and benevolent slave owners who sacrifice themselves for their slaves, however, were entirely fictional. As C. Vann Woodward explains in *The Strange Career of Jim Crow* (1974), freemen fled from their former owners, white people lived in fear of insurrection after Emancipation, and the distrust between the races contributed to segregation, Jim Crow laws, and lynching.[72] The revised narrative runs directly contrary to reality, but the nation preferred the fiction to the truth, and the fiction legitimated the continued exploitation of laborers by landowners.

## Black Codes

In the imaginations of many American readers, reconciliation narratives and plantation fiction normalized the ideology of sharecropping as a form of racialized labor exploitation in the decades after Emancipation. These racist works suggested that Blacks and whites had a special relationship based on benevolent paternalism and that they had a functional labor arrangement that ultimately benefitted the American economy. A number of African American writers, however, used literature to challenge the ideology of exploitation by exposing the violence inherent in the system. Following Emancipation, former slaves reasonably expected a significant degree of control over their own lives, their families, and their labor. While it may be difficult to imagine how people who lived in slavery conceived of freedom, one can fully expect that they anticipated that it would be tangibly different than their previous condition. As Reconstruction came to an end and as sharecropping and black codes infringed on civil rights, in spite of the Fourteenth and Fifteenth Amendments, the optimism that African Americans felt about freedom turned to resentment, resignation, and hope for revolution. African Americans after Emancipation were subject to exploitation, disfranchisement, and violence, and they had few forms of redress available to them, leaving them in a condition comparable to slavery but without the inherent moral outrage of slavery. Gene Jarrett contends in *Representing the Race* (2011) that literature was one of the few means of transforming society available to African Americans in the decades both before and after Emancipation, but whereas abolitionist writers before Emancipation could directly confront slavery, post-Emancipation writers wrote about the exploitation of Black people in code.

In *Iola Leroy* (1892), the novel that epitomizes the uplift movement, Frances Ellen Watkins Harper depicts Black intellectuals discussing the post-Emancipation fate of the race in a set of hypothetical position papers presented in a converzazione. Although published in 1892, the book is set at the transition from slavery to freedom, and the participants in the conversation reflect a sense of optimism about the possibilities of freedom. One character, for example, says, "Just now we have the fearful grinding and friction which comes in the course of an adjustment of the new machinery of freedom in the old ruts of slavery. But I am optimistic enough to believe that there will yet be a far higher and better Christian civilization than our country has ever known."[73] The novel's overarching message concerns the responsibility of African American leaders and intellectuals to commit themselves to improving the condition of their fellow men, a struggle that had gained relatively little traction in the generation after Emancipation.[74] Another character, however, blames young Black men, expressing concern about "the lack of home training for those for whom the discipline of the plantation has been exchanged for the penalties of prisons and chain gangs."[75] This is one of the few expressions of racial pessimism in the novel, and soon after this exchange the novel's protagonists marry and move to North Carolina to fight for racial uplift. But the cause of racial uplift that the book champions is in itself a form of racial self-blaming because it suggests that African Americans are responsible for their own condition. By 1892, any rational person would recognize that African Americans were victims of an elaborate socioeconomic matrix that deliberately delayed their political agency, legal authority, academic achievement, and financial power in order to exploit their labor. It was obvious in Jim Crow laws, in poll taxes, in sharecropping contracts, and in lynching. Thus, the novel's bootstrap moralizing appears naïve.

Yet in the context of the 1890s, the book's naïveté functions as an appeal to pathos. Gerald David Jaynes documents in *Branches without Roots: Genesis of the Black Working Class in the American South, 1862–1882* (1986) that the southern labor market after Emancipation was initially unstable. Sharecropping arrangements emerged quickly after the war as laborers and planters alike eschewed wage labor, but laborers continued to retain a degree of autonomy through microaggressions, such as slowing their work, withholding labor, or pitting one planter against another for better arrangements. Incrementally, the labor system became more repressive as debt became a means of control and bondage. Sharecropping contracts enforced by the Freedmen's Bureau devolved into unenforceable oral agreements, merchants developed crop lien contracts to provide food and supplies for a usurious interest rate, and whites used wanton violence to diminish Black social and political freedom. Laborers who could not repay the lien would have their debt carried over to the next year making them unable to seek new arrangements and effectively holding them in bondage. Meanwhile, Jim Crow laws became more repressive, limiting African Americans' movement through public space and their social agency, and even more overt forms of debt bondage became commonplace. In some cases, laborers were held in peonage to landowners who paid their fines for petty crimes; in other cases, African Americans were convicted of breaking black codes, crimes such as vagrancy, and leased to companies and plantations to work out their sentences. In the most horrific cases, African Americans were lynched to demonstrate that the white community held ultimate authority over life and death. By the 1890s, all of these repressive practices functioned within an ideological framework of white supremacy that permitted no criticism, not even from white writers, as George Washington Cable learned, and certainly not from Black writers without serious consequences.[76]

In his last novel, *The Colonel's Dream* (1905), Charles Chesnutt critiques the culture of labor exploitation in the post-Emancipation South.[77] A light-skinned African American, he passed through the nation's complicated, racist literary marketplace, publishing stories in high-profile journals and novels with established presses when few other African American writers were able to do so.[78] His most famous works, the conjure tales featuring Uncle Julius McAdoo, challenged the plantation romances and dialect stories that portrayed Black characters as simpleminded by depicting Uncle Julius as a trickster figure who uses his stories to manipulate the white power structure. His novel *The Marrow of Tradition* exposes the means whites in the South used to intimidate Blacks by recounting the gruesome Wilmington Massacre of 1898, when racist whites violently overthrew a democratically elected fusion government, eliminating the last trace of Black political participation in the South. Chesnutt was himself a trickster figure in American literature who used his stories to critique the white power structure, but he knew how to use patrons for protection and how to critique indirectly rather than openly antagonizing. In *The Colonel's Dream,* he uses a white protagonist and a cast of stereotypical African American characters to depict the problems with labor exploitation in the South.[79] According to William L. Andrews, the book asks, "could an enlightened and fair-minded white man, blessed with economic power and moral influence, help the southern black man win what he could not achieve alone?"[80] The answer, of course, is no because no single person, no matter how privileged, could change the South's ideological structure alone, but Colonel French's story achieves its effect by exposing how the ideology of exploitation affects African Americans. He makes his agenda clear in the book's dedication "to the great number of those who are seeking, in whatever manner or degree, from near at hand or far away, to bring the forces of enlightenment to bear upon the vexed problems which harass the South."[81]

Colonel French, the eponymous dreamer, is an idealized protagonist in the novel. Chesnutt borrows from the hyperbolic masculine tropes of plantation tales to endow him with all of the characteristics of a postbellum planter—courage, honor, nobility, and a profound allegiance to the southern cause. Consider, for example, the story of how he became a colonel: "He had served in the Southern army, in a regiment that had fought with such desperate valour that the honour of colonelcy had come to him at nineteen."[82] Chesnutt signifies on Page and the other plantation writers by depicting this character as an idealized aristocrat, reflecting the fiction of white aristocracy. The colonel meets all the requisite qualifications of noblesse oblige, but there is one problem. After the war, his one remaining relative brought him to New York, where he became a man of business, growing wealthy in the process, and where he learned the values of progressive northern industrialism. The people of his hometown regard him somewhat suspiciously because of his career in the North, but they are willing to accept him because of his family's status. He, thus, becomes a planter/carpetbagger hybrid. This proves inevitably to be his downfall, suggesting that southern values are incompatible with mainstream American values.

When Colonel French returns to the South, he is ensnared in the lingering legacy of paternalism. He takes his young son to visit his family's cemetery plot to connect him with the family's noble history, and they encounter "a very black and seemingly aged Negro" cleaning the family plot.[83] The man is Uncle Peter, who had been Colonel French's slave in his childhood. As they reminisce about their lives before the war, Peter says, "'Deed dem wuz good ole time!" uttering almost exactly the same risible statement as Sam in "Marse Chan."[84] Chesnutt found the conventions of plantation fiction useful, according to William L. Andrews, but he subverts the message of plantation fiction by drawing attention to why Uncle Peter might make such an absurd statement.[85] Page suggests that former slaves would miss the supposed contentment of slavery, where all their needs were met by the benevolent and adoring masters, but Chesnutt illustrates that freedom has been problematic. As Peter tells him about his life after the war, the colonel wonders, "What good had freedom done for Peter?"[86] While he recognizes that a petted house slave might have lived more comfortably than Peter, he decides that "Peter had been better free," and he realizes that he is also better off because of Emancipation.[87] "Had Peter remained a slave," he thinks, "then the colonel would have remained a master, which was only another form of slavery."[88] Because he is not dependent on slaves to work for him and because his capital is not invested in humans, he is free to earn a living of his own and to amass wealth in financial investments, so Emancipation, according to Chesnutt's subtle suggestion, is a benefit to the former slaveholders, even though the former slaveholders probably would not recognize the advantage themselves. Freedom, meanwhile, has not helped Peter because he remains at a social disadvantage. He had no abilities, education, or resources at his disposal at the time of Emancipation, and repressive structures developed over time that prevented him from ever recovering from his disadvantage.

Chesnutt uses Peter to demonstrate how the repressive structures function to exploit African Americans. Soon after the reunion scene at the cemetery, a constable arrests Peter on charges of vagrancy. Because Peter does not have a job or a protection of a white person, he is subject to be arrested for one of the most transparent black codes, vagrancy, the supposed crime of unemployment. This notorious law was intended to force former slaves to work for landowners who needed cheap labor, and Chesnutt uses Peter to describe the process. Peter is taken to jail where he is held until his bail is paid or until court meets. In most cases, a person arrested for vagrancy would be given a sentence of extended hard labor, often a few years for a minor offence, but in some cases, a landowner would pay the bail of an alleged criminal in return for a period of contracted labor. Landowners could thus purchase cheap labor "til the cotton crop is picked" in lieu of taking on sharecroppers.[89] To make the comparison to slavery completely apparent, Chesnutt depicts an auction at which landowners bid on the prisoners' labor, where the person willing to pay the alleged criminal's fine in exchange for the shortest period of work wins. Inmates accused of serious crimes come at high prices requiring long contracts that virtually replicate slavery. Peter, an elderly man, does not attract much interest until Colonel French happens upon the auction taking place in the street. "Fresh from the land of labor unions," he finds the sight of the auction odious, and he intervenes to purchase Peter, "a purchase which his father had made, upon terms not very different, fifty years before."[90] He thus finds himself shackled, because he cannot immediately release Peter, as he will be re-arrested for vagrancy, so he is forced to take Peter on as a servant, essentially unraveling Emancipation for both of them.

The colonel has a dream of a New South. Stirred simultaneously by a sense of nostalgia and affection for the South and a sense of outrage and pity for southerners, he decides to apply his Yankee ingenuity to reforming the South:

> He dreamed of a regenerated South, filled with thriving industries, and thronged with a prosperous and happy people, where every man, having enough for his needs, was willing that every other man should have the same; where law and order should prevail unquestioned, and where every man could enter, through the golden gate of hope, the field of opportunity where lay the prizes of life, which all might have an equal chance to win or lose.[91]

His plan is to reopen a dilapidated textile mill—C. Vann Woodward's so-called "symbol of the New South, its origins, and its promise of salvation"—and to pay his workers a fair wage, regardless of their race.[92] The basic outline of his plan is a caricature of the New South Creed, the movement to cultivate northern investment in southern industry to improve the region's overall quality of life. To counterpoint this creed, however, Chesnutt describes an ordinary southern cotton mill owned by a man named Fetters that is a Dickensian nightmare of despair and brutality, where women and children work grueling shifts under vicious overseers. Undeterred, the colonel persists in his plan, but he encounters resentment from townspeople who disapprove of Black workers being paid the same wage as white workers for the same work, and local opinion turns against him when he makes a Black mason foreman of a crew with white workers. Every attempt he makes at reform in the best interests of his community meets resistance, even when his motives are good, if somewhat naïve. Chesnutt makes clear that the southerners do not actually want progress, in spite of the New South Creed. The South has a habit of killing dreams.[93]

Fetters, the mill owner, is the antagonist in the novel. In addition to owning the mill, he owns the bank, mortgages on most of the farms in the area, a large plantation, and the political will of most of the people in North Carolina. Because of his control, the large farmers are in debt, and "the small farmers, many of whom were coloured, were practically tied to the soil by ropes of debt and chains of contract."[94] Fetters, whose name suggests bondage, embodies the repressive structures and ideologies of the New Old South. He uses credit and debt, rather than slavery, to maintain control of every element of the community. Most of the farms actually belong to him, but he rarely forecloses, preferring to allow the farmers to fall deeper into debt and then claim the property when they are completely destitute or dead.[95] The most abject people in the novel are the convicts whom Fetters leases to work on his desolate plantation, where they work in gangs under the supervision of overseers who use the lash to manage their labor, placing these peons in a condition even worse than slavery. Chesnutt's characterization of Fetters as omnipotent yet mostly invisible in rural North Carolina suggests the insidious pervasiveness of labor exploitation in the South.

At the beginning of the twentieth century, the United States saw a shocking revelation of southern depravity. In 1903, the Justice Department brought charges of peonage against several farmers in Alabama, accusing them of holding laborers in debt bondage, as Fetters does on his plantation. The charges shocked the nation, and the northern press pilloried the South, leading to a new, short-lived wave of neoabolition.[96] Chesnutt wrote an article about the cases, titled "Peonage, or the New Slavery," that explains the ideology of peonage:

> Under the renting system, the crop mortgage laws leave the laborer but little more than a slave to the soil, while at the worst the Southern labor system presents peonage, or the new slavery. The old habit of making the Negro work for the white people for their board and clothes has in large measure survived. Enough Negroes have risen above this level to present a remarkable average of industrial progress, but the majority are still subject in one way or another to the old rule. This continuity of social custom is sufficient in part to account for the survival of slavery in some modified form. When to this is added the temptation of greed and cunning to take advantage of poverty and ignorance, it is not strange that peonage should exist. Taking into account the artificial solidarity of the white South on all questions relating to the rights of the Negro and in all matters between white and black, it is easily seen why the State Courts were inadequate to cope with the evil. The individuals who bribe constables and justices to arrest ignorant and friendless Negroes and sentence them to servitude, are the same men who, in a more Northern latitude, would exploit imported foreign workmen in factories and sweatshops, or immature white children in the cotton mills, and bribe legislatures and city councils to betray the rights of people and grind the faces of the poor in the interest of their own selfish greed.[97]

His recognition that northern laborers are not immune to exploitation is important because the labor union movement was gaining momentum at the same time, but the peonage cases proved to be a lost cause for the Justice Department. While strikes and labor organization led to better conditions for factory workers in America, the justice department quickly realized that the practice of peonage was too widespread and too deeply ingrained in the South, and the prosecutions ended with minimal sentences for the offenders.

*The Colonel's Dream* ends with a sense of resignation about the South's future. Uncle Peter dies trying to save the colonel's son from a train. They both die in the accident, and the colonel has them buried in the family plot in the cemetery where he reunited with Peter, but burying a Black person in the white section of the cemetery enrages the white community. The next day, the colonel finds Peter's coffin on his front porch with a note nailed to the lid, "upon which were some lines rudely scratched in a handwriting that matched the spelling," telling him to "berry yore ole nigger somewhar else," and signed "Cumitty."[98] The symbolism here is heavy-handed: the South has resurrected the corpse of slavery. Colonel French leaves, his dream deferred, burying both Peter and his son in the North and never returning to the South. The book ends with a rueful benediction. Progress in the South moves slowly, "here and there a brave judge has condemned the infamy of the chain gang and convict lease systems," but no great change has been made, and the community lags farther and farther behind: grass grows in the streets, the schools fall into disrepair, weeds grow over the graves, and "vines soon overgrew the unfinished walls of the colonel's cotton mill."[99] The conclusion is lugubrious, and Matthew Wilson argues that "Chesnutt self-destructs as a writer" because the book "so contradicted conventional understandings of the time and did so in a form that was purposely self-defeating."[100] (149). This assessment goes too far, and the fact that a book that makes a modest proposal for social reform ends tragically only substantiates the force of the ideology of exploitation. Even in fiction, it cannot be challenged, and the book's supposed self-destruction is, in fact, the point of the book.

At a time when racially repressive structures were rife in the US South, relatively few African American intellectuals dared to criticize the white power structure, focusing instead on advocating for reform and uplift from within the African American community, and of those African American writers who did challenge white hegemony, most focused their critiques on political disfranchisement, educational inequality, or lynching. Works by African Americans analyzing racialized labor exploitation in the decades after Emancipation, thus, are rare. *The Colonel's Dream* is probably the best example in fiction, and *Black and White: Land, Labor, and Politics in the South* (1884) by T. Thomas Fortune is probably the best example in nonfiction. Editor of the most prominent African American newspaper of the 1880s and 1890s, *New York Age,* Fortune was a prominent activist for civil rights who helped found several African American organizations, ghostwrote for Booker T. Washington, and eventually edited *The Negro World,* newspaper of the UNIA. In *Black and White,* he eschews rhetorical dissembling, the kind of coded messaging that Chesnutt uses, and writes aggressively about the situation of Black life in the South.

He argues that sharecropping is an evil greater than slavery. In a biting and cogent analysis, he contends that sharecroppers are "more absolutely under the control of the Southern whites; they are more systematically robbed of their labor; they are more poorly housed, clothed and fed, than under the slave regime."[101] Sharecroppers have no legal protection, no status as citizens, and no political franchise. The problem, he asserts, is that African Americans are alienated from the land. Their labor produces commodity crops that support the landowners, but they do not own the land themselves, and they do not directly benefit from the products of the land. He exclaims, "The real grievance is the false system which makes the landlord possible."[102] Sharecropping, he writes, is "the great social wrong which has turned the beautiful roses of freedom into thorns to prick the hands of the black men of the South; which made slavery a blessing, paradoxical as it may appear, and freedom a curse."[103] Under sharecropping, laborers have been detached from the means of production, thus, dehumanizing their labor.

Although he never advocates Communism *per se,* his critique of sharecropping has strong Marxist influences. He uses Marxist vocabulary, such as referring to laborers as a "proletariat," and he calls for a revolution among the sharecroppers.[104] Echoing *The Communist Manifesto,* he tells all workers to unite to throw off the landlords who control the means of production. He exhorts, "the condition of the black and white worker is the same, and that consequently their cause is common; that they should unite under the one banner and work upon the same principles for the uplifting of labor."[105] In the course of arguing for laborers to recognize a common cause, he makes a number of predictions that prove to be false. For example, he asserts that "the future struggle in the South will be, not between white men and black men, but between capital and labor, landlord and tenant" and that eventually laboring classes in all parts of the country "will recognize that they have a common cause, a common humanity, and a common enemy."[106] While he correctly diagnoses the problem of sharecropping, he underestimates the persistence of white supremacist ideology. In a few exceptional cases in the coming decades, white and Black sharecroppers would find common cause, but these instances are rare, and the ideology of exploitation defined the dominant labor paradigm in the post-Emancipation South. Fortune's book is valuable primarily for its unusual aggressiveness on economic issues, and it is unsurprising that Fortune would cycle through several ill-fated civil rights organizations over the course of his career in an attempt to find a solution to exploitation.

In 1935, W. E. B. Du Bois wrote a retrospective history of African Americans since Emancipation, *Black Reconstruction in America* (1935), and he sounded a sanguine note. Describing the collapse of Reconstruction in the 1870s, he writes, "It must be remembered and never forgotten that the civil war in the South which overthrew Reconstruction was a determined effort to reduce Black labor as nearly as possible to a condition of unlimited exploitation and build a new class of capitalists on this foundation."[107] He goes on to assert that all of the repressive social structures that developed after the war, including disenfranchisement, sharecropping, and peonage, were deliberate strategies to debase African Americans and to "beat the black laborer into submission."[108] Echoing the sentiments of Chesnutt and Fortune, he suggests that Emancipation has made race relations more antagonistic, because it "loosed the finer feelings of some Southerners toward Negroes."[109] In this context, the likelihood of racial advancement was negligible, yet he argues that African Americans have made progress, but it is important to recognize the forces that push back against that progress. For most Americans, the ideologies that repressed racial economic advancement were so deeply ingrained that they were invisible, and most Americans then, as now, were likely to blame African Americans for their own lack of progress. But this is the false promise of Emancipation: it freed masters from slaves, but it did not free the slaves from masters.

During the Civil War, the cause of Emancipation was a moral crusade to rid the United States of a great national sin and to extend the promise of freedom and democracy to all of the American people. After the war, during the so-called "radical" phase of Reconstruction, the federal government extended protection to African Americans in the form of the Freedmen's Bureau to provide legal representation and educational resources, and the Thirteenth, Fourteenth, and Fifteenth Amendments to the Constitution to abolish slavery, establish citizenship rights, and extend the franchise. Yet at the same time, the overriding economic priority to redevelop cotton production allowed for economic practices that exploited labor, initially as a form of expedient compromise and eventually as a form of hegemonic repression. "A response to the new working arrangements that arose after emancipation," Laura Edwards writes, "sharecropping effectively defined most African American agricultural workers as common laborers and denied them the relative independence associated with tenancy."[110] Reestablishing white supremacy required making former slaves dependent upon landowners for food, shelter, and legal protection, which involved a massive socioeconomic shift to generate a system that limited the agency of laborers and empowered landowners.

In the imaginations of many American readers, reconciliation narratives and plantation fiction normalized the ideology of sharecropping as a form of labor exploitation in the decades after Emancipation. These racist works suggested that Blacks and whites had a special relationship based on benevolent paternalism and that this functional labor arrangement ultimately benefited the American economy. A number of African American writers, however, used literature to challenge the ideology of exploitation by exposing the violence inherent in the system. In *The Literature of Reconstruction: Not in Plain Black and White* (2017), Brook Thomas states, "attention to works of literature can enhance our historical understanding of Reconstruction."[111] Since this historical period is often shrouded in myths about the Lost Cause and federal intervention, reading works of Reconstruction literature is vital to understand the ideological maneuvers that took place after the Civil War to redevelop the southern economy, reinstate white supremacy, support the passage of the Black Codes, and convert former slaves and poor whites into sharecroppers.

Then, as now, America valued commerce over human rights, and sharecroppers were left to languish in their condition, falling deeper and deeper into exploitation. Meanwhile, America could simultaneously assert the moral authority of abolishing slavery and the economic authority of producing the majority of the world's cotton. Yet the United States was not the only nation to use sharecroppers to produce cotton. The practice was common in most cotton-producing areas, including India, Mexico, China, and Egypt, as a means of coercing and controlling labor, but in the United States, sharecropping originated distinctly from the end of slavery, marking a transition from one exploitative labor paradigm to another.[112] Soon, however, sharecropping in America extended beyond the boundaries of race, and eventually millions of white southerners found themselves victims of the ideology of exploitation. Rather than being a transitional solution to a short-term problem, sharecropping became the foundation of the way of life in the US South.

→ 3 ←

# The New Slavery

In 1919, an insurrection broke out in Arkansas. A group of sharecroppers in Elaine, Arkansas, created the Progressive Farmers and Household Union of America, a fraternal organization for mutual protection of laborers from the exploitation of landowners intent on cheating them from the value of their cotton. When they met with an attorney's representative in a rural church, a group of white police officers fired into the building. Armed men inside the church returned fire, killing one officer and wounding another. Over the next few days, an enormous posse descended on the community, including units of veterans newly returned from World War I. In the ensuing violence, hundreds of Black sharecroppers and their families were killed, with estimates ranging from as few as two hundred to as many as eight hundred dead. Hundreds more people were detained, interrogated, and tortured. The local landowners and the Arkansas government attempted to cover up the massacre, claiming that only a few people were killed, but Walter White and Ida B. Wells-Barnett investigated the incident. White used his ability to pass as a white man to interview the governor about the state's martial response to the incident, and he was nearly lynched when he went to Elaine to investigate further. Wells-Barnett recorded witnesses' accounts of the massacre in the pamphlet "The Arkansas Race Riot" (1919), in which she argued for clemency toward twelve men sentenced to death for their role in the union.[1] White officials in Arkansas deliberately used the language of slave uprisings to describe a labor dispute and to legitimate their brutal response to it. They contended that it "was not a race riot. It [was] a deliberately planned insurrection of the negroes against the whites."[2]

Sharecroppers in Elaine unionized to protect themselves from systematic exploitation by landowners. Elaine is a small community in Phillips County, and in the early twentieth century, it was a hub of New South plantation development. Investors purchased the swampy, heavily timbered delta land on the west side of the Mississippi River, used heavy equipment to clear and drain it, and established hundreds of sharecropping plots growing thousands of bales of cotton. The area transformed from a swamp to a cotton empire within a few years, but labor tensions were quickly evident. A 1916 federal report on tenancy in the Southwest, including Arkansas and Texas, presciently stated that "as a result of both of the evils inherent in the tenant system and of the occasional oppression by landlords, a state of acute unrest is developing among the tenants and may result in civil disturbances of a serious character."[3] Landowners in Phillips County were using the same methods as landowners across the South to exploit their laborers. Sharecroppers could only sell their cotton to their landowner, who could in turn sell it on the open market; sharecroppers could not break or renegotiate contracts, most of which were oral and legally unenforceable; sharecroppers could not determine how to use their land without explicit permission from the landowner; and sharecroppers had essentially no political, legal, or social standing even though they composed the majority of the county's population. To correct these circumstances, laborers formed a union based on the model of a fraternal order, pooled their meager resources, and attempted to hire an attorney to represent their interests. A few days after the initial contact with the attorney's office, hundreds of people were dead, and the remaining workers were forced back into the fields to pick cotton.

The Elaine massacre took place immediately after World War I. Many of the sharecroppers had recently returned from service in the military where they had been involved in an international fight for freedom and democracy. These veterans likely expected to find some degree of freedom and democracy for themselves in America. At the same time, the end of the war brought a spike in cotton prices, making that year's crop the most profitable in decades. Both landowners and sharecroppers wanted a share of those proceeds, but the brutality with which the landowners met a relatively small request for self-determination suggests that the issue was much bigger than a share of the profits. Nan Woodruff writes in *American Congo* (2003), "the wholesale massacre in Phillips County indicated how fearful planters and their allies had become of the changes the war had brought, and it revealed their determination to destroy the aspirations of Delta black people."⁴ The local planters, the state government, and the federal government cooperated to make clear that any deviation from the current system of labor would not be tolerated. The Elaine massacre indicates the explosive level of tension between planters and laborers in one specific time and place, but the same tensions were persistent and endemic to the sharecropping system practiced throughout the South. By the beginning of the twentieth century, relations between landowners and laborers reached a peculiar détente, in which planters influenced every element of the social structure for the purpose of exploiting labor. They limited laborers' social, political, and economic agency as means of extracting labor as free from cost as possible. Decades after Emancipation, sharecropping persisted as the dominant system of labor in the US South, a paradigm that simultaneously ensnared Black laborers in systemic racism and embedded laborers—regardless of their color—in a pernicious cycle of labor exploitation.

By the early twentieth century, many Americans were aware of the South's numerous social problems. In 1924, sociologist Frank Tannenbaum published *Darker Phases of the South*, a provocative analysis of the region's major problems. He observes that the South's single-crop commodity system "leads to a concentration of land, of economic power, and of political influence in the hands of a small group of creditors, and reduces the actual growers of cotton to a state of dependence upon them," reducing the laborers to a "slave status."⁵ By the 1920s, rates of tenancy had grown significantly, and the majority of farms in South Carolina, Georgia, Alabama, Mississippi, Arkansas, Louisiana, and Texas were worked by tenants rather than by landowners.⁶ At that time, tenants cultivated more than fifty percent of the improved land in Georgia and South Carolina and more than forty percent in Texas, Louisiana, Arkansas, Mississippi, and Alabama, and across the South there were roughly as many farm tenants as farm owners. The 1920 agricultural census paid special attention to the circumstances of southern sharecroppers because their condition impacted the overall agricultural composition of the nation. The census states that unlike farm renters in other parts of the nation, southern sharecroppers did not expect to ever own their own land. The census figures could be lower than the actual figures, as many sharecroppers may have been unlikely or unwilling to respond to census takers. Yet the existing data makes clear that by the early twentieth century the South developed a vast underclass of laborers who were landless yet tied to their crops; who were nearly half the population but who had very little political, economic, or social agency; and who were only slightly better off than slaves.

Sharecropping was a problem not only for sharecroppers but also for the entire South. Sharecropping enforced poverty for millions of southerners, which in turn lowered the region's rate of economic development and per capita income. It also substantially lowered the region's literacy rates, access to healthcare, life expectancy, and infant mortality. Disenfranchising millions of African Americans, meanwhile, greatly hampered the region's political influence and moral authority. With the exception of number of bales of cotton picked, every aspect of sharecropping was deleterious. Occasionally, the government or reform agencies attempted to intervene on behalf of the laborers or the benighted South, but as William Link documents in *The Paradox of Southern Progressivism* (1992), their attempts were often thwarted, both through the opposition of laborers who resented paternalistic intervention and landowners who opposed outside meddling. Similarly, southerners largely ignored the government's call to diversify agriculture in the face of imminent threats, including drought, flood, and the boll weevil. In *Boll Weevil Blues* (2011), James Giesen describes one especially telling incident. In a campaign to encourage farmers to prepare for the advancing insects, a train bearing several agronomists and extension agents intended to cross the Mississippi Delta, but it was stopped by planters who prevented their workers from attending the demonstrations. Giesen explains that planters feared losing control of their laborers more than they feared losing their crops.[7]

In the years between the *Plessy v. Ferguson* ruling in 1896 and the collapse of the stock market in 1929, sharecropping ossified into a rigid system of persistent labor exploitation. As the Elaine massacre illustrates, any challenges to the system would not be tolerated, and, furthermore, any changes to the system, even those that would otherwise benefit the entire region, would not be allowed. The ideology of exploitation encompassed white supremacy, and it allowed for the transracial exploitation of poor whites and Latinos. It permitted ritualistic, orgiastic violence, in addition to dozens of forms of coercion, limitation, and manipulation that infringed on human rights. For many exploited laborers in the South, the only ways to resist exploitation were to leave the South or to die. The ideology penetrated every element of southern culture, everyday life, and social order. History and economics can describe many elements of the southern system of agricultural labor, but literature reveals many of the subtle, frequently irrational, aspects of the system, humanizing the exploiters and the exploited, both of whom often worked directly against their own best interests for a host of complex reasons.

## Rise of the Merchant Class

The southern plantation in the early twentieth century served the same economic purpose as the antebellum plantation, namely, to generate profit through the cultivation of commodity crops. Antebellum plantation owners often invested their proceeds in capital investments, usually land and slaves. The finance structure of the modern, postbellum plantation system was quite different. Slaves, a form of capital, were replaced with laborers, a liability, and modern plantation owners, faced with the uncertainty of debt and fluctuating commodity prices, extracted as much labor from their workers as possible for as little cost as possible, using contracts, laws, and debts to manipulate and exploit the laborers. The locus of capital in the modern South shifted from large planters to furnish merchants—store owners who provided tools, seed, fertilizer, and food to laborers in exchange for a lien on the crop. In many cases, furnish merchants were also landowners, such as Jody Varner in Faulkner's *The Hamlet* (1940) and Militiades Vaiden in T. S. Stribling's *The Store* (1932). A furnish merchant in *The Store* explains how the system developed: "the war ushered in a new method of accumulating money. This was the method of working negroes under mortgages instead of under simple chattel slavery. Handback and thousands of other merchants just like him perfected this method. It did away with the great landowners, or, rather, it shifted the proprietorship in the land from the manor to the store."[8] The war mostly eradicated the South's banking system, leaving the region without capital and financing, so furnish merchants emerged as a grassroots network of credit providers to finance the planting of a crop. The system was inherently unstable because it perpetually financed next year's crop at the expense of this year's crop, preventing the possibility of profit taking at settlement time, and because it required the consistent exploitation of laborers, who were the most persistent fixed cost in the system.[9]

Amassing a fortune in this precarious economic system required risk, ruthlessness, and audacity. The most famous literary character to make the difficult journey from rags to riches in the literature of the early twentieth-century South is Faulkner's Flem Snopes, the son of a sharecropper, who uses his father's reputation for barn burning to get a position in a crossroads store and then uses his uncanny knack for accounts and market manipulation to rise to bank president in Jefferson in the Snopes trilogy. Faulkner's account of Flem Snopes corresponds with his younger brother John Faulkner's novel *Dollar Cotton* (1942), the story of a Tennessee hill farmer, Otis Town, who builds and loses a vast alluvial empire encompassing thousands of acres of the Delta. The novels of both Faulkner brothers echo Stribling's Pulitzer Prize-winning novel *The Store,* in which Miltiades Vaiden swindles his business partner to take control of a store and several plantations. Critics have noticed the connections among the texts, and they share a similar narrative arc from poverty to bourgeois success to tragedy.[10] Vaiden and Town are the unambiguous protagonists of their stories, which invites the reader to identify with their success and failure. The story of Snopes's rise, in contrast, is told indirectly from the perspective of the community at Varner's crossroads in *The Hamlet,* foreclosing the reader's ability to identify with him and making him appear manipulative and callous. In most narratives of sharecropping, the landowner or furnish merchant appears as the antagonist embodying the socioeconomic forces that exploit the sharecroppers. In these three novels, however, the landowners and furnish merchants exploit the laborers, but they are also the protagonists who are themselves subject to socioeconomic forces.

The typical path to wealth in the antebellum South was through the accumulation of land and slaves, but the path to wealth in the postbellum South was through the accumulation of other people's mortgages and laborers' debts. Furnish merchants provided laborers with goods—including seed, fertilizer, tools, food, clothing, medicine, and any other item a family might use—on credit using the laborers' share of the crop as collateral.[11] This method of credit was known as the crop lien. In some cases, a landowner would provide furnish directly to his own tenants through a commissary. Otis Town furnishes his own laborers, and his commissary is a key source of revenue. When the cotton is ginned, he calls his workers "into the commissary one at a time and settled with them. After having charged for everything he thought they would stand, he added ten percent as fair interest, then sold them cheap whiskey at bonded prices for what little money they did draw."[12] Other merchants would furnish materials for laborers working for landowners in the vicinity, some of which might be working on land they owned. Will Varner's store provides this service, and it is highly significant in the novel that Varner allows Flem Snopes to help him calculate settlements soon after he comes to the store. Because settlement determines both the maintenance of a labor force for another year and the profit margin for this year's crop, it is an extremely sensitive process, and the fact that Will allows Flem to calculate settlement rather than his own son signals "the usurpation of an heirship."[13] By the holding laborers' accounts, merchants effectively functioned as financiers in their communities, and they would often hold mortgages to landowners' farms, which they could acquire through foreclosure if the landowner defaulted in the debt. In this way, merchants could become plantation owners. Miltiades Vaiden learns the principles of southern commerce by supervising the farms owned by his employer. He learns, for example, that Black sharecroppers are cheaper than white sharecroppers and that it is cost effective to push sharecroppers off their plots at the end of each season.[14] Ultimately, the entire system depends upon the price of cotton on the international commodity market, so it is highly unstable and prone to default. Furnish merchants, thus, provided credit and financing because banks were unwilling to invest in cotton growers.

The system also had minimal oversight, and the laws on the books greatly benefited the furnish merchants and landowners, giving them nearly absolute control over their laborers.[15] They could determine when, where, and what was planted; how it was fertilized, cultivated, and harvested; and what kinds of cabin, tools, animals, and food laborers could use. Vaiden, for example, visits a sharecropper's home and inspects his manure pile, telling him that he came "not just to see it, to tell you where to put it, and I'll be around every week or so to see that you put it there."[16] Their control over the laborers was a function of the system of credit. The land, housing, seed, fertilizer, and all other elements of crop production were debits on the potential crop that would diminish the value of the harvest, so landowners had an interest in minimizing investment to maximize return. While the crop lien laws protected the landowners and furnish merchants, they provided no protections to prevent the landowners from cheating their laborers. In one particularly creative means of swindling laborers, Otis Town tricks his laborers at settlement. For a laborer named Henry, he tabulates the amount of cotton picked, $8,000, and then subtracts the value of furnish and debts, leaving $600. He then tells Henry that he can take a check for $600 or take a hat filled with cash money, and Henry's "unhesitating hand took the hat full of quarters and halves from the counter," totaling $135.[17] As a result of this exchange, Town receives his share of the crop, recovers the cost of his investment in the growing of the crop plus interest, and cheats the laborer out of an additional $435. His means are brazen, but cheating laborers was not unusual.

Some landowners defended the practice of sharecropping and castigated landowners who cheated their laborers. In his memoirs, *Lanterns on the Levee* (1941), William Alexander Percy, who inherited an enormous plantation in the Mississippi Delta from his father, describes the practice as an equitable arrangement, in which the landowner takes more risk than the laborer because in a bad year the landowner is likely to lose the land while the laborer is likely to lose nothing because he has nothing to lose.[18] Percy continued the arrangement as his father and grandfather had developed it, and he believed "that profit-sharing is the most moral system under which human beings can work together."[19] He describes it as superior to any other labor arrangement. "Our plantation system seems to me to offer as humane, just, self-respecting, and cheerful a method of earning a living as human beings are likely to devise," he claims. "I watch the limber-jointed, oily-black, well-fed, decently clothed peasants on Trail Lake [his plantation] and feel sorry for the telephone girls, the clerks in chain stores, the office help, the unskilled workers everywhere—not only for their poor and fixed wage but for their slave routine, their joyless habits of work, and their insecurity."[20] His preposterous, racist statement echoes the arguments comparing slavery to wage earning made to legitimate slavery before Emancipation, and he feigns deep offense at the accusations that sharecropping is an exploitative system. Instead, he attributes the system's failures to human nature, and he suggests that laborers should boycott unworthy landowners, as if that were a possibility.

Although Percy's rationalization for sharecropping reeks of paternalism, he is correct that landowners face a significant risk with each crop. The title of John Faulkner's *Dollar Cotton* refers to a magical and imaginary price for cotton per pound. The story takes place during the period surrounding World War I, and during the war, the price of cotton skyrocketed from seven cents a pound in 1914 to thirty-six cents a pound in 1919 as the closure of foreign markets and wartime demand drove prices up, making many southerners wealthy—temporarily. The next year, the price plummeted to sixteen cents a pound, and it did not approach thirty cents a pound again until the 1950s. In the book, Otis Town sells his cotton for a dollar a pound during the war, becoming fabulously wealthy with all the trappings of bourgeois success—expensive homes, fast cars, venal children, and nouveau riche status. When the price of cotton falls, his family abruptly loses everything. Miltiades Vaiden experiences a similar arc in *The Store*. Using the proceeds he swindled from his employer, he purchases a plantation, but a shady attorney contrives to usurp the deed and foreclose on the mortgage, leaving him destitute. Flem Snopes fares somewhat better, eventually becoming a bank president, putting him in a less precarious position financially, yet even he falls victim to his career of manipulation when he is murdered by one of his own relatives in *The Mansion* (1959).

Vaiden's decline leads to an especially revealing insight about the ideology of exploitation. Vaiden seizes his sharecroppers' tools and mules to liquidate his final assets before foreclosure, but one of the sharecroppers—who happens to be his own mixed-race son—files an injunction. A former governor of Alabama defends Vaiden in court, and he makes an impassioned speech about the system of sharecropping:

> Your honor, it is a well known fact in Alabama that no negro tenant obtains any further returns for the crop he raises than his board and keep.
>
> At the end of any agricultural year, your honor, the negro sharecropper comes out exactly even. His account at the store balances with his share of the crop. No one owes him anything.
>
> Therefore a negro tenant's connection with a plantation may be severed by the landlord at any stage of the planting because the negro has had his board and keep up to that point, and that is as much as he will ever get, no matter how long he toils.
>
> In brief, your honor, the negro share cropper in Alabama has no share in the crop he cultivates. And any contract which contemplates the negro as having a share in such a crop cannot be made the foundation of a suit in equity.[21]

The governor argues "sharecropping is a de facto perpetuation of slavery" because laborers receive food and board in exchange for their labor.[22] The only difference between sharecroppers and slaves is that slaves also have value as capital. His speech articulates a hard position on sharecropping as a form of exploitation, but it is consistent with the practice in which sharecroppers were systematically cheated out of the products of their labor. Many landowners, in fact, felt a strong disincentive to provide their laborers with remuneration because paying laborers both gave the workers an opportunity to purchase farms of their own and cut into the landowners' profit from the crop—if the crop made a profit.

Each year's crop was a gamble for the landowners, and securing financing for the crop was a challenge. Before the Civil War, cotton factors were the primary source of financing for plantation owners. They provided lines of credit, using crops and slaves and collateral, and they acted as brokers selling cotton and buying slaves on commission for the plantation owners. They were middlemen in the cotton economy, connecting the cotton growers with the textile mill owners who purchased the cotton. After the war, "new forces tended to undermine the factors' hegemony in cotton marketing. Slowly, but steadily, factors were replaced in the cotton trade by furnishing merchants, merchant-buyers, and by a new breed of speculators."[23] Otis Town uses one of the remaining cotton factors in Memphis to finance the purchase of huge tracts of land, using his crop and existing plantations as collateral. In return, the factors act as his agent, negotiating terms for the sale of his cotton and handling his accounts with banks. While the price of cotton remains high, they support his drive to expand, but when prices fall, they force him to sell his crop on unfavorable terms and foreclose on his plantations.

With his empire in ruins, Town takes the extraordinary measure of pleading his case to the New York Cotton Exchange, the world's largest and busiest commodities exchange at the time. Cotton lots and futures were sold at several commodities exchanges around the world, including exchanges in Memphis, New Orleans, and other trading centers, and buyers and sellers on the floor of the exchanges set the price of cotton. In the imagination of most cotton growers, the New York exchange would have been analogous with Wall Street, so Town's journey to the exchange is a metaphorical attempt to speak truth to power. He barges onto the trading floor and into the office of the president, the person he holds most responsible for setting the price of cotton. The president tries to explain the law of supply and demand to him, and Town tells him, "'Hit's wuth a dollar. Hit was then and we growed better cotton this past year than we did two year ago. Hit ain't right fer no one nor nothing to say cotton is wuth a dollar one year and then turn right around and say better cotton ain't wuth as much the next year.'"[24] He argues that the commodities brokers "never put no seed in the ground" and cultivated it into a crop, so they cannot know how much a crop is worth.[25] The episode is absurd, useful primarily for its symbolic value, and Town suffers a stroke in the middle of his speech, signifying the impotency of his confrontation. The commodities market was volatile, leaving cotton growers vulnerable to wild swings in the value of cotton on the international market, and this confrontation reveals the limitations of the landowners' power.

Cotton growers, landowners, and furnish merchants faced several forces beyond their control that effectively dictated the value of their crop and, thus, the stability of the southern economy. In this precarious system, credit and financing were unsecure. Because most banks were unwilling to lend money directly to cotton growers, an informal and insecure system of local credit emerged in which merchants and landowners passed their risks onto their laborers. Under this arrangement, the landowners and merchants were "virtually forced to exploit the tenant if [they are] to survive."[26] Landowners exploited laborers because they had to, because they could, and because they had every incentive to do so. Ultimately, the harder question to answer is why they remained committed to growing cotton and other commodity crops when the risks were so great and the potential returns were so low? Would they not have been better served to use the natural resources and labor force available to diversify the economy? A 1935 study of the cotton industry states, "The explanation is obvious. Unsatisfactory though the returns on cotton are, on an average, cotton is usually the most remunerative cash crop which can be produced on southern farms."[27] The existing apparatus of credit, precarious though it was, was constructed entirely on the production of commodities; the local infrastructures of trade, primitive though they were, were designed to carry specific commodities to market; and the local systems of labor, exploitative though they were, were created to control laborers by limiting their opportunities, social mobility, and access to education, thus forcing them into poverty. Landowners and merchants exploited laborers because they could, and laborers submitted to exploitation because they had to.

## Sharecropping and Social Death

"In cultural terms," Orlando Patterson writes in *Slavery and Social Death* (1982), "enslavement, slavery, and manumission were symbolically interpreted as three phases in an extended rite of passage. Enslavement was separation (or symbolic execution), slavery was a liminal state of social death, and manumission was a symbolic rebirth."[28] When a slave is freed, they are ordinarily reintegrated into the social structure through a process of transformation, yet Patterson finds that the process "deepened the ties of dependency between ex-slave and ex-master" in ways that invariably benefited the former master class.[29] While the former masters maintained dominance in the postslavery relationship, the process in the US South was deliberately extended in a way that limited the former slaves' agency for generations, forcing Blacks into a set of social relationships that replicated the conditions of slavery for several decades after Emancipation. Most Black southerners in the early twentieth-century South were free in name only, and they continued to live under the nearly totalizing domination of landowners who held all of the means of production as well as all of the social and political agency. The Black laborers in the period between Emancipation and the civil rights movement existed in a state of social limbo, not entirely dead yet far from alive.

The federal government did not officially recognize the existence of southern sharecroppers until the 1910 census, so evaluating the numbers of people caught in the system is difficult. In 1910, the census commissioned a special survey of sharecroppers in 325 counties in eleven southern states to gather a snapshot of data, and the survey revealed that in large segments of the South the plantation system continued to hold sway.[30] The 1920 census offered a more systematic and thorough counting of southern sharecroppers, and Carter G. Woodson used the data as the foundation of his study *The Rural Negro* (1930). He documents that in 1920, 636,248 Blacks were landless farmers working as tenants, sharecroppers, or wage hands, and the average farm plot for a family was approximately thirty acres.[31] In 1920, approximately 75 percent of Black farmers in the South were landless. Sharecropping of some form, thus, was pervasive for Black southerners in the first part of the twentieth century, and the dynamics of sharecropping suffused the social construction of the region. The ideological necessity to limit African Americans' social and political agency and to maintain a vast, inexpensive labor force defined the region's racial structure. Books about the lives of Black southerners during this period depict the experience of social and economic oppression and the ways that Blacks attempted to resist the new slavery. These works include W. E. B. Du Bois's first novel *The Quest of the Silver Fleece* (1911), Welbourne Kelley's *Inchin' Along* (1932), George Washington Lee's *River George* (1937), and George Wylie Henderson's *Ollie Miss* (1935). The vast majority of African American southerners in the first part of the twentieth century lived the lives of labor and struggle represented in novels about sharecropping.

As an ideological system, sharecropping was an insidious means of limiting African Americans' social, political, and economic agency based on the drive to minimize the cost of agricultural labor and on white southerners' resurgent racism. Slavery was a totalizing system in which the slave's agency was erased. Sharecropping was similar to slavery, but to overemphasize the relationship between them "deprives intervening generations of the credit they deserve for the substantial progress they were able to achieve in the faces of overwhelming obstacles."[32] Hypothetically, a sharecropper could aspire to own land and the economic agency of selling his own crop, and, theoretically, a Black southerner had a claim to the rights of American citizenship, but, practically, through legal restrictions, repressive customs, and systematic dehumanization, these rights and aspirations were diminished. The everyday life of a sharecropper was highly similar to the everyday life of a slave, making it impossible to escape the "hopeless cycle of work debt and poverty that so sharply circumscribed the economic freedom of Black southerners." In *Trouble in Mind*, Leon Litwack writes, "in reality most of them worked the white man's land, planted with the white man's seeds, plowed with the white man's plow and mules, and harvested a crop that they owed largely to the white man."[33]

The fundamental difference between sharecropping and slavery for Black southerners was that, despite the realities, a sharecropper had the option to dream of a better life, and the key to a better life was education. Yet schools for African Americans were scarce, and children who had the opportunity to attend school often had an abbreviated school year because tending the crops took priority over education. In *The Quest of the Silver Fleece*, Du Bois offers a vision of postbellum African American education similar to the Rosenwald schools funded by a wealthy northern businessman.[34] In the novel, Mrs. Smith runs a school that employs northern white women to teach the Black children, but the local planters resent the school, which, according to the most prominent plantation owner, threatens "to ruin the whole labor structure."[35] Du Bois illustrates that the philanthropic scheme is comparatively effective because it does not depend upon the local structure for funding and support.[36] In *Inchin' Along*, on the other hand, Dink Britt is forced to contribute tax money toward constructing a school for white children, but his own children are not allowed to attend school.[37] Aaron George manages to go to college in *River George*, although the book never explains how this remarkable achievement was possible. The book does make clear that the benefit of his college education, however, is negligible. He learns that "in the breast of good men whether white or colored there burned a passionate love for democracy and justice," but his return to Beaver Dam plantation makes clear that both the whites and the Blacks resent his education, and they mutually regard him as subversive.[38] For African Americans, education signified the possibility of social mobility, but most white plantation owners continued to follow the adage that too much education would spoil a good plow-hand. White landowners believed that keeping laborers illiterate and ignorant kept them more isolated, more compliant, less capable of challenging the white power structure, and, thus, more easily exploitable.

Many sharecroppers harbored ambitions to become landowners and to produce their own crops. Some African Americans managed to achieve this goal, but it was difficult. In the early twentieth century, approximately 25 percent of Black farmers owned their own land. In *The Bottom Rung*, Stewart Tolnay writes, "When compared with white-owned farms, however, an average Black-owned farm was smaller, had fewer farm implements and machinery, and was located on poorer soil."[39] In most cases, whites intentionally refused to sell land to Blacks, and when they did, they often intended it as a form of exploitation. The white plantation owner in *The Quest of the Silver Fleece*, for example, sells a piece of swamp land to a Black person because he expects the "fool darkey" to clear the land and then default on the debt, returning the improved land to the seller in the process.[40] In *Ollie Miss*, the title character, Ollie Miss, works on a Black-owned farm, and the owner, Alex, has two sharecropping families and three wage laborers in addition to Ollie working on the farm, which makes him fairly prosperous.[41] Dink Britt manages to become extremely prosperous by exceeding the white plantation owners' expectations. He initially purchases land with cash when most African Americans would purchase on credit, in which case the seller, similar to the plantation owner Du Bois describes, "would have it back in two years, with the nigger working for him as a share-cropper to boot." Britt's purchase makes some whites nervous, but one plantation owner explains that if he becomes too successful, "we'd run him clean out of the country. As far as niggers in this part of the country are concerned, there's never been a such thing as the Civil War."[42] Britt, however, does manage to keep his farm and buy even more land, eventually becoming one of the largest landowners in the county, but in the process he is cuckolded by a white man, his wife loses her sight, he is cheated in a land purchase that bizarrely works out in his favor, he is regularly intimidated and ridiculed, his best friend is lynched, and he barely escapes lynching himself. Even in cases where Black farmers are successful, the success is often limited and contingent.

The vast majority of Black farmers were sharecroppers who existed in a perpetual state of debt slavery. When William Pickens was a child, his family sharecropped in Arkansas, and the experience made him a radical activist for racial justice. He was a founding member of the NAACP, and he wrote passionately and perceptively about the conditions of Africans Americans in the South, which he labeled the "American Congo." In one pamphlet, he writes, "The quest of this Congo is not for rubber and ivory, but for cotton and sugar. Here labor is forced, and the laborer is a slave. The slavery is a cunningly contrived debt slavery to give the appearance of civilization and the sanction of law. A debt of a few hundred dollars may tie a Black man and his family of ten as securely in bondage to a great white planter as if he had purchased their bodies."[43] Pickens's rhetoric sounds like hyperbole, but in effect, it is true. In the sharecropping arrangement, the landowner had authority to determine the laborer's debt, and laborers determined to be in debt were bound to work off their debt. Just as the disposition of the owner often determined the condition of the slave, the disposition of the landowner determined the condition of the laborer. When Aaron George returns to Beaver Dam plantation, for example, he laments that the kind landowner had sold the plantation to a cruel man. "For in those days," he remarks, "a vicious share-cropper system open to so much abuse on the part of the white overlords and offering so little recourse against the wrong to the negro was, nevertheless, administered with kindliness and an underlying sense of justice. But since King had sold the plantation the negroes had been in as sorry a state as their ancestors had been under slavery."[44] The frequent comparisons between sharecropping and slavery in literature about sharecropping indicate both the immediacy of slavery in African American memory and the similarity between the systems of labor.

In *The Souls of Black Folk* (1903), W. E. B. Du Bois describes the people and the farms of Dougherty County, Georgia, a postbellum landscape of cotton and poverty, which Du Bois traces directly to slavery: "Here in 1890 lived ten thousand Negroes and two thousand whites. The country is rich, yet the people are poor. The keynote of the Black Belt is debt; not commercial credit, but debt in the sense of continued inability on the part of the mass of the population to make income cover expense. This is the direct heritage of the South from the wasteful economies of the slave regime; but it was emphasized and brought to a crisis by the Emancipation of the slaves."[45] Du Bois argues that the poverty in the area is intentional. By limiting the alternative economic opportunities in the area, the landowners can force the laborers into exploitative arrangements. He identifies the merchants as the center of the economic structure, "part banker, part landlord, part contractor, and part despot," and he explains that the merchants deliberately keep the laborers in debt.[46] "The widespread opinion among the merchants and employers of the Black Belt," he writes, is "that only by the slavery of debt can the Negro be kept at work."[47] The new slavery in the South that emerged out of the dissolution of the old slavery was debt slavery, a multifarious system of limiting economic agency for the deliberate purpose of maintaining a large supply of inexpensive labor.

Du Bois's perceptive study of life among rural Blacks in south Georgia—the chapter is titled "Of the Quest of the Golden Fleece"—inspired his first novel, *The Quest of the Silver Fleece,* which attempts to imagine a form of economic empowerment for sharecroppers. Borrowing from the techniques of muckraking novels such as Upton Sinclair's *The Jungle* (1906) and Frank Norris's *The Octopus* (1901), Du Bois uses the novel to expose the economic forces that determine the sharecroppers' lives and to propose a way for sharecroppers to achieve financial independence through collectivization.[48] "In contrast to the exploitation of sharecropping and tenant farming," Jarvis McInnis states, "he explores the aesthetics of cotton cultivation to imagine Zora and Bles's burgeoning romance and to evince black people's contributions to the global economy. In so doing, he offers a vision of cotton cultivation that is rooted in human need instead of global capitalist accumulation."⁴⁹ In the book, southern plantation owners and northern mill owners collude to corner the cotton crop, earning high profits for themselves but creating low prices for everyone else. Du Bois counters this plot with the story of an illiterate Black girl, Zora, whose mother is a conjure woman, who grows a magical crop of cotton, the silver fleece, in a swamp outside the white sphere of influence. The stories intersect when Zora brings her cotton in for sale, and Du Bois portrays settlement as an outright theft. The plantation owner, who has no legitimate claim to the cotton, calculates its value as seventy-five dollars and charges Zora one hundred dollars for rent and rations, levying a twenty-five-dollar debt on her. Bewildered, she wonders, "What should she do? She never thought of appeal to the courts, for Colonel Cresswell [the plantation owner] was Justice of the Peace and his son was bailiff. Why had they stolen from her? She knew. She was now penniless, and in a sense helpless. She was now a peon bound to her master's bidding."⁵⁰ Here, Du Bois illustrates the mechanism of debt slavery and the lack of agency available to Black farmers. He goes on to describe Zora getting an education, which gives her a degree of autonomy, and establishing a collective farm on the same land that produced the silver fleece to empower a community of self-sufficient Black farmers. But even in this quasi-utopian scheme, Du Bois capitulates to futility, and a white mob overruns the farm. The novel suggests that there is no possibility of freedom for Black farmers in the South.

Aaron George has a similar experience in *River George*. When his father dies, he takes over his father's sharecropping contract, determined to use his education and work ethic to produce a profitable crop and buy a farm of his own. He naively believes that most farmers are swindled because they are uneducated, but he realizes that his education is no advantage when he visits the plantation commissary to buy work clothes and encounters the "coldness and unfriendliness" of the white clerks who resent his education. They serve him because "they were instructed to do so. Negroes could get what they pleased—the more the better—so that it would be unnecessary to pay them anything in the Fall settlement. The amounts charged for the goods, including large profits, would be entered and interest added," converting the laborers' commodity consumption into material debt. "And if, as so often happened, the fall reckoning would show, by the owner's figures, that there was a balance in favor of the owner instead of the share-cropper, the interest would go into the next year," trapping the sharecropper in debt. "If there happened, by some rare chance, to be a little money coming to one of the Negroes at the Fall settlement, so that he owed the owner nothing, the owner would make him a little loan for Christmas, advance him a little money for repairs—anything to get the debt back on the books and to tie him up for another year," making it impossible for the sharecropper to escape the cycle of work and debt. "The share-croppers were virtually peons," he concludes, "their bodies and souls the property of their masters as effectively as they had ever been in slave times."[51] In this exchange, the sharecropper is powerless, and the adverbs Lee uses to describe the sharecropper's victimization—"virtually" and "effectively"—signal the sharecropper's social limbo, not quite slave but far from free. Aaron George raises an excellent crop, and when he brings it in for settlement, he is told that his account is even and offered a loan of seventy-five dollars for Christmas. When he protests that he should have made a profit and asks to see the figures, the bookkeeper pulls out a gun, illustrating the violence inherent in the system.

Sharecroppers in debt to the landowners were not virtually peons; they were actually peons. In *The Shadow of Slavery* (1972), Pete Daniel writes, "peons existed at the core of concentric circles of oppression, their entire world circumscribed by exploiters. Defrauded of their wages and deprived of their mobility either by threats that they could not legally move until their debts were paid or by actual force, they lived in a vortex of peonage."[52] Because they are in debt to the landowner after settlement, both Zora and Aaron George are obligated to either pay the debt, which is usually impossible, or work it off through the next year's crop. If they leave the plantation, then they are subject to arrest and sentence to a chain gang. Many sharecroppers found themselves trapped in this cycle. In other cases, plantation owners could purchase a person's labor by paying their bond to get them out of jail and then requiring the laborer to work off the debt for a period of time, usually left to the landowner's discretion. Peonage violated the constitutional prohibition on involuntary servitude, so it was technically illegal in the United States, and it was challenged in federal court in several cases.[53] For this reason, it is difficult to estimate the number of people who were peons in the South, and it is difficult to know how many sharecroppers were held in debt servitude. Peonage does not appear frequently in southern literature, but it is mentioned in some books about sharecropping. Sutton Griggs, for example, mentions it in *The Hindered Hand* (1905) in which a character goes to Mississippi because "she had heard much of the practice of peonage."[54]

Du Bois also includes a brief digression about peonage in *The Quest of the Silver Fleece*. A woman explains to the schoolmistress that her family will not be allowed to move because Colonel Cresswell is holding them in debt for paying her son's bail. The schoolmistress objects, "Why, Aunt Rachel, it's slavery!"[55] To a great extent it is an extension of slavery. Peons could not be sold on the open market as slaves could, but their labor is stolen in an extreme form of exploitation, and they cannot do anything to stop it.

For most African Americans involved in the sharecropping system, any form of resistance was futile. Minor acts of transgression such as petty theft or deliberately slow work were common and often tolerated.[56] Breaking a contract by leaving before the crop was harvested, selling the landowner's cotton, or entering a new contract before settlement, however, could lead to the chain gang. Acts of physical resistance would lead to disproportionate violence, including lynching. William Pickens argues that "lynching and mob violence are only methods of economic repression. Lynching is most prevalent where Negro labor is most exploited; and the spread of mob violence against colored people has followed the spread of the exploitation."[57] In the period between Emancipation and the civil rights movement, more than three thousand Africans Americans were lynched in the South, and many of them were sharecroppers. In some cases, allegations were made about crimes against whites as a pretext to lynching, but in other cases lynching was a form of labor control. It used violent spectacle to demonstrate the landowners' authority over the laborers, and the specter of lynching looms over most novels about sharecropping. In *The Hindered Hand*, a man and woman are lynched "on general principles";[58] in *Inchin' Along*, Dink Britt is nearly lynched for "trying to be the rich nigger";[59] and in *The Quest of the Silver Fleece*, a white mob overruns Zora's school. Aaron George in *River George* gets into a fight with a white man and flees the plantation, but he is pursued for years, and at the end of the novel his body is found hanging in a cabin on the plantation. These novels all send the message that any challenge to the landowners' control would inevitably lead to violent retribution.

Most Black laborers had only two courses of action available to them, work or leave. After settlement, laborers not bound in debt servitude often moved to another plantation in hopes of better prospects, to escape a bad situation, or simply to exercise the only freedom available to them. Most families moved within a small geographic area to maintain social and familial connections, yet between 1910 and 1960, millions of African Americans migrated out of the South. Those who stayed in the South were resigned to a life of labor exploitation, hoping at best to work in peace.[60] At the end of *Ollie Miss*, Alex promises Ollie, who had worked only as a day laborer, to rent her ten acres to work, "and that had made her feel happy in a way that she had felt before."[61] As a single Black woman in the sharecropping system, Ollie has been extremely marginalized, and a plot of her own effectively integrates her into the social order, making her part of a community, but the fact that her hopes extend no farther than this highly circumscribed condition illustrates the effect of exploitation on her state of mind.[62] Possibly the most profound example of resignation in sharecropping literature is Arna Bontemps's short story "A Summer Tragedy" (1931).[63] In the story, an elderly couple dresses in their best clothes, gets in their ragged Model-T Ford, leaves the farm they have worked for forty-five years, and deliberately drives into a river. They kill themselves because they can no longer work, because they have lost five grown children, and because they have no prospects for comfort in their old age. Their entire lives have been toil on Greenbriar Plantation, and after a lifetime of work in a state of social limbo, they can only expect the solace of death. For millions of Black laborers in the South in the decades after Emancipation, a lifetime of labor exploitation was the only viable option available.

## White Slavery of Cotton

In the antebellum South, white people were not enslaved, but Emancipation created the opportunity to exploit white laborers in the same way as Black laborers, greatly expanding the potential labor force and shifting the region's social stratification. Before the Civil War, the South's social order was broadly divided into slaves and some free Blacks, white yeoman farmers who comprised the majority of the region's population, a small merchant and professional class, and a small yet powerful class of planters. After the Civil War, without slavery as a laboring category, the region divided into a large class of Black and white landless farmers, a smaller class of Black and white landowning farmers, a small class of merchants and professionals, and a small yet still disproportionately powerful class of planters. The upshot of Emancipation was to put whites on relatively equal economic footing with Blacks at the bottom of the social hierarchy. The disenfranchisement of Black voters and the passage of Jim Crow laws guaranteed that Blacks and whites would be unequal politically and socially, and racial antagonism continued to define the region's social order, but in the fields, whites and Blacks would work in similar conditions, often for the same landowners, in what Harry Harrison Kroll describes as "the white slavery of cotton."[64] The key difference between Black and white sharecroppers is that white sharecroppers could imagine the possibility of social mobility, climbing the agricultural ladder from sharecropping to landowning, which is the predominant theme in novels about white sharecroppers set before the Great Depression.

According to the 1920 census, 39 percent of white farmers were sharecroppers, 887,566 out of 2,283,750. White sharecroppers significantly outnumbered Black sharecroppers, comprising two-thirds of the region's sharecroppers.[65] In *One Kind of Freedom* (1977), Roger Ransom and Richard Sutch explain that whites became sharecroppers in part for an economic opportunity. Most antebellum yeoman farmers raised subsistence crops, growing their own food and a few commodity crops that could yield cash. Growing cotton required a significant amount of capital, and sharecropping allowed white farmers an opportunity to use the landowners' capital with the potential of generating a cash profit.[66] Gavin Wright suggests that the development of white sharecropping had an overall negative effect on southern agriculture. "Southerners associated the decline of self-sufficiency with a fall in standards, a loss of prudence and thrift, or, at the very least, with an unfortunate falling behind financially," he writes.[67] Although the possibility of earning money was an attractive opportunity, white sharecroppers were vulnerable to the same forms of exploitation, coercion, and debt as Black sharecroppers, and their race had little, if any, impact on their working conditions. Many of them endured in debt from year to year without any social movement. In the best-case scenario, a sharecropper might earn enough money to purchase an independent farm of his own, but small farms were susceptible to the vicissitudes of market forces, so they were constantly in danger of default and foreclosure, leading back to the mire of sharecropping.

Several novels about white sharecroppers were set before the Great Depression, and they share a similar plot structure that illustrates the ambitions and obstacles white sharecroppers faced. The books typically follow the progress of a young man born into a sharecropping family who, through a strong work ethic and/or unusual intellect, manages to rise above his station and to marry or court a beautiful woman before economic forces inevitably lead to his downfall or death. These books include *The Cabin in the Cotton* (1931) by Harry Harrison Kroll, *This Body the Earth* (1935) by Paul Green, *In the Land of Cotton* (1923) and *Can't Get a Redbird* (1929) by Dorothy Scarborough, and *Cotton* (1928) by Jack Bethea. Collectively, these books suggest that sharecropping, while not as oppressive for whites as for Blacks, was a nearly insurmountable social condition that trapped generations of families in a system of labor exploitation. These books, however, have not attracted a significant amount of critical attention, leaving the stories of white sharecroppers shrouded in silence.

The protagonists in white sharecropping novels are typically sympathetic males who embody appealing personal traits of ambition and hard work. The protagonist of *The Cabin in the Cotton*, Dan Morgan, aspires to have "a plantation of his own some day," and he recognizes the importance of money in determining a person's social outcomes, so he attempts to make money by teaching himself accounting and working as the plantation's clerk.[68] Ben Wilson in *In the Land of Cotton* is born into a sharecropping family, and he befriends the landowner's precocious daughter. His ambition and work ethic impress the landowner, who pays his tuition to Baylor University, which allows him to get a good job running a cotton gin. In *Can't Get a Redbird*, Johnny Carr is born into a family of Irish immigrant sharecroppers, but he works hard and manages to purchase a farm for his parents and to make a home for his family. Alvin Barnes in *This Body the Earth* aspires to be "the best farmer the Little Bethel Country has ever seen," a feat he accomplishes temporarily while his body is young and strong.[69] Larry Maynard in *Cotton* comes from a poor white family, and he works his way into an executive position with a textile company that sends him back to his hometown to run an experimental plantation. Because these characters share attributes consistent with the hero of the typical rags-to-riches story, they give the reader an interior perspective on the experience of sharecropping, but their stories deviate from the ordinary rags-to-riches story. Rather than following an upward curve of social mobility, they follow a symmetrical arc from rags to riches back to rags.

One of the obstacles the protagonists in these novels face is limited access to education. The planters' ideology that a good education spoils a good field hand extended to the children of white sharecroppers. Kroll explains that planters would deplore the children's poor attendance at school, but they would also enforce the truancy because "a tenant brat picking cotton was doing something worth doing. A tenant brat reciting a grammar lesson—well, that was something different."[70] A tenant child receiving an education was an exceptional circumstance. Somehow, Larry Maynard in *Cotton* receives an education, although the book does not explain how this improbable feat occurred, and Ben Wilson in *In The Land of Cotton* goes to college through the beneficence of an unusually generous landowner. More often, a sharecropper's child would, like Alvin Barnes, be virtually illiterate, or would, like Ben Wilson, be forced to leave the classroom for the fields. Johnny Carr's story is especially illustrative on this point. As a child, he "craved to 'learn books.' Schooling was an invisible, intangible something that was to make life easier and happier for him than life could otherwise be—that would be like giving him a horse to ride, when otherwise he must trudge through his days."[71] But his father's ill health forces Johnny to take over responsibility for the plowing when he is eleven years old, and "the gaping furrows opened up to swallow all his school, his Professor, his dreams, his boyhood."[72] When he is an adult, this loss weighs on him, and it motivates him to get involved in organizing sharecroppers for social change. His loss of education influences his perception of cotton and sharecropping: "Beauty and cruelty—that was what cotton meant. He visioned thousands of children, sent into the fields as he had been, taken out of school to toil, kept at work when they should have had happy play-time; they became stunted in body, untrained in mind, warped in soul, many of them, so that the cotton crop might be gathered. Everywhere little children, girls as well as boys, were cheated of an education, robbed of their right to play and sent into the world with scant chance for success."[73] The limited access to education impeded generations of sharecroppers' social mobility.

The antagonist in white sharecropping novels is a vast system of economic exploitation personified in the form of a landowner. In some cases, such as gracious plantation owner Jack Llewellyn in *In the Land of Cotton*, the landowner is portrayed as a subject of the same system, forced to use sharecroppers for lack of any other opportunities to make a living under the circumstances. In most cases, however, the landowner is portrayed as a malevolent and scheming figure eager to grow his own wealth through the exploitation of other people. Alvin Barnes in *This Body the Earth* gets his first sense of the landowner's role in sharecropping when his friend Rassie dies, and he realizes that "it was not God that had taken Rassie, but Mr. Byrd, the great landlord who lived in riches and let flies and filth bring destruction on the poor people."[74] In *The Cabin in the Cotton*, Dan Morgan learns how Mr. Lord manipulates his sharecroppers' contracts by charging up to 20 percent interest on the accounts of workers he wants to control through debt, and in *Can't Get a Redbird*, the Carr family works tediously on the plantation of Bill Chisholm, failing to make a profit at all until Johnny, through Herculean effort, manages to pull the family out of debt. Most of these landowners are benignly or passively antagonistic, operating primarily as a signifier for economic forces that steal the sharecroppers' lives and labor. The most malevolent character is Evan Shelby in *Cotton*. When Larry Maynard is a child, his father works for Shelby, and Shelby "cheated him on his accounts, cheated him in the money he advanced, made him pay outrageous interest for it and forced him to sell his cotton as soon as it was ginned."[75] When Larry Maynard attempts to implement changes in the community's economic structure, Shelby resorts to bribery, arson, kidnapping, and attempted murder to prevent it, illustrating how deeply the white power structure is invested in maintaining the social order.

This social order based on the exploitation of white laborers by white landowners hinges on the distinction between whiteness and poor whites.[76] In *Cotton*, Larry Maynard, who was born a sharecropper but becomes an educated cosmopolitan representative of a northern industrial entity, is shamed when a white businessman who knew his father calls him "poor white trash," revealing that his social mobility is hampered by the perception of class.[77] The sensation of being called poor white trash eats "into him like acid," and Alvin Barnes has a similar experience, feeling "suddenly blasted with shame and humiliation," when he hears Mr. Byrd describe his family as low-down.[78] After Mr. Lord calls Dan Morgan "damned white trash" in *The Cabin in the Cotton*, Dan also stings: "Damned white trash . . . His sick soul said it over and over, as he went through the cotton in the dying light of evening."[79] This incident leads him to ruminate over the social order of sharecropping:

> There they were, thought Dan—the three biological groups: nigger, pore white, and planter. Dan did not have much abstract sense, but his study of biology and social science in high school—studies in which he took an intense interest—gave him to know that here was a situation

so complex as to defy analysis: The aristocrat looking upon the black man with a mixture of racial antipathy, and in proportion to the black's docility, a gentle, wise paternalism; the pore white viewing the nigger with the antipathy but not the paternalism; the aristocrat looking at the pore white with mixed tolerance and disgust, mostly disgust; the nigger looking up at the grand aristocrat but down upon the pore white; and all of them driving mules to skin the land of cotton, more cotton, and still more cotton. It was a chase in mad circles, with cotton the center. The nigger, the pore white, the planter. A vast business with no method or sense of business. The system—that was it.[80]

Dan's perception effectively summarizes the social relations that circumscribed the South's agricultural commodity economy. The system was self-perpetuating, and it resisted social mobility by any members of the structure.

White sharecroppers were subject to the same system of exploitative contracts and corrupt settlements as Black sharecroppers. Larry Maynard disrupts the system when he chooses to pay his laborers wages, and he finds that some of his laborers are quick to leave after their wages are paid, but many more are willing to remain when they know that they will be paid consistently and reliably. Virtually all other landowners follow the standard system of annual contracts based on shares and debts. Mr. Byrd in *This Body the Earth* never gives written contracts, but all of his tenants are required to purchase their supplies and goods through his commissary run by Mr. Joe. He charges the tenants a time price, a surcharge added to each purchase on which interest is based, so "fat side meat could be bought over in town for twelve cents a pound, but every pound the tenants got from Mr. Joe was entered on the books for twenty cents. . . . So when every fall came around and settling up day was at hand, the tenant farm laborers found themselves owing the landlord everything down to the shirts on their back."[81] Harry Kroll documents the practices in *The Cabin in the Cotton*, including an example contract and an explanation that the landlord manipulates the contract, the interest rates, and the price he pays for cotton to the laborers. "It was assumed," he writes, "of course, that Lord's price would not vary greatly from the prevailing market price at the moment, but the contract did not specify such an assumption."[82] Dan eventually learns that Mr. Lord used the same means to cheat his own family, including one instance when his father should have cleared $300 but was in debt at settlement for $1.47.[83] For sharecroppers, each year's work was virtually wasted, trapping them in a repetitive cycle of labor and poverty, leaving "the average cotton renter no better off than a peon, a slave to the landlord and the storekeeper."[84]

Even though Black and white sharecroppers were equally exploited, white sharecroppers felt themselves to be socially superior to Black sharecroppers, as Dan Morgan's social hierarchy illustrates. In *Can't Get a Redbird,* Johnny Carr uses a racial epithet to describe labor when he asks, "did a landlord mind if a renter's girl had to nigger in the field?"[85] This usage is telling because it suggests that the white sharecropper considers exploitative labor as normal for Blacks yet unjust for whites. This perception contributed to racial tension among the sharecroppers, and Black sharecroppers in these novels typically occupy an abject position. A Black sharecropper is lynched in *The Cabin in the Cotton* for killing a white store owner, even though the evidence clearly indicates that a white man committed the murder, and a Black inmate attempts to escape from the chain gang in *In The Land of Cotton,* begging for mercy and sanctuary from the white landowner. The dramatic tension in these novels, however, rarely focuses on race, shifting the focus on race relations into the background of the narrative. Instead, the books foreground the tension between white laborers to the exclusion of Black laborers and the system of exploitation.

White sharecroppers had more opportunities available to them to escape labor exploitation than Black sharecroppers, such as the option to leave the farm to work in a textile mill. The Barnes family in *This Body the Earth* contemplates moving to a mill, but mill work does not differ significantly from farm work. "Reports conflicted among the tenant farmers as to the hardship in the mill," Green writes. "Some said it was better to have your pay certain on Saturday night, small as it was, than to have to plow all summer, sweating your liver out, and then freeze in the summer for an uncertain return."[86] Life in a textile mill was different but not necessarily better. Similar to landowners, mills hired entire families as units of labor, using women and children in tedious and dangerous positions.[87] The work in the mills was difficult, the pay was low, and mill owners maintained strict control over the mill hands, just as landowners controlled laborers. Ben Robertson, who descended from a long line of landowners in South Carolina, expressed sorrow over the sharecroppers who went into the mill because they made him "feel that they had been captured, that they were imprisoned, that they had given up being free."⁸⁸ Considering his perspective as a person responsible for the exploitation of sharecroppers, his comments are quite ironic, but they are also somewhat sincere because the living and working conditions for mill hands were equally difficult as they were for sharecroppers. The key difference is that mill hands were exploited by the hour while sharecroppers were exploited by the year.

Each of the white sharecropper novels offers their own solution to the problem of labor exploitation. In the dramatic final scene of *The Cabin in the Cotton*, Dan Morgan exposes the landowner for extortion and the laborers for theft, indicating that the sharecropping system was unjust for both parties. Alvin Barnes in *This Body the Earth* attempts to return to subsistence farming as a way to remediate his debt and live independently, and in *In the Land of Cotton*, Ben Wilson advocates for cooperatives to organize the cotton farmers and market their crops directly to the cotton exchange, freeing them of the burden of the crop lien. Dorothy Scarborough advances the idea farther in *Can't Get a Redbird* with the fictional American Cotton Planters' Exchange, whose mission is "not only to reduce speculation and to stabilize prices to assure the farmer the largest possible return for his cotton, but also to improve standards of living among the farmers."⁸⁹ Larry Maynard in *Cotton* attempts to apply both scientific and economic principles to farming by using agricultural research to determine his fertilizer use, yield per acre, and harvest cycle; by using industrial labor practices to harvest his crop; and by organizing a cooperative warehousing scheme to market the crop when the commodity prices are at their highest. All of these suggestions are effectively critiques of the existing system of cotton production, which exacerbated the exploitation of labor through massive inefficiency and diminished the commodity value of cotton for the producers by flooding the market with the crop immediately after harvest. The crop lien system of credit, however, dictated the farmers produce as much cotton as possible and that they sell it as quickly as possible. The expedient system that emerged during Reconstruction by this time had evolved into a self-perpetuating economic hegemony that forced landowners and merchants to exploit laborers and that forced laborers to submit to exploitation regardless of their race.

None of the resolutions proposed in the novels change sharecropping, which proves impervious to progress. *Cotton* ends with Larry Maynard's wedding, which may be the most hopeful resolution, but the wedding follows his near lynching at the hands of his fellow townspeople, and the wedding itself signifies he "belongs to Aarons County now."[90] At the end of *The Cabin in the Cotton*, Dan Morgan quietly returns to the plantation having said his peace but having little long-term impact, and *Can't Get a Redbird* ends with the collapse of the cotton exchange and Johnny Carr's bankruptcy, sending the message that little will repay the "countless sacrifices that men and women in the South had made, were making, to help the farmer give himself a chance."[91] *In the Land of Cotton* concludes with Ben Wilson killed in a shootout while protecting a cotton gin, and *This Body the Earth* closes with a scene of Alvin Barnes's grave, a spot in the field "where a clump of cotton grew higher than the surrounding stalks."[92] This image may be the most resonant for white sharecroppers, who effectively gave their lives to raise cotton. White sharecroppers had the potential to try to advance their social status, but they had little likelihood of making the advance a reality.

## Sharecropper Migration Novels

The sharecropping system trapped millions of white and Black southerners in an intractable system of poverty and labor exploitation, leaving them virtually no means for social advancement, subject to coercion and violence, suffering and toiling in abject poverty, and with little human dignity. One of the most reasonable responses to living in such a situation was to leave. Every year, millions of sharecropping families did try to leave, usually by moving from one farm to another. After settlement, sharecroppers faced a set of limited options. Those left in debt were forced to remain on their current plantation, but those who made a profit could either remain on their current plantation or move to another plantation in hopes of finding a better landowner, more fertile ground, or a nicer cabin. Landowners, meanwhile, could determine to retain some tenants and to evict others to maintain a docile and productive labor force. The result is that each winter a large proportion of the agricultural laborers in any given area would move from one farm to another, usually within a radius that allowed them to maintain community and kinship bonds, but moving farms simply perpetuated the system with little likelihood for social mobility. In some cases, a family might move into town to find work or to a textile mill, but the majority of sharecropping families moved frequently within their local area, from farm to farm, from field to field, and from plow to plow.

Some families, meanwhile, took the risk of moving out of the South to seek opportunities in another part of the United States in hopes of escaping the cycle of exploitation. Many of these families were part of the enormous domestic population shift known as the Great Migration, a phrase that usually refers to the movement of about six million African Americans out of the South between 1910 and 1970.[93] While this migration significantly changed the racial composition of the country, it was only part of the larger movement of southerners out of the South. In *The Southern Diaspora* (2005), James N. Gregory calculates that twenty-eight million southerners moved out of the region during the twentieth century.[94] More than three times as many whites left the South as Blacks, but among the whites who left, "farmers were, if anything, underrepresented in comparison to their presence in the southern population," and "the composition of the black diaspora also varied," consisting of sharecroppers, blue-collar workers, and professionals.[95] Although sharecroppers were part of the movement out of the South, they did not dominate it. They were, in fact, less likely to leave than other middle-class or working-class southerners. This may be because they often lacked the resources to leave the region or because they were more likely to move from rural areas into one of the growing urban centers within the region. Or sharecroppers may have been reluctant to leave in spite of all of the compelling reasons to go because of their attachments to family and community, because they recognized that they were just as likely to exploited outside the South as in the South, or because they were deeply embedded in the ideology of exploitation as a result of manufactured dependency. Novels about sharecroppers who migrated out of the South indicate that the reasons for leaving were often complicated.

The historical reasons for the migration have been thoroughly investigated, and they are usually grouped into push and pull factors. The pull factors include the lure of employment, social equality, and the hope for prosperity outside the South, and the push factors include the persistent poverty, racial discrimination, limited access to educational opportunity, and unchecked violence in the South. There were plenty of compelling reasons to leave the South, and the system of sharecropping itself, which embodied many of the regressive social practices that impeded progress and prosperity in the region, was a reason to leave. The decision to leave, however, was often much more personal and complicated than the systemic forces would suggest, and the fact that millions of southerners, including millions of sharecroppers, remained in the South indicates that there were also compelling reasons to stay. The mass migration of people out of the South, ultimately, had marginal impact on sharecropping, leaving behind millions of laborers languishing in the fields.

Literature about sharecroppers leaving their fields to migrate out of the South makes some interesting revelations. First, there are relatively few books about sharecroppers leaving the South. Considering that millions of people left the South, it is not surprising that there are many works about displaced southerners creating new lives outside the South, but only a few books depict sharecroppers actually departing the South.[96] These sharecropper migration novels include *The Dollmaker* (1954) by Harriette Arnow, *Blood on the Forge* (1941) by William Attaway, *The White Face* (1943) by Carl Offord, and *The Grapes of Wrath* (1939) by John Steinbeck. Second, books about sharecropper migrants follow a nearly identical narrative arc beginning with families leaving their farms either reluctantly or by force, making a difficult journey to a new city, mounting challenges with acclimating to a new life, facing exploitation in an industrial labor system, and leading to a tragic conclusion. This narrative arc suggests that sharecropping families are destined to be exploited labor, regardless of the setting. Third, the protagonists in these books tend to be constituents of family units who migrate as a group, and, as the narrative unfolds, members of the family succumb to the pressures of the migration, usually manifesting in the death of children, which suggests that the next generation of laborers will be foreclosed. Fourth, books about sharecropper migrants appeared relatively late in the history of migration. Most scholars date the beginning of the migration period with the 1910 census, when population numbers began to shift, with a noticeable surge during World War I and a much larger surge during World War II and with the migration reaching its peak during the 1950s before receding in the 1970s. Books about sharecroppers migrating clustered during the peak of migration. *Blood on the Forge* is set in 1919, but the others are set during the Great Depression or World War II, which reinforces the impression of sharecroppers succumbing to economic forces.

The huge numbers of people who moved within the United States in the twentieth century led to the emergence of a literary subgenre of migration narratives. In *Ain't Got No Home*, Erin Battat argues, "migration narratives—both internal and transnational—brought regional differences into broad relief, tying human difference to place rather than bloodlines or skin color."[97]

In her analysis, migration narratives yield a vision of "interracial working-class solidarity."[98] Within African American literature, meanwhile, the trope of a fugitive from the South escaping to freedom in the North has a long tradition beginning with fugitive slave narratives published before the Civil War. Farah Jasmine Griffin asserts in *Who Set You Flowin'?* that African American migration narratives in many genres share a "notion of ascent from the South into a 'freer' North."[99] Ascent in this case implies both the geographic movement northward and an upward social trajectory moving from poverty to prosperity. Many works of African American literature about the Great Migration use a recurring narrative pattern in which a protagonist leaves the South to escape an oppressive situation and create a new life in the North, but the protagonist experiences difficult and degrading circumstances in the urban environment that often lead to a tragic conclusion, such as Richard Wright's *Native Son* (1940) or Ralph Ellison's *Invisible Man* (1952). Lawrence Rodgers analyzes this pattern in *Canaan Bound* (1992), and he also identifies a variation of the pattern that he describes as fugitive migrant novels.[100] He notes that these novels challenge the themes of interracial solidarity and ascent because they hinge in racial violence and because they end with the protagonists' dispossession from the supposed promised land.

Sharecropper migration novels are a specific niche within migration novels, and they include a couple of important deviations from the usual narrative pattern of migration novels. First, in sharecropper migration novels, the laboring families are forced to leave their homes, which changes the dynamic from escape to exile. Second, in these novels, the laboring family leaves one exploitative economic system in the South only to find themselves mired in another exploitative economic arrangement outside the South. While the hope of ascent plays a role in the narrative arc of sharecropper migration novels, actual social mobility proves to be elusive. The fact that this pattern appears in novels about both whites and Blacks indicates a form of transracial solidarity in experience and dispossession, but the novels show few signs of interracial cooperation.

In sharecropper migration novels, the laboring families leave the South when they are forced off their farms, not of their own volition. In *The White Face*, Chris Brown dreams of going North, but he hesitates to leave until he has a fight with his landowner over settlement. The landowner hits him with a whip, and he punches the landowner, then flees, taking his wife, child, and best friend to Harlem. The landowner dies, and Chris and his family remain pursued by southern authorities on charges of murder. Similarly, in *Blood on the Forge*, the brothers Big Mat, Melody, and Chinatown leave after Big Mat nearly kills their overseer in a fight over a mule. In *The Grapes of Wrath*, the Oklahoma tenant families argue with the landowners to stay on their cotton plots, the landowners blame the banks for pressuring the tenants off the land, and then tractors come through and plow the tenants' fields and cabins under, forcing them to leave. The Nevels family in *The Dollmaker* comes closer to leaving of their own volition. They are tenant farmers in Kentucky, and Gertie, like most protagonists in white sharecropping novels, saves her money to buy a farm of their own, but her husband, Clovis, decides instead to move the family to Detroit against her wishes, and the remainder of the novel reads like an object lesson in the foolishness of his decision. This dynamic of forced departure makes one wonder why laborers who recognize their own exploitation would remain in the same circumstance. Bizarrely, it is because the laborers are dependent on their own exploitation, and the series of tragic events that transpire in each of these novels after the families leave the South is evidence that sharecroppers—at least in works of fiction—were unprepared for life outside the South. This is largely the result of the same social forces used to manufacture dependency in order to maintain a docile labor force, such as limited access to education and diminished personal agency, so sharecroppers were essentially unprepared to be anything other than sharecroppers.

Partly because of their docility, sharecroppers were an attractive source of labor for industries seeking cheap workers at a time when labor was in short supply. When world war staunched the flow of European peasants immigrating into northern labor markets, some industries sent recruiting agents into the South to entice workers to move. "Labor agents did operate effectively in the Deep South," James Grossman writes, but their actual impact was limited, and by 1917, "northern employers had virtually ceased sending agents south."[101] A labor agent appears in only one of the sharecropper migration novels, *Blood on the Forge*, which is set in 1919. In the story, a jackleg agent makes it possible for the brothers to leave by providing them ten dollars and instructions to meet a train headed north at a specific time. Even with the offer, the brothers are still reluctant to leave. The agent attempts to persuade the brothers with a rational economic argument. He asks them how much land they farm and how much money they make, and Melody responds that they don't know because "Mr Johnston keeps the book. He don't let us see what's writ in it."[102] Yet the agent's argument appealing to their exploitation and his monetary enticement are insufficient to convince the brothers to leave. In truth, the labor agent's argument is insincere because the brothers will be equally exploited by the Pennsylvania steel mills that the agent represents, but they will be paid a wage for their labor rather than being held endlessly in debt and thrall.

In sharecropper migration novels, the laboring families are ruthlessly exploited for their labor outside the South, where they become pawns in labor conflicts. The Joads in *The Grapes of Wrath* are forced off their farms in Oklahoma, and they go to California seeking work, but they find a glutted labor market where farm owners are exploiting the new arrivals. Near the end of the book, Tom Joad kills a strikebreaker in a clash between union workers and scabs. The Nevels family in *The Dollmaker* moves to Detroit, where they live in a crowded tenement while Clovis works in a factory until he is laid off. In a pattern similar to *The Grapes of Wrath*, the book climaxes with Clovis killing a management goon in a fight between union workers and strikebreakers. In *Blood on the Forge*, the brothers work in a steel foundry where tension between labor and management is rising. The sheriff recruits Big Mat as a strikebreaker, and he is killed in a fight with union workers. The Browns in *The White Face* struggle to find work in Harlem, and they move from flophouse to flophouse living on Nella's income as a domestic worker until Chris is enlisted as an enforcer for a gang of thugs. He dies in prison, shot in the back by guards as he tries to attack his wife. In all of these books, the family units disintegrate as family members leave or, more often, die in accidents or violence. None of these families find acceptance, prosperity, security, or any other indicators of social ascent outside the South.

One clear message from sharecropper migration novels is that workers are expendable and exploitable. Sharecroppers were especially vulnerable to predatory labor systems because of their experience with manufactured dependence, which left them without the resources or the agency to find a path to prosperity outside the South. More than other blue-collar southern workers, sharecroppers were subject to control by their landowners because landowners could deny sharecroppers ready access to money, which tied the sharecroppers to the crop until settlement, so sharecroppers were less likely to leave until they were forced to leave. Unless they were fleeing lynching, sharecroppers in these novels were unlikely to leave until they were turned off the land by the landowners when finances or technology made them unnecessary. However, it is crucial to remember that employers, whether southern landowners or northern industrialists, were dependent on laborers, and all of these novels are ultimately books about labor control. It is to the employers' benefit to maintain a consistent supply of workers, to pay them poorly, and to keep them docile. In these books, the workers flow from one place to another, responding to economic conditions beyond their control. They are enticed into exploitive conditions, they are forced out of their positions, and they are subject to violence and coercion regardless of where they are.

The sharecroppers' experience outside the South undermines the myth of southern exceptionalism, the distorted notion that the South has been the primary site of racism, violence, and systems of exploitation in the United States.[103] It challenges the imaginative association of the North with freedom and the West with opportunity. While sharecropping is distinctively and historically associated with the South, it is far from the only means of exploiting workers, and factories, farms, and mines across the country have found effective means of extracting undercompensated labor from workers. In time, the descendants of sharecroppers who migrated out of the South amalgamated into other regions with many whites assimilating into local communities and many Blacks remaining de facto segregated in inner cities.[104] The migration of southerners changed American demographics, but the impacts, ultimately, were more significant outside the South than inside the region. Other than a temporary scarcity of laborers in some areas of the South, relatively little changed in the South.

By the early twentieth century, sharecropping transformed from an expedient system of economic redevelopment into an elaborate, intractable social hegemony based on commodity production that exploited Black and white laborers at the expense of its own financial efficiency. Sharecropping limited the agency of everyone involved in the system, including landowners, who had every incentive to exploit their laborers. Laborers, meanwhile, had little recourse but to accept their own exploitation, even the rational choice to leave was not a sure means of escaping exploitation. The system used debt to coerce and manipulate workers, tying them to crops for an entire year to reach settlement, and the landowners and merchants control of settlement and usurious practice of furnish allowed them to manipulate laborers into peonage and involuntary servitude. Sharecropping aligned with the culture of Jim Crow in the South, so Black laborers had virtually no legal, political, or economic agency, and no recourse to avoid or protest wanton violence. In many pragmatic and realistic terms, sharecropping was a direct extension of the culture of slavery.

One of the clearest illustrations of how sharecropping limited agency is the uniformity of narrative patterns about sharecropping. Depending upon the perspective of the protagonist, the novels follow predictable and consistent patterns with few deviations and with few examples of actual social mobility. In the novels about landowners and merchants, the means the protagonists use to acquire wealth prove to be temporary and based on the rapacious exploitation of laborers through debt control. Novels about Black sharecroppers depict conditions that have evolved only minimally beyond slavery, leaving them vulnerable to exploitation and violence. Novels about white sharecroppers, meanwhile, show that climbing the agricultural ladder from sharecropping to land ownership was virtually impossible. Sharecropper migration novels illustrate that escaping labor exploitation for people conditioned to sharecropping was also nearly impossible because workers were as likely to be exploited in the North or West as in the South. Works depicting sharecropping set between the beginning of the twentieth century and the Great Depression suggest that labor exploitation and alienation were unavoidable because of overwhelming systemic structures.

Only a major set of social upheavals would change the exploitive system of sharecropping. As long as the United States depended upon cotton production as a major global export, the federal government was reluctant to intervene in the system of labor, turning a blind eye to human and civil rights violations in the South. The region's dependence on commodity crops, however, made it vulnerable to economic instability, and its lack of investment in education, infrastructure, and diversification left it in a highly precarious position. In the event of a severe economic downturn, the South would be in a difficult position, and its vast exploited labor force would be a liability that would affect the entire country. When the stock market fell, sharecropping became America's problem.

→ 4 ←

# America's Number One Economic Problem

The first issue of *LIFE* magazine featured pictures of sharecroppers. In September of 1936, two months before the actual first issue was published, Henry Luce commissioned a dummy issue of the magazine to demonstrate to advertisers how the actual issue would look.¹ The issue contained a range of photo-laden articles about news and celebrities, but its lead article was a photo-essay by Alfred Eisenstaedt about sharecroppers on the nation's largest cotton plantation, the Delta and Pine Land Company (D&PL) in Scott, Mississippi. The actual article was not published in *LIFE*, which began production two months later, but it did appear in one of Luce's other magazines, *Fortune*, as "Biggest Cotton Plantation," a profile of Oscar Johnston, president of the plantation. The article gushes about the plantation's success in the depths of the Depression, comparing D&PL to Steinway & Sons as a commercial outlier, and Eisenstaedt's photographs appear as a series of images of Lonnie Fair and his family. One caption comments that "Lonnie Fair is a paragon of good fortune, as U.S. sharecroppers go. Last year he got $1,001.10 from D.P.L. (credit—$482.76, cash—$518.34)," and the pictures, which also appeared in the dummy issue of *LIFE*, show his home, his family picking cotton, and scenes of community life among the sharecroppers on the plantation.² The fact that the publication that would become the nation's leading news magazine began with a feature article about sharecroppers is highly significant because it demonstrates how ubiquitous images of southern sharecroppers were during the Great Depression. When America was at its economic nadir, sharecroppers were signifiers for the nation's poverty, objects of both pity and blame, and a symbol of the South as a social problem.

The magnitude of sharecropping as a social problem during the Great Depression is difficult to comprehend. "Although poverty was not confined to any particular area in the South," Paul Mertz writes in *New Deal Policy and Southern Rural Poverty* (1978), "privation was most widespread, and probably most intense, among several million tenant farmers, sharecroppers, and agricultural wage workers."[3] According to the 1930 census, there were 1,091,944 white families and 698,839 Black families working as landless farmers in the South. This group was a quarter of the region's population and more than half of its agricultural workers. Altogether, they totaled about 8.5 million individuals, about 5.5 million whites and 3 million African Americans, and they were "the most impoverished and backward of any group of producers in America."[4] At the beginning of the Depression, when this census was taken, their numbers were growing both because they had the nation's highest birthrate and because more farmers were losing their land and moving down the agricultural labor ladder. These families lived on some of the lowest incomes in the nation. Many of them earned only the value of their own subsistence or less. One government study of cotton plantations found that sharecropping families earned an average of $312, or $71 per person, in 1934, and this sum includes both the value of the family's debt to the landowner for food and other necessary expenses and their profit, if any, on the crop.[5] Their dire situation was made even more precarious by the unstable price of cotton, which fell from twenty cents a pound in 1927 to six cents a pound in 1933.

The decline in cotton prices and the rise in landless farmers made southern sharecroppers a national problem. Sharecroppers had been living in abject poverty on southern plantations for more than two generations before the Great Depression, and during this time, they had received relatively little national attention, even as the Progressive movement focused attention on the conditions of labor in the nation's industrial centers. Why, one might ask, were sharecroppers important now? This question has a few important answers. First, as the census numbers indicate, the proportion of white and Black sharecroppers reversed by 1930. Up to 1920, Black sharecroppers significantly outnumbered white sharecroppers, so a relatively small percentage of poor whites worked on land they did not own, but predatory credit practices and falling cotton prices caused many white families to lose their land and move down the agricultural ladder into tenancy and sharecropping. White sharecroppers, unlike Black sharecroppers, could vote, so sharecropping became a major political issue in southern states. Second, sharecroppers produced the cash crop—cotton—that continued to be one of America's leading export commodities, and cotton production and textile manufacturing constituted a significant component of the US gross domestic product. Sharecroppers' poverty also impeded their ability to contribute to the economy through consumerism. Third, as the federal government pressed an agenda of Keynesian investments in poverty alleviation, images of sharecroppers living in squalid, primitive conditions aroused public support for political solutions. This served a social agenda because it established a baseline quality-of-life expectation for Americans, indicating that access to food, shelter, education, healthcare, and basic services was considered essential for all citizens.

With America mired in its greatest economic catastrophe, southern sharecroppers became a synecdoche for poverty. Stories were told about southern sharecroppers in a dazzling array of media, including reams of government documents, scores of journalistic exposés, stacks of social science research reports, scores of newsreels and film documentaries, rolls and rolls of photographs, and dozens of works of nonfiction and fiction. All of these works, I contend, use the image of sharecroppers to serve a deliberate purpose, often to further a social agenda that politically or economically empowers an entity that claims to advocate on behalf of the sharecroppers. Government documents, for example, use sharecroppers to make a case for federal relief programs. In *They Must be Represented: The Politics of Documentary* (1994), Paula Rabinowitz makes the case that documentary forms are inherently political tools because they remake "the relationship of truth to ideology by insisting on advocacy rather than objectivity."[6] In addition to various forms of documentary, proletarian novels depicted the struggles of workers to make the case for reforms of an ideological system that subordinated vast groups of people into enforced poverty.[7]

Representations of sharecroppers during the Depression emerged in a fraught political climate that demanded action to address social and economic inequalities. These representations are important because they make the experience of rural agricultural poverty in the South during the 1930s visible, but these representations often seem to obscure the same people who they intend to expose. The pictures used for the prospectus of

*LIFE*, for example, depict the sharecropping family as contented laborers toiling productively on a Mississippi cotton plantation. The article published in *Fortune*, however, uses them as a background for its discussion of the planter, shifting the focus to finance and profitability and missing the opportunity to humanize them or even to recognize that their living conditions are barely deviated from those of their ancestors who worked as slaves on cotton plantations in the Delta. During the Depression, sharecroppers were used consistently as vehicle for projection to support numerous social and political agendas, but they rarely had an opportunity to tell their own stories. Thus, the attention focused on them distorts their experiences as much as or more than it illuminates their struggle.

### Men Working: Tenant Farmers and the Federal Government

One August 11, 1938, President Franklin D. Roosevelt gave a speech in Barnesville, Georgia, about the economic conditions in the South. In that speech, he said, "It is my conviction that the South presents right now the Nation's No. 1 economic problem—the Nation's problem, not merely the South's. For we have an unbalance in the Nation as a whole, due to this very condition in the South itself."[8] He was quoting himself from the introductory letter to "The Report on the Economic Conditions in the South," a controversial document that described the social, political, and economic challenges the region continued to face nearly a decade into the Great Depression, including persistent poverty, soil erosion, out-migration of labor, usurious credit, illiteracy, and poor public health. The report and the president's speech were political tools designed to reinforce a political agenda to expand New Deal reforms in the region. In particular, the president used the speech in Barnesville, colloquially known as "the purge speech," to denounce conservative southern Democrats, such as Georgia senator Walter George, who was seated directly behind him as he gave the speech, who were resistant to expanding federal legislation for relief initiatives. As the crowd watched, President Roosevelt endorsed Senator George's opponent in the upcoming primary, state attorney general Lawrence Camp. Although Roosevelt enjoyed tremendous personal popularity in Georgia, his speech backfired, and Walter George was reelected easily.

The two obvious lessons from the speech are that southern poverty was an issue of national concern during the Great Depression and that political narratives serve political purposes. The government response to southern poverty was often controversial. As Sidney Baldwin writes in *Poverty and Politics: The Rise and Decline of the Farm Security Administration* (1968), the New Deal program was alternately villainized as "a dangerous, radical, and un-American experiment in governmental intervention, paternalism, socialism, or communism" and lauded as "a heroic institution designed to secure social justice and political power for a neglected class of Americans."[9] Because any form of government intervention into labor markets and social welfare was politically divisive, the government needed to make the case that intervention was necessary and that it was successful. To do this, the federal government employed social scientists who were tasked with studying rural poverty and producing documents that delineated the government's policy on addressing poverty. While rural poverty was widespread across the country, it was most acute in the South among sharecroppers and tenant farmers living precariously on the unstable and unreliable whims of the cotton commodities market. "The Report on Economic Conditions of the South" that Roosevelt referenced in his Barnesville speech, for example, found that "the paradox of the South is that while it is blessed by Nature with immense wealth, its people as a whole are the poorest in the country."[10]

Between Roosevelt's election in 1932 and America's entrance into World War II in 1941, the federal government mounted numerous attempts to improve the South's economy. Soon after Roosevelt's first inauguration, Congress passed the Agricultural Adjustment Act (AAA), which was intended to increase the depressed price of commodities, particularly cotton, that glutted the marketplace. By the time the bill went into effect in the late spring of 1933, the season's cotton crop had already been planted, so a scheme was developed to plow under every third row of cotton. According to the plan, "farmers were to receive $7 to $20 for every acre plowed under, depending on their estimated yield," and landowners were supposed to divide the government allotment with their tenants according to the usual terms of their contracts.[11] The program did decrease the crop, and "in 1933 the AAA paid farmers $161,771,697 to remove 10,487,991 acres of cotton from production, reducing the yield by an estimated 4,489,467 bales," which increased the price of cotton from five cents a pound to ten cents a pound.[12] The next year, Congress passed the Bankhead Cotton Control Act, which limited the amount of cotton a planter could grow in a year, and the Federal Emergency Relief Administration was established to provide credit to some of the region's poorest farmers. In 1935, President Roosevelt used an executive order to create the Resettlement Administration, which was intended to help landless farmers purchase small farms. Congress passed the Bankhead-Jones Farm Tenant Act in 1937, which enacted the Farm Security Administration (FSA), a new office in the Department of Agriculture. The FSA absorbed the work of the Federal Emergency Relief Administration and the Resettlement Administration, and the FSA invested hundreds of millions of dollars into grants, low-interest loans, and relief projects for farmers to alleviate rural poverty.

These programs had mixed results, especially for southern sharecroppers. The AAA, in particular, may have made conditions worse for many sharecroppers and tenant farmers. According to the terms of the 1933 legislation, the government allotment was to be shared according to the tenants' share of the crop, but checks were distributed directly to landowners "who were left to distribute them appropriately with no federal oversight."[13] In many cases, landowners deducted the allotment from the tenants' debt, and in other cases, they simply took the money. "A tenant was lucky if he received any cash from the 1933 plow up," David Conrad concludes in *The Forgotten Farmers: The Story of Sharecroppers in the New Deal* (1965).[14] The government contracts gave landowners an incentive not to enter into sharecropping contracts, thus increasing their own acreage and their allotment from the government. In many cases, families who had previously worked on tenancy contracts were reduced to day laborers, which gave them little access to housing or provisions, or they were turned off the land altogether. Gunnar Myrdal described the AAA as "an American enclosure program" because it forced people off of their land and into cities, thus, increasing rates of poverty.[15] A key government study of the need for government intervention after the AAA drily states, "it appears that the AAA to some extent 'froze' the number of croppers employed in cotton culture in the Southeast at something like the 1932 figure." The programs that followed the AAA, such as the Resettlement Administration and the Farm Security Administration, were deliberately intended to move more tenant farmers up the agricultural ladder into farm ownership, but their results were also mixed and complicated.[16]

The federal government articulated its own narrative about rural relief in several government studies and pieces of outright propaganda that made a case for the need for and the efficacy of rural relief programs. The government reports were written by a group of liberal southern intellectuals who were affiliated with the Commission on Interracial Cooperation and the Institute for Research in Social Science, a group of sociologists based at the University of North Carolina. Thomas Jackson Woofter was the lead author of *Landlord and Tenant on the Cotton Plantation,* published in 1936, a study of the AAA, and a follow up analysis, *The Plantation South, 1934–1937,* which laid the sociological foundation for the FSA. He also wrote a pamphlet for the Works Progress Administration titled "The Plantation South Today" that was published in 1940 near the end of the Farm Security Administration's implementation. Woofter was a Georgia native who studied sociology at Columbia and worked both for the Commission on Interracial Cooperation and the Institute for Research in Social Science, and his progressive attitudes on racial uplift and social inequality color the reports.[17] Clark Foreman was the principal architect of the 1938 *Report on Economic Conditions in the South* that labeled the South as America's No. 1 economic problem. He was also a Georgia native, and he studied economics at Harvard and then worked with the Commission on Interracial Cooperation and the Julius Rosenwald Foundation before joining the Department of the Interior after Roosevelt's election. In 1937, The President's Committee on Farm Tenancy published an omnibus report that drew heavily from Woofter's previous work to produce a document titled *Farm Tenancy* that lays out the outlines for the Bankhead-Jones Act that led to the creation of the Farm Security Administration. The committee included many notable southern liberals, including Will W. Alexander, executive director of the Commission on Interracial Cooperation; Edwin Embree, president of the Julius Rosenwald Foundation; and Howard Odum, director of the Institute for Research in Social Science. These leading southern liberal intellectuals were responsible for making the government's case for rural relief.

The case for relief was based on large-scale studies of southern poverty. By 1930, tenancy was pervasive and growing in the South. Since 1880, the percent of tenants had grown from a national average of just over 25 percent to more than 40 percent, with the highest concentrations in the South, where more than half of all farmers were tenants. In Mississippi, nearly 70 percent of farmers were tenants.[18] While tenants provided inexpensive labor, the concentration of tenants was a problem because it mired a large swath of the population in poverty and impeded economic growth. Woofter's

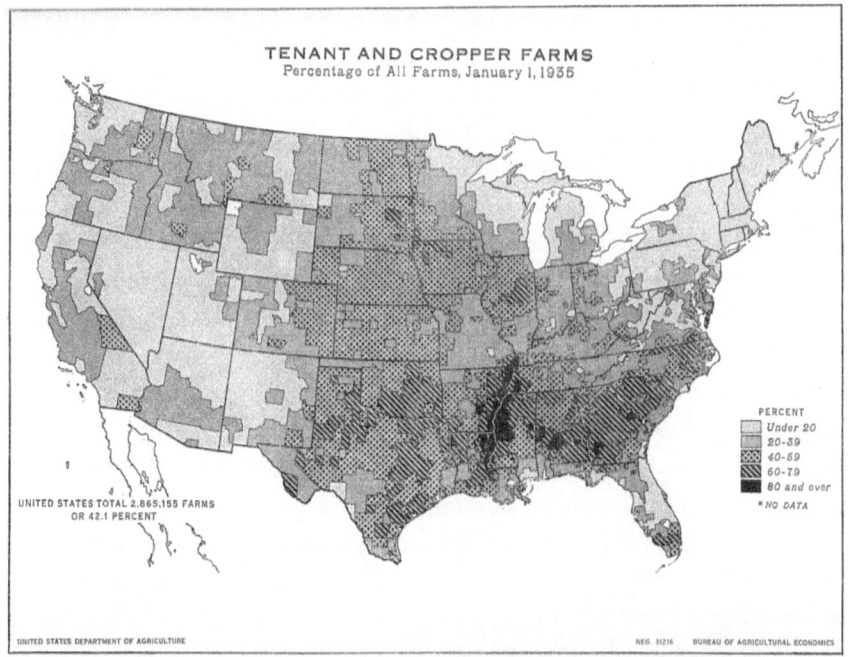

FIGURE 1.—The percentage of farms operated by tenants is highest in the areas where the major staple cash crops are grown, and lowest in the areas where livestock, specialized fruit and vegetable production, and subsistence farming are important.

FIGURE 3. Map of Farm Tenancy 1935. (President's Committee on Farm Tenancy)

study of tenant families on 646 plantations found that they had an average income of $122 after debts for furnish were settled.[19] "On the basis of such low incomes," Woofter and A. E. Fisher write in *The Plantation South*, "it is clearly impossible for the average tenant to raise his level of living above mere subsistence or to accumulate resources with which to improve his tenure status."[20] Because of this precarious economic position, tenants were unable to acquire land, and small landholders were constantly in danger of falling into tenancy from which they were unlikely to emerge. The problem was made even more intractable because "plantation customs and ideology set the pattern for relationships within smaller farm units."[21] Woofter goes on to explain that local plantation owners "persistently emerge as the political and economic leaders in the cotton areas," and they are unlikely to disrupt the system of labor exploitation because of their self-interest. Government intervention was necessary, according to this narrative, because by "whatever criterion is used, the number of needy is stupendous and offers convincing proof of the inadequacy of present programs to cope completely with the widespread destitution in the rural South."[22]

The reports offer some important findings about the tenant families' living conditions to make the case that intervention was necessary. Woofter and Fisher's report *The Plantation South Today* argues that the AAA improved living conditions so families "were a little better off" even though thousands of families were still living in "poverty and deprivation."[23] Because children were expected to work in the cotton fields during the spring and fall, education was frequently interrupted and school systems were poorly funded, so millions of southerners were illiterate. They also had less access to medical care, and they ate a monotonous, nutritionally deficient diet, so they were susceptible to disease and had shorter life spans than other Americans. They were likely to live in "an unpainted shack in a bare eroded field" without access to electricity, running water, adequate sanitation, refrigeration, sufficient insulation, or window screens, leaving them exposed to the elements.[24] Their living conditions were a result of their poverty, but their poverty was a result of sharecropping. "Fundamental to the understanding of the living habits of tenants is the realization that they exercise a relatively limited choice in determining these habits, and have been supervised for so long that if they did have a freer choice they would not have the knowledge of other ways of living essential to change," Woofter and Fisher write. They go on to explain that "the system of agriculture determines" that sharecroppers grow cotton exclusively and "the landlord determines" what houses the families live in, how they eat, and whether they have access to education and healthcare.[25]

The government studies indicate several characteristics of tenant farming that undermine social stability. First, the usurious system of credit created a disastrous cycle of planting and debt because pressure to pay off debts incurred to raise cotton led tenants to plant even more cotton, which lowered cotton prices on the global market and was "a strong influence against diversification and the production of varied field and garden crops for home consumption," which, in turn, increased the families' debt and decreased their self-sufficiency.[26] Second, the system of tenancy encouraged tenants to have large families in order to produce more laborers while simultaneously limiting the children's access to education because the plantation system "thrived on masses of ignorant workers."[27] Third, tenant farming made families more likely to move and less stable because families often moved at the end of a contract either to find better arrangements or because their landlords were unwilling to keep them. They mostly moved from farm to farm within the county in which they lived, so the distances were not great. The average period of residence per farm was 5.9 years, and white families moved more frequently than African American families.[28] This instability meant that families were unlikely to make long-term improvements to their land, less likely to gain favorable credit, and more likely to have unstable social and community relationships. Fourth, plantation owners tended to prefer African American tenant families, even though white tenant families were more prevalent, because African American families were less likely to leave, were more likely to live on poorer farms, and were less likely to apply for relief.[29]

Relief proposals were designed to reduce the rate of poverty, improve living conditions for the tenant families, promote social stability, and enhance the overall national economy. In *Landlord and Tenant in the Cotton South*, Woofter notes that the federal government had no policy toward the tenant system and the cotton economy before 1932 and that this laissez-faire approach was partly responsible for the current situation.[30] He outlines a set of constructive measures that could be implemented to improve the situation, including legislation to protect the rights of tenants; retirement of submarginal land wasted through erosion; crop diversification; limits on cotton production; credit assistance, direct relief, and work relief for tenant families to provide economic stability; and low-interest loans to promote tenants moving up the agricultural ladder to land ownership.[31] In the follow up study, *The Plantation South, 1934–1937*, he echoes the same proposals, some of which had been implemented to varying degrees of effectiveness through programs such as the Federal Emergency Relief Administration, and he adds a suggestion for housing programs. The authors of the study *Farm Tenancy*, who were making the case for the Farm Security Administration to carry out many of these proposals, argued that secure tenancy, which means either long-term contracts or land ownership, would encourage farmers to improve their homes and land, invest in machinery, and build stable community relations. They assert that "secure tenure does not produce large speculative profits, but greatly increases the opportunity for a steady income to the owner-operator, tenant, and landlord."[32] All of these proposals, obviously, call for federal solutions to the problem with no attention given to local or state-level interventions and no recommendations for investment in education or healthcare to improve the tenant families' living conditions. In effect, the constructive measures suggested still leave the tenant families dependent, merely shifting the dependency from the landowner to the government.

To be fair, the purpose of government studies is to promote government solutions. They make the case that tenant farming is an economic and social crisis, and they also indicate that federal interventions produce positive results. In the South, federal relief funds were crucially important because the state and local governments had no funds to disburse, so the South paradoxically received a lower percentage of federal funding than any other region while also receiving nearly all of its relief funding, "more than 96 percent," from federal sources, particularly AAA, FERA, and FSA.[33] These reports also make the case that the southern economy is a national problem because slow recovery in the South delays economic recovery for the entire country. *The Report on Economic Conditions of the South* gives two specific reasons that the South is a drag on national economy. First, although the South is an agricultural region, it "is failing to raise the things it needs. Southern farmers grow at home less than one-fifth of the things they use; four-fifths of all they eat and wear is purchased."[34] This dependency of goods from outside the region makes the South essentially a colony of the United States that is dependent on the nation for food, services, and economic relief. Second, the South's dependency suppresses its purchasing power, cutting off the nation's most accessible growth market, because "the people of the South need to buy, they want to buy, and they would buy—if they had the money."[35] Therefore, investments in stabilizing and developing the southern economy should benefit all American taxpayers. The actual relief programs had mixed results, often creating as many problems as they addressed, but the government studies of the tenant farming are unquestionably important because they represent the most significant engagement between the federal government and southern cotton farmers since the demise of the Freedmen's Bureau. "Although marked progress has been made in meeting certain problems and little in meeting others," Woofter concludes in *The Plantation South*, "the numerous books, reports, and discussions of the past few years dealing with conditions in the South have stimulated public opinion to such an extent that it is far more enlightened and unified than ever before with respect to Southern needs."[36]

The problem with government reports, however, is that they have a limited audience of policy makers, politicians, and bureaucrats, so the government needed a propaganda campaign to affect public opinion. After the Bankhead-Jones Act was signed creating the Resettlement Administration, Pare Lorentz, a young filmmaker from West Virginia, was appointed as film consultant and charged to make a documentary that explained the need for rural relief. His first film, *The Plow That Broke the Plains*, released in 1936, focused on the Dust Bowl in the Great Plains. The film brought attention to the government's intervention, but it was controversial because of its cost. Nonetheless, Lorentz was contracted to make a second film about the Mississippi River Valley that focused on the relief programs designed to improve conditions for southern farmers through conservation, river management, electrification, and rural relief. This film, *The River*, released in 1938, was highly successful, earning praise from President Roosevelt, southern audiences, and film critics.[37] It was distributed nationally through Paramount Films, so it was screened in theaters across the United States, and it was also widely screened in England. Although it was snubbed for an Academy Award nomination, it won the award for best documentary at the Venice Film Festival, beating *Olympia*, Leni Riefenstahl's film about the 1936 Olympics, and the script was nominated for the Pulitzer Prize for Poetry.

As a work of political propaganda, *The River* invites comparison to the work of Leni Riefenstahl. Beyond the fact that they were contemporaries and the coincidence that they both released documentary films at the same time, they also used similar language and images to tell political narratives. Lorentz makes some strong connections between the land, the people, and the state that are not overtly fascist, but they make similar emotional and imaginative appeals. *The River* features a strong masculine voice-over by Thomas Hardie Chalmers speaking in poetic verse that echoes the populistic vision of Walt Whitman and Hart Crane with long lines that build connections among the Mississippi River's many tributaries, the states it flows through, and the people who occupy the land it drains. Southern tenant farmers figure prominently in the film's narrative, particularly in the refrain "men and mules, mules and mud" about the levee system in the lower Mississippi that made the Delta cotton plantations possible. The film includes many shots of cotton fields and sharecroppers picking cotton and bales of cotton being loaded into riverboats. The story builds to a climactic crisis of economics and conservation because "poor land makes poor people and poor people poor land," which the narrative blames for the increasing numbers of sharecroppers in the Mississippi Valley, illustrated with scenes of poor whites pulling cotton sacks through fields and white families "ill-housed, ill-clad, and ill-fed" living in squalid conditions. Resolving these problems, the film asserts, will require an interlocking set of government interventions to stabilize the river, the land, and the people. The film praises the Tennessee Valley Authority's campaign of dam building—the names of dams rattled off like a list of Civil War battles—because it will tame floods and produce electricity. Civilian Conservation Corps programs that replanted forests and Extension Service initiatives to promote contour plowing will ameliorate erosion and stabilize the land, and the Farm Security Administration will build cooperative communities of farmers who build their own homes and work together to raise diversified crops.

*The River*, ultimately, is a work of propaganda designed to make the case for government intervention and to illustrate the efficacy of government programs. Steven Knepper describes the film as "a moving visual poem, an epic of the Mississippi, and a savvy piece of propaganda—a mix of conservation science and poetry, of national boosterism and critique of nation. Lorentz sought to dramatize the problems plaguing the Mississippi watershed, but like all documentary films there is a politics to *The River*'s representations. Lorentz does not present unvarnished facts and images; he presents a highly stylized, symbolically rich, and rhetorically sophisticated film."[38] The film echoes the case for New Deal programs laid out in the government reports, but it had a much broader impact with audiences. It defined perceptions of the southern economy as a national problem much more effectively than President Roosevelt's speech in Barnesville or *The Report on Economic Conditions of the South*. Jack Temple Kirby, in fact, claims that *The River* was "arguably the best-known, most widely seen portrait of the South during the 1930s," which means that the documentary did as much as any other form of media to make images of southern sharecroppers ubiquitous and to influence how Americans perceived southern sharecroppers.[39] Notably, the film presents sharecroppers as predominately white, and it suggests that their impoverishment is the result of vast social forces beyond their control, not their own ignorance and depravity, which challenges the common misperception that sharecroppers were mostly Black and inherently indolent. The film's narrative promoting New Deal programs makes appeals to the nation's conscience to promote a political agenda.

Not everyone concurred with the government narrative. New Deal programs were frequently controversial, and their results were often mixed, so they were an open target for satire, such as John Faulkner's novel *Men Working* (1941). In 1939, Faulkner worked as an engineer for the Works Progress Administration, a program designed to create job opportunities for destitute workers across the nation, and the following year he wrote a novel based on his experience that satirizes both the tenant families who receive federal relief and the government programs that supposedly helped them. His novel tells the story of the Taylors, a white north Mississippi tenant family, who leave their farm and move to an unnamed small city to take relief work. Their decision to leave their farm is the result of push and pull factors related to New Deal programs. "Why, hell, paw. What is there left for us out here?" Hub asks his father. "Mr. Young, the old bastard, taking the whole par'ty check and paying us day wages. What are we going to do after the crop's laid by? There will be a dozen farmers then trying to git on the WP and A for every job there is."[40] In this case, Mr. Young, their landlord, has changed their contract from sharecropping to wage laboring, which allows him to pocket the farm's entire AAA allotment, so the family will receive no payment for their crop at settlement, leaving them destitute over the winter. Meanwhile, the WPA offers the possibility of work and steady pay. For the Taylors, and many other tenant families, the decision seems to be simple.[41]

The results of their decision, however, prove to be complicated. Mr. Taylor files a 402 work assignment form, which places him on the government payroll for eighteen months. The family moves to town, rents a room "in a huge old vacant house" along with several other families, gets an account at a grocery store, and buys a radio.[42] The family replicates the relationship they had with their landlord with the local merchants, and the merchants are eager to ensnare them in debt, effectively taking on the role of furnish merchants: "Hell, yes. Charge the stuff to 'em, said the merchants. They get one of them blue government checks every two weeks. . . . Add about half onto everything they buy and it's cheap at that. They been used to running one of them furnish accounts and them rich furnish merchants add three hundred percent to every one of their accounts and then charge them eight per cent interest to make it legal."[43] The merchants and rental agents exploit the workers in the same ways that their landlords did, and the only difference is that the money comes from the government rather than from cotton. The government contracts, however, are designed to be short-term relief, and they expire after eighteen months, which leaves the family destitute. They spend days waiting outside the office of the social worker in the county courthouse while evading rental agents and debt collectors.

Although the Taylors in *Men Working* are exploited workers, Faulkner does not present them sympathetically. In his depiction, they are rural rubes, whose depravity makes them a social menace. The novel includes several passages narrated from the perspective of scandalized members of the community who comment on the family. For example, in one passage, a voice describes "that bunch of WPA folks in that big house below the City Hall" and recounts a grotesque anecdote about the horrifying smell coming from the family's room.[44] The entire family lives crammed into one room. When the daughter has a baby, a doctor is brought in to help with the delivery, and he discovers the smell coming from the infected body of the family's oldest son, Reno: "this thing, whatever it was, was about seven foot tall even all crumpled up like a bundle of sticks and had a big dirty white head about as wide as it was long and a black beard right around its mouth and looked like pig bristles sticking flat out from the top of its head."[45] Much like Vardaman in *As I Lay Dying* (1930) and Dude in *Tobacco Road* (1932), Reno is the character who embodies the family's deviation from social norms. The product of a botched abortion, he is born prematurely but survives and grows to be more than six feet tall, although severely mentally and physically disabled. As the family devolves over the course of the novel, his condition worsens, until he dies, and the family keeps his corpse in a homemade coffin kept under a bed. The other characters in the novel are physically functional, and one could easily see how they might be integrated into the community, but Faulkner uses this character to indicate that the Taylors are not a functional family because they are too depraved and ignorant to understand basic social conventions.

The satire, however, reflects more on the inherent depravity of tenant farming and federal relief programs, both of which force the family in an intractable cycle of manufactured dependency, leaving them as abjectly deformed as their grotesque child. As tenant farmers, the family is utterly dependent upon Mr. Young for land, a home, food, work, direction, and support. On federal relief, the family is dependent upon the WPA and government officials for all of the same things. In the absence of a landlord, Mr. Taylor focuses his dependency on a midlevel government official at City Hall named Mr. Will who makes unreasonable promises to the men on relief. When their permission to work expires, he promises to get them back on the rolls and then disappears to Hot Springs to treat his neuralgia, leaving them with false hope. The men return to city hall every day, waiting to be returned to work, blocking the hallways and harassing the government officials. As a WPA administrator, John Faulkner likely identified with the government workers who find the workers detestable, and his novel depicts government officials consistently rescuing the family from their own ignorance, such as when the mayor finds them a new place to live or when the health department finds them access to water and sanitation. Yet these interventions do not improve the family's condition. Instead, the family dissolves as the children leave, some returning to tenancy and others leaving for industries in the North, and the book ends with Mr. Taylor, still living on relief, showing up for another cycle of WPA work, "bewildered no longer but vaguely concerned at being once more engulfed into a time-ordered existence and shackled to the security of two moving clock hands by the magic of his name on a slip of paper in impersonal print, drawn to a fate that he did not recognize as unkind."[46]

In 1935, Erskine Caldwell published a pamphlet titled "Tenant Farmer" that also critiques government intervention in sharecropping. "The FERA [Federal Emergency Recovery Act] in many southern counties is inadequate to help [sharecroppers]," he writes.[47] FERA provided federal funding to the states for distribution to infrastructure projects and other work programs, but Caldwell argues that southern governors, such as Georgia governor Eugene Talmadge, mismanaged the funding so that it never reached the people it was intended to help. At the time this pamphlet was published, Caldwell was a famous, or notorious, documenter of poor white southerners as a result of the commercial success of his novel *Tobacco Road* (1932) and the Broadway play based on the novel. He substantiates his criticism of government programs in the pamphlet with descriptions of impoverished sharecropping families in East Georgia suffering from unemployment, malnutrition, disease, and privation, similar to the Jeeters in his novel. He mentions, for example, women suffering from pellagra, a sickly child licking a bag that had contained a piece of meat, and an elderly farmer evicted when he could no longer produce a crop. He states, "This section of East Georgia is the scene of cases of human want that no relief agency, government, county, state, or private charity has touched."[48] He proposes that the solution to southern poverty is landownership: "until the agricultural worker commands his own farm, either as an individual or as a member of a state-allotted farm group, the Southern tenant farmer will continue to be bound hand and foot in economic slavery."[49]

The results of government intervention in tenant farming during the Great Depression were mixed at best. The government narrative that southern tenant farming was a national problem and that something had to be done to help tenant farmers was correct, but the reports about the impacts of AAA, FERA, FSA, and WPA were inconclusive. In some cases, the interventions created more problems than they solved. AAA benefited landowners much more than sharecroppers, and FSA and FERA programs offered short-term solutions that were rendered moot by World War II. However, Roger Biles claims that "New Deal programs became most important in the long-term conduct of southern farming."[50] (53). The AAA set a precedent for government subsidies in agriculture that continue to underwrite industrial agriculture, supporting farm owners and corporations at the expense of workers. In spite of campaigns to increase small farm ownership, government intervention actually encouraged landowners to grow the size of their operations and to shift more and more families into wage laboring. The challenges of tenant farming during the Great Depression were much too complex to be solved with top-down solutions.

## Southern Pathology: Social Science and Tenant Farming

In 1932, Hortense Powdermaker, an anthropologist affiliated with the Institute of Human Relations at Yale University, began an ethnographic study of people in the Mississippi Delta. Her previous work had been a study of leadership in a primitive society, and she had conducted fieldwork among the Lesu in Papua New Guinea. She came to Mississippi, to a place that she identified as "Cottonville," to bring the analytical tools of anthropology to bear on a segment of modern America because "problems of race, of minority groups, of a region like the South, are among our most pressing issues."[51] Before going to Mississippi, she met with African American sociologist Charles Johnson at Fisk University, who gave her some useful advice about interacting with white southerners. While in Cottonville, which was actually

Indianola, Mississippi, she befriended poet William Alexander Percy, who helped her find a place to live, was vetted by a panel of the community's leading citizens who were concerned that she would agitate the local African Americans, pretended to be a Methodist to gain access to church congregations, and spent a considerable amount of time driving around Sunflower County with domestic workers.[52] Her ethnographic research, published as *After Freedom: A Cultural Study of the Deep South* (1939), develops some interesting implications about the South during the Great Depression. Similar to the government reports analyzing the region, it suggests that the South was a site of social problems, that it deviated significantly from the mainstream of US culture, and that it was primitive relative to the rest of the country. Powdermaker was one of more than a dozen social scientists who analyzed the region's systemic problems during the Great Depression, and these works collectively constitute an intricate narrative of sharecropping as a distinctive sociocultural system.

These studies mostly emanated from a few of sources. Howard W. Odum established the Institute for Research in Social Science at the University of North Carolina a few years before the Depression began, and it produced a cadre of liberal sociologists interested in diagnosing the region's problems. Odum produced *Southern Regions of United States* (1936), a vast compendium of data about the South's environmental, economic, and human resources, packed with hundreds of maps, charts, and graphs, and he inspired a generation of young sociologists to study the region. His protégés Rupert Vance and Arthur Raper "shared a determination to understand southern society by probing to a deeper level than had ever been attained before through social science."[53] Another source of research was the Commission on Interracial Cooperation, an organization based in Atlanta that advocated for an end to lynching and better racial relations.[54] The commission's director, Will W. Alexander, lobbied New Deal agencies for more programs for African Americans, and Arthur Raper joined the organization as research director. The third source of research on southern agricultural communities was the Institute of Human Relations at Yale University, an interdisciplinary group of social scientists interested in using social research to understand modern civilization. These groups shared a common commitment to liberal politics, faith in the emergent methodologies of social science, and an interest in understanding and improving the economic and social circumstances in the South.

Sociologists studying the South generated data-driven holistic studies of representational communities to analyze the region's problems. Rupert Vance published two important studies during the Great Depression that analyze much of the data reflected in Odum's *Southern Regions of the United States*. His 1929 book, *Human Factors in Cotton Culture*, argues that the lower South is a closed system devoted to cotton cultivation. "There exists a kind of natural harmony about the cotton system," he writes. "Its parts fit together so perfectly as to suggest the fatalism of design . . . a complex whole that is so closely interconnected that no one can suggest any place at which it may be attacked except the grower; and the grower is to change the system himself, cold comfort for advice." His 1935 book *Human Geography of the South* gives a broader analysis of the connections between the South's agricultural subregions and its social systems. Arthur Raper, another of Odum's students, published *Preface to Peasantry* in 1936, a detailed comparative study of two counties in Georgia that argues that tenant farming creates a culture of dependency.[55] Margaret Hagood, a research associate with Odum's Institute for Research in Social Science, published *Mothers of the South: Portraiture of the White Tenant Farm Women*, a study that details the difficult lives of women in sharecropping families, in 1939. Charles S. Johnson, a sociologist at Fisk University who was affiliated with the Commission on Interracial Cooperation, published *Shadow of the Plantation*, a study of Macon County, Alabama, in 1934. His study claims that "the Negroes in areas of the South, notably in the cotton and cane belts, represent an American type which can most nearly be described as 'folk,' and so far as their lives are rooted in the soil, they are, perhaps, the closest approach to an American peasantry."[56] Johnson, who would later become president of Fisk University, collaborated with Will W. Alexander and Edwin R. Embree, president of the Rosenwald Fund, to produce *The Collapse of Cotton Tenancy* in 1935. This brief study of southern agriculture was extremely important and "had an immediate effect on government policy," even though it was critical of the New Deal, "and it directly influenced the reformist shape and substance of the Bankhead-Jones Act and the second Agricultural Adjustment Act."[57]

These works suggest that the tenant farming system in the South is "a new kind of slavery."[58] Charles Johnson articulates this most clearly in *Shadow of the Plantation*. "The essential observation of this study," he writes, "is that the Negro population of Macon County has its own social heritage which, in relatively complete isolation, has had little chance for modification from without or within. Patterns of life, social codes, as well as social attitudes, were set in the economy of slavery."[59] Johnson conducted his study in Macon County, Alabama, the site of Tuskegee Institute, because it was a representative lower South agricultural community, which suggests that his assertion applies to the rest of the lower South. Rupert Vance explains that this exploitative socioeconomic system continues to exist for a specific reason: "cotton cannot be grown at a profit *if all the labor it requires has to be paid for*" (italics in original).[60] Tenant farming in all of its permutations was a means of extracting virtually free labor from cotton growers, and this economic paradigm instantiated "a total socio-cultural system" that produced numerous social problems while resisting any intervention.[61]

The sociological studies emphasize the economic foundations of sharecropping, but the ethnographic studies focus on the culture of segregation. Three anthropological studies were conducted in Mississippi during the Great Depression, plus an additional study conducted in Alabama soon after World War II. While researching *After Freedom*, Hortense Powdermaker spent several months living in Indianola, Mississippi, posing as a visiting teacher, and she conducted interviews with nearly two hundred Black and white members of the community while actively participating in the community's social life. Her book explains the elaborate and sometimes subtle system for maintaining segregation and examines the effects of this system on both Blacks and whites. At the same time that Powdermaker was in Indianola, John Dollard, another researcher from Yale, was also in Indianola, which he labels "Southerntown," conducting a separate ethnographic study, *Class and Caste in a Southern Town* (1937).[62] His book also focuses on the social apparatus of segregation, and he offers a theory about how white people benefit from the system through social gains. Meanwhile, a team of two married couples, one Black couple and one white couple, studied the social structure of "Old City," Natchez, Mississippi, for *Deep South* (1941). The teams, Allison Davis and his wife Elizabeth and Burleigh and Mary Gardner, were students of Lloyd Warner, an anthropologist at University of Chicago, who sponsored the study. They lived in Natchez for two years, and they were able to infiltrate the community more thoroughly than Powdermaker or Dollard and produce a nuanced study of segregation that examines its effects on each level of social stratification. Finally, Morton Rubin, an anthropologist affiliated with the Institute for Social Science Research at the University of North Carolina, conducted a study of *Plantation County* (1951) in Wilcox County, Alabama, in 1947 that indicates some of the effects of post-World War II industrialization on the rural plantation South.

These anthropological studies use a divergent set of methodologies, but they share a perspective that race relations in the South are based on a caste system. Dollard, in fact, claims that "caste has replaced slavery as a means of maintaining the essence of the old status order in the South."[63] Borrowing the idea of caste structure from Indian culture, in which social mobility is limited by birth into a particular social stratum, the anthropologists extend the social stratification into a racialized class structure that "is pinned not to cultural but to biological features—to color, features, hair form, and the like."[64] Dollard investigates the sociosexual characters in great detail, dilating on the function of the color line and explaining that white men may have sexual relationships with African American women but that African American men are forbidden from having relationships with white women. The prohibition on intermarriage and the complications of incorporating interracial offspring are the key issue for the discussion of caste in the South, and the Davises and Gardners expand on the issues to describe how to enforce economic subordination. They explain that caste subordination keeps the tenant dependent on the landowner and maintains the landowner's dominance.[65] The problem with their use of caste as a term for racial segregation in sharecropping communities is that it flattens the more complicated social structures. In these studies, "whites were prototypically planters and wealthy businessmen, and blacks were prototypically sharecroppers," but across the South more white people were sharecroppers than Black people, and the systems of social controls were modified and adapted to accommodate intraracial social dominance.[66]

Read together, these social science texts offer some important insights about the culture of sharecropping during the Great Depression. They confirm the extensive data offered in government reports about the sharecroppers' living condition, and they describe poor nutrition, substandard housing, lack of healthcare, and diminished educational opportunities. These works, meanwhile, offer much more detail about the social institutions that constitute the sharecropping community, such as families, churches, and social organizations. The strongest social institution for tenant farmers was the family, which tended to be large because families were economic units. Larger families could work more land and produce more labor. According to Powdermaker, "A man and wife together work from fifteen to twenty acres. If they have three children, the acreage is twenty-five to thirty.... A child of ten to twelve is a worker, and is counted as half a hand. A sixteen year old boy or girl is a full hand."[67] Because of this economic incentive, family units tended to be cohesive because all family members were needed to work from an early age, and children had fewer opportunities for education or recreation because they were expected to work. This family structure put enormous pressure upon the mothers, whom Raper calls the "chief burden carrier," because they were often pregnant, they were expected to perform all of the laborious domestic tasks, including feeding a large family, in addition to the emotional labor of raising a family in persistent poverty, and they were often needed to help with work in the fields during planting and harvest.[68] Sharecropping families also had few sources of social support in the community. "Although the lives of most women are somewhat affected by the occupations of their husbands," Margaret Hagood writes, "there is probably no group where the influence is more profound than in the case of tenant farm women," and she explains that in addition to providing domestic labor and assisting with the family's farm labor, they are dependent upon their husbands to negotiate a contract that determines their housing, food supply, income, and social status.[69] Even during the New Deal, government support was scarce, and other sources of social connection tended to be weak. Schools, obviously, were insignificant, and families living on rural farms were often distant from their neighbors. The one social institution available to tenant farmers was the church. Charles Johnson explains that "it is in a very real sense a social institution," and he goes on to state that churches offered not only spiritual guidance but also an opportunity for families to have face-to-face interaction, to have social events, to enjoy recreation, and to maintain social order.[70] With the exception of church, social relationships outside the family tended to be weak.

The most important relationship for tenant families was with the landowner, which determined where they would live, how they would work, what they would eat, and whether they would make money. The landowners' power in the relationship was absolute, and Morton Rubin describes it as the "last vestige of beneficent despotism" because tenants had little recourse for grievance against the landowner.⁷¹ Johnson, Embree, and Alexander extend this point, explaining "The status of tenancy demands complete dependence; it requires no education and demands no initiative, since the landlord assumes the prerogative of direction in the choice of crop, the method by which it is cultivated, and how and when and where it shall be sold."⁷² They go on to enumerate the landowners' control over the children's education, the families' accounts, their government relief, and their access to the courts. In *Shadow of the Plantation*, Johnson describes tenant farming as a system in which both the landowner and the tenant are locked because the landowners are obligated to sell cotton to satisfy the banks and tenants are obligated to grow cotton to satisfy the landowners. "In this desperate struggle both may lose," he writes, "but the advantage is always with the white landlord."⁷³ Tenant farming was a highly asymmetrical power relationship that left sharecropping families with very little leverage, but there were a few opportunities for resistance.

One form of resistance was mobility. During the Great Depression, millions of Black and white southerners left the region altogether, but millions more stayed in the South and continued working on annual contracts. After a contract ended at settlement, families were faced with the decision to leave, provided they weren't forced into peonage through debt. Those who could leave often did, if only out of a sense of hope. Powdermaker documents, "During December and January the roads are filled with wagons piled high with household goods, the families perched on top. They are hoping to find something better, but they seldom do. Two years on one plantation is considered a good average."⁷⁴ The annual migration was a fixture in sharecropping communities, but Johnson explains that sharecropping families tended to stay within a specific area. "Year after year these families continue to live and move about within the county, but rarely leaving it," he writes. "The tenant turnover is high. Their one outstanding means of asserting freedom is this mobility, although within an extremely narrow range."⁷⁵ They stayed within the area usually because of their extended family relationships in the area and also because of the value of reputation. Tenants within a small area often knew landowners by reputation, including which ones were fair and which ones were violent, and "one of the bases of competition between landlords for tenants was the landlord's reputation among the tenants."⁷⁶ A landowner known to intimidate tenants would have a more difficult time finding workers, and a landowner known for fairness would be more likely to keep tenant families with greater stability for longer time. Of course, mobility worked both ways, and landowners often discharged families from their land at their whim, but voluntary mobility was one of the few ways that families could assert control over their own lives.

For tenant families, small acts of disobedience, deliberate indolence, and seeking small pleasures were also forms of resistance. Powdermaker, for example, explains that "now and then a sharecropper may cripple a mule or make an animal sick; or he may 'tie up' farm implements, do damage to his house, harm his employer's property in any possible way. This sort of thing is the only feasible revenge, but is seldom occurs and never does anything except harm."[77] More often, sharecroppers would demonstrate their frustration through indolence, working slowly or inattentively to sabotage the landowner's crop. The tenant system, which was designed to cheat the tenants of their labor, provided little incentive for industry. In fact, a highly productive sharecropper was even more likely to be cheated at settlement, so sharecroppers had no motivation to work much beyond making a bare living. This mindset contributed to a reputation for shiftlessness and an attitude among landowners that "the typical wage hand or tenant will work when he has to—when he is hungry or about to get hungry."[78] Shiftlessness was a natural result of the system. As Vance explains, "possessing by law no right in his tenancy and no claim for improvements made, the cotton renter has acquired a shiftless attitude toward the place in which he lives."[79] Tenants had no reason to maintain the homes they rented or the tools they borrowed, no motivation to work harder than absolutely necessary on their crops, no purpose to develop their communities, and little reason to make long-term investments. On the rare occasions when they had any money, they had good reason to spend it as quickly as possible. Tenants often had a reputation for being spendthrifts in addition to being shiftless, but their "love for material goods of the moment is conditioned by the insecurity of [their] position in society. Since [they] move about considerably, there is little incentive to invest in objects of permanent value."[80] The profound imbalance of power in the tenant system left tenant families few ways to assert their independence beyond these small symbolic actions.

During the Great Depression, the federal government attempted to intercede on behalf of sharecroppers, but the social scientists indicate that government intervention disproportionately benefited the landowners. Raper finds that New Deal programs have affected the economy in the counties he studied, improving the overall standard of living, but sharecroppers were least affected, which left them highly vulnerable. He writes: "Inadequate relief will continue the rickets and pellagra, the high morbidity, the high mortality among the landless farmers of the South. Adequate relief will disturb labor conditions in many communities, because it will offer more than many of the landless farmers have been receiving from their employment."[81] Herein lies the dilemma of government intervention in sharecropping: the landowners demanded a depressed, exploitable labor market, but the tenant families hoped for a means of survival. The authors of *The Collapse of Cotton Tenancy* conclude, "It is the blunt truth to say that under the present system the landowner is more and more protected from risk by government activity, while the tenant is left open to risks on every side. Only after he first forfeits what property he may possess and then his tenure, does the tenant come to the form of insurance designed for him—relief."[82] One of the challenges for the federal government was finding a way to add economic incentives to a system that was predicated on economic exploitation. The result was that many sharecroppers were willing to accept government relief, so for some sharecroppers, "the government has taken over the role of 'good white folks' appearing almost more beneficent and more paternalistic than they."[83] The end result of the New Deal for many sharecroppers was substituting one form of dependency for another.

Many of the social scientists who studied the system recognized that it was untenable, but as long as the cotton-based economy required vast amounts of manual labor for brief periods at virtually no cost, sharecropping would continue to exist as it did for nearly a century. However, they also realized that a problematic shift was imminent as mechanization replaced manual labor, which had the potential to create as many problems as it solved. As Rupert Vance presciently summarizes the situation, "The invention of a practicable cotton-picker, often announced but never quite realized, will serve to lower the cost of production, extend acreage, consolidate holdings, and reduce the demand for labor.... The transitional period will find the South full of cotton tenants with no place to turn."[84] Johnson, Embree, and Alexander, meanwhile, predict that when the mechanical cotton picker goes into production "it will automatically release hundreds of thousands of cotton workers particularly in the Southeast, creating a new range of social problems," and John Dollard echoes the sentiment, warning if the mechanical cotton picker is implemented, "the South would face a radically new problem as regards the Negro."[85] By the Great Depression, people studying the South could foresee the inevitability of mechanization changing the tenant farming system, as mechanization had already changed many other sectors of the American economy, but they could not clearly predict how those effects would play out, although the general consensus was that it would not be immediately beneficial.

The social science texts catalog many of the problems associated with tenant farming in the South, and they attempt to propose some solutions. Margaret Hagood indicates that "until the agricultural system of the South is successfully rehabilitated, or until family limitation practices become more universal than at present, Southern farm tenant mothers will continue to supply a disproportionate share of children who will be disadvantaged from birth."[86] Rupert Vance suggests greater agricultural diversity, such as "stock raising, fruit farming, or dairying," but he recognizes that economic and physical infrastructure would need to be rebuilt entirely to accommodate new crops.[87] Cotton persisted in part because of inertia, because the system of credit was based on cotton crops, because the network of production and distribution was established for cotton, and because farm workers knew how to raise cotton and not much else. Charles Johnson proposes decreasing cotton production, similar to the AAA, but he notes that the AAA resulted in increased production on smaller acreage, which led to the displacement of many sharecroppers and the exacerbation off many social problems.[88] Arthur Raper considers increasing Black landownership, but the culture of white supremacy severely limits the possibility of Black landownership, so "there is a high probability that Negroes will be able to purchase land in this area only as the plantation system crumbles."[89] Finally, Johnson, Alexander, and Embree give a plan for land distribution through the federal government, reviving the promise of forty acres and a mule, but again they explain that the existing structure of the plantation system, not to mention the need to confiscate private property, make this plan untenable.[90] The social science narrative of tenant farming indicates that the system presents many problems, enough problems to make its survival doubtful, but the potential solutions are not practical, primarily because of the systems intractable culture of cotton and racism.

## Have You Heard Their Voices?
## Sharecropper Photo Documentaries

Gladys Reed sued *The Saturday Evening Post* in 1939 for mislabeling her photograph. The previous year, Arthur Rothstein, a photographer for the Farm Security Administration, had visited the family's cabin in Arkansas and taken photographs of her standing in the doorway of her cabin, visibly pregnant, wearing a threadbare dress, and surrounded with three sickly, wan children. The pictures were published several times in national publications, including *the New York Times, the Boston Sunday Post, Look*, and Archibald MacLeish's long illustrated poem *Land of the Free*, in addition to *the Saturday Evening Post*. She sued the publisher of *the Saturday Evening Post* for libel over the caption that accompanied the picture, which said, "'They don't know how to use a doctor; they've never had one'; An Arkansas Sharecropper's Family."[91] She contended that the caption identified her incorrectly because her family were not sharecroppers; they were tenants. The case did not go to trial, but it exposed "a tension between the [Farm Security Administration's] mission on behalf of the South's underprivileged and the necessity of having to work through the established media to achieve a high visibility for its programs."[92] During the Depression, pictures of sharecroppers and tenant farmers were ubiquitous in print media, and the political need to tell the story of America's rural poor led to the emergence of a distinctive genre—full-length photo documentary texts.

These picture books of poverty were plagued with an inherent problem, as the Reed case indicates. They told the story of southern sharecroppers to further a political agenda designed to increase support for New Deal programs, but they did not allow poor southerners to tell their own stories. This mode of speaking for rather than listening to is implicit in the title of the text that established the conventions of the genre, Erskine Caldwell and Margaret Bourke-White's *You Have Seen Their Faces* (1937).[93] Between 1937 and 1943, almost a dozen photo documentaries were published, many with the direct support of the federal government, that focused on the experiences of southern tenant farmers. The genre of documentary photography began with Jacob Riis's revolutionary work *How the Other Half Lives* (1890), which illustrates the squalid lives of urban tenements during the Gilded Age. Since then, many important documentary works paired photographs of people living in difficult circumstances with text that attempts to explain

FIGURE 4. Arthur Rothstein, "Wife and children of sharecropper in Washington County, Arkansas," August 1935. (US Farm Security Administration; Library of Congress)

and contextualize the images, and "the point of all of these books was the same," William Stott writes, "to make the reader feel he was a firsthand witness to a social condition."[94] Caldwell and Bourke-White, capitalizing on the success of Caldwell's novels about poor white southerners, collaborated to produce a highly successful work that adapted documentary photography to the conditions of rural poverty and established the conventions of Depression-era sharecropper photo documentaries.[95] These works pair images of sharecropping families with text that explains the family's living conditions and economic circumstances, draw upon appeals to pathos to help the audience sympathize with the sharecroppers, reinforce the need for government intervention to ameliorate the squalid conditions, and participate in a problematic process of middle-class voyeurism that reifies southern poverty.

While Caldwell and Bourke-White's book developed from an opportunistic impulse to use Caldwell's celebrity to sell books while establishing the credibility of his depiction of poor southerners in *Tobacco Road*, its success led to a series of works that followed the same conventions, most of them involving direct collaboration between writers and the Farm Security Administration.[96] In 1938, Herman Clarence Nixon, a onetime Agrarian turned New Dealer, published *Forty Acres and Steel Mules*, an idiosyncratic analysis of southern poverty that blends autobiography with sociology and uses panels of photographs to illustrate the issues in the book. The next year, Dorothea Lange, who would become the most famous photographer working with the Farm Security Administration, and her husband, agricultural economist Paul Schuster Taylor, collaborated on *American Exodus*, a photo documentary of displaced laborers that begins in the South with images of sharecroppers facing the imminent threat of mechanization. Edwin Ware Hullinger published *Plowing Through: The Story of the Negro in Agriculture* in 1940, and Richard Wright and Edwin Rosskam, a Farm Security Administration staff member, collaborated on *Twelve Million Black Voices*, a photo documentary of African Americans moving from southern farms to northern slums, in 1941. That same year, James Agee and Walker Evans published *Let Us Now Praise Famous Men*, which has become the most famous work of the genre. Arthur Raper moved from sociology to public commentary with two photo documentaries: *Sharecroppers All* (1941), a general analysis of sharecropping's effects throughout the southern social structure that he cowrote with Ira De Reid, and *Tenants of the Almighty* (1943), a photo documentary of the history and economy of Greene County, Georgia, with special emphasis on the New Deal, which includes dozens of photographs by Farm Security Administration photographer Jack Delano.

The Farm Security Administration's photographic division, a government agency established to publicize the plight of the rural poor, provided most of the photographs in these works. In 1935, Roy Stryker joined the Resettlement Administration, a New Deal agency, and created a photographic division to document and promote the agency's work. Although the agency employed some of the greatest American photographers of the time, including Dorothea Lange, Walker Evans, and Gordon Parks, Stryker maintained that the unit's focus was not on aesthetics but on documentary.[97] Edwin Rosskam, Stryker's editorial assistant, explains that the unit's mission was "to document the living and working conditions of America's rural lower third" and that photographers were instructed to "point their cameras not merely at government projects but at anything in the rural scene which seems significant to them. Nevertheless the FSA file has managed to remain amazingly homogenous and purposeful. The reason: an inclusive attitude which makes photographer, eye and camera into an instrument of social science."[98] Although Rosskam diminishes the propaganda role of the unit, it had a clear purpose to document both the dire need for government intervention in the rural South and the beneficial impacts of interventions in the lives of poor southerners. "It is no coincidence that nearly one-fifth of the RA/FSA photographs concerned subjects useful for agency promotion efforts," such as land reclamation projects, construction, and resettlement camps, and clients being assisted by agents.[99] The unit's objectives aligned well with the photo documentary genre because they allowed the unit to make its case for intervention in the rural South by pairing photographs with text that explained and amplified the images.

The photo documentary genre, however, has a fundamental flaw. As a medium designed to communicate a message to provoke an intended response, it manipulates both the subject of the message and the receiver of the message. In *Documentary Expression and Thirties America* (1973), William Stott explains the means that documentarians use to communicate their messages through appeals to the intellect and to emotion. He concludes that "the practitioners of the documentary genre in the thirties realized, if dimly, the same thing: emotion counted more than fact."[100] As such, documentary, even when it appealed to objectivity, could be used to sway perceptions, which is the foundation of propaganda. Paula Rabinowitz voices a similar concern in *They Must Be Represented: The Politics of Documentary*. She argues that documentary is a form of voyeurism that reinforces the viewer's power differential because it inspires feelings of sympathy in the "bourgeois subject" based on material inequality between the object of the documentary and the viewer.[101] Jeff Allred, meanwhile, reinforces the "strangeness" of the documentary form in *American Modernism and Depression Documentary*

(2010). While documentaries give the viewer the sense of being a witness to the human condition, they also underscore the inherent sense of difference between the viewer and the object, which he traces in the "uneasy encounters between metropolitan artists and denizens of underdeveloped hinterlands; the ethical, aesthetic, and political problems of representation that emerge from these charged encounters; and the fraught attempts to use the documentary text as a means to the political ends of fostering new collective subjects."[102] All of these concerns echo James Agee's metanarrative preoccupation with documentary in *Let Us Now Praise Famous Men,* in which he described himself and Walker Evans as spies sent by an industrial economy and a bureaucratic government to observe families living in poverty. In spite of the impulse to identify with the sharecroppers through images and text, the documentaries expose the distance between the viewer and the image, and they reveal the fundamental fact that documentaries speak for tenant families, rather than allowing them to speak for themselves.

The images in the photo documentaries play a prominent role. Often taken from the FSA's library of images, they illustrate the experience of rural southern poverty by allowing the viewers to see living conditions directly, which no amount of description in government documents and social science narratives could make possible. The photograph's ability to tell a story is limited, however. An image without context does not explain who or what the image depicts, what caused or contributed to the conditions pictured, or tell the viewer how to understand the image. The pictures in sharecropper photo documentaries are paratextual illustrations that amplify the text and work in conjunction with the text to enhance the effects on the reader. While all of the photo documentaries used text to explain the system of tenant farming, most of them also used captions with the pictures to enhance the reader's perception of the images further, making the relationship between text and image inseparable. In the epigraph to *You Have Seen Their Faces,* Caldwell and Bourke-White signal the value of images and text and their ability to manipulate the viewer. "The legends under the pictures," they state, "are intended to express the authors' own conceptions of the sentiments of the individuals portrayed; they do not pretend to reproduce the actual sentiments of these persons."[103] They have been rightly criticized for caricaturing their subjects, such as a caption beneath a picture of an older African American woman that read "ATOKA, TENN. 'I reckon I forgot to remember how old I is.'"[104] In many cases, their captions reek of minstrel ventriloquism, projecting racist and classist attitudes onto the people in the images. At the same time, they expose the facility with which images and text can be used to influence viewers, which was the ultimate goal of Depression-era photo documentaries of tenant farming. As a genre, they worked to demonstrate the need for government intervention into southern agriculture.

Most of the criticism of the genre has focused attention on the images, which are the most obvious identifying characteristic, but the text in these works also deserves attention because it raises several questions. How, for example, does it function differently from text in the other nonfiction narratives about tenant farming? Also, how does it cooperate with the images? And how does it describe the sharecroppers' living conditions? These questions are important in part because this is a unique genre of works that are on the same topic, that share some of the same material, and that share similar goals. But they approach the material in different ways, and, while many of the works are highly conventional, some of the texts engage in remarkable forms of experimentation to affect the reader/viewer. Arthur Raper, whose *Preface to Peasantry* was a straightforward work of narrative sociology, uses different techniques in *Sharecroppers All* and *Tenants of the Almighty*. In these photo documentaries, he uses character sketches and elements of creative nonfiction to connect with the reader. In *Twelve Million Black Voices*, Richard Wright attempts to articulate the perspective of a race, using the words "we" and "our" to indicate the plural possessive voice. He explains, for example, how words indicating racial difference have been used to isolate African Americans socially and politically: "The word 'Negro,' the term by which, orally or in print, we black folk in the United States are usually designated, is not really a name at all or a description, but a psychological island whose objective form is the unanimous fiat in all American history . . . which artificially and arbitrarily defines, regulates, and limits in scope of the meaning the vital contours of our lives."[105] Wright's first-person plural, however, emphasizes the distance separating the purported Black voices in the text from the reader/viewer. The most experimental of these texts, *Let Us Now Praise Famous Men*, attempts to blur the boundaries of genre and convention, but for all its surrealist aesthetics and existential rumination, it only reinforces the same separation as Agee realizes that he is fundamentally different from the sharecropping families whose lives he infiltrated.[106]

The photo documentaries portray the same squalid living conditions described in the government documents and the social science narratives, but where those texts use charts, graphs, data, and an objective third-person perspective, the photo documentaries use appeals to pathos to allow the reader/viewer to identify with the sharecroppers and imagine the difficulty of their lives. Herman Nixon, for example, describes his approach in *Forty Acres and Steel Mules* as "a hillbilly's view of the South . . . based partly on research, partly on general reading, and largely on direct observation."[107] He explicitly states that his observations are based on growing up in a country store, where he learned about crop liens and settlements, and on working as a relief agent for a New Deal agency, although he does not mention his career as a political scientist at Vanderbilt University or Tulane University.[108] Caldwell and Bourke-White established the convention of alternating pages of black and white images plates with passages of text in *You Have Seen Their Faces*, which creates the effect of a contrapuntal narrative. Caldwell's sketches offer imaginative descriptions of sharecroppers' lives, such as "Arnold Berry[,] a Negro tenant farmer on a plantation in Eastern Arkansas in the Delta country."[109] He describes Berry's living conditions, his contract, and his relationship with his landlord, and he also describes his thoughts and feelings as if he has unfettered access to Berry's interior states of mind, inviting the reader/viewer to identify with the sharecropper vicariously. James Agee uses a similar technique in *Let Us Now Praise Famous Men* by interweaving meticulously detailed descriptions of the families' meager material possessions with sketches of their behavior and scenes of imagined interior dialogue. The most obvious example of his projection onto the sharecroppers is his use of second person to describe Mrs. Ricketts's reaction to meeting him: "You realized what the poor foolishness of your husband had let you all in for . . . to you it was as if you and your children and your husband and these other were stood there naked in front of the cold absorption of the camera in all your shame and pitiableness."[110] Here even as he projects his own perceptions onto Mrs. Ricketts, he telegraphs the same concerns to the reader/viewer, portraying the sharecropping families as self-conscious and abject.

In all of the photo documentaries, the sharecroppers are portrayed as victims of an economic system that exploits their labor and limits their agency. Caldwell explicitly states that "the Negro tenant farmer on a plantation is still a slave."[111] Nixon blames the system for being "disadvantageous to both landlord and tenant."[112] Wright indicts the economic power structure for holding laborers in thrall. "The Lords of the Land hold sway over the plantations and over us," he writes, "the Bosses of the Buildings lend money and issue orders to the Lords of the Land. The Bosses of the Buildings feed upon the Lords of the Land, and the Lords of the Land feed upon the 5,000,000 landless poor whites and upon us, throwing to the poor whites the scant solace or filching from us 4,000,000 landless blacks what the poor whites themselves are cheated of in this elaborate game."[113] According to Agee, the sharecroppers are drudges, and work is "the very essence of their lives."[114] He goes on to suggest that the work dehumanizes them, "into this work and need, their minds, their spirits, and their strength are so steadily and intensely drawn that during such time as they are not at work, life exists for them scarcely more clearly or in more variance and seizure and appetite than it does for the more simply organized among the animals, and for plants." Paul Taylor, meanwhile, explains that sharecroppers are being replaced with machines as "plantation landlords have begun to question the paternalism which since slavery has laid upon them the responsibility of caring for their people from one crop to the next."[115] All of the photo documentaries suggest that sharecroppers are pitiful people who are hopelessly mired in an endless cycle of debt and dependency, a narrative that fits with the images of squalor and suffering.

The texts explain that an elaborate system of debt bondage limits the sharecroppers' agency. Agee, who offers excruciating detail on most aspects of the sharecroppers' lives, finds himself unable to adequately describe the system, so he gives "as extreme a precis as [he] can manage."[116] He offers a sketch of the contracts and their terms with differentiation between tenants and croppers and an explanation of contingencies and indebtedness with the assessment that "what is earned at the end of a given year is never to be depended on and, even late in a season, is never predictable."[117] Nixon describes the crop lien system and indicates that it is designed to place risk on the tenant who "became the ultimate shock absorber, going from year to year with little or no money."[118] Wright describes the extractive system of debt poetically: "after we have divided the crops we are still entangled as deeply as ever in this hateful web of cotton culture. We are older; our bodies are weaker; our families are larger; our clothes are in rags; we are still in debt; and, worst of all, we face another year that holds even less hope than the one we have just endured.... The land upon which we live holds a promise, but the promise fades with the passing seasons."[119] Raper and De Reid extend the cycle of exploitation in *Sharecroppers All*, stating that "planters are themselves little more than sharecroppers to their creditors" and that the South, "victimized by modern American feudalism," is essentially a sharecropper to the United States.[120] They blame the South's colonial economy in which southern cotton is sold to repay debts from northern banks, leaving the profit from the system in the hands of the financiers. The colonial economy thesis, which was popular in the early twentieth century, suggests that southerners were powerless to change the system even if they wanted to, so the government would have to intervene.

Yet, even though most of the photo documentaries were published in direct collaboration with the Farm Security Administration, they seem to be ambivalent about the effectiveness of New Deal interventions in the southern economy. Edwin Hullinger offers the most positive assessment of the programs in *Plowing Through*, summarizing the results as increases in landownership among African American famers, better farming methods, improved living conditions, and "increased self respect."[121] Nixon offers a more mixed position, noting the haste with which well-intentioned programs were implemented and their ultimate expediency, which risked the "danger of perpetuating poverty."[122] In *Sharecroppers All*, Raper and De Reid dismiss the effectiveness of the linchpin New Deal program, the Agricultural Adjustment Act, because it had not "done more for the plantations that keep them propped up season by season."[123] Wright indicates that the programs have been virtually irrelevant to Black sharecroppers because "you sign it entirely over to the Lords of the Land and forget about it."[124] Agee also points out the irony that work relief programs are not available to sharecroppers because "they are, technically, employed, and thus have no right to it."[125] This political ambivalence seems curious considering that all of these texts were produced in direct partnership with the FSA, whose agenda was to generate public support for political programs, and it implies tension between the purpose of the photographs and the purpose of the text. It also raises the question of whether the photo documentaries are themselves a form of government intervention, which suggests a direct political agenda, or if they should be seen as independent works of art, which may be political or may be critical of the government's agenda. As a genre, these texts seem to fall along a spectrum with *Plowing Through*, which is perhaps the weakest of the works, leaning more in line with the government and *Twelve Million Black Voices* being the most critical.

While these books are frequently critical of government interventions, they are reluctant to offer their own solutions to the problems. The photographs make an implicit case that something must be done, and the texts describe a litany of issues, so the reader is likely to have an impulse to seek a resolution, but the problems of sharecropping were seemingly intractable. "There have probably been as many methods offered for the elimination of economic distress among field hands, renters, and sharecroppers as there are known cures for warts," Caldwell writes, "and none of them has proved to be any more effective."[126] He proposes unionization and government intervention, but he notes that these approaches have not been effective in the past. Nixon suggests "regional and intra-regional planning," Taylor argues for agricultural diversification and "self-support," and advocates "programs of *action* which will release to growth the South's disinherited masses."[127] None of these ideas, however, come with systematic development or assessments of efficacy. With a tone of resignation, Agee explains that proposed solutions are "dangerous because by proposing wrong assignment of causes it persuades that the 'cure' is possible through means which in fact would have little effect save to delude the saviors into the comfortable idea that nothing more needed doing."[128] Most interventions, in other words, only serve to assuage the reader/viewer's sympathetic sense of guilt at seeing the sharecroppers' wasted bodies and squalid homes, and simple solutions, including existing government programs, would have no real impact.

Agee's comments about the role of the saviors highlights an important element of sharecropper photo documentaries that he articulates better than any of the other writers. He recognizes the reader/viewer's voyeuristic perspective on the sharecropper's lives, and he speaks directly to the audience, acknowledging their position in relation to the sharecroppers. He writes:

> This is a book about "sharecroppers," and is written for all those who have a soft place in their hearts for the laughter and tears inherent in poverty viewed at a distance, and especially for the those who can afford the retail price; and in the hope that the reader will be edified, and may feel kindly disposed toward any well-thought-out liberal efforts to rectify the unpleasant situation down South, and will somewhat better and more guiltily appreciate the next good meal he eats.[129]

*Let Us Now Praise Famous Men* is as much about modern American capitalism, which profits upon and relies upon the exploitation of workers, as it is about the lives of the sharecroppers. Their existence is a reflection of capitalism's disrespect for labor. The reader/viewers are staring into a mirror even as they feel guilt and pity for the sharecroppers.

This effect—or, rather, this affect—is the point of sharecropper photo documentaries. By combining documentary photographs of people living and working poverty with text that explains the material circumstances and imaginatively depicts their interior states of being, the books allow the reader/viewer to participate in the experience of sharecropping vicariously. These books accomplish something that government documents and social science texts with their charts, graphs, and quantitative data cannot do; they personalize sharecropping. But they have an inherent problem. All of these texts obliterate the sharecroppers' voices by speaking for them rather than allowing them to speak for themselves, which distorts their perspective. Raper, for example, expands the meaning of the term "sharecropper" to include any exploited workers: "For the real meaning of the term 'sharecropper' look to such matters as low wages, insecurity, and lack of opportunity for self-direction and responsible participation in community affairs. A sharecropper shares in the risk without sharing in the control."[130] Although this polemical statement exposes the inequality endemic to modern capitalism, it also glosses over the unique experiences and circumstances of landless agricultural workers in the South. One might wonder why the voices of actual sharecroppers would not be used to cultivate sympathy and support for government interventions, but as the case of Gladys Reed indicates, the actual voices of sharecroppers were unruly and complicated.

In sharecropper photo documentaries, the sharecroppers are symbols. Raper writes that "the most typical scene in the South . . . is a cotton field with a solitary man—a sharecropper—plowing in it. He stands between the handles of a single-stock plow pulled by a mule."[131] This man, alienated from his labor, systematically exploited by systems of debt and finance, and utterly vital in a globalized commodity economy, is a signifier for the inequitable system that led to the Great Depression. "The everyday sharecropper is anything but a heroic figure at present," Caldwell writes, referencing the same symbolism, "if he continues being the nation's under-dog, that is what he will become. As an individual, he would rather be able to feed, clothe, and house his family properly than to become the symbol of man's injustice to man."¹³² In the photo documentaries, the sharecroppers serve someone else's agenda, and Caldwell, who literally spoke for the sharecroppers by putting his own thoughts on their pictures, gestures toward the tension between the sharecropper's needs and the author's use of him. One might wonder if the sharecropper photo documentaries exploit the sharecroppers for their own purposes because, as Raper himself observed, they shared in the risk of the text without sharing in the control. In the photo documentaries, the reader/viewer may see their faces, but their voices are not heard.

## "Raggedy, Raggedy Are We": Sharecropping Unionization Narratives

In Tyronza, Arkansas, a crossroads town about thirty-five miles northwest of Memphis on the alluvial Mississippi floodplain in eastern Arkansas, is a museum inside a building that once housed a gas station and a dry cleaner. Today, the building houses the Southern Tenant Farmers Museum, a collection of artifacts that tells the story of the Southern Tenant Farmers Union (STFU), but when the Great Depression began, it was the businesses of H. L. Mitchell and Clay East, two men who helped to found the union. During the Depression, many groups claimed to speak for sharecroppers, ventriloquizing their voices for political and economic influence, but unions offered sharecroppers an opportunity to speak for themselves. According to Howard Kester, one of the union's leaders, through unionization sharecroppers "found a new voice, created a collective will, discovered a forgotten hope, brought to life new impulses, . . . forged a new dream for the oppressed and disinherited and brought forth a song from lips where once hung lamentation."¹³³ During the Great Depression, sharecroppers organized into short-lived Socialist unions in Alabama and Arkansas, and they staged labor events, such as strikes and protests, that expressed their frustration with their exploitation at the hands of avaricious landowners and with government policies that failed to ameliorate their condition. While unionization could be seen as a form of speaking truth to power, the narrative record of sharecropper unions leaves an ambiguous legacy of who speaks for whom and why.

By the end of World War I, many American industries developed unions that advocated for workers' rights and won some major concessions during the Progressive era, but agricultural workers were slow to unionize.[134] Communist organizers worked in areas of the South, and they successfully organized textile mill workers in some areas, specifically western North Carolina, and even larger progressive unions, such as the United Textile Workers, held an enormous nationwide strike in 1934 that involved many textile mills in the South.[135] With the exception of textile workers, however, unions were scarce in the South even during the Progressive Era, and organizing rural agricultural workers who lacked a centralized employment structure and who were likely to divide along racial lines was difficult. Meanwhile, southerners, who were likely to be highly religious and individualistic, were unlikely to align themselves with the ideologies of collective action, much less Socialism or Communism, which were integral to many union organizations. Yet the unions that developed among sharecroppers borrowed from socialist ideas. The leaders of the Southern Tenant Farmers Union were self-professed Communists who sold copies of *The Daily Worker* in their stores, and the Sharecroppers' Union in Alabama was affiliated with Communist party organizers who attempted to organize steel workers in Birmingham. While the Alabama union had direct connections to the Communist party, the Southern Tenant Farmers Union had no clear affiliation with Communists or Socialists. The union's leaders denied that they had any direct connection to Socialists or the Communist Party, and "almost anyone who professed sympathy for the working class and volunteered to help organize the union was accepted," David Conrad writes in *The Forgotten Farmers*.[136] Except for some ideological influence, however, the unions of sharecroppers in the South during the Great Depression were homegrown organizations that reflected the distinct conditions, needs, and values of sharecroppers and tenant farmers.

Narratives of sharecropper unionization record a unique rhetoric of resistance, describing the events that led to union organizing and articulating sharecroppers' grievances against an overwhelming and dehumanizing system of political economy. Government and social science narratives consistently represent sharecroppers as objects of pathos who required external intervention to ameliorate their exploitation, but unionization narratives depict sharecroppers as sufficiently empowered to challenge their working conditions. These narratives follow some of the familiar contours of the government, social science, and photo documentary narratives by offering ample evidence of sharecropping as a system of exploitation that forces people into squalid and inhumane living conditions, but they advocate labor organization and disruptive action, such as strikes, to challenge the labor system and to draw attention to their cause. They also usually describe the violence inherent in the system, as planters used overwhelming force—with either implicit or explicit government support—to break the unions. Three of the key leaders of the Southern Tenant Farmers Union published narratives that serve as valuable indicators of the union's progress. Norman Thomas, a Socialist activist and frequent candidate for president of the United States, published a brief pamphlet in 1934, *The Plight of the Sharecropper*, that explains the urgent need for a union. In 1936, Howard Kester, a Socialist minister and social activist, wrote *Revolt Among the Sharecroppers*, which gives more detail about the sharecroppers' living conditions, the problems with the Agricultural Adjustment Act, and the union's agenda for change. H. L. Mitchell, one of the union's founders and most active members, published an autobiography in 1979, *Mean Things Happening in this Land*, that describes and revises his work with the union. These works are useful to understand the perspectives of the union's leadership, but they tend to gloss over the immediate concerns of the members. Two oral histories taken decades after the unionization movement, however, fill in these stories. Theodore Rosengarten interviewed Ned Cobb, a member of the Sharecroppers Union in Alabama, for *All God's Dangers* (1974), and Michael Honey interviewed John Handcox, an important organizer and songwriter for the Southern Tenant Farmers Union, for *Sharecroppers' Troubadour* (2013).[137] Although mediated somewhat by the interests and perspectives of the interviewers, these works offer a valuable account of sharecropper's experiences. Charlie May Simon's 1937 novel *The Sharecropper*, meanwhile, is a fictional narrative of a white Arkansas sharecropper who joins the union out of desperation.

These works describe the sharecroppers' exploitation as a rationale for unionization. Norman Thomas analyzes the structure of sharecropping contracts, explaining that the contracts, which are often oral and, thus, unenforceable, arrogate all rights to the landlord, leaving the sharecropper dependent for food and shelter yet responsible for exorbitant furnishing costs. The contracts allow landlords to evict tenants at will and to confiscate tenants' possessions for debts, and "a share-cropper may live on the same plantation all his life and acquire no rights outside the terms of the contract."[138] Howard Kester emphasizes the inherent dehumanization in the system, asserting that "a sharecropper is worth less in the eyes of many a landlord-planter than a good mule."[139] H. L. Mitchell, whose parents were sharecroppers and who sharecropped himself, describes sharecroppers as economically abject, held completely at the mercy of landowners, who could "pass out the word that the sharecropper was unreliable, and no one would let him have a place where he could make a crop. When that happened, his only hope was to find part-time work as a wage laborer, but that was a downward step to an agricultural worker."[140] Handcox and Cobb, meanwhile, suggest that sharecroppers had some modest means of personal agency. Handcox tells a story about standing up to a landowner at settlement for a fair price for his cotton, and he says, "'Course, that was the biggest things about livin' on those farms and things, you had to stand up for your rights."[141] Cobb, who Rosengarten renames Nate Shaw to protect his family's identity, tells how he toiled as a sharecropper under crooked landowners in an unfair system, but he also represents himself as an honest, industrious man who managed to acquire two mules, pay his debts, and provide for his family. Charlie May Simon's novel *The Share-cropper* is a declension novel that opens with Bill Bradley's marriage to a frugal and level-headed woman named Donie and follows their struggle through failed crops, cruel landowners, floods, and enduring poverty.

Exploitation is important in all of these works as a rhetorical device to establish the necessity of forming a union to ameliorate the sharecroppers' inhumane living conditions. Conventionally, union organizers used an argument like this to develop credibility and public support, which could be used as leverage against factory owners. Stories of sharecropper exploitation, however, were ubiquitous during the Great Depression, and the problem of sharecropper exploitation could not be localized to a specific set of landowners. The purpose and goals of a union of sharecroppers was inherently nebulous, so some of these narratives, specifically Norman Thomas's *The Plight of the Share-cropper* and Howard Kester's *Revolt among the Sharecroppers*, attempt to make the case for unionization and explain the function of a union, such as the methods of collective bargaining or the ideology of Socialism. Most of the people who joined the union were not interested in ideology or methodology, however. They joined most often out of desperation. During the Depression, many landowners, who were also facing economic pressure, provided their sharecroppers with less food, charged higher interest, confiscated parity payments, evicted families, and demoted sharecroppers to wage laborers. In *The Rise and Fall of the Southern Tenant Farmers Union in Arkansas* (2018), James Ross explains that "immediate concerns about food, clothing, and a place to live were very important to sharecroppers and tenant farmers that joined STFU."[142] Charlie May Simon depicts this sense of desperation in *The Share-cropper* when Bill Bradley joins the union. He tells an organizer:

> "I wonder," Bill spoke slowly, for thoughts did not come fast to him. "Last month before you came along, I was hungry all the time. It seemed all I ever thought about was food. If you'd a mentioned a union to me then, the first thing I'd wanted to know would have been, 'Is there anything to eat in it for me and mine?' Now that I've enough to eat, and I'm not hungry any more, I can think of other things. But for the rest of these people, nearly all of them, I reckon, I just wonder if they would even feel like starting anything and keep it up. They are too tired to fight, and too hungry, too, to think any further ahead than their next meal."[143]

Bill joins, and he works to recruit other sharecroppers to join the union, all of whom join to find food for their families, focusing more on immediate concerns than ideology. For most members, the unions were expedient means to meet immediate needs.

Desperation among sharecroppers in Alabama led to the emergence of the Sharecroppers Union in 1931. Tommy and Richard Gray, two sharecroppers, contacted Communist activists in Birmingham to help form a union to demand continued food advances from planters, who had stopped providing food to sharecroppers between settlement and planting, leaving families hungry from October to March. The union also asked for sharecroppers to have the right to sell their own cotton and to grow vegetable gardens on their plots. Although the union had minimal support from the Communist party and a loose system of organization, it recruited eight thousand members, nearly all of whom were African American, and held strikes in 1932 and 1934 that won some concessions from landowners. Landowners responded to these labor actions with brutal violence. Richard Gray, one of the original founders of the union, was assassinated, several men were lynched, and dozens of people were beaten. By 1935, the union's effectiveness had waned, and as Robin D. G. Kelley writes in *Hammer and Hoe* (1990), "thousands of families found themselves landless in the harsh winter of 1934–35. The eight thousand strong union stood helpless in the face of New Deal-induced evictions, and no antifascist slogans or demands for self-determination could solve their quandary."[144]

Ned Cobb joined the Alabama Sharecroppers Union in 1931. In his oral history, he explains that he joined for mutual protection.[145] While he had been industrious and managed to provide for his family, he saw that many of his neighbors were being mistreated and that his landlord, Mr. Watson, was cheating him at settlement. He told Rosengarten:

> Weren't no use under God's sun to treat colored people like we'd been treated here in the state of Alabama. Work hard and look how they do you. Look how they done my daddy in his time and look how Mr. Watson tried to do me. Dug at me and dug at me, couldn't handle me, then he made me bring him the cotton. I carried it to him—I was workin for a easy way out—didn't carry him all of it but I carried him more than enough to pay him what I owed him. Still he dug at me.[146]

When Mr. Watson sent sheriff's deputies and a posse to confiscate goods from Virgil Logan, a sharecropper who owed Watson money, Ned Cobb and other union member went to Logan's home to defend his property. A shootout ensued. Cobb fired at a sheriff's deputy, and he was wounded in the shootout. He was arrested and sentenced to thirteen years at a labor camp. His story illustrates both the motivation of union members and the risks that people took to join a union.

In 1934, a group of "eleven black men and seven white men met to found the Southern Tenant Farmers Union," writes H. L. Mitchell, one of the men present at the founding.[147] Similar to the sharecroppers in Alabama three years earlier, the sharecroppers in Arkansas were desperate. Many of them had recently been evicted from Hiram Norcross's farm. In the previous year, Norcross restricted credit at his plantation's commissary and evicted about forty families, and when the AAA began making parity payments, Norcross, like many planters, withheld payments from sharecroppers.[148] The sharecroppers from Norcross's plantation asked Mitchell and East to help them create a union because, as Howard Kester writes, they "were known as 'square-shooters' who always gave the underdog the benefit of the doubt, and who were, to the amusement of most people, always discussing strange ideas about labor, politics, and economics."[149] The STFU had some similar objectives to the Sharecroppers Union. Their purpose was "to secure better living conditions by decent contracts and higher wages for farm labor," and they asked for legal distribution of AAA parity checks, schools for sharecroppers' children, the right to organize, decent wages, and land to grow vegetables on their plots.[150] While their demands were modest, they caused a significant disruption in American agricultural policy during their brief tenure, and their labor actions led to violent and bloody backlash by planters.

Unlike the Sharecroppers Union, the STFU was interracial for both ideological and strategic reasons, but its interracial composition was not without problems. Howard Kester, in a story that may be embellished, relates that the question of race was raised at the union's first meeting, and he describes "an old man with cotton-white hair overhanging an ebony face" who had been a member of the earlier union formed in Arkansas in 1919 that led to the infamous Elaine massacre who gave a speech appealing to their common humanity and their common cause.[151] When the "old man sat down," Kester writes, "the men decided that the union would welcome Negro and white sharecroppers, tenant farmers and day laborers alike into its fold." Including both Black and white members was important because sharecroppers faced the same issues regardless of their race, and, perhaps more importantly, interracial membership prevented planters from simply pitting one race against another. As Norman Thomas wrote, "the organization to be effective must be of white and Negro sharecroppers together."[152] Interracial membership, however, was more complicated in practice. Even though they shared the same concerns, white sharecroppers were as racist as other white southerners, and they were reluctant to join integrated locals, so many locals were organized into a white unit and a Black unit. Some locals were biracial, but the union reflected many of the racial issues in the South. Jason Manthorne argues that the STFU "was effectively a black organization."[153] The exact racial composition of the union is unclear, but one union member estimated the white membership at 15 percent. "Of those who responded to the union's own survey, completed in June 1937, only 12 percent were white," Manthorne writes. "A more generous estimate might grant that at its peak the STFU membership was approximately one-third white."[154]

Although racial issues were challenging, the Southern Tenant Farmers Union successfully organized thousands of members. Charlie May Simon portrays a scene of a union organizer appealing to an integrated group of sharecroppers. "Negroes and whites together, forgetting for the time their race barriers, listened intently as Young [the union organizer] talked to them, telling them of his plans for banding them together to give them the strength to stand up and demand justice for themselves and their children," she writes. "And as he talked, his heart was touched, looking upon these men before him, friendless and homeless; old women with beaten and cowed looks, looking ever toward the door in fear, and young men still with dreams and hopes of better conditions in the future, all wearing worn and faded clothes, and many, no doubt, with empty stomachs."[155] Her description captures the sense of desperation and possibility that many sharecroppers may have felt when they learned of the union. Many organizers appealed to the possibility of hope and of gaining a voice. Howard Kester explains that "through the Southern Tenant Farmers Union the disinherited sharecroppers, tenant farmers and day laborers of both races are becoming increasingly articulate and gradually thrusting themselves into a nation's conscience. Through this united struggle they will either climb out of the hell of misery in which they have been floundering or they will be more completely submerged as America battles and blunders for a way out of the present chaos."[156] Considering the destitution they faced, many sharecroppers found the appeal persuasive, and by 1937 the union had more than thirty-four thousand members across six states.[157] Unionization gave sharecroppers the unusual opportunity to speak persuasively with a collective voice.

The union's primary audience was the U.S. Department of Agriculture. The Agricultural Adjustment Act, which was intended to raise the price of cotton by taking one third of the nation's crop out of production, had a deleterious effect on sharecroppers. Although the legislation required that no sharecroppers be displaced by the act and that parity payments be shared between landowners and sharecroppers, the law was observed most often in the breach, and thousands of sharecropping families were evicted and thousands more were cheated out of their parity payments in nefarious ways. In many cases, "the checks went to the landlord and were credited by him to the tenants' accounts at the commissary" where they were often used either to cover existing debt or held against future charges or simply confiscated.[158] Simon depicts this scenario in *The Share-cropper*, where the landowner claims that the parity payment has not been received until "bit by bit all the money earned that year was taken up in credit at the plantation store, with the usual ten percent added, until at last there was no more credit due them."[159] According to H. L. Mitchell, "this program wrecked the already desperate lives of nearly a million sharecropper families who were no longer needed on the land; they were evicted and set adrift to roam the countryside."[160] In *Cry from the Cotton* (1971), Donald Grubbs gives a more sober, yet still disturbing, assessment of the AAA's impact on sharecroppers. The AAA fell short of its goal of taking one third of cotton land out of production, coming closer to one quarter of production: "There was a proportionate reduction in the total cash return to labor, despite AAA pittances. A study which reached fairly typical conclusions could 'state with authority' that the AAA had caused unemployment, displacing at least 15 and probably 20 percent of all sharecropping families."[161] In 1930, there were approximately eight million sharecroppers in the South, and 20 percent of that number is 1.6 million, which is greater than the population of the State of Connecticut in 1930. The Department of Agriculture responded to STFU's allegations by commissioning Mary Connor Myers "to investigate the union's complaints of AAA violations."[162] She traveled to Arkansas, interviewed sharecroppers and landowners, and concluded that there was "enough evidence of contract violation and evasion with hardship to tenants to warrant a full-scale investigation."[163] The Department of Agriculture, however, suppressed the report and expunged it from the archival record, effectively ignoring the pleas of more than a million and a half sharecroppers.

STFU organizer John Handcox wrote a song, "Landlord, What in the Heaven is the Matter with You?" that describes the effect of the AAA on sharecroppers. The lyrics give a narrative history of the AAA from the perspective of a union member:

> In nineteen thirty-three when we plowed up cotton,
> Some of that money your labor have never gotten.
> You pledged the government your labor you would pay;
> You put it in your pocket and you went your way.
> And in the AAA contract in nineteen and thirty-four
> You chiseled your labor outta some more.
> And in nineteen and thirty-five
> The Parity money your labor you deprived.
> And in the AA in nineteen and thirty six
> You all are trying to fix.

> We hope that it'll be so:
> You'll get yours and no more.
> Your labor you've always robbed.
> Because they want their rights, you want them mobbed.
> You disfranchise us and won't let us vote,
> When we have all the load to tote.
> Your labor never have had anything to do with what you join,
> Neither broken into your meetings or your church or barn.
> From none of your meeting by your labor have you ever been hailed,
> Shot in the back, beaten with axe handles, or put in jail.
> You are not honest enough to do right,
> Your labor never shot in your homes neither throwed dynamite.
> Now Arkansas would be a fine place to live you bet,
> If the sod didn't have such a bad set.
> Landlord, what in the heaven is the matter with you?
> What have your labor ever done to you?
> Upon their backs you ride,
> Don't you think that your labor never gets tired?[164]

This song is addressed to the landowners, and it accuses them, rather than the government, of exploiting sharecroppers. Since the STFU got little recourse directly from the government, the union's leaders focused their strategy on the landowners, setting a course for inevitable conflict.

In 1935, the Southern Tenant Farmers Union staged a strike. That year, landowners reduced the amount paid to day laborers from eighty cents per hundred pounds picked to sixty cents. H. L. Mitchell and union leadership called a wage conference, and they established a demand for one dollar per hundred pounds and instructed union members not to work until landowners met the demand. In spite of violent opposition, the strike was successful. "In ten days, wages rose everywhere," H. L. Mitchell writes. "It had been agreed upon that whenever the rate reached 75 cents per hundred pounds, the workers could decide if they would accept that. In most places they did accept the 75 cents rate, but in other, the pickers held out longer and won the dollar."[165] The strike brought national attention to the union, leading to a surge in members, fundraising, and media attention, and it was repeated the following year. A 1936 March of Time newsreel titled "King Cotton's Slaves" depicts the union's strikes, showing footage of sharecroppers working in fields. The newsreel, however, suggests that planters are as much in thrall to sharecropping as their laborers, and it attributes the flaws in the AAA to political maneuvers. It dramatizes the strike with scenes of union members singing union songs and marching in protest and workers throwing down their tools in the fields. The landowners retaliate with a campaign of terror, and the newsreel shows a white male and female couple of union investigators being flogged by a group of strikebreakers. The newsreel's voiceover sternly intones that "it is not the planter who is at fault in the Southland, but the one-crop system which has both planter and sharecropper in peonage," and it concludes that "the planter and sharecropper alike are the economic slaves of the South's one-crop system."[166] The newsreel, which offers a glimpse into the way that American media in the 1930s portrayed labor tension in the South, blames both sharecroppers and planters for participating in cotton production. The newsreel's deliberate naïveté indicates that most Americans did not fully understand the sharecroppers' concerns or the extent of their exploitation and deprivation.

Landowners, however, paid attention to the union's demands. While they conceded to the demands by raising wages for day laborers, they also used violence to undermine the union and coerce laborers into working. H. L. Mitchell quotes a newspaper report that illustrates the de facto martial law that descended upon Arkansas during the strike: "The strike of cotton choppers goes on with Union members hunted down with dogs, beaten, jailed and driven from the state. Bands of armed planters patrol the roads and highways turning back all workers who attempt to leave plantations. Men arrive in Memphis singly, only to be arrested on charges of vagrancy."[167] The newspaper account understates the situation gravely. According to David Conrad, "the reign of terror lasted two and one-half months," and he catalogs a list of acts in one ten-day period that included an attempted lynching, hooded night riders firing machine guns into the home of a union leader, the abduction of another union leader, numerous acts of mob violence, churches burned, and "T. A. Allen, a Negro preacher and organizer of the union, found shot through the heart and weighted with chains in the Coldwater River, near Hernando, Mississippi."[168] In Marked Tree, Arkansas, a mob chased Clay East, one of the union's founders, into the office of attorney C. T. Carpenter, and the men threatened to shoot him on sight. John Handcox was also threatened. In his oral history, he tells the story that "them planters had made a threat, they had the rope and the limb, and all they wanted was me."¹⁶⁹ Howard Kester explains that planters also used other forms of coercion and pressure against the unions. "A type of violence frequently used by the plantation interest against the union members, and particularly against active organizers, was to cut off their access to food clothing, and other necessaries," he writes.¹⁷⁰ In sharecropping territories, the planters' power was absolute, so people who joined a union and who participated in labor action took an enormous risk, but this was one of the only ways that they could make their voices heard.

The violence in Arkansas inspired some poignant literary responses. In *The Share-cropper*, Charlie May Simon depicts a scene of a mob surrounding a union attorney's office, inspired by the mob that chased Clay East into the office of C. T. Carpenter. In her novel, a thug named Dan Amos, working for local planters, riles a group of "river rats" to confront Abner Young, an attorney and union organizer, and Bill Bradley stands with Abner during the engagement.¹⁷¹ In her story, the only violence actually perpetrated is a brick thrown through the window transom, but the referent to actual violence is obvious. Sterling Brown also wrote a powerful poem about the strikers. In the poem "Sharecroppers," a group of night riders, including the landlord and the sheriff, surround a union member's shack and demand information, "But he wouldn't tell, he would not tell. / He was Union, the Union was his friend."¹⁷² The mob ties him up, drags him into the woods, and beats him, "And cursing, they left him there for dead." He told his attackers nothing, but "He gave up one secret before he died: / 'We gonna clean out dis brushwood round here soon, / Plant de white-oak and de black oak side by side.'" This cryptic final couplet implies that the brushwood—a reference to nuisance plants—are the planters and the white oak and black oak are the integrated members of the union, who are strong trees able to endure calamities.

As STFU held strikes in Arkansas, representatives from the Sharecroppers Union in Alabama raised the possibility of merging. The organizations shared similar goals and methods, but there were some obstacles to their joining. The Sharecroppers Union was closely aligned with the Communist Party, but the STFU was independent, although it leaned toward socialism. The Sharecroppers Union was almost entirely African American, and its members "existed mainly on paper," but the STFU was interracial, and its membership was growing substantially in the mid-1930s.¹⁷³ "Throughout the winter of 1935–36, STFU leaders privately opposed organizational unity but still kept up a façade of friendly relations with SCU," and by mid-1936, "STFU leaders vehemently rejected the idea of merging and dividing the two agricultural organizations."[174] The Sharecroppers Union later merged with another Communist organization, the American Farmers Union, that effectively disregarded their concerns, and by 1938, the union dwindled to nearly nonexistent numbers. SCU was never as large or as well organized as STFU, but its very brief history illustrates the inherent difficulty of labor organizing in the cotton South.

While the STFU's leaders leaned toward Socialism, its members tended to be more ambivalent about ideology. In *Revolt among the Sharecroppers*, Howard Kester proposes a socialist solution to sharecropping. He suggests creating a National Land Authority that would acquire large areas of agricultural land and allow small farmers to grow diversified crops for self-sufficiency and for sale on the land. His plan is similar in some respects to the Resettlement Administration, but he has in mind a much larger initiative that "would set as its task the abolition of tenancy in all of its forms."[175] By the time the book was published, Kester, Mitchell, and other STFU leaders raised funds to purchase a two-thousand-acre piece of land in northwestern Mississippi where they created Delta Cooperative Farm, a social experiment in alternative agriculture. As Robert Martin recounts, "Planners hoped to train relocated sharecroppers in diversified scientific agriculture so that they could achieve self-sufficiency and a decent standard of living. However, they also wanted to school residents and observers alike in the virtues of democratic socialism and interracial cooperation."[176] The experiment never achieved its goals because poor management and high expenses sank it into bankruptcy after just over a year of existence. Delta Cooperative Farm's problems were both practical and ideological. While many sharecroppers in the 1930s were seeking shelter, support, and opportunity in any available setting, most of them preferred private land ownership to collectivization. In 1934, STFU distributed a survey to its members asking them to indicate their first and second preferences among four options: (1) small farm ownership through government loans with a low interest rate, (2) farming with a long-term lease on government land, (3) cooperative farming, (4) or sharecropping with a union contract. Small farm ownership was the overwhelming first choice, which indicates that even the union's members preferred private property and individualism to socialism.[177]

The union's last major labor action took place in the bootheel of southeast Missouri in the winter of 1939. In January of that year, hundreds of sharecropping families were evicted from their farms, and STFU organizer Owen Whitfield arranged a form of protest to draw national attention to their plight. On the morning of January 10, 1939, more than 1,000 people evicted from their homes moved their meager possessions to the side of Highway 61, where they camped for everyone to see. According to Louis Cantor, "there were 251 families, comprising 1,161 individuals. These people, the [FBI] report states, formed thirteen camps located intermittently along seventy miles of Highway 61 north and south between Sikeston and Hayti, Missouri."[178] The media covered the protest, drawing newspaper headlines across the country, and FSA photographer Arthur Rothstein took some moving photographs of homeless families. By January 15, however, the Missouri State Health Commissioner declared the camps a public health hazard and ordered the Highway Patrol to remove the campers and move them to less conspicuous tracts of land. The federal government sent supplies, tents, and food to the makeshift camps, but local authorities continued to disperse the groups into smaller and smaller camps until they were no longer visible, leaving only the photographs as a record of their protest.[179] Radical intellectual C. L. R. James observed the bootheel strike, and in an essay titled "With the Sharecroppers," he describes the impact of the strike.[180] "The action itself has had a tremendous moral effect on the Negroes themselves, on the landlords, and on the government," he writes.[181] He offers a Marxist prophecy based on the strike: "Despite their many limitations, these workers, in a fundamental sense, are among the most advanced in America. For, to any Marxist, an advanced worker is one who, looking at the system under which he lives, wants to tear it to pieces. That is exactly what the most articulate think of capitalism in southeast Missouri."[182] Events, however, contradicted James's vision of the future.

By the time of the Missouri bootheel strike, the STFU was already in decline. In 1939, the union had about three thousand members, less than 10 percent of its peak two years earlier.[183] While the cotton pickers' strikes in 1935 and 1936 made an impact, the violent backlash dissuaded many people from continuing to participate in the union. On the national level, the Supreme Court had ruled the AAA unconstitutional, so the union had no clear government policy to protest, and as cotton prices slowly moved back toward their pre-Depression levels, labor relations across the South returned more to their previous status, with landowners furnishing sharecroppers during the winter months. Since few sharecroppers held strong ideological convictions, not many were inclined to remain in the union. The union's leaders, meanwhile, affiliated with other labor unions, which diffused the purpose and effectiveness of the STFU. The Congress of Industrial Organizations established an agricultural workers union, the United Cannery, Agricultural, Packing Allied Workers of America (UCAPAWA), under the leadership of Donald Henderson in 1937. STFU joined the new union, but there were ideological and practical tensions from the beginning. UCAPAWA leaned more toward Communism, its base of strength was with immigrant migrant workers on the West Coast, and its tactics were based on trade unionism. STFU leaders, on the other hand, were wary of Communism, their members were an interracial group of people, and their tactics were based on protest. A few weeks after the roadside strike in Missouri, UCAPAWA attempted to purge STFU leadership, which caused a schism. By the end of the year, STFU was effectively defunct, and the start of World War II and the development of the mechanical cotton picker rendered the need for a sharecroppers' union moot.

Socialist and Communist unions among sharecroppers in the South were unlikely to be successful because most sharecroppers wanted private land ownership rather than collectivization. As James Ross explains in *The Rise and Fall of the Southern Tenant Farmers Union*, "The idea that only a man who owned land was free died hard with these poor southerners, white and black. The men and women who joined the STFU sought two goals. First, they wanted their immediate needs met. They could not live without food and without shelter. . . . [Second,] these sharecroppers and tenant farmers wanted to own their own land."[184] The union helped sharecroppers achieve their first goal to a limited extent, but it could not help them achieve their second goal. At the end of Charlie May Simon's *The Share-cropper*, Bill Bradley, who has been beaten and jailed for his involvement in the union, returns to his family. In spite of his own enduring exploitation and the violence he has witnessed, he stubbornly imagines a better future for his children. "There would come a change, he knew, though he might not live to see it himself," he thinks, "and it would be possible, somehow, for them to have land of their own. Land that would not be taken away for mortgages or debts. Or if they were renters . . . it would be an honest system, one that would not drag them down to where they could never rise up."[185] Simplistic though it may be, Simon's description of the sharecroppers' desires is much more accurate than the prophecies of Marxist revolution. Perhaps the most important effect of unionization was the opportunity for sharecroppers, who had been diagnosed as a social problem, to speak for themselves through labor action and protests that drew attention to their exploitation and to their agency.

### "The Richest Land, The Poorest People": Great Depression Sharecropper Fiction

"The Crop" (1947), one of the stories Flannery O'Connor wrote while an MFA student at the University of Iowa, uses the common conceit of writing about a writer writing a story. In this case, O'Connor's protagonist, Miss Willerton, wants to write a story about a social problem. Sitting at her typewriter, she muses, "Social problem. Social problem. Hmmm. Sharecroppers! Miss Willerton had never been intimately connected with sharecroppers but, she reflected, they would make as arty a subject as any, and they would give her that air of social concern which was so valuable to have in the circles she was hoping to travel! 'I can always capitalize,' she muttered, 'on the hookworm.'"[186] O'Connor's story satirizes a genre of Depression-era novels about sharecroppers that portrayed the system of labor as a social problem. O'Connor's story focuses the satire on the writer, but Erskine Caldwell's infamous novel *Tobacco Road* (1932) and the Broadway play based upon it (1933) satirized the lives of sharecroppers, portraying them as ignorant, depraved, and complacent.[187] His pejorative depiction of the Lester family suggests that they are responsible for their own squalor, but his harmful depiction contrasts with a much broader genre of novels that portray sharecroppers as victims of systemic forces designed to exploit their labor. Beyond *Tobacco Road* lies several mostly forgotten texts that collectively offer a narrative of sharecropping as a social problem that demands external intervention in the form of unionization or government programs to alleviate poverty. These novels fit within the broader Depression-era narratives from the government, social scientists, photo documentaries, and unionization by dramatizing the experiences of southern farm laborers.

As writers responded to the economic catastrophe during the Depression, social novels depicting labor exploitation were common, but novels representing the experiences of factory workers and urban dwellers have received the majority of the scholarly attention, and scholars of Depression-era social fiction have mostly ignored novels about sharecroppers. Michael Denning's landmark study *The Cultural Front* (1997) explores the relationship between the Communist Party and other leftist groups and American writers during the Depression, but it only mentions one text that depicts sharecroppers—John L. Spivak's *Hard Times on a Southern Chain Gang*. In *Radical Representations* (1993), meanwhile, Barbara Foley establishes several criteria for proletarian literature, including authorship, audience, subject matter, and political perspective, yet she finds tremendous inconsistency among the criteria, because a work of proletarian literature was not necessarily written by working-class writer, for a working-class audience, or in support of Communist ideology. The most consistent criterion is that the work treats "the subject of working-class experience," which opens the category to a broad range of texts, including works that depict the experience of agricultural workers.[188] The idea of a cultural front can be expanded to include not only writers who have direct connections to leftist organizations but also writers addressing the social and economic conditions that contribute to exploitation. In *The Black Cultural Front* (2012), for example, Brian Dolinar extends the term to several African American writers that Denning omitted, including Langston Hughes and Chester Himes, and he explains the Communist Party had a complicated relationship with African American writers, which often left the writers feeling marginalized. While African Americans were disproportionately exploited in the labor force, leftist organizations in the United States tended to focus their attention on white workers. Social novels published in the 1930s, however, were not limited to any particular group or any specific political agenda as writers from a broad range of perspectives and backgrounds portrayed the living conditions of people enduring economic hardship. "Rather than merely evoking the present epoch, social novels of the Depression portrayed immediate tragedies like hunger and unemployment as the cumulative products of centuries of capitalism," writes David Peeler in *Hope Among Us Yet* (1987).[189] The defining characteristics of Depression-era social novels are their depiction of social problems and their implicit call for change.

Depression sharecropper novels focus on the experiences and exploitation of southern farm laborers. These books offer a sympathetic portrayal of sharecropping families mired in a matrix of systemic forces that impede their agency, leaving them at the mercy of a rapacious, totalizing power structure that uses debt, coercion, and violence to determine their living conditions. The novels share characteristics of literary naturalism and realism because of their emphasis on external forces, but they also share characteristics of modern proletarian literature because they make at least an implicit argument for external intervention to change the system, usually aligned with socialism. These novels include *Hard Times on a Southern Chain Gang* (originally published as *Georgia Nigger*) (1932) by John L. Spivak, *Deep Dark River* (1935) by Robert Rylee, *A Sign for Cain* (1935) by Grace Lumpkin, *Uncle Tom's Children* (1938) by Richard Wright, *Land Without Moses* (1938) by Charles Munz, *The Stricklands* (1939) by Edwin Lanham, *The White Scourge* (1940) by Edward White, National Book Award winner *Hold Autumn in Your Hand* (1941) by George Sessions Perry, *High John the Conqueror* (1948) by John W. Wilson, and *A Wind is Rising* (1950) by William Russell. Most of these books were published before the United States entered World War II, but a couple of works that depicted the Depression era and that focused on the lives of laborers and otherwise shared the same characteristics were published after the war.

These novels share a common set of genre conventions. The protagonist is usually a male sharecropper, nobly working the land to provide for his family and struggling against the coercive pressures of the despotic, malevolent landowner antagonist. Both the sharecropper and the landowner are part of a larger system of economic pressures that involve both juridical power and macrofinance. The novels typically have a cast of supporting characters, including a supportive and long-suffering wife or mother, dependent children who amplify the story's pathos, and functionaries, such as a sheriff or banker, who embody the local power structure. The plotline in these novels is usually straightforward and predictable: the landowner exploits the sharecropper, and the sharecropper resists, which leads to an inevitably tragic result for the sharecropper. The distinctive twist in the Depression-era sharecropper novel is that the sharecropper's resistance involves some form of external intervention in the system to alleviate the obvious pattern of exploitation. Charles Munz's *Land Without Moses* is an exemplar of the cultural poetics of sharecropping. In this novel, Kirby Moten works for Aaron Longnecker on his plantation in Renfro County, just as his father had. Trapped in an unending cycle of farming and debt, compounded by Longnecker's unscrupulous bookkeeping, Moten dreams of escaping his debt and moving to Habishaw County, where he believes there are no plantations. Moten and the other sharecroppers on the plantation write a letter appealing to President Roosevelt for relief, but Longnecker learns of the letter and uses it as a pretext to turn several of the sharecroppers off the plantation and punish others, including Moten. The book ends with Moten and his wife having a baby, a new sharecropper to work on Longnecker's plantation, implying a new iteration in the ongoing cycle of exploitation.

These novels are consistent and explicit about depicting sharecropping as system of exploitation. Robert Rylee, for example, describes the inevitable cycle of work and debt: "If [the cotton crop] is sold at a good price, the negroes are robbed and excessive commitments are made in the sudden vision of wealth. If the price is low, as it usually is, cruelly high land taxes are left unpaid and the ever-present mortgage interest lapses."[190] There is, in other words, no viable means to escape the cycle. In *Hold Autumn in Your Hand*, George Perry dispassionately explains the landowner's role in the system. Sam Tucker works for a man named Ruston:

> He was not, like some of the others, known as an especially bad man to work for. He paid trifling wages because it was customary and because a man working in a cotton field was not doing a very valuable thing. He was not known to be vicious or dishonest with his workers beyond the conventional banditry of the commissary system. Neither he nor any of his foremen had killed any Negroes or even quirted [beaten] any. Grapevine talk said that everything he had was mortgaged to the hilt.[191]

Perry's description indicates how imbricated the landowner is in the system. While he owns significant amounts of land and has almost complete control over his sharecroppers, who he pays in commissary tokens that can only be used at his store, he is himself mortgaged and, thus, completely in debt, so he has no choice but to exploit his workers. What makes Ruston better than most landowners is his reluctance to use violence.

The sharecroppers live in abject poverty, as thoroughly documented in the social science narratives and the photo documentaries, because the system of pervasive debt determines it. In *Hold Autumn in Your Hand*, Sam Tucker moves his family into a dilapidated cabin on Ruston's land, and both he and Ruston understand that nothing will be improved. "When you are a tenant," Tucker thinks, "you know you'll be gone next year anyway, and somebody else will inherit your lack of care for the land and the houses on the land. If she wants to wash away, let her wash. The landlord will never make any repairs, because the next fellow might want it different; so that in the end these things amount to a conspiracy against the land which feeds the people."[192] Since the landowner has no incentive to improve the land or the laborers' living conditions, the farms fall into disrepair, and since the sharecroppers have no funds to invest in the homes and no motivation to provide maintenance, the condition steadily worsens. In the introduction to his novel *The White Scourge*, Edward Davis, who was dean of the North Texas Agricultural College (now the University of Texas at Arlington), blames cotton for devastating the social structure. He writes, "poverty and ignorance have always clung to the cotton stalk like iron filings to a magnet. . . . Cotton culture is simple, an elemental means of subsistence for that portion of the South's rural proletariat composed of lowly blacks, peonized Mexicans, and moronic whites numbering into the several millions."[193] In his novel, which is a thought experiment in social Darwinism, cotton farms move into Texas ranch land, displacing cattle, ruining the soil, and devastating the population.[194] All of these novels are filled with examples of run-down cabins, meager food, threadbare clothes, sickly children, spavined mules, eroded soil, sweat, toil, and hardship.

Work and poverty, however, are not the chief concerns in these novels. During the Depression, millions of Americans lived in poverty on worked for minimal wages. The greater problem for the sharecroppers is debt, which inhibits their agency, leaving them in thrall to the landowners. In the sharecropping system, landowners had complete control over the sale of the crop and the sharecroppers' accounts, so they could determine a sharecroppers' profit or loss at settlement arbitrarily, and they had motivation to keep sharecropping families bound to them through debt. In *A Wind is Rising*, William Russell describes debt as inevitable, "no matter how much cotton they raised and no matter how much it sold for, Seabury King [the landowner] would always say the owed him more than they had coming. Still, you might as well spend your time hoping as doing anything else."[195] On King's plantation, sharecroppers "did not keep their own record, nor could they," of the amount of cotton they produced or its sale price, so they do not know either how much they earned or how much they owe at settlement.[196] To compound the issue, debts from the previous year carried over to the current crop, so sharecroppers often found themselves deeper in debt each year. Russell writes, "as the fortunes of both the past and the future depended upon the generosity of the settlement, the Negroes assembled around the commissary on that important morning with mingled feelings, the certainty of their disappointment overlaid by the pleasure of receiving any cash at all, no matter how little, no matter how soon spent."[197] Unlike wage workers during the Depression, sharecroppers received their payment only once per year, so they were obligated to stay under the control of one landowner for an entire year without the ability to move or seek a better opportunity, and if a landowner claimed that a laborer owed money on their account, then the sharecropper could be arrested for leaving the property, leaving them effectively trapped.

Munz offers a particularly graphic depiction of debt slavery in *Land Without Moses*. The book opens with a scene of Kirby Moten's father returning home enraged at a bad settlement: "In fifteen years as a sharecropper on Aaron Longnecker's plantation, Tamp Moten had never once been out of debt. Once every four or five years, when the crop was good and the price was high, he climbed high enough out of the well of debt to make him think that next season he would get all of the way out; but then a bad year or two would sink him deeper into debt than ever before."[198] Longnecker uses the family's debt to exert complete control over them. In one case, he notices that Tamp is wearing a new pair of overall that did not come from his store, and he fumes, "You know damn well you're supposed to buy everything you eat and wear in my store. Don't I support you the whole damn year? You'd starve to death if I didn't furnish you cornmeal and bacon every week."[199] He cuts the overalls to pieces and forces Tamp to walk to the store naked to buy new overalls and charge them to his account, humiliating him in front of his family and the other sharecroppers. Later, after Kirby learns some arithmetic in school, he demands to see the family's account in Longnecker's ledger, but "with tears of shame rising up in his eyes, Kirby discovered that he couldn't make head nor tail of these figures. They might be all right, or they might be all wrong, but he didn't know."[200] The tally, nonetheless, shows the family in debt to Longnecker by more than $500, and Kirby accuses Longnecker of "using the crooked pencil" on the accounts and cheating the family, and he goes to the sheriff with his allegations.[201] When Longnecker learns about the incident, he goes to the Moten's cabin with a whip and forces Tamp to beat his own son with it. Later, after Tamp dies, Longnecker transfers the family's debt to Kirby, keeping him trapped in the same cycle, and when Kirby tries to leave the plantation, he has him arrested and adds the fine to his debt, keeping him tied to the plantation seemingly forever.

While Longnecker is a vile and ruthless depiction of a landowner, Munz indicates that he is also part of the system of debt. Landowners, such as Longnecker and Ruston, are usually in debt to banks through mortgages on their land or loans to finance their crops. "He knew that most of the planters in Renfro County were in debt to the banks," Munz writes, "that if they didn't pay they lost their land; that cotton prices were as slippery and treacherous as a freshly caught bullhead; that a planter had to get every last bit of work out of his sharecroppers, every last cent out of his cotton, or he couldn't pay his loans; that even with the best of luck, at the end of the season, a planter might be deep in the hole."[202] Longnecker, in fact, is in debt to the First National Bank of Renfro for "fifty thousand dollars," with no clear path to get out of debt, so he also shares in the sense of economic anxiety.[203] In *Land Without Moses*, and all of the other Depression-era sharecropper novels, the characters are signifiers for a vast system of economic pressures, which reflects the common sense of economic anxiety among Americans at the time.[204] Longnecker may be a cruel person who exploits his workers with impunity, but, at least as far as his debt is concerned, he is also a victim of broad systemic forces.

In these novels, landowners, banks, and law enforcement represent the socioeconomic power structure, and they embody the deterministic forces that circumscribe the sharecroppers' lives. In *Hard Times on a Southern Chain Gang*, John L. Spivak portrays the power structure in the character Jim Deering, the county's largest landowner and owner of the bank. Deering's power is virtually unlimited: he has the ability to order the local sheriff to arrest men at his request, which allows him to force men into debt slavery by paying their bond, and he kills two men on his farm without being charged. Richard Wright depicts the local power structure in "Fire and

Cloud" in the form of three men who come to meet Reverend Dan Taylor to coerce him to stop a planned protest march. The three men—the mayor, the police chief, and the head of the industrial squad—represent political, legal, and economic power, and they have immense authority, including the ability to have Reverend Taylor killed. These characters are synecdoche for the entire system of power in the United States, demonstrating how politics, courts, and banks worked together to consolidate and maintain social control. In all of these books, when the sharecroppers resist local control, they are metaphorically resisting national systems.

Resistance comes with risk. Sharecropping is a form of debt bondage, and it is reinforced by cruel and inhumane methods of punishment and incarceration. Nearly all of these novels include scenes of incarceration in which a sharecropper challenges the power structure and is then arrested, jailed, and usually tortured until they acquiesce. In *Land Without Moses*, Kirby Moten attempts to leave Aaron Longnecker's plantation, but he is arrested almost as soon as he leaves the county and taken to jail, accused of walking out on a debt of more than $600 and stealing Longnecker's mule. Longnecker leaves him in jail over the winter and then pays his bond and adds it to his debt. Denis Gault, an African American union organizer in *A Sign for Cain*, is arrested on false charges of murder, and he is beaten until he signs a confession and is eventually killed in jail by a white man. Incarceration in these novels is an extension of the system of labor exploitation. Sharecroppers can be jailed at the landowner's request, and incarcerated sharecroppers find themselves in circumstances that mirror sharecropping. All southern states used inmates for forced labor in the first half of the twentieth century, so a person serving a prison sentence may spend their time working on a state-owned plantation.[205] In *Deep Dark River*, Mose is sentenced to hard labor for murder, and his lawyer tells him what to expect in the prison camp. "Now I want to tell you a little about life on the farm," she says. "The work will not be unlike the work you knew at the plantation. Only of course you will be in a prison. They will guard you in the fields. You will have to work hard. If you should be disobedient; they would whip you; if you tried to run away, they would shoot you."[206] Her description of his living conditions in the labor camp illustrates that the gap between sharecropping and slavery was narrow. Indeed, southern prison systems deliberately took advantage of the loophole in the Thirteenth Amendment to the US Constitution, which outlaws involuntary servitude "except as punishment for a crime." Sharecropping as a system of labor exploitation came close to involuntary servitude, blurring the line between freedom and slavery, and the forced labor system of incarceration erased the distinction altogether.

These novels expose how the system of debt and labor exploitation demeaned and dehumanized workers, depriving them of due process and civil rights. One novel, in particular, delves deeply into the human rights violations inherent in sharecropping as a system of labor, *Hard Times on a Southern Chain Gang* by John L. Spivak. One of America's most prominent journalists, Spivak was involved with several Communist causes and Leftist publications, and in the 1930s he became interested in the southern penal system after covering the trial of the Scottsboro Boys. He investigated chain gangs in Georgia, gaining access to interview wardens, guards, and inmates, and he took photographs of inmates being tortured. Rather than write a journalistic exposé, however, he wrote a novel that allowed him to illustrate the totalizing nature of southern labor. In this novel, David Jackson, born into a family of sharecroppers, is effectively a slave, mired in a system of debt, bondage, and torture. The book illustrates the relationship between sharecropping and labor laws, such as vagrancy and false pretenses, that make it illegal for a Black person to not have a job or to negotiate for a new job while working a current job. These crimes were punishable by extended sentences in labor camps, trapping workers in an inescapable system. The book also explicitly describes peonage, the practice of holding workers in bondage through debt. Peonage was the practice of forcing sharecroppers into debt and then adding the total of each year's debt to the next year's contract, keeping the workers tied to the landowner in a state of virtual slavery. In *The Shadow of Slavery: Peonage in the South, 1901–1969*, Pete Daniel asserts that "peonage infected the South like a cancer, eating away at the economic freedom of blacks, driving the poor whites to work harder in order to compete with virtual slave labor, and preserving the class structure inherited from slavery days."[207] Jim Deering holds David Jackson in peonage, Aaron Longnecker holds Kirby Moten in peonage in *Land Without Moses*, and John Chaney holds Cleveland in peonage in *High John the Conqueror*. The practice was not uncommon, and it gave landowners near absolute control over their workers.

When a landowner determined that a sharecropper was no longer useful or was otherwise problematic, they could have the sharecropper and their family turned off the land. While being held in debt bondage was tantamount to slavery, being turned off meant destitution and potential starvation. Since landowners controlled the labor markets and the food supply, workers were dependent on landowners for food and shelter—a form of forced dependency that landowners deliberately cultivated and exploited. When Mose in *Deep Dark River* arrives in Lisbon, Mississippi, he immediately seeks work on a plantation because there are no other options available to make a living, and since he arrives after the planting season has begun, he has to accept a contract that only offers him food and shelter but no promise of payment. If a landowner chose to dispossess a sharecropping family during the planting cycle, they would lose their crop, their home, and their only source of food. After a group of sharecroppers resists the planters' scheme to seize Agricultural Adjustment Act payments in *Land without Moses*, the landowners turn the families off of their farms in droves. "Everywhere you go, sharecroppers being turned off," one sharecropper says despondently. "Some of 'em goin' to the Florida turpentine camps, some to the steel mills in Birmingham, or the cotton mills in Atlanta; some goin' to Memphis, or Little Rock, or New Orleans; some tryin' their luck in the oil fields in East Texas. But most of 'em ain't goin' no place in particular, goddam hit to hell, they don't know where they're goin'; they're just goin.'"[208] The combination of debt, incarceration, and dependency left sharecroppers powerless to challenge the landowners and to change the cycle of exploitation. These novels make the case that external intervention would be necessary to change sharecropping.

These works are mostly ambivalent, however, about the value of New Deal government programs to improve the economy and sharecroppers' welfare. Government relief programs designed to provide income for displaced sharecroppers created a new form of dependency. In *High John the Conqueror*, a family of sharecroppers expresses concern about government programs. They welcome the "gov'ment check," but they are reticent about the plan to plant less cotton under the Bankhead Cotton Control Act. They plan to plant less cotton and use their mules to plant peas and corn and to raise hogs, but the plan has an obvious problem. "Us can't do no good sellin' hogs," one says, "but they sho' worth somethin' to put in yo' belly."[209] Planting more food can provide means for subsistence, but it does not allow for income, so it does not improve the family's economic condition. Sam Tucker in *Hold Autumn in Your Hand* works on relief for a while, but he becomes dissatisfied with the work, so he returns to sharecropping. When he struggles to feed his family, "he applie[s] to the relief agency, but its rolls [are] full."[210] In these novels, government relief is inadequate to solve the problems of the southern economy, and the plan to take one third of cotton farming land out of production makes them worse. In *Land Without Moses*, a county agent tells the sharecroppers on Aaron Longnecker's plantation about the oversupply of cotton and the government's plan to pay farmers to take land out of production by plowing up every third row of planted cotton with the promise that the government check "will be divided between you and Mr. Longnecker just the same as the money you get from selling cotton: half and half. Mr. Longnecker will get half and you will get half."[211] The promise, predictably, never comes to fruition. Longnecker and the other planters in the area claim the checks as rental for their land from the government, so the sharecroppers get no compensation for their diminished crops. Some of the sharecroppers on the plantation send a letter to the Agricultural Adjustment Administration in Washington, DC, complaining about their lack of payment. Munz depicts the government bureaucrat receiving hundreds of similar letters, indicating that "one way or another the cotton reduction program was not being carried out as the government intended it to be."[212] The bureaucrat writes to the county agent, who goes to Aaron Longnecker, who tells the county agent to mind his own business. The end result of the program is that Longnecker gets a better price for his crop, his sharecroppers get nothing, and those who complain get turned off the plantation. In these novels, government programs are insufficient to solve the intractable problems.

Some of these proletarian novels suggest that the sharecroppers should participate in a Communist revolution to overthrow the landowners. In *Hold Autumn in Your Hand*, Sam Tucker takes in a family of migrant farm workers trapped in a flood. They tell him that they had to leave California, reversing the Joad's course in *The Grapes of Wrath*, because they were involved in a strike. One of the family members is a preacher who came under the influence of Communist organizers in California, and he recognizes that Christianity and Communism have some interesting parallels. "I commenced to preaching Jesus and the brotherhood of man and then I seen how things was and mixed it up kinda with Communism," he explains, but his followers double-cross him, so he ends up in jail.[213] This side plot, with its heavy-handed allusions to flood, Judas, judgment, and exile, is incidental to the book's overarching plot, but it demonstrates the affinity between sharecroppers and other exploited workers. Grace Lumpkin, who worked as a Communist organizer among sharecroppers and textile workers in North Carolina, includes Communist organizers in *A Sign for Cain*.[214] In her book, an African American organizer, Denis Gault, returns to his hometown, where he works with a sympathetic white newspaper publisher to spread Communist ideas among the sharecroppers and organize resistance. He succeeds in organizing workers on one plantation to demand better conditions, but when the local power structure realizes his project, he becomes the scapegoat for a false murder charge. In one scene, the sheriff reads to a landowner from one of Denis's leaflets, which had been discovered along with a copy of *The Communist Manifesto* in a sharecropper's cabin: "'"We have a right to bread and clothing and books for our children. By a mean trick, getting a so-called health officer down to inspect the shacks we call homes, those who are in power have cheated our women out of the means to make a livelihood." It goes on like that,' the sheriff said, swallowing in his excitement."[215] The leaflet references a plan to prevent African American women from taking in laundry, and the fact that Lumpkin puts these words in the mouths of a representative of the power structure, who nearly chokes on them, indicates their subversive power. The most radical work of sharecropper fiction is Richard Wright's story "Bright and Morning Star" in *Uncle Tom's Children*.[216] In this story, Sue, a laundress, worries for her son, Johnny-Boy, a communist organizer. Wright uses Sue to illustrate Communism's compatibility with African American liberation theology, and he describes her as thinking, "The wrongs and sufferings of black men had taken the place of Him nailed to the Cross; the meager beginnings of the party had become another Resurrection; and the hate of these who would destroy her new faith had quickened in her a hunger to feel how deeply her new strength went."[217] Her faith is tested when a sheriff's posse comes searching for Johnny-Boy, whom they eventually capture and torture, interrogating him for the names of other communists. In all of these stories, the prospect of Communism is as much anathema to landowners and the power structure as insurrection had been to slaveholders because it suggests the overthrow of the existing power structure.

Other works of Depression-era sharecropping fiction stop short of Communism but suggest the possibility of organizing sharecropper unions to negotiate less exploitative conditions for the workers. Beal goes to New York to implore the Association, an allusion to the NAACP, to defend his brother on false charges of murder in *A Wind Is Rising,* and while in the city, he meets some white liberal intellectuals who encourage him to "start a sharecroppers' union."[218] The idea, however, does not advance far because cooler heads point out that "organizing sharecroppers against the planters is nothing like organizing factory workers. The whites always have race supremacy to fall back on."[219] The sharecropper labor struggle demonstrates the validity of this point, but in *The Stricklands,* Edwin Lanham depicts a white union organizer who works tirelessly, perhaps maniacally, to organize an integrated union in Oklahoma. Jay Strickland makes his pitch to everyone he meets. "Our slogan is land for the landless," he tells a Native American tenant, and "some day we aim to abolish farm tenancy altogether." He goes on to outline a plan to create cooperative stores that allow farmers to purchase goods at a fair price without interest and loans through Farm Security to finance land purchases.[220] Later, he has delusions of grandeur when he imagines that "Nothing ain't going to stop us and the Southern Tenant Farmers' Union will git to be a power in this here state. We'll band them tenants and sharecroppers together and we'll demand land fer the landless and a WPA job fer every man that can work and we'll get it."[221] In his vision, the tenant farmers become a major political unit that dictates the terms of labor in the state, but, predictably, the landowners in the area oppose the plan, and they are willing to use violence and intimidation to stop it. The plans for unionization do not come to fruition in either of these works, partly because the books reflect the actual history of Depression-era sharecropper unionization.[222]

One of the key problems for sharecropper unions was race, which is also reflected in the fictional depiction of unionization. Black and white sharecroppers "lived in the same kind of cabin[s], ate the same kind of food, and wore the same kind of clothes," but finding a common cause was challenging in the Jim Crow South.[223] In *The Stricklands,* Jay struggles to convince a white sharecropper that he should join an integrated union. The man firmly states that "if we're going to have a union it's got to be a union of white men."[224] Jay tries to explain that a segregated union will allow the landowners to pit the races against each other to undermine their bargaining power, but the man balks, claiming that the races do not belong together.

"They belong together economically," Jay says, frustrated. "It's economic equality we want fer everybody. We ain't talking social equality."[225] In this revealing exchange, Jay implies that the Southern Tenant Farmers' Union intends to exploit Black workers to achieve its goals to benefit white farmers, not to promote racial equality among the workers. Notably, interracial unions do not develop in these novels, so even in works of fiction, where a writer could imagine the possibilities of a functional interracial union that achieves the goals of land distribution and no-debt contract, race impedes economic progress in the South.

Appeals for external intervention fail because the landowners' power structure uses coercion and violence to disrupt intervention. Beyond the social and economic methods of control, including debt bondage, peonage, vagrancy laws, turning off, and imprisonment, landowners in the novels often use violence and murder to maintain their control, sending the message to any sharecroppers or labor organizers that the system would not permit intervention. In *The Stricklands,* for example, Rocky Jones, Jay Strickland's African American comrade, is captured, severely beaten, and eventually dies from his injuries, and in *Land without Moses,* Keet Riffle, the African American schoolteacher who helps the sharecroppers write a letter to President Roosevelt, is burned to death in his cabin. Richard Wright's short story "Bright and Morning Star" ends with an extended scene of gruesome violence. After terrorizing Johnny-Boy's mother, Sue, the sheriff's posse captures Johnny-Boy and tortures him for the names of the other organizers. Sue, carrying a white sheet, finds them, intending to cover Johnny-Boy's body, which invites comparisons to the crucifixion of Christ. She watches as they break his legs, rupture his ear drums, and shoot him before they kill her. In this story, describing the gruesome extent of the violence is crucial to exposing the depravity of the power structure and the immense danger sharecroppers face for resisting. These scenes of violence answer the implicit questions about why sharecroppers would have been reluctant to challenge the power structure. Any challenges to the system triggered coercion, violence, and possibly death.

Depression-era sharecropper novels do not have happy endings. These are social problem novels that rarely offer effective solutions or imagine future resolutions that alleviate exploitation. The one exception to this rule is Wright's story "Fire and Cloud" in which Reverend Taylor endures a severe beating but still collaborates with Communist organizers to lead sharecroppers in a march for food, which draws the mayor, a signifier for the landowners' power structure, to ask for negotiations. This story offers a potential blueprint for massive resistance that resonates in uncanny ways with the Montgomery bus boycott more than two decades later, but this story also immediately precedes "Bright and Morning Star" in *Uncle Tom's Children,* so the story of gruesome violence undercuts the potential for optimism. Perry's *Hold Autumn in Your Hand* also ends on a slightly optimistic tone, but the ending is more complicated than it appears. In the final scene, Sam Tucker looks out on the fields that he cleared to raise a crop, and says to his wife, "there's always another day," implying that they will try sharecropping another year with hopes for eventually having their own farm.[226] This, however, is a change from the book's original ending in which Sam, defeated, decides to move the family to Houston to find work in a factory because "it was the only way in which a man with no education, no capital of land or money, could any longer support his family in anything but squalor."[227] The original ending, which Perry changed at the direct request of his publisher, changes the tone of the entire book, making the work much more bleak and fatalistic than the published version. *Land without Moses* also ends with a pessimistic vision, as Kirby Moten, compliant and broken, presents Aaron Longnecker with his son, who Longnecker describes as "another sharecropper," suggesting that their family will continue to struggle in debt bondage for another generation.[228] At the end of *Deep Dark River,* Mose learns that his appeal his been unsuccessful, so he will have to spend the rest of his life on the prison farm, but he realizes that his sentence is irrelevant because sharecropping is a prison from which he can never escape.

As a genre, Depression-era sharecropper novels present agricultural labor exploitation as an intractable problem with no clear solutions. External intervention appears to offer sharecroppers a means to challenge the landowners' power structure, but in these novels, the attempts to resist succumb to coercion and violence. To the extent that these works present a social agenda, they dramatize the exploitation and abjection of sharecropping families in a way that cultivates sympathy for the sharecroppers' plight, similar to the methods used by narrative photo documentaries. The books' political objectives, however, are ambiguous. While Grace Lumpkin and Richard Wright were directly involved with the Communist Party during the Depression, the other writers were less engaged, and their objectives were likely more aesthetic than political. They were not writing in support of government programs, nor were they writing to further academic inquiry, but this lack of predetermined objectives makes the novels even more affecting for their representation of southern poverty. The novels substantiate the data represented in government and sociological studies, and their descriptions of sharecroppers living in squalor resonate with the images captured by documentary photographers. In this sense, they hold a mirror to reality, reflecting the pervasiveness and magnitude to sharecropping as a social problem. The fact that these books have been mostly forgotten by readers and critics, meanwhile, indicates that agricultural workers are often overlooked in labor struggles and also that conditions in the South changed rapidly in the years after World War II. Coming back to these novels reveals important stories of "the richest land, the poorest people."[229]

The Great Depression made sharecropping in the US South a national issue. At a time when the nation experienced unprecedented levels of poverty, sharecroppers became signifiers for deprivation. By 1929, when the stock market fell, sharecroppers had been performing the exploited, alienated labor that was essential to the nation's agricultural export market for more than six decades. But when the racial dynamics of sharecropping shifted as white laborers outnumbered Black laborers, the concerns of sharecroppers became a political issue of national significance. The federal government offered several interventions in agricultural policy that were intended to alleviate sharecroppers' plight, but the initiatives, such as the Agricultural Adjustment Act, largely backfired because landowners found ways to use their control over local systems of finance to manipulate government payments. In many cases, landowners outright pocketed the payments; in other cases, they took payments out of the sharecroppers' debt; and in some cases, landowners turned sharecroppers off the land to keep the payments. While federal intervention did little to address the actual needs of sharecroppers, it made them ubiquitous in national media. "The depression was the decade of the Southern tenant farmer," Charles Aiken writes. "Never before or since have tenants received the attention they were given during the 1930s."[230]

The attention directed toward sharecroppers, however, was problematic. Several genres depicting sharecroppers emerged during the Depression, each intending to describe their experience, but they co-opted the sharecroppers' perspective to serve a particular agenda. Government documents present enormous amounts of data and information that quantify and document the sharecroppers' living conditions and economic struggles to support federal interventions, but their collective narrative, while highly illuminating, ultimately functions as a form of government propaganda. Social science narratives, meanwhile, catalog a vast array of social problems that stem from sharecropping, but they project external attitudes onto the sharecroppers' lives in a way that tends to demean and marginalize them. The distinctive genre of photo documentaries that emerged following the precedent of Caldwell and Bourke-White's *You Have Seen Their Faces* humanized and publicized the experiences of sharecroppers, bringing an enormous amount of national attention to the exploitation they endured, but the books often ventriloquize their perspectives, using them as symbols for poverty without allowing them to speak for themselves. Sharecroppers had a greater opportunity to speak for themselves through labor action during the unionization movements in Arkansas and Alabama, and their strikes sent a potent message about their exploitation that attracted national attention. Ideological issues, however, complicated the message because union leadership supported collectivization while rank-and-file members preferred independent land ownership. Proletarian sharecropper novels portray sharecroppers as helpless in the face of overwhelming economic forces that obliterate their agency and their humanity. While all of these types of works focused national attention on the plight of sharecroppers, they tended to put political agendas ahead of the individualistic and humane concerns of the actual sharecroppers who wanted, for the most part, to own their own land, to not be exploited, and to live with dignity.

The abundance of works depicting sharecroppers during the Depression provides important context for southern literature of the 1930s. When works such as *Absalom, Absalom!* and *Gone with the Wind* were published in 1936, most people in the United States would have been thoroughly aware of the struggles sharecroppers faced, and these images of rural poverty were synonymous with the image of the South in the minds of most Americans. This powerful pejorative association may help to explain why midcentury scholars of southern literature endeavored to shift the focus from images of poverty to yeoman farmers who, in the context of Cold War America, offered a more empowering, capitalist representation of the region. At the same time that Cold Warriors were shaping depictions of southern culture, however, sharecropping was undergoing radical transformations. The development of a reliable, cost-effective mechanical cotton picker obviated the need to maintain a vast, inexpensive labor force. In the years after World War II, sharecropping came to an end as technology replaced the need for human labor, but the end of sharecropping raised new issues for the people displaced from farms, leading to major changes in the region's economy, population structure, and race relations.

## → 5 ←
# The End of Sharecropping

A scene in the 1967 film *In the Heat of the Night* shows the sharecropping system in decline. The film's premise, in fact, reflects the region's post-World War II economic development, as Virgil Tibbs, an African American police officer from Philadelphia, Pennsylvania, is mistakenly arrested for the murder of a Chicago industrialist who is building a factory in rural Sparta, Mississippi. Tibbs has returned to Mississippi to visit his family, and once his identity as a police detective is confirmed, he assists the local police chief with the investigation. In this mystery, both the murder and the detective demonstrate the dynamics of industrialization and population migration on the rural community, which is involved in an agricultural transition from manual labor to mechanization. As the murder investigation unfolds, Tibbs suspects a plantation owner named Endicott who embodies the traditional southern economic power structure. Endicott is a racial paternalist who opposes the opening of a factory in the community, likely because he recognizes that a new factory will create competition in the local labor pool. The establishing shot as Tibbs and local police chief Bill Gillespie drive up to Endicott's plantation, however, reveals that the system of labor on the plantation is already in transition. As they drive through the field in the police car, sharecroppers pick cotton by hand as tractors also pull wagons full of cotton. This symbiosis of laborers and machines indicates a new paradigm in sharecropping that eventually led to the end of sharecropping and the displacement of millions of southern agricultural laborers. The film does not dilate on the nuances of labor arrangements on Endicott's plantation, but many landowners made investments in machinery to replace labor in the decades after World War II, leading to new transitional sharecropping contracts, such as the "through and through" arrangement. In this system, a certain acreage is assigned to a family, but the entire plantation is worked with tractors for plowing and some other tasks and with manual labor gangs for chopping and picking.[1] This scene sets the film within the period of transition from manual labor to agricultural mechanization that eventually led to the end of sharecropping and massive social changes in the South.

Since the end of the Civil War, sharecropping had been a pervasive labor arrangement in the South, undergirded by an elaborate set of social, political, economic, and cultural control systems that limited nearly every aspect of the sharecroppers' lives. Over of period of about thirty years from the end of World War II to the civil rights movement, however, new machines, chemicals, and practices incrementally eliminated the need for cheap and abundant labor, so millions of sharecroppers either left or were forced from farms. While sharecropping was itself a complex social problem, the end of sharecropping created a cascading set of additional social problems as people who had limited education, financial means, and cultural capital were displaced from the only homes and occupations they knew. Many of these displaced people migrated to cities in the South and the North, where they sought out housing and work in manufacturing and industries. This movement, which Donald Holley calls "the second great emancipation," contributed to the emergence of the civil rights movement, diversification in southern agriculture, and the development of the region's industrial economy and urban infrastructure.[2] While the end of sharecropping instantiated the long-delayed modernization of the South, it also left behind a set of entrenched social structures, including institutionalized racism, educational inequality, and intergenerational poverty, that continue to hamper the region's social progress.

The process of agricultural mechanization in the South was slow, but the effects of the process were revolutionary, affecting every aspect of life in the region. As cotton farming mechanized and as the region's system of agriculture diversified, less of the region's population was directly engaged with agriculture. The shifting economic and population paradigm is reflected in the region's literature. After World War II, fewer literary works were set on farms and fewer texts focused on the experiences of sharecroppers, diminishing the attention on agricultural labor. The focus of southern writing shifted to the processes of social change, with more works set in urban spaces, more focus on domestic and occupational issues outside agriculture, and more focus on issues of civil rights. While many of these books do not focus on sharecroppers in the South, they do depict a social structure built on the detritus of sharecropping, and many of the social problems represented in the works have their roots in sharecropping. The key works of southern literature that focus on sharecropping after World War II represent the long process of mechanization, the effects of sharecropping on the civil rights movement, and the impact of sharecropping on the life stories of many southerners. Even as sharecropping came to an end, it continued to define the South.

## The Death of Cotton: Mechanization and the End of Sharecropping

Because the mechanization of southern agriculture and its attendant social effects manifested incrementally over three decades, literary works that follow a long temporal scope offer the most illuminating perspective on the process. Alice Walker's first novel, *The Third Life of Grange Copeland* (1970), chronicles three generations of a Georgia sharecropping family from the 1920s to the 1960s. The book opens with a scene that evokes the interwar migration of African Americans to cities in the northeast, and it ends during the civil rights movement. The book focuses on Grange Copeland's son, Brownfield, who spends much of his life working as a sharecropper, even though he says, "I never did want to be no sharecropper, never did want to work for nobody else, never did want to have white folks where they could poke themselves right into my life and me not have nothing to do with it."[3] Ernest Gaines's novel *The Autobiography of Miss Jane Pittman* (1971) follows an even greater scope, a century that extends from the end of the Civil War to the civil rights movement, and it makes clear that sharecropping is an extension of slavery. When the title character's master informs his slaves, "y'all free," he immediately adds, "y'all can stay and work on shares."[4] The book uses the fictional life of centenarian Jane Pittman to reflect the slow pace of social change in the century after slavery, a process delayed by sharecropping. Dale Maharidge and Michael Williamson's Pulitzer Prize-winning nonfiction narrative *And Their Children After Them* (1989) revisits the same community and the same families that James Agee and Walker Evans described in *Let Us Now Praise Famous Men* (1941), tracing the changes that have elapsed between 1936, when Agee and Evans visited Hale County, Alabama, and 1986, when Maharidge and Williamson visited. Their work, which includes photographs of many of the same people and places that Walker Evans photographed during the Great Depression, illustrates how the end of sharecropping affected the families and the community in mostly negative ways. Reading these works in context with the history of mechanization demonstrates that the end of sharecropping was incremental, complicated, and sometimes counterproductive.

Sharecropping ended slowly because cotton picking was difficult to mechanize. The first patent for a mechanical cotton picker was issued in 1850, but mechanical devices could not replicate the nimble, delicate motions needed to extract fibers from the cotton boll, which meant that hand picking was necessary to produce a crop. This required the maintenance of an enormous, inexpensive labor force and a set a repressive social and economic practices to tie the laborers to the crop. Landowners, thus, had relatively little incentive to make capital investments in mechanization. James H. Street writes in *The New Revolution in the Cotton Economy: Mechanization and Its Consequences* (1957), "it is sufficient to note that in most parts of the Cotton Belt before World War II the coming of mechanized farming, rather than being widely welcomed, was anticipated with considerable dread of its economic and social consequences."[5] During the Great Depression, several companies worked on developing mechanical cotton pickers, and tractors came into use on some farms. Landowners, government officials, labor activists, and sharecroppers could all discern the inevitability of mechanization and its consequences for sharecroppers already struggling for opportunity and income. Yet, as late as the 1940s, cotton farming was almost exactly as primitive as it had been in the eighteenth century. Alice Walker describes sharecroppers before World War II laboring in the fields by hand: "planting chopping, poisoning and picking in the cotton field, which ran for half a mile along the main road. Brownfield had worked there too now, for four years, since he was six, in the company of other child workers. His father worked with men and women in another part of the field. The cotton field too was generally silent."[6] The field is silent in part because the children have been taught not to play in the cotton fields, and they are forced into the cotton fields and out of school because their primary value to the landowners is manual labor, the same as it had been for their great-grandparents.

World War II disrupted the dynamics of labor in the South. According to Gavin Wright, three million young men, nearly a quarter of the agricultural labor pool, left the South either to join the military or to work in wartime industries. "Most of the departures," he notes, "were not by owners or tenants, but by farm laborers and sharecroppers."[7] The war created a labor vacuum as demand for cotton increased for military purposes, so available townspeople were lured into fields to work for triple wages. The war temporarily solved the problem of excess agricultural labor in the South, and it generally changed attitudes about the utility and necessity of mechanization. Many landowners, facing labor scarcity, began investing their capital into machines to replace labor, but the overall landscape of labor relations changed slowly. Brownfield Copeland stays on the farm during the war in Walker's novel. In one scene, he prepares to move from one farm to another, and the landowner pays him a visit before his departure, speaking condescendingly to him, which makes Brownfield seethe. "But this is 1944!" Walker writes, "Brownfield wanted to scream; instead he said 'Yassur,' and waited until Captain Davis was three yards away before he moved."[8] For sharecroppers who remained on the farm during the war, the scarcity of labor did not improve working conditions, and the imminent onset of mechanization created at least as many problems as it solved. "The war reconfigured the southern rural labor system," according to Pete Daniel, "phasing out sharecropping and utilizing wage labor, and many people who did not fit into the new scheme fled the land—and often the South—forever."[9]

After the war, a set of push and pull factors restructured sharecropping.[10] Dale Maharidge explains that these factors drew many of the descendants of the sharecropping families in Hale County, Alabama, away from the farms. "World War II, of course, altered American expectations and the economy of the world. Here was what is called a 'pull' factor," he writes.[11] Other pull factors include the increase in nonagricultural jobs in growing cities across the United States, as well as the urge to provide a better life with greater equality for one's family. For an enormous number of southerners who had been born into sharecropping, this lure was more than sufficient to induce hundreds of thousands of them to leave the fields. Those who remained faced another force. "Then there were the machines," Maharidge writes, "a 'push' factor to force them off the land. The machines came and the tenants had little choice in the matter. Some had nothing to go to."[12] For many families, the end of sharecropping was a blessing, creating opportunities for more secure and more remunerative employment and better living conditions off the farms. For others, however, who were unable to adapt to the changing conditions, it meant homelessness and destitution and generational poverty. In the absence of social safety nets and programs to reintegrate sharecroppers into an industrialized economy, families were left to fend for themselves. Landowners, meanwhile, had good reason to continue to maintain cheap and expendable labor.

The process of mechanizing southern agriculture extended incrementally for several decades after World War II. The first step of mechanization was the introduction of ordinary tractors that were used to plow fields at planting time, but these machines could not complete the specialized tasks of chopping a field of cotton to remove weeds or picking cotton in time for harvest. Dale Maharidge recounts that the landowner Floyd Gudger worked for bought a tractor in the 1950s, "giving up on mules."[13] They displaced several sharecropping families, and "Floyd became a tractor man. With the tractor, Floyd plowed 134 acres of corn and cotton, five times the amount of land a man could plow with a mule."[14] The emergence of tractors made the dehumanization of sharecropping labor even more evident. For example, Brownfield Copeland's landowner, Mr. Davis, swaps him to another landowner, Mr. J. L., and "in return Captain Davis had let his tractor go for a season. The swap had been made exactly as if he and his family were a string of workhorses."[15] The trade here evokes the sale of slaves from one plantation owner to another, but rather than trading humans for humans, the landowners trade sharecroppers for tractors. The implication is that even in the supposedly modern South, humans were still implements for labor.

The process of agricultural mechanization eventually eliminated the need for human labor. Economic historian Richard Day segments the process into four stages: stage one is mule-powered cultivation with no mechanization, stage two is partial mechanization using a tractor for plowing and other nonspecialized tasks, stage three is mechanization of the preharvest operations, and stage four is complete mechanization using a mechanical cotton picker.[16] Charles Aiken documents that this process developed incrementally. Tractors for plowing, planting, and cultivating came into common use soon after World War II. As wartime industries shifted back to manufacturing domestic products, they mass-produced tractors, which made them affordable for most landowners. Mechanical cotton pickers were more cost prohibitive, however. They entered mass production in the 1950s, but they were adopted more slowly because of their price. Herbicides to kill weeds were also developed in the 1950s and were in extensive use by the 1960s, which reduced the need to chop cotton by hand.[17] The increase in mechanization led to a reduction in manual labor. Producing one bale of cotton using mules required 150 hours of labor, and using tractors for cultivation reduced the required hours of labor to 120 hours. This was still a considerable requirement, particularly during the labor-intensive and time-sensitive harvest season, which led to transitional forms of agricultural labor, such as "through and through" arrangements and increased use of day labor during harvest. Mechanical cotton pickers drastically reduced the required hours of labor needed to produce a bale of cotton to about thirty hours per bale, and complete mechanization, including the use of herbicides to control weeds, brought the total number of hours to produce a bale of cotton down to about fifteen, so one person could effectively produce ten times more cotton with machines than with mules.[18] By 1972, all cotton in the United States was harvested mechanically, ending sharecropping as a system of labor.[19]

The key to mechanizing southern agriculture was developing an effective and efficient mechanical cotton picker. As long as the region maintained a cheap and abundant labor pool, mechanizing the harvest was not a crucial priority, so relatively little capital was invested in developing a mechanical cotton picker. Picking cotton with a machine was an extremely complicated task for several reasons. The most obvious reason is the inherent challenge of gently removing a small clump of fiber from a tough, woody boll. A mechanical picker needed not only to remove the cotton lint but also to remove as little of the leaves, stems, and other trash as possible. Also, since cotton plants are not naturally determinate, they do not produce all of their blooms at the same time, so a mechanical picker needed to remove the fiber from the mature bolls without destroying the undeveloped bolls. A mechanical picker would also have to negotiate a range of difficult terrains, from broad, flat fields in east Texas and the Mississippi Delta to hilly fields in the Piedmont areas of South Carolina and North Carolina.[20] Making a picker effective would require developing a new technology, a new cotton plant, new agricultural practices, new terrains, and a new workforce. Many individuals, hoping to make a fortune on a new technology, experimented with cotton pickers in the decades before World War II, but neither the market nor the labor supply demanded it. With the destabilization of the labor market during the war, however, conditions were ripe for a mechanical cotton picker, and several models entered the market after the war. The largest segment of the market went to International Harvester, which built a factory in Memphis in 1948. That year, the factory produced 766 spindle-type pickers, and five years later, it manufactured 3,741.[21] Each mechanical picker produced marked a further incremental step toward the end of sharecropping.

The individual who contributed most to the development of the mechanical cotton picker was John Rust. With the assistance of his brother, Mack, he produced the first viable method to pick cotton with a machine. The brothers were raised on a cotton farm, they grew up picking cotton, and John was determined to find a way to simplify the process. "One night, while lying in bed, John remembered how cotton clung to his fingers in the early morning dew. Water attracted the fiber. That was the secret!" Maharidge writes.[22] Rust conceived of his idea to use a moistened spindle to remove cotton fiber from a boll in 1927, but he struggled to develop a working prototype until 1936, when he demonstrated a machine that could pick four hundred pounds of cotton in an hour. The machine proved to be controversial, alternately hailed and reviled as a revolution in southern agriculture that would either free sharecroppers from their bondage or cast them into destitution. During the Great Depression, there was relatively little incentive to make large investments in relieving labor, so the Rust brothers' picker languished. John Rust, meanwhile, realized the potential consequences of his invention. In a *Time* magazine article, he worried that "75 percent of the labor population could be thrown into unemployment," so he contrived to develop conditions in which the machine would benefit labor.[23] He refused to sell his idea to a large corporation, and, as Maharidge documents, he proposed "to lease rather than sell the machines, and to do so to large growers under restrictive rules. Those rules required the lessee to pay his workers minimum wages, to set a maximum number of work hours for all adult workers, and to eliminate child labor altogether."[24] He also collaborated with the Southern Tenant Farmers Union to create collective farms where all farmers could use the mechanical picker freely. None of these schemes were successful, and the development of other models of mechanical cotton picker made the Rust brothers' machine dispensable, but the Rust brothers offered the only set of policy ideas that ameliorated the socioeconomic impact of the end of sharecropping.

After the Great Depression, the federal government largely vacated its involvement in social issues concerning sharecropping. The host of New Deal programs and interventions that had been designed to provide economic support for sharecroppers vanished during World War II. As the government abandoned social interventions, "the federal government heavily subsidized and coordinated the mechanization of cotton production, but failed to absorb the adjustment costs of those harmed by the results."[25] The key objective of the postwar government agenda was to invigorate the nation's economy by investing in production, so the government invested in cotton mechanization and supported subsidies to help American cotton compete in an increasingly global agricultural market. These same programs, however, contributed substantially to the eventual decline of the cotton labor market. In *And Their Children after Them,* Maharidge explains that former sharecroppers who were unable to integrate into the developing economy depended upon a new form of federal entitlement programs, such as welfare, Medicaid, and housing projects. He describes a barracks-style housing project, writing, "In 1960, when these projects were much younger and had not yet trampled the many souls they would in time crush, they looked grand to white cotton refugees who had never lived in anything more substantial than sharecropper shacks. There must have been quite an army of these sharecroppers passing through these projects: by 1964, so many tenant farmers would have left the land that the Census Bureau would decide it was no longer worth counting them."[26] To the government, sharecropping ceased to be a social or political problem because sharecroppers ceased to exist as an employment category, but the consequences of generational poverty and labor exploitation remained.[27]

The sharecropping families in *The Third Life of Grange Copeland* and *The Autobiography of Miss Jane Pittman* labor inexorably for generations, continuing a labor paradigm that extends unbroken since Emancipation. Gaines and Walker both use their characters as metaphors for the systemic exploitation of sharecropping, and their stories reflect the rise and fall of sharecropping as a system of labor. Jane Pittman's life indexes the historical scope of sharecropping, and her story reflects the false promise of Emancipation, which devolves into Reconstruction and Jim Crow and a century of labor exploitation. The only escape from sharecropping in the book is the possibility of escaping the South, but Jane herself fails to escape immediately after Emancipation, and over the course of the novel, she and others make various attempts to leave, including her move to Texas with her husband, but she inevitably returns to sharecropping, which suggests that the circumscribed demand for labor limits agency and mobility.[28] In *The Third Life of Grange Copeland*, meanwhile, Grange's son, Brownfield, embodies sharecropping. When he is born, he is named for the first thing Grange sees from the door of their cabin, "sort of brownish colored fields."[29] At his birth, Grange and his mother are utterly demoralized, and they feel "hopelessness, when cotton production was all that mattered in their world (and not ever their cotton!), even love had stopped."[30] His birth represents a repetition of an inescapable cycle in which Brownfield repeats the pattern of his father's life and his daughter, Ruth, appears to be on course to repeating his life, if not for the intervention of her grandfather and civil rights activists.[31] Despite the oppressive cycle of exploitation, Brownfield "loved the South. And he knew he loved it because he had never seriously considered leaving it. . . . It was a sweet, violent, peculiarly accommodating land. It bent itself to fit its own laws."[32] His perverse affection for the South, which signifies his resignation to a life of exploitation, may be the greatest irony in the work because Brownfield, like millions of other sharecroppers, would inevitably be dispossessed from the fields.

Sharecroppers were evicted or displaced in proportion to the progress of mechanization. Maharidge accounts that mechanization resulted in millions of acres going out of production, much of it in the Piedmont areas where the uneven terrain was more difficult to farm with machines. In 1936, the US produced fourteen million bales of cotton on forty-three million acres, but the same amount of cotton was produced on just seventeen and a half million acres in 1960. As efficiency increased, "fewer people were needed. One million farms had vanished since 1940, representing a loss of the majority of the nine million cotton tenants."[33] Gaines describes this process taking place on the Samson plantation, where Jane Pittman works. During the war, the Cajuns on the plantation bought plows and tractors, "and the better the plows and tractors, the more they got. After a while they wanted more land. That's when Robert [the landowner] started taking acre by acre from the colored and giving it to them. He took and took till there wasn't enough to support a family, so the people had to give up and leave."[34] As one of the families moves away from the Samson plantation, they hang signs on the sides of their wagons, saying "AFTER FIFTY YEARS, ROBERT SAMSON KICKED US OFF. BLACK PEOPLE FATE."[35] Increasing mechanization changed the dynamics of labor management on southern plantations, eroding the manufactured dependency that landowners had exploited for generations. With less demand for labor, landowners had less reason to use debt, violence, and other forms of manipulation to keep laborers tied to the land, so they gradually either let them leave or forced them off. Jay Mandle argues that displacement was a revolution in southern labor relations. "The plantation economy rested not merely on coercion," he writes, "but also upon deference. It was dependency as well as control which characterized the organization of production on the estates."[36]

The same process that displaced sharecroppers also dispossessed small landowners, particularly African Americans. When Grange Copeland returns to Baker County, Georgia, in Walker's novel, he buys a small farm with money he takes from his girlfriend, Josie. This farm represents self-determination, autonomy, and the potential for intergenerational wealth, and he intends to pass it down to his granddaughter, Ruth, but he realizes that his claim to the land is continually under threat. In one scene, Grange and Ruth put up a barbed-wire fence around their property, and he explains to her that "good fences don't make neighbors."[37] The fence protects the property from white folks who would be eager to claim it. "Those people over there," he tells Ruth, "you give 'em a chance, they try to take our land, never mind it belong to us. They want hit, they take hit. They been that way since histr'y. They the cause the fence was invented."[38] The fact that African American landowners struggled to maintain their landholdings against an elaborate system of racist policies is not surprising, but mechanization and changing agricultural programs accelerated the rate of dispossession. Pete Daniel documents that "when the U.S. Commission on Civil Rights released *Equal Opportunity in Farm Programs* in 1965, it revealed that between 1935 and 1959 white full owners declined by 28 percent and black by 40 percent. The lack of equal opportunity for African Americans showed up in 1959 statistics: black farms averaged 52.3 acres, and white ones averaged 249 acres. Whites earned $2,802 per year; blacks $1,259."[39] Mechanization shifted the fundamental nature of southern agriculture from labor-intensive to capital-intensive, and the farms with capital that invested in mechanization absorbed many of the smaller farms, particularly the farms owned by African Americans, often using predatory means.

As southern farms mechanized, the region's economic infrastructure diversified. Growing cotton became difficult without substantial investment, and displaced farm laborers glutted the labor market. Some cotton fields went out of production, and farmers looked for new sources of income, which resulted in new forms of labor. Brownfield, who embodies sharecropping, has a couple of other occupations that reflect the diversification of the southern economy: "When cotton declined in Georgia and dairying rose, he tried dairying. They lived somehow."[40] As his marriage with Mem declines, she manages to rent a house in town, and Brownfield gets a job in a factory, which reflects the movement of millions of southern sharecroppers into southern cities, where they sought out new forms of work in industries and manufacturing. He works in a frozen pie factory, which he detests because he would prefer to be in the fields, despite his own best interests. "He was in a rage against his own contentment," Walker writes. "It did not seem fair to him that the new work should actually be easier than dairying or raising cotton or corn."[41] Brownfield has difficulty adjusting to factory work, and he returns to sharecropping both for his own comfort and to humiliate his wife. His commitment to sharecropping proves to be malignant, however, making him the antagonist in the story because he impedes progress. His efforts would be in vain, as mechanization would inevitably force laborers off the land, diversify agriculture, and change the economy. The land would also find new uses. Maharidge recounts that Chester Boles, the landowner of Hobe's Hill, "sold the ground to a timber company, which planted pine trees, maybe the best use for this mineral soil. The [sharecropper's] home either fell or was pushed over, and the trees have done well, growing thick."[42] Today, thousands of acres of pine trees cultivated for paper products stand on former cotton fields across the Southern Piedmont.

At the same time that mechanization was bringing sharecropping to an end, the civil rights movement was gaining momentum. These two events were related in several ways. The displacement of millions of African Americans from rural communities into southern cities helped to establish the political and economic capital that made mass movements effective in Montgomery, Birmingham, Atlanta, and other cities. Also, decreased demand for manual labor allowed more children to attend school, such as Ruth Copeland in *The Third Life of Grange Copeland* and Jimmy Aaron in *The Autobiography of Miss Jane Pittman*. In these books depicting the long scope of African American history since Reconstruction, these two characters represent the future, and they are both involved with the civil rights movement. After Ruth encounters a march in Baker County, an interracial group of activists visits her at Grange's home and encourages him to register to vote. Jimmy, meanwhile, attempts to organize a march in Bayonne, but he is murdered on the morning of the march, so Miss Jane leads the remaining sharecroppers on Samson's plantation in the march. These events, which happen at the conclusion of the respective books, signal the end of sharecropping and the beginning of a new chapter in the history of southern African Americans. In 1957, James Street gave an optimistic assessment of the relationship between mechanization and race relations:

> Among the most interesting aspects of the changes in southern agriculture are the decreased dependence on the use of child labor and the eventual reduction of interracial tensions long present in the South. One may easily overrate the importance of a single factor in its effect upon a social attitude so widely held and emotionally rooted as racial discrimination. Yet there is no doubt that the peculiar relation of southern Negroes to cotton as a cheap-labor crop has long fostered the more coercive forms of racial exploitation in the region. A redistribution of the population and a general increase in the standard of living should ease the economic competition which intensifies group hostility. While recent events have shown that these changes can be very disturbing at the outset, the longer run effects are certain to be beneficial.[43]

In retrospect, Street's vision seems prescient yet naïve. The end of sharecropping, which came about fifteen years after he made this statement, did change labor dynamics in the region and did propel the movement for civil rights by African Americans, but racial tensions have proven to be persistent.

In the wake of mechanization, the South changed, and many displaced sharecroppers suffered, at least in the short term. Maharidge opens *And Their Children after Them* with the story of Maggie Louise, who as a young girl charmed James Agee. At about the same time sharecropping came to an end, she committed suicide. "By the time she drank the arsenic, cotton fields were a memory in most of the Old South," he writes. "Maggie Louise's life had transcended the death of cotton, but not by much. Over her four and a half decades, she and most of the other nine million cotton tenants were forced off the land. The journey was harder for some than for others."[44] By the time she died in 1971, southern agriculture used very little manual labor, so African Americans and poor whites were pushed almost entirely out of farming to compete for new jobs. The transition was difficult for some, and the poverty that continues to linger in former cotton plantation areas throughout the South indicates that the transition is still not entirely complete. However difficult the end of sharecropping may have been for many people, it was necessary to create the possibility for a new future. According to Jay Mandle, "The plantation economy did not collapse at once. The diffusion of the new technology was uneven and took time. Nonetheless, the technological requirement for a mass, docile labor force in agriculture had come to an end, thus opening the possibility of the development of a truly new South."[45]

One might wonder if the end of sharecropping left the South better off. Sharecropping was an entrenched system of labor exploitation that institutionalized ignorance, poverty, racial antipathy, and a host of coercive practices, including violence. There was no reason to mourn its demise. For the millions of people who had worked as sharecroppers, however, there were no transitional programs, no opportunities for job retraining, no social safety net, and no politicized attention to their plight to ease their shift into the modern economy. At times, their story emerged as part of broader social agendas such as the Great Society or the War on Poverty, but for the most part, they were ignored. The challenges former sharecroppers faced after mechanization shines a stark light on the political and economic manipulation of sharecroppers between Reconstruction and World War II. After sharecropping, there were new opportunities, and in the long term, the South has collectively developed into a modern, urbanized, industrialized region, although it still bears marks of its extended agricultural primitivism. Looking at the youngest child born to the descendants of the sharecroppers from Hobe's Hill, Maharidge asks some questions about the future. "What kind of world will their unborn heirs face?" he asks. "And what of the millions of others of this same generation who have inherited the legacy of cotton sharecropping? Will they be free of its effects by the time they reach adulthood? Will we as a nation have done right by them? Will they themselves have done enough to purge their lives of the malignancy?"[46] He asked these questions in 1986, and the answers to many of them are still inconclusive.

## Sharecropping and Literature of the Civil Rights Movement

The end of sharecropping had a profound effect on race relations in the South. During the Great Depression, Black and white sharecroppers shared a common economic cause that sometimes superseded racial segregation, as in the case of the interracial Southern Tenant Farmers Union, but the rapid displacement of sharecroppers in the 1950s and 1960s eroded interracial mutuality, leaving African American sharecroppers and day laborers without white economic and political allies. This same time period coincides with the civil rights movement, when African Americans used legal cases, civil disobedience, economic pressure, political suasion, and media exposure to advance the cause of racial equality. The movement's greatest successes occurred in the form of legal decisions in the Supreme Court and in the form of economic boycotts in larger southern cities, such as Atlanta, New Orleans, Montgomery, and Birmingham, that had a sufficient African American population to exert influence. In rural areas, where African American populations were more diffused, the movement struggled, and organizing among sharecropping communities in the 1960s proved to be challenging. Yet sharecroppers and displaced sharecroppers contributed to the movement in some significant ways. Those who migrated into southern cities increased the population density substantially, making the urban movement more effective. The diminished need for manual labor meant that children in sharecropping families were not required to work in the fields during the fall and spring, allowing them the possibility to attend school and placing more pressure on school systems to integrate. Displaced sharecroppers competed with white people for jobs, they used public transportation systems, and they challenged all of the other existing forms of social segregation. Residual sharecroppers working on plantations in rural areas also demonstrated for civil rights in some crucial events of the movement, such as Freedom Summer, showing a will for self-determination, social equality, and economic opportunity.

Several novels published during the years of the civil rights movement fictionalize the movement in the rural South, offering imaginative renderings of the movement that either demonstrate the hardship and pathos that Black southerners endured or create alternative spatiotemporal settings that revise the social circumstances in the rural South. Melvin Kelley describes an alternative version of the South set in an imaginary state in his novel about mass migration, *A Different Drummer* (1959). Carter Brooke Jones's obscure novel *The White Band* (1959) tells the story of a white supremacist organization run by a southern senator, similar to the White Citizens' Council, and its campaign to maintain segregation in the wake of the Supreme Court's decision in *Brown v. Board of Education*. In *Many Thousand Gone* (1965), Ronald Fair imagines a county in Mississippi that Emancipation did not reach, coming very close to describing actual conditions in many benighted parts of the rural South. Ernest Gaines's novel *Of Love and Dust* (1967) is set in the immediate post–World War II period when plantations were transitioning, and it projects much of the tension of the civil rights movement on the plantation as a microcosm of the South. John Oliver Killens's highly underrated novel *'Sippi* (1967) portrays the effects of the civil rights movement on an insular plantation county in Mississippi, and Alice Walker's novel *Meridian* (1976) offers a retrospective on the movement informed by her own experience as an organizer in Mississippi. Collectively, these novels indicate that mechanization changed the culture of sharecropping in the South, eroding the manufactured dependency that planters cultivated to maintain a large, docile labor force and creating some marginal space for social and political agency in rural areas that both revealed the magnitude of racial antipathy and led to some slow, grudging advances in racial equality.

These works are set against the backdrop of civil rights organizing in the rural South. In *You Can't Eat Freedom: Southerners and Social Justice after the Civil Rights Movement* (2016), Greta de Jong explains that one of the key issues for the region's white power structure, which had been dependent on African American labor for decades, was "whether there was a place for African Americans at all" in the South.[47] Between dwindling employment opportunities and powerful resistance to civil rights, millions of African American sharecroppers were displaced, some by force, and many made the decision to leave the South altogether. Those who remained faced the challenge of making a home in their native communities with limited economic opportunity and open, often violent, opposition from white people. This tension between leaving and staying animates the novels set in the South during the civil rights movement. In a scene from *'Sippi*, for example, the protagonist Charles Othello Chaney interviews displaced sharecroppers who have been evicted from their plantations, living in a tent city, and they share their experiences of utter destitution with him. One of them tells him that he lived on the Watson plantation his entire life before being pushed off at fifty-five years old. Exasperated, he says to Charles Othello, "Cropping shares is the only work I ever known. What is we going to do?"[48] Other displaced families echo the same sentiment, indicating their vulnerability, which the tent city, whose makeshift composition suggests a refugee camp, amplifies powerfully. Many rural African American southerners at the end of sharecropping were left with nothing, and in some cases, these desperate people worked with civil rights organizations to demonstrate for their rights. Displaced sharecroppers contributed to the Albany Movement in 1961, Freedom Summer in 1964, the Lowndes County Freedom Organization in 1965, and the Selma to Montgomery Freedom Marches in 1965. For displaced sharecroppers, the issues of economic opportunity and racial equality were joined under the banner of freedom.

The civil rights movement made working on plantations highly precarious, leaving workers vulnerable to exploitation, expulsion, and violence. The novels that depict life on transitional, post-World War II plantations illustrate the dangers of sharecropping during the period of increasing mechanization. Ernest Gaines's novel *Of Love and Dust* is set on Marshall Hebert's plantation in south Louisiana in the late 1940s. The plantation uses a combination of sharecroppers and day laborers, and Hebert has invested in tractors for general use but has not yet purchased specialized equipment for harvesting. The novel's narrator, James Kelly, drives a tractor that he calls Red Hannah, and he describes driving her to the fields in the morning with the day laborers to pull corn while the sharecroppers went "out to their own little patches" to pick cotton.[49] The novel's main character is a man named Marcus, whom Hebert bonds out of jail on a murder charge to work on his plantation as a peon for an extended term. Hebert's overseer does his best to break Marcus, and after a few weeks, Marcus tells James, "I'm a slave here now. And things can't get harder than slavery."[50] Labor conditions are similar on the Wakefield Plantation in Mississippi in the 1950s in John Oliver Killens's novel *'Sippi*. The book opens with the news of the Supreme Court's decision reaching the plantation two weeks after it was handed down, as Jesse Chaney, "the best cotton picking cottonchopper in all of Wakefield County," runs to the big house to share the news with Charles James Richard Wakefield, the plantation owner.[51] Wakefield, "a modernistic Mississippian" who counts "Willie Faulkner" among his friends, runs a transitional plantation using day laborers who "only had to work sixty hours a week" because he believes that "cropping shares is tantamount to slavery."[52] On these transitional plantations using labor-saving machines, laborers still worked on exploitative terms in deplorable conditions with an even greater degree of occupational insecurity.

As grim as these realistic novels appear, other novels offer alternate realities based on sharecropping that emphasize and exaggerate the workers' exploitation. Ronald Fair's novel *Many Thousand Gone* is set in Jacobs County, Mississippi, a vast plantation founded by Samuel Jacobs, whose descendants still run the plantation with slaves as they had before the Civil War. Jacobs "succeeded in isolating Jacobs County from the rest of the world by donating enough land to the state so that all roads in the area, except one well-hidden dirt road, could be detoured around it."[53] The isolation allows Jacobs to keep his slaves in thrall until "they forgot that they had been emancipated. Slavery to them was better than death. They ceased to resist."[54] In this case, spatial isolation allows Jacobs to continue using African American laborers as literal slaves, but the thought experiment here only extends slightly beyond the actual experience of millions of sharecroppers who, though ostensibly free, were held in bondage through debt and coercion. William Melvin Kelley also creates an alternate space in *A Different Drummer*, which is set in "An East South Central state in the Deep South" that borders Tennessee, Alabama, Mississippi, and the Gulf of Mexico. Kelley situates his unnamed state in a space within the deepest part of the South, and he gives it a mythical history that focuses on a Confederate general named Dewey Willson who was elected governor of the state after Reconstruction. Kelley's unnamed state serves as a synecdoche for the South, which makes the book's primary action highly symbolic. In 1957, all of the state's African American inhabitants leave after Tucker Caliban, a descendant of a defiant African king sold into slavery, sows his fields with salt, destroys all of his possessions, and burns his house. The book's overall conceit is that African Americans have no place in the South and should sever all connections with the region.

Whether or not Black people should remain in the South was an important question during the civil rights movement. Between 1940 and 1970, more than five million African Americans left the South, which Killens calls the "Cotton Curtain."[55] In *Of Love and Dust*, Marcus aspires to go to California to work in the shipyards, and in *Many Thousand Gone*, the idea of escaping to Chicago is compared to going to "Hebbin."[56] The vast exodus in *A Different Drummer* reflects the waves of families who left the region. At one point in the book, a white person asks a Black person why he is leaving, and he responds, "It ain't worth fighting because things ain't getting any better for us here."[57] The push and pull factors that contributed to the migration of Africans Americans out of the South have been discussed extensively, but the mass exodus raises several issues that apply specifically to African American sharecroppers during the civil rights movement.[58] Since landowners had used coercive and exploitative means to compel workers to raise crops, workers who were displaced had little reason to remain after mechanization. However, many displaced workers had strong family and community ties that would be broken by leaving the region. Were these connections worth fighting for? Did displaced African Americans have a home in the South? Could they live an equitable and productive life in the South? For millions of African Americans, the answers to these questions was, evidently, no. They did not believe they had a reason to remain in the South. But millions more did remain, either because they saw no significantly better opportunities elsewhere or because they saw something worth fighting for in the South. Those people who saw something worth fighting for, including thousands of current and recently displaced sharecroppers, contributed to the civil rights movement in the South.

Kelley's book heightens the issue of attachment to the land because Tucker Caliban is a landowner. His family worked on the Willson plantation for generations "as slaves and then as employees," one of the Willson descendants explains, "until my grandfather Demetrius broke up the plantation into small sharecropping plots."[59] Tucker purchases seven acres of the plantation from the current landowner, David Willson, initially telling him that he intends to farm and eventually admitting that he sees the land as his birthright: "I want that land on the plantation because it's where the first Caliban worked, and now it's time we owned it ourselves."[60] Willson, who calls the deal "a very strange kind of agreement," explains that he does not know why he sold the land to Caliban, except that "each of us wanted so much individually we helped each other to do."[61] The sale signifies the value of the generations of Calibans who worked on the land, and Tucker's purchase of the land manifests a vision of Black self-determination in the South. Willson's ambiguous reasons for selling the land, however, hint at some underlying problems. As southern farms mechanized, many small farmers who were unable to invest in machines lost their land, which was often purchased and amalgamated into larger farms, so the number of farms dwindled as the average acreage increased. In *Dispossession: Discrimination against African American Farmers in the Age of Civil Rights* (2013), Pete Daniel explains that the number of African American farmers fell by more than 90 percent between 1940 and 1974 due to economic pressures from mechanization and racist policies from the United States Department of Agriculture that limited their access to loans and other forms of government support. Caliban's connection to the land is doubly fraught. As much as he feels that his family deserves to own the land where his ancestors have worked and died, external forces undermine his ability to make the land productive, so his departure suggests that African Americans do not have a viable claim to the South as long as white people dominate the power structure. Eric Sundquist observes that "by buying and then destroying and abandoning his property, Tucker declares that what has been taken from Africans can never be given back," undermining the legitimacy of the white power structure.[62]

The Supreme Court's decision in the *Brown v. Board of Education* case challenged the white power structure. The decision applied specifically to segregated schools, but it effectively overturned *Plessy v. Ferguson*, rendering the practice of separate but equal invalid, paving the way for more legal challenges to racial inequality, and making the civil demonstration phase of the civil rights movement possible. Killens indicates the significance of this decision in the prologue to *'Sippi* when Jesse Chaney approaches the front door of Wakefield's plantation house and shouts at the landowner, "The Supreme Court done spoke! . . . Ain't going around to the back door no more. Coming right up to the front door from now on!"[63] Jesse's exuberance, however, would be short-lived, as the white power structure mounted a response to the decision. In *The White Band*, Senator Joe Duffield organizes a white supremacist organization to challenge the Supreme Court decision and preserve segregation. At a rally, he rants, "I take it most of you have heard what the Supreme Court did back in May. . . . Our granddaddies had hoped back in eighteen sixty-five that the War Between the State was over. But we see we was wrong. They're invadin' the poor old South again. Trying to dictate to us how we'll live our daily lives."[64] The organization, which is modeled on white supremacist organizations such as the White Citizens' Council, recruits thousands of members within weeks, and it uses legal and political means to challenge desegregation in public and violence and intimidation to challenge it in private.

Those who chose to remain in the South and fight for racial equality faced enormous opposition. Jesse Chaney's son, Charles Othello, joins an organization similar to the Student Nonviolent Coordinating Committee while at college, and he is highly aware of the racial tension developing in his hometown during the summer of 1964. "There were wars and rumors of war between the colored and the white all over peaceful Mississippi," Killens writes sarcastically. "Some folks said the trouble started when the Supreme Court struck its first blow for 'Commonism' way back there in 1954," others in the community blame outside agitators, such as the "EN-DOUBLE-A-SEE-PEE," who are plotting "against the genteel southern way of life."[65] The tension mounts when organizers arrive in Wakefield County to register African Americans to vote. Keith Gilyard explains that Killens wrote *'Sippi* to dramatize the civil rights movement in the South. "*'Sippi's* characters," he writes, "are working to seize political power through the ballot box and eliminate the African American casualties at the hands of white supremacists."[66] The novel serves as template for fiction about the civil rights movement because it articulates not only the sense of righteous frustration that African Americans felt after years of coercion and exploitation but also the outrageous ignorance of white people who failed to recognize their common humanity. In the South, racial oppression and economic exploitation were related, and the end of sharecropping heightened the racial tension in rural areas.

During the summer of 1964, Freedom Summer, several civil rights organizations, including Congress on Racial Equality (CORE), the Student Nonviolent Coordinating Committee (SNCC), and the Council of Federated Organizations (COFO), organized hundreds of college students, most of whom were white, to register voters in rural Mississippi. At the time, Mississippi had one of the lowest rates of registered African American voters in the nation, and the goals of Freedom Summer were to register new voters, teach them how to vote through Freedom Schools, and create a slate of candidates who represented their interests through the Mississippi Democratic Freedom Party. From the outset, the organizers faced violence and intimidation, and three organizers—Michael Schwerner, Andrew Goodman, and James Chaney—were abducted, beaten, and murdered. Charles Othello Chaney's name in *'Sippi* recalls James Chaney and his sacrifice, and the title character of Alice Walker's *Meridian* shares the same name as the city from which the organizers were abducted. Meridian Hill in Alice

Walker's novel volunteers as an organizer.[67] A Mississippi native, she notices the interracial group of young people gathered at a nearby freedom house one afternoon, which piques her curiosity, and she later sees on the morning news that the freedom house has been bombed, killing one adult and three small children. Walker uses this scene to foreground Hill's engagement with the movement to illustrate the danger of being involved. Civil rights workers faced considerable risk, yet a month after the bombing, she goes to a freedom house to volunteer. "What was she volunteering into?" the narrator asks. "She had no real idea. Something about the bombing had attracted her, the obliteration of the house, the knowledge that had foreseen this destruction. What would these minds, these people, be like?"[68] Initially, the civil rights workers give her gendered tasks, such as typing, but she eventually takes on leadership roles, such as registering voters.[69]

The registration drive during Freedom Summer was a limited success because many Mississippians recognized the dangers of voting, which made them afraid to register.[70] In one scene in *Meridian*, Meridian and a white female organizer, Lynne Rabinowitz, visit an African American woman, Mrs. Mabel Turner, to register her to vote, but Mrs. Turner is skeptical. "Y'all must be them outside 'taters," she says. "Jooz and runnin' dogs. Y'all hungry?"[71] She feeds them "butterbeans, collards, cornbread, the works," and then tells them, "I wants to feed y'all real good, 'cause I don't believe in votin.'"[72] Meridian and Lynne argue with her, but she refuses to listen. Killens illustrates the perils that African Americans faced for registering: "Cracker plantation owners in nearby counties were running Negro croppers off the land for registering to vote. Churches were dynamited. Four Negroes in Barksdale County found murdered."[73] Killens also demonstrates that, despite the danger, registering to vote was essential not only for equality but also for survival. Charles Othello spends the summer visiting rural families to register voters, where "he saw poverty in its utter nakedness, ignorance in its purity, despair at its greatest depths. He saw people dying of starvation."[74] In one case, he knocks on the door of a family in a remote location and finds "the entire family lying together on a single bed. The coroner's verdict was Death Due to Starvation."[75] Likely, this is a family of displaced sharecroppers who were left to fend for themselves in a place with no opportunities or support for African American families.[76] The right to vote and, thus, the ability to influence the political process was one of the few ways that African Americans could determine their own fate.

In some cases, survival was a form of resistance. Possibly the most abject depiction of African Americans in the rural South during the civil rights movement is Ronald Fair's *Many Thousand Gone*, which is set in a county where slavery never ended. Yet even here, in an isolated community where white people exercise complete authority, people find ways to resist. One of the community elders, known as Granny Jacobs, contrives to subscribe to *Ebony* magazine. The postmaster confiscates the magazine and shows it to the sheriff, who finds the images of successful African Americans in the North infuriating and dangerous. As local white people learn of the magazine, he senses a conflict: "The sheriff realized that something had to be done to stop the people from discussing the magazine. He knew that sooner or later they would decide that the conditions it showed really existed and that some Negroes up north did live better than the whites of Jacobs County."[77] The sheriff fears a riot, but the magazine is itself a form of resistance. An African American lifestyle magazine challenges the notion of white supremacy, and it presents a vision of African Americans as successful and glamourous that runs counter to the culture of segregation. In the context of the civil rights movement, references to the magazine allude to the coverage of Emmett Till's funeral in *Jet* and *Ebony*, which brought national attention to the brutal violence of white supremacy in Mississippi. Emboldened by the images in the magazine, African Americans in Jacobsville send a letter to the president describing their plight and telling him that they are still held as slaves.[78] The letter signifies African Americans in the South petitioning the federal government for civil rights protection, in spite of the risks.

The movement for civil rights prompted an enormous backlash from the white power structure. In *Many Thousand Gone*, federal agents come to Jacobs County to investigate the claims made in the letter, and the county sheriff has them arrested. "The vulgar, illiterate sheriff had outwitted the entire United States government because all the time he had known something they didn't know," Fair writes. "He knew he was at war with Yankee forces; he knew he was fighting the same war his great grandfather had fought."[79] White southerners mobilized to oppose the movement in numerous ways, using their political and economic power to impede progress and using violence and intimidation to prevent people from participating in the movement. One example of white resistance is the White Citizens' Council, a white supremacist organization founded in 1954 in response to the Brown decision. The organization had more than sixty thousand members in the South, and it pressed state and local politicians to oppose desegregation and encouraged business owners to fire African American employees who participated in civil rights activities. In Carter Brooke Jones's book about a fictional white supremacist organization, the White Band, the organization uses all of these tactics, and it also organizes marches through African American neighborhoods of white people wearing masks and carrying placards that read "COLORED FRIENDS, STAY IN YOUR PLACE AND ALL WILL BE WELL" and other harassing slogans.[80] The White Citizens' Council also appears in *'Sippi*. As African Americans register to vote, the council stirs into action to derail the process, led by a local congressman who realizes that African Americans outnumber whites in the county. In a conversation with a plantation owner, he explains the logic of segregation in the postsharecropping South:

> The profit system in Mississippi is based on segregation. If you admit a nigger is your equal, then you've got to give him equal pay for equal work. You take away the poor peckerwood's white superiority, and you got to give him some other kind of compensation. By God, you desegregate the sunny Southland and inside of a decade, the niggers and the peckerwoods will take over everything. Can you imagine how powerful the damn labor unions would be in Mississippi if niggers and peckerwoods got together? How come you think all that new industry is coming down here out of the North? It ain't 'cause they like the smell of honeysuckle. Power, I'm talking 'bout. Political power! Economic power![81]

Even as sharecropping came to an end, obviating the need for abundant agricultural labor, the white power structure had reason to maintain racial inequality for economic purposes. The congressman's statement prophesies the political strategies of the Sun Belt economy that emerged in the South in the last decades of the twentieth century. After sharecropping, white people resisted the civil rights movement to maintain their hold on power.

Killens dramatizes the dangers of the civil rights movement for an African American sharecropper in the story of Luke Gibson. A "quiet faced sharecropper" who works on a plantation belonging to the congressman's brother, Luke decides to register to vote after meeting with civil rights workers.[82] He tells the landowner, "I b'lieve I'll make myself a citizen. I b'lieve itta be the best thing for us, specially my chillum."[83] Enraged, the landowner responds, "You do, boy, and I'll run you offa this farm, you hear me? Run you and your family clean out the county?"[84] Undeterred, Luke registers, and the landowner has him evicted, but Luke refuses to leave, so the sheriff removes all of his possessions from the property, but Luke moves back in, claiming to have a contract from the landowner's first wife that guarantees him a place to work for the remainder of his life.[85] This contract gives him some leverage with the legal system, so he remains on the plantation for a while longer while all of the other sharecroppers who attempt to register to vote are evicted. His act of defiance earns him a reputation as a local folk hero for standing up against "one of the 'baddest' Mister Charlies the state had ever known."[86] Charles Othello Chaney calls him "an example of courage" who "inspired every black man in this county."[87] Later that night, Luke Gibson's cabin is bombed, killing him and his entire family.[88] His story indicates that no African American workers were safe from the white power structure, and his murder inspires both fear and determination, leaving some activists resolved to fight in his memory.

Charles Othello Chaney recognizes that the only viable means to overthrow the white power structure is through the vote, especially in areas where African Americans outnumber whites. "If all the black folk registered who are eligible, we could outvote the white man three to one," he tells a reluctant deacon.[89] In some areas of the South, African American voting had the potential to shift the power structure completely, and characters in *'Sippi* contemplate the possibility of electing a Black sheriff and mayor, which would overthrow the political regime and open the possibility of economic reforms. The campaign to register voters in Mississippi in 1964, however, had limited success. While African Americans had good reason to register to vote to protect their own self-interest, the campaign of white intimidation was overwhelming. In *Freedom Summer* (1988), Doug McAdam accounts that 17,000 people attempted to register to vote during the campaign, but "only 1,600 of the completed applications were accepted by state registrars."[90] While the number of actual registrations was low, the campaign succeeded in exposing the violent and coercive means that whites used to maintain power, such as the murders of the Schwerner, Goodman, and Chaney, and this exposure aroused national support for the Voting Rights Act of 1965. The act made the discriminatory practices that registrars used to deter voter registration, such as poll taxes, literacy requirements, or constitutional quizzes, illegal. In this respect, the campaign was successful, although changes in political and economic power in former plantation areas have been slow.

Some activists demanded more than voting rights. They demanded Black Power. After working to register voters in Mississippi, Charles Othello Chaney encounters a new, radical ideology on Black equality. He meets Stokely Carmichael, who counters Dr. King's mantra of nonviolence with the right of self-defense.[91] The Black Power movement proposed a more assertive form of racial self-determination and autonomy.[92] Even in most plantation areas of the South where Black populations were historically dense, African Americans were a minority population, so voting rights would not be sufficient to secure equality. Advocates for Black Power proposed that minority rights would be better protected through arms and separatism, detaching communities from the white power structure and threatening to counter violence and intimidation with violence. In 'Sippi, an African American minister advocates Black Power: "Did you think all this fighting and struggling over voter registration was just to keep the white man happy? Did you think all this sacrificing was to keep white folks in power? Is that why Luke Gibson gave up his precious blood? Black Power means love of our black selves. It means pushing our black selves up the ladder."[93] His congregation is reluctant, but they eventually join in a chant of Black Power, yet "some faces were frightened even as they shouted Black Power, as if they uttered blasphemy, and perhaps they did."[94] Asserting equality within the power structure was a challenge for many people who had spent their lives in manufactured dependency to landowners. The further assertion of independence and self-reliance was even more difficult for people who lacked education, capital, and resources. Progress required leadership to motivate displaced sharecroppers toward freedom.

Nearly all of the novels about African Americans in the rural South during the Civil Rights Movement feature characters who take on leadership responsibility by challenging the white power structure. In *Of Love and Dust*, Marcus refuses to conform to regimentation on Marshall Hebert's plantation. While most of the workers wear khaki outfits and boots, signifying their role as laborers, he continues to wear flashy clothes, and he seduces the overseer's wife despite the immense risk. He is a problematic leader, however, because he works to liberate himself with no regard for others. Bennett T. Bradshaw in *A Different Drummer* creates a separatist religion, the Black Jesuits, claiming, "We have declared war on the white man! To the white world and all it stands for, we vow death!"[95] He sees Tucker Caliban's act of defiance as a model for other African American communities across the country. Ronald Fair depicts a child known as the last of the first born in *Many Thousand Gone*. The child is special because both of his parents are completely of African American descent. The rape of black women by white men in Jacobs County is so rampant that "many Jacobsville Negroes were light enough to pass for white."[96] The last Black woman in the community has a child by the last Black man in the community, and this child is "a prince who would someday . . . go up north" and find freedom.[97] The leader in *The White Band* is Ned Tarver, the son of sharecroppers, who went to law school with Joe Duffield at Georgetown and is general counsel of the League for Racial Justice, an organization advocating for equal rights. His position pits him against Duffield, with whom he was a close friend in law school. In *'Sippi*, Killens creates a fictional civil rights leader named David Woodson who is modeled on other charismatic figures in the movement, such as Malcolm X and John Lewis. Woodson is a native Mississippian, and he is highly invested in making progress toward racial equality in the state, which leads to tragic consequences. In almost all of these novels, the leader plays a determinant role as a symbolic sacrifice to the movement.

The narrative structure of almost all of these novels leads to racial violence involving the assassination of the leader. The prospect of violence looms over each of the books, with frequent references to lynchings and beatings foreshadowing the inevitable outcome.[98] In *Of Love and Dust*, Marshall Hebert manipulates Marcus to kill his overseer, Sidney Bonbon, which leads to the climactic scene where Marcus attempts to leave the plantation with Bonbon's wife, and Bonbon kills Marcus. By killing Marcus, Bonbon puts an end to the disruption on the plantation. At the end of *A Different Drummer*, a white mob lynches Bennett Barrett because they blame him for causing African American workers to move away, and in *The White Band*, a group of violent thugs affiliated with the White Band kidnap, beat, and murder Ned Tarver. In *Many Thousand Gone*, a lynching party gathers to punish those they believe to be responsible for writing to the president and bringing federal agents to Jacobs County. "They were going to set an example for all Negroes the world over," Fair writes. "They were going to roast Granny and Preacher Harris alive, slowly, as they would barbecue a hog, and then they were going to destroy every single possession owned by any Negro in Jacobs County."[99] Fair, however, inverts the trope of racial violence. The Black people dynamite the town while the lynching party is getting organized, which leaves the sheriff "dumbstruck."[100] Despite the campaign of terror that whites systematically carried out on African Americans in the county for generations, he refuses to believe that they would fight back. "They couldn't do this to us!" he shouts.[101] This book, notably, is the only one that ends with African Americans committing acts of violence against whites. The others end in a way similar to 'Sippi, in which a white man takes aim on David Woodson with a high-powered rifle and assassinates him in public outside Good Hope Baptist Church.[102] This pattern of violence suggests that African American novels about the civil rights movement are tragic and, possibly, defeatist. The books, however, have another message. They assert that sacrifice for the cause of freedom is valid.

The murder of David Woodson is uncannily prophetic because it seems to anticipate the murder of Martin Luther King Jr., who was assassinated a year after the book's publication. 'Sippi concludes with an epilogue that describes the events after Woodson's murder: "Within an hour the news went out around the world. Riots broke out in all the major cities of the United States. Black American soldiers deserted all across the earth. Some of the Black leaders went on national television, looking as if they were in a state of sustained shock, as they undoubtedly were, and called on all Black Americans to stick by their dedication to the Christian principle of nonviolence."[103] Killens's depiction of Woodson's murder predicts the riots and unrest that followed the murder of Dr. King and foreshadows his funeral. "Woodson's body lay 'in state' for five days in the Good Hope Baptist Church," Killens writes. "From morning till late at night when the church closed, the people came, black folks from all walks of life. A long line of blackness that stretched around the church and up the road for ten long blocks. Quiet people, angry people. They came to stare briefly upon his face, and go away perhaps changed forevermore. From his death they hoped to gather strength to live."[104] His description of the mourners searching for meaning in his death resonates with Walker's depiction of King's funeral in Meridian, which was published a few years after Dr. King's murder. Meridian attends the funeral, and she describes the crowds who arrived early "to see, just for a moment, just for a glimpse, the filled coffin."[105] But after the funeral, as the dignitaries leave and the crowds thin, she feels that the attendees miss the meaning of the service. "Those who had never known it anyway dropped the favorite song, and there was a feeling of relief in the air, of liberation, that was repulsive," she thinks.[106]

After Dr. King's murder, the movement lost some of its momentum. Activists and organizers continued to make the case for equality, but the major court decisions, legislative actions, and demonstrations for civil rights came to an end, leaving a complicated legacy. At the federal level, African Americans received a great deal of protection that ended the most overt forms of segregation in schools, businesses, and public places, but these advances ended far short of equality or freedom. In *Meridian*, Lynne and Meridian, who had worked together to organize voters in Mississippi, watch a documentary television show about the movement, "one of those southern epics about the relationship of the Southern white man to madness, and the closeness of the Southern black man to the land."[107] A scene in the show focuses on a beautiful young Black man, "with eyes as deceptively bright as dying stars," who asks a question that evokes Killens's explanation of the logic of segregation in *'Sippi*: "Now that he had just about won the vote, he was saying, where was he to get the money to pay for his food?"[108] Walker, illustrating the complicated legacy of the movement, explains that to Meridian and Lynne "this was obvious" because power has not shifted from white people to Black people even after the movement.[109] "That the country was owned by the rich and that the rich must be relieved of this ownership before 'Freedom' meant anything was something so basic to their understanding of America they felt naïve even discussing it. Still, the face got to them. It was the kind of face they had seen only in the South. A face in which the fever of suffering had left an immense warmth, and the heat of pain had lighted a candle behind the eyes," Walker writes.[110] This beautiful young man symbolizes the rural South after the civil rights movement—traumatized, confused, and abandoned. The collapse of sharecropping and the end of the civil rights movement left many African Americans in the South with more freedom but less opportunity.

### Up from Sharecropping: Postsharecropping Memoirs

The end of sharecropping left an indelible imprint on the southern landscape and population. In *Throwed Away* (1990), Linda Flowers describes driving along miles of mechanically cultivated fields dotted with abandoned shacks. She explains that by the 1960s, "once a tenant farmer died or became too old to farm or the family moved, the land owner would no longer seek a replacement."¹¹¹ As a result, "tenants increasingly found themselves to be unnecessary; owners, especially if they were also farmers, came to rely overwhelmingly on machines, which meant both an unprecedented increase in the number of acres they could farm and a sharp and immediate decrease in the number of people needed to help them."¹¹² She uses the term "throwed away" as the title of her autobiography because it means a thing that "can be in no worse shape. Fields left unattended and overcome with cockleburs are 'throwed away.' Ramshackly houses with boarded-up windows and rotten porches, or country stores that have bitten the dust are 'throwed away.'"¹¹³ For sharecroppers, mechanization progressed slowly during the 1940s and 1950s and then rapidly during the 1960s and early 1970s, pushing millions of workers out of the fields and away from rural communities with surprising haste. Since the 1860s, the system had resisted change as it developed economic, political, and social systems that deliberately ensnared huge numbers of laborers into manufactured dependency by limiting their agency. Because of these systems, the South at midcentury had an ossified one-party political system, rampant illiteracy and poverty, minimal social safety net, and deeply entrenched white supremacy. Through a process of attrition, generational shift, population migration, and economic change, sharecropping wasted away, leaving a new generation to face an uncertain future. The generation of southerners who came of age at the end of sharecropping confronted the frightening yet exhilarating prospect of writing a new story.

Several southerners who lived through this transitional period wrote memoirs and autobiographies that depict how the end of sharecropping and the momentous social forces at play affected their lives and personal development. The postsharecropping memoirs tell stories of trauma rooted in economic exploitation, adaptation to social instability, activism for civil rights, and personal uplift and mobility. These works fit within the broader genre of southern autobiographies that, to use Fred Hobson's phrase, "tell about the South," articulating the region's complicated culture in acts of personal self-discovery. Since the antebellum period, the personal narratives of people from the South have explained the relationship between the individual and the region, often either defending or indicting the region's racial antagonism and social problems in the process, and the prevailing characteristic of southern autobiography is the sense that the region's culture influences the individual's development. J. Bill Berry, for example, states that "family and a sense of place are wedded in southern autobiography."[114] William L. Andrews explains that "the fundamental difference that the southern system of social difference makes in much modern autobiography from the South is this: it makes the notion of individuation—the achievement of personal indivisibility—a persistent, though not always recognized or acknowledged, ideal."[115] Postsharecropping autobiographies illustrate the formative effect of a regionalized system of economic exploitation on the individual and the growth of personal agency that occurs when the exploitative system recedes. Most of these works follow a trajectory of uplift as the individual is born into a sharecropping family and follows a path to personal success. In this sense, these stories are exceptional because only a relatively small number of people born into sharecropping went on to successful careers, but those who did indicate that sharecropping was an impediment to development. In addition to Linda Flowers's *Throwed Away*, postsharecropping autobiographies include *An Hour Before Daylight* (2001) by Jimmy Carter, *A Childhood: The Biography of a Place* (1978) by Harry Crews, *Daddy King* (1980) by Martin Luther King Sr., *Walking with the Wind* by John Lewis (1998), *Separate Pasts: Growing Up White in the Segregated South* (1987) by Melton McLaurin, and *Coming of Age in Mississippi* (1968) by Anne Moody.

The foundational text for this subgenre is *I Was a Sharecropper* (1937) by Harry Harrison Kroll. After he achieved a modest amount of fame and income with his novel *The Cabin in the Cotton* (1931) and the subsequent movie of the same name, he wrote an autobiography that describes his life trajectory from sharecropper to writer. His book establishes many of the normative conventions of postsharecropping autobiographies. He describes his nomadic childhood as his parents move seasonally searching for a favorable sharecropping arrangement. They eventually settle in Cottontown, his depiction of Dyersburg, a small town in western Tennessee. They arrive after the harvest, when landowners are unwilling to take on croppers, so they live in a stable on the city's fairgrounds and subsist on charity from the Ladies' Aid Society. While they live in the stable, a flash flood nearly carries the family away, leaving him traumatized. "To this day, at night when I get chilled," he writes, "I dream of water—of flood waters, eddying suddenly about me in the darkness, while I cling to cotton weed, or grope for a lost road, and cry out for help in the rain."[116] The trauma stemming from economic vulnerability is a common feature of sharecropping autobiographies. Kroll also describes the family's life of ceaseless toil, their inevitable exploitation by landowners, their constant poverty, and their squalid living conditions. The narrative hinges on his decision to escape a life as a sharecropper by becoming a teacher, so he studies on his own to take the state teacher's examination. When he turns twenty-one, he becomes a teacher, and he works his way up to a successful school principal with a family and a middle-class income, while he writes novels and short stories. He receives an unexpected windfall from *The Cabin in Cotton*, which leads predatory family members to seek shares of his income, suggesting that he is unable to escape the effects of sharecropping on his life trajectory.

The autobiographies of people who grew up in sharecropping families relate similar experiences of childhood trauma stemming from economic precarity. Anne Moody's autobiography opens with the sentence, "I'm still haunted by dreams of the time we lived on Mr. Carter's plantation."[117] She tells the story of how her eight-year-old cousin George Lee watched her and her sister, Adline, while her parents worked in the fields. One day, George Lee, who would rather spend his time playing in the woods, sets their cabin on fire and places the blame on Anne, so her father gives her a severe beating. She connects her father's violent reaction to problems with the crop. "A week or so after the fire," she writes, "every little thing began to get on Daddy's nerves. Now he was always yelling at me and snapping at Mama. The crop wasn't coming along as he had expected. Every evening when he came from the field he was terribly depressed."[118] In another traumatic incident, Martin Luther King Sr. recounts seeing a white mob lynch a Black man to steal his pay. Looking at the man hanging from a tree by a belt, he writes, "suddenly I could hear my breathing coming through me harder and harder, and then there was a scream pouring through my lips that nobody could hear but me."[119] John Lewis grew up in an insular, predominantly African American community in Alabama, but he describes having a similar response to the murder of Emmett Till, who was the same age as Lewis. Harry Crews's autobiography catalogs an array of wounds and illnesses affecting both himself and nearly everyone else in his community.[120] He recollects an early childhood memory, for example, in which he nearly blinded himself with lye, and, while his parents rush him to a doctor's office, their cows die from drinking the pesticide his father had been spraying on the crops. After being told the story about the cows years later, Crews reflects, "I have thought a great deal about my daddy in that time, of how tragic it was and how typical. The world that circumscribed the people that I come from had so little margin for error, for bad luck, that when something went wrong, it almost always brought something else down with it. It was a world in which survival depended upon raw courage, a courage born out of desperation and sustained by a lack of alternatives."[121] Sharecropping made people highly vulnerable, making traumatic incidents almost inevitable, and these traumas influenced the individual's course of development.

These traumatic experiences are the result of poverty endemic to sharecropping. John Lewis explains the system's function in *Walking with the Wind*. After the end of slavery, "the plantation owners, of course, remained rich, controlling the tenant farmers by leasing land and furnishing their supplies, then 'settling up' each harvest season at rates that put the farmer— Black or white—further in the hole each year. For most men and women working under this system, it was hardly better than slavery. Everyone worked for 'The Man,' and they were still working for him well into the twentieth century when I was born."[122] Lewis, who would go on to be one of the leaders of the civil rights movement and a congressman, makes several crucial connections in this quote. First, sharecropping is a direct extension of slavery. Second, sharecropping ensnares farmers regardless of their race, although it exploits Black farmers more acutely. Third, the system remained in place for a century after the end of slavery, affecting the lives of people born in the middle of the twentieth century. Finally, and most important, sharecropping is a system of exploited labor that illustrates the connections among economic, social, and political power. In the United States, people in poverty almost always lack power. These points would be important to Lewis's activism during the movement when he and others sought ways to organize people who had lived their entire lives in poverty to assert their rights and seek empowerment. People living in poverty are unlikely to resist power structures and are more likely to be compliant, but the end of sharecropping also eroded the region's entrenched power structures, creating the possibility for activism and change.

Before the end of sharecropping, crops determined the conditions of sharecroppers' everyday lives. Since sharecroppers raised commodity crops for the global market, external market forces regulated their income and their labor, leaving them with little economic agency. John Lewis explains how cotton determined living conditions for his family: "If that farmer was black and living in Alabama in the middle of this century, the rhythm he understood better than any other was the tedious, grinding monotonous rhythm of cotton. He might have raised other crops—maybe some corn, probably some peanuts—but nothing came close to the amount of his land and his time and his energy that was devoted to cotton."[123] In eastern North Carolina, tobacco exerted the same type of force on sharecroppers' lives. Linda Flowers writes, "Farmers on the edge of going under, as tenants always were, had no choice but to grow mostly tobacco and corn and soybeans, and as usual raise a few hogs, since they knew that with its government support tobacco would always sell."[124] Growing up in sharecropping families, these autobiographers experienced the alienation of their families' labor, which left their families dependent on crops for their existence, leading them to internalize a diminished sense of personal agency and value and portray themselves as helpless in the face of overdetermining economic forces.

One of the clearest indicators of the sharecroppers' economic subjectivity was their homes. The autobiographers who grew up in sharecropping families describe their childhood homes as squalid and decrepit. Harry Crews recounts living in a house "made out of notched logs, but instead of being mud-sealed, it was board-sealed, which meant the wind had a free way with it in the winter. My brother had a case of double pneumonia that year and almost died."[125] Most sharecropper's homes were inadequate, and Flowers explains that landlords had no incentive to provide adequate housing for their laborers. "Houses in the worst shape, the porches rotted and rags sometime over where windows had been, houses without underpinning or septic tanks, running water or electricity, more often than not, were tenant homes," she writes. "Not many tenants had the money for fixing up another man's home, even if they had the will and saw the need; most, because they could do nothing else, took the house that came with the land and lived in it. Besides the lack of money there was, too, an unvoiced but determined resistance to doing anything much to a house that didn't belong to you, and from which you might be told to move after the crop was made."[126] The sharecroppers' houses were a tangible indication of their economic subjectivity, which left them in a take-it-or-leave position regarding not only their income but also their living conditions. Their willingness to endure squalor was, in some respects, a form of passive resistance to their subjectivity, but their acts of resistance were frequently misinterpreted as resignation or laziness.

This is clearly a misapprehension because sharecroppers were conditioned to work. Anne Moody describes working in the fields to exhaustion. On her first day chopping cotton, she recounts, "I was scared to look up at the sky because I knew the sun had come up. My heart began to beat like a loud drum. I shook all over. I could almost feel the sun rising in the sky."[127] Working in the fields causes her to have nightmares and anxiety attacks until she develops a tolerance for the work: "After a couple of days and didn't anybody die, my dream began to fade. Soon I even began to like the work. I'd pull off my shoes and let the hot earth fall over my feet as I was hoeing. It sent a warm feeling over my whole body."[128] After working the entire season, however, the family makes no money, and she claims that if "mama's garden hadn't been so good, we would have starved to death that winter."[129] John Lewis also despised agricultural labor. He writes: "I hated picking cotton, and not just for what it was—literally backbreaking labor: planting, picking, chopping, fertilizing, row after row, often on your hands and knees, from one end of a field to the other, sunup to sundown, year in and year out, the blazing Alabama sun beating down so hard you'd give everything you owned for a little piece of shade and something cool to drink."[130] Lewis and Moody were both young children when they first went to work in the fields, and their families depended upon their contributions to produce the crop, but they were not compensated in any way for their work. Instead, they were conditioned to labor exploitation from childhood.

Sharecropping was designed to extract as much labor as possible from workers for the least amount of compensation possible. John Lewis explains the futility of sharecropping, writing, "I hated the work itself, but even more than that, from a very early age I realized and resented what it represented: exploitation, hopelessness, a dead-end way of life."[131] According to Martin Luther King Sr., racism amplified the inherent exploitation. "There was no way to make any money sharecropping," he writes. "Owning your mule, maybe a few cows, this was about as much as a farmer working shares could hope to achieve."[132] He recounts that his father was a hard worker who "never shirked," but to the "whites who owned land around Stockbridge," he states, "a Negro wasn't a human being, but just a thing. Our lives were never real as far as they were concerned and so nothing that might be done to us, no matter how cruel or savage, was real either."[133]

Lewis and King demonstrate how the process of acculturating people to sharecropping strips them of personal agency and aspirations, leaving them to accept a form of economic victimization in order to exist within a highly asymmetric system of power. Looking back on the system, Linda Flowers comments, "nobody wants those days to come again, not the heyday of tenantry in the early 1950s and not the years of its decline once everything changed, once the machines came in, in the 1960s. At best, tenantry still was exploitative; at its worst, it was a kind of slavery."[134]

To illustrate the dangerous inequities in the system, King tells a story about a time when his father was cheated at settlement. When he was twelve years old, he went with his father to deliver the cotton crop to the landowner, Old Man Graves, who had a notorious reputation for cheating his tenants. After weighing the family's cotton and tallying their debts, Graves tells them that they cleared thirty dollars for the year. King, to his father's horror, says out loud, "ain't nothing been said 'bout the cotton seed!" implying that Graves has taken the seed in the cotton without paying for it.[135] Graves threatens to "kick his little butt," but the other white men around the commissary begin to tease Graves about cheating the family out of their money, so he pays them the full amount for their seeds, which brings their income to ninety dollars. This result makes King happy because he believes that he has helped save the family, but it makes his father furious, and the next morning he learns why. Graves and some men come to their cabin, confiscate their mule and tools, and kick them off the land. They pack everything they own into a wagon, but they have no mule to pull it, so they are left completely destitute. King writes, "The look on Papa's face told me we were in trouble. He was in pain. For getting only what was right, what was due him, he now had to get off the shares he'd been working. His family was without a home. What did being 'right' mean, I wondered, if you had to suffer so much for it?"[136]

King's story gives a clear example of how sharecropping demeaned tenant families, leaving them at the mercy of landowners, but even supposedly fair landowners were complicit in a system of exploitation. In *An Hour Before Daylight*, his memoir of growing up on a small plantation in rural Georgia, Jimmy Carter invokes several paternalistic defenses of sharecropping. Ignoring the inherent exploitation in the system, he asserts that "the essence of sharecropping, during the Great Depression as it had been a century earlier, was the freedom of both parties to accept or reject any proposed arrangement."[137] While Carter may have been sincere in this statement, it seems utterly risible in the history of sharecropping, which stripped laborers of any agency to reject a proposed arrangement and empowered landowners to dictate any terms that they chose or to break a contract at any time. Carter does admit that the system could be abused, but he shifts the primary blame for abuse to the sharecroppers. "In all too many cases," he claims, "the poorer sharecroppers failed to produce an adequate cash crop to pay their accumulated debts," implying that sharecroppers are solely responsible for the value and quality of their crops, which are susceptible to weather, pests, fluctuations in the global market, and numerous other external factors beyond the sharecropper's control.[138] When a sharecropper falls into debt, Carter admits, "their negotiating freedom was lost," and he acknowledges that landowners kept the books, which gave them the ability to determine how much a sharecropper earned, and that Black sharecroppers were unable to question the word of white landowners.[139] These two points substantially diminish the ability of a sharecropper to negotiate an arrangement, leaving them vulnerable to exploitation and mired in poverty. Carter eventually asserts that landowners were subject to the same economic forces, leaving them unable to treat their sharecroppers fairly. "Even honest landlords like my father," Carter writes, "who treated tenant farmers with a scrupulous fairness, found it impossible to alleviate their plight."[140] Carter writes fondly of the sharecropping families who lived on his family's plantation, but he fails to recognize the inherent inequities that bound them to his father, the landowner.

The Carter plantation included a commissary, and one of the mechanisms that bound the sharecroppers to the landowner was credit. "On Saturdays," Carter recalls, "Daddy always paid the field hands and gave credit or cash loans to tenants at the commissary store, where he kept careful records of all advances and sales. The poorer farmers who had minimum weekly draws never bought the more costly items."[141] They bought fatback instead of bacon, cornmeal rather than flour, and molasses instead of syrup, and he calculates that more than half of every dollar spent in the store went to food, and a quarter of every dollar went toward interest on the debt. In *Separate Pasts*, Melton McLaurin recounts growing up in a small community in eastern North Carolina where his grandfather ran a store. His grandfather "came through the Depression by selling gasoline to the occasional tourist and to Clarence Lee Tart [the local landowner] for his lumber trucks, 'furnishing' supplies and provisions on credit to farmers who he prayed could and would repay their debts at harvest time, and encouraging the 'trade' of the black community that practically surrounded the store."[142] McLaurin's memoir connects his childhood at the store with his developing racial consciousness because he has the opportunity to grow up in proximity to Blacks, helping them in the store and studying their accounts. He attempts to position himself outside the community's racist dynamics, but he represents himself as using his whiteness to probe into the lives of Black people. "Because they were different," he writes, "outside the white power structure, and because they questioned its values, they more than any other group, except my immediate family, shaped my concept of who I was and my hopes about who I would become."[143] His memoir contains several sketches of his relationships with African Americans that he developed through his grandfather's store. Yet he seems to overlook the key point that the store itself embodied in the white power structure and the middle-class lifestyle that his family lives, with new cars every couple of years and investments in the stock market, is based on the labor of the Black farmers who may or may not be able to pay their debts at harvest time.

As mechanization obviated the need for massive amounts of manual labor, the mechanism that tied people to the fields loosened, forcing many people into destitution, amplifying migration out of the region, and creating a new set of opportunities. People coming of age after World War II had more opportunity than previous generations to attend school, which became a vehicle of social mobility for some children in sharecropping families. When Martin Luther King Sr. was growing up in the 1910s, "a child was always looked upon first as a worker, then as a youngster. . . . As a result, school became a luxury."[144] He was unable to complete school until he was in his twenties and became a pastor. John Lewis recounts that he would sneak out of his house before his father woke up to go to school rather than going to work in the fields. "No one needed to convince me about the value of learning," he writes. "I was absolutely committed to giving everything I had to bettering myself in the classroom. I had no doubt that there was a way out of the world I saw around me and this was the way."[145] Linda Flowers documents that between the mid-1950s and late 1960s, the number of high school graduates pursuing higher education in North Carolina increased by more than 20 percent. While the numbers in rural areas lagged behind the state average, more children of sharecropping families not only graduated high school but also went on to college, often at community colleges or technical schools that opened across the state.[146] Increasing opportunities for education prepared the children of sharecropping families for new occupations, but the occupations they needed were not necessarily available, and much of the racist power structure that had undergirded sharecropping was still in place. The people of the generation coming of age as sharecropping ended were forced to either adapt to a new economy or leave the South and also to dismantle the existing power structure.

Millions of people who worked as sharecroppers made the transition from agriculture to industry. Linda Flowers perceptively assesses this process and its mixed impacts on former sharecroppers. She describes the children of sharecroppers "making the transition from farm to factory. Their parents saw such profound changes in agriculture that they left farming altogether, taking up the jobs that the new industry of the mid-to-late 1960s and 1970s made available."[147] She calls these new jobs "public work," meaning nonagricultural, nonprofessional jobs involving a workplace such as a factory or job site.[148] The economic transition often labeled the Sun Belt brought manufacturing and processing jobs to southern states as companies took advantage of cheap labor and low taxes to grow their workforces.[149] According to Flowers, however, this new employment paradigm followed the contours of sharecropping. She writes, "Public work changed a way of life: in just twenty years from roughly 1960 to 1980, habits and attitudes bred of generations were transformed, and necessarily so. Yet if we but scratch the surface of contemporary life, we'll find much of the tenant and hand, the small landowner—of farmers dispossessed—from whom so many people nowadays in the factory trace their heritage."[150] She admits that southern labor has evolved beyond analogies to slavery, which were frequently invoked to describe sharecropping, but the rigid asymmetries of power that undergirded sharecropping are still discernible. "Tenantry is the compelling metaphor," she claims, because it "evokes the right alembic of pride and abjectness, hardheadedness and compliance, faith and resignation."[151] The results of the economic transition for workers were complicated. On one hand, quality of life and income improved for most working families, but Flowers notes that jobs in southern factories paid low wages, so "public work has no more liberated workers from a debt-ridden, ill rewarded life than did the fields of another era."[152]

As sharecropping ended and the economy transitioned, the region's population shifted, with millions of southerners leaving the South for opportunities outside the region and millions more leaving depressed rural areas for jobs in rapidly growing southern cities.[153] Like many other farmers from south Georgia, Harry Crews's family moved to Jacksonville, Florida, where they lived in a low-rent, industrial neighborhood known as the Springfield Section. He writes, "I had spent a lifetime hearing about the city. Jacksonville came up in conversation like the weather. Farmers' laconic voices always spoke of Jacksonville in the same helpless and fatalistic way. It was a fact of their lives. They had to do it. *Everybody* had to do it. Sooner or later everybody ended up in the Springfield Section, and once they were there, they loved it and hated it at the same time, loved it because it was hope, hated it because it was not home."[154] Moving to the city meant both opportunity and failure for many sharecropping families, signifying an end to a way of life and substituting one form of economic exploitation for another. Crews's mother took a low-paying job rolling cigars in a factory, moving from the cultivation end of tobacco production to the manufacturing end. More recently, however, the migration trends have shifted. Since the 1990s, more people have moved into the South, many of them the children and grandchildren who left the region. John Lewis sees "some hope in that movement, in the belief that the better life so many dreamed of when they left the ugliness and oppressiveness of the South and headed north thirty and forty and fifty years ago might now be found in a place they left behind, in a South that has changed—or been changed—for the better in terms of its treatment of *all* humans."[155] Lewis is correct that the South has changed as the repressive legal, political, economic, and social systems that enforced sharecropping and white supremacy have slowly eroded. He deserves a great deal of credit for that progress personally, but mechanization and the end of sharecropping were necessary conditions for the civil rights movement in the South.

The civil rights movement progressed in tandem with the end of sharecropping. Martin Luther King Sr. recognized that racism was directly connected to economic control. As a young pastor in Atlanta, he "began uncovering the mysteries of the South's racial arrangement."[156] He explains that segregation allowed for the possibility of Black success as long as it did not affect the white power structure, so he could build a prosperous ministry as long as he did not interfere in politics or labor. Challenging the structure, however, would lead to retribution. Melton McLaurin, meanwhile, claims that most white people in his rural community were oblivious to the impending challenges to white supremacy "during the 1940s and 1950s when rumblings of racial change were in the air but before the tumultuous civil rights struggles of the 1960s."[157] He claims that whites in his community expected that any challenges would ultimately fail because challenges to white supremacy had always failed, but as the economic controls of sharecropping weakened, African Americans agitated for civil rights and made tangible progress. Anne Moody grew angry in the 1950s as she learned more about white supremacy. "I was fifteen years old when I began to hate people," she writes. "I hated the white men who murdered Emmett Till and I hated all the whites who were responsible for the countless murders Mrs. Rice told me about . . . but I also hated Negroes. I hated them for not standing up and doing something about the murders."[158] Moody and thousands of other African Americans of her generation eventually channeled their anger and frustration into organization and protest.

John Lewis and Anne Moody were personally involved in the civil rights movement. Lewis's autobiography, *Walking with the Wind,* recounts his childhood in a sharecropping family in Alabama and his heroism during many of the key events of the movement, including the Nashville Student Movement, the Freedom Rides, the Student Nonviolent Coordinating Committee, the March on Washington for Freedom and Jobs, Mississippi Freedom Summer, and the Selma to Montgomery March. Like Moody, Lewis found Emmett Till's murder profoundly affecting. He and Till were the same age, and Lewis realized "he could have been me," which made him feel anger—"anger not at white people in particular but at the system that encouraged and allowed this kind of hatred and inhumanity to exist."[159] He committed to join the movement after hearing Dr. Martin Luther King Jr. preach and realizing that the Supreme Court's decision in *Brown v. Board of Education* signaled a change in race relations. Moody became involved with NAACP and SNCC while she was a student at Tougaloo College. She and a white student, Joan Trumpauer, and Rev. Ed King staged a sit-in at the Woolworth's in Jackson, Mississippi, and Moody helped to register voters in the Delta during Freedom Summer. While working there, she recognized that sharecropping and white supremacy had conditioned African Americans to avoid confrontation. "Most of these old plantation Negroes had been brain-washed so by the whites, they really believed that that only whites were supposed to vote," she writes. "The only thing most of them knew was how to handle a hoe."[160] Making progress for civil rights would take great personal risk and many years to undo the legacy of sharecropping. To a great extent, this process remains unfinished.

The movement did make some tangible progress, changing policies and raising consciousness. Melton McLaurin's *Separate Pasts* describes the racist power structure in rural eastern North Carolina, and McLaurin strenuously attempts to describe his divergence from the community's prevailing racism. The book, for the most part, is an example of what Fred Hobson describes as a "racial conversion narrative." In *But Now I See: The White Southern Racial Conversion Narrative* (1999), Hobson analyzes several post-World War II autobiographies by middle-class white southerners that seek redemption, either personally or collectively, for the region's racism. Many of the authors he discusses, such as Lillian Smith, James McBride Dabbs, Katharine Du Pre Lumpkin, and Willie Morris, came of age before the civil rights movement but were not directly involved in the movement, although they were sympathetic with its objectives. McLaurin was not personally involved in the movement either, but his autobiography indexes the South's progress on issues of race and economics. In an epilogue to the book, he returns to his hometown in 1997, and he describes the community's economic devolution as much of the population and business has moved from the rural areas into surrounding cities, such as Fayetteville, Raleigh, and Wilmington. What remains in his hometown, however, is a newly ascendant Black power structure, with an African American mayor and some successful Black-owned businesses. He ends the book with a conversation between himself and an African American childhood friend who remained in his hometown, and he asks about the residue of racism in the community after segregation. His friend states, "It's in you, and it's in me, and that's the truth, down there inside us. That's just the way it is."[161] His statement affirms McLaurin's sense that racial progress remains incomplete decades after the end of sharecropping and the civil rights movement.

Postsharecropping autobiographies as a genre reflect the region's progress in the second half of the twentieth century. For the most part, these books are success stories, reflecting the author's uplift from impoverished sharecropping families to productive careers. Martin Luther King Sr. grew a thriving ministry among the African American community in downtown Atlanta, became a major figure in local politics, and raised a son who probably had a greater impact on the twentieth-century South than any other individual. Harry Crews, Linda Flowers, and Melton McLaurin went on to careers as professors teaching at universities in the South, which positioned them to contemplate the region's development. Anne Moody, traumatized by her childhood in Mississippi, settled in New York, where she lived quietly before returning to Mississippi to be near her family in the 1990s. John Lewis went from cotton fields to Congress, becoming one of the most revered figures in the United States House of Representatives. Jimmy Carter went from a modest plantation in rural Georgia to the White House. For each of these people, the opportunities that emerged as a result of the end of sharecropping contributed to their success, which forms the crux of their personal stories. Notably, with the exception of Kroll, sharecropping autobiographies were effectively nonexistent in the generations before the end of sharecropping, partly because the lack of access to education and economic opportunity made writing life stories difficult. However, these stories are also exceptional. Many people struggled to adapt to the changes taking place in the South, and their stories are rarely told.

Linda Flowers assesses the legacy of sharecropping on her generation astutely. "Looking back, however," she writes, "the remarkable thing finally is not how much at loose ends this generation of workers was, but how resilient they were" as they adapted to dynamic circumstances for which they were unprepared.[162] Despite the exploitation, trauma, and oppression, sharecroppers adapted the best they could out of necessity, usually with minimal resources, and often with mixed results. The children of sharecroppers lived very different lives from their parents, and the grandchildren of sharecroppers would be effectively unrecognizable to their grandparents. "These are proud people," Flowers writes. "Throwed away they may be, but it won't do to count them out. Men and women, who have seen how, in the 1960s, machines pushed up the demand for land, even as they made farm laborers increasingly obsolete, who have experienced the breakup of smalltime agriculture, yet who have kept going nonetheless, kept looking ahead—they know they're up against a hard time, but they know, too, they'll make it somehow: they always have."[163] In the long term, the end of sharecropping has led to the emergence of a different, more diverse South, but the region still bears vestiges of its repressive, exploitative past, and many southerners still carry the physical, psychological, and sociological scars of sharecropping.

The mechanization of sharecropping radically altered labor relations in the US South. After centuries of intensive manual labor producing commodity crops, the paradigm shifted as tractors, mechanical cotton pickers, and herbicides eliminated the need for enormous pools of exploitable labor. The end of sharecropping revealed the underlying structure of debt, coercion, paternalism, and violence that reinforced the system, as well as the function of manufactured dependency in southern labor. While landowners depended upon sharecroppers' labor, they devised an elaborate series of controls to make the sharecroppers dependent upon the crop. Once landowners no longer needed the sharecroppers' labor, they ended the arrangement, either letting families leave through attrition or forcing them off the land. The displacement of millions of sharecroppers reshaped the South's social structure. A large percentage of displaced sharecroppers moved into southern cities, leading to an urbanization boom in the South, where they competed for jobs in industries and services, which drove down wages and furthered the growth of the Sun Belt economy. The population shift also contributed to the civil rights movement as concentrations of African Americans in southern cities exercised sufficient social and economic force to end some segregation practices and create more opportunities for social equality.

Southern literature reflects the profound impact of mechanization and the end of sharecropping on the region. The extended scope of *The Autobiography of Miss Jane Pittman* and *The Third Life of Grange Copeland* capture the process of mechanization as it unfolds, reflecting the instability and precariousness that sharecroppers endured during this period, and *And Their Children after Them* offers a direct comparison with a small sharecropping community fifty years after the Great Depression, revealing how their lives have changed, mostly for the worse, after the end of sharecropping. Novels of the civil rights movement set in the rural South, meanwhile, indicate that the struggle for civil rights for rural Blacks was difficult. Mechanization made them even more vulnerable to displacement and violence, and the novels that portray this process, such as John Oliver Killens's *'Sippi*, tend to have tragic endings. The autobiographies and memoirs of people who lived through the transition from sharecropping to mechanization illustrate the instability of the process as they left the communities and circumstances that their families had endured for generations. The end of sharecropping led to new opportunities for the autobiographers personally, but their stories demonstrate that their stories are exceptional because most sharecroppers making the transition to the postsharecropping economy struggled. All of these texts reveal that the end of sharecropping was complicated for people who had been conditioned for agricultural labor for generations.

While mechanization ended sharecropping as a system of labor, the social and cultural effects of generations of labor exploitation continue to affect the South. The residue of sharecropping lingers in numerous persistent ways in the landscape, in the population distribution, in race and class relations, in immigration patterns, and in new forms of labor exploitation. Although sharecropping effectively ended by the early 1970s, it continues to influence southern culture today, and understanding the cultural history of sharecropping is critical to understanding the South. Southerners are living in the afterlife of sharecropping.

→ 6 ←

# The Afterlife of Sharecropping

Tim Scott, the first African American Republican senator to represent a southern state since Reconstruction, gave a keynote speech at the Republican National Convention in 2016. He used his family story as an example to illustrate his confidence in the viability of class mobility under a Republican administration, saying that his family "went from cotton to Congress in one lifetime."[1] Four years later, Raphael Warnock, the first African American Democratic senator to represent a southern state, used a similar reference in his victory speech in 2020. He discussed his mother, Verlene Warnock, who worked in cotton fields in the 1950s, and to illustrate the racial progress that had taken place in her lifetime. He said, "The 82-year-old hands that used to pick somebody else's cotton went to the polls and picked her youngest son to be a United States senator. The improbable journey that led me to this place in this historic moment in America could only happen here."[2] In both of these speeches, picking cotton as a synecdoche for sharecropping serves as a trope to indicate an overwhelming system of racial oppression and economic stagnation that contrasts with the symbolic accomplishments of these two exceptional individuals. Their success appears to indicate that the end of sharecropping has led to the possibility of social mobility in the South, but the enduring legacy of racism, social inequality, and rural population decline in the region indicates that the afterlife of sharecropping still influences the social, economic, and cultural patterns in the US South.

The landscape of the rural South has changed since mechanization eliminated the need for massive manual labor. In the middle of the twentieth century, a nearly unbroken network of fields dotted with meager cabins punctuated with crossroads communities, stores, and churches stretched from southern Virginia to eastern Texas. Over the past several decades, the cabins have been removed as laboring families have been pushed out of sharecropping, the stores have closed, and many of the church congregations have dwindled. In some areas, the fields of cotton and tobacco have been replaced with soybeans, corn, and commodity pine trees as cotton production has shifted to the Southwest. The crossroads communities show signs of depopulation and decay as millions of people from rural areas have moved to cities, leaving agricultural work for manufacturing or service industry jobs.[3] The changes in the landscape reflect changes in the socioeconomic system, but, like a palimpsest on the land, vestiges of sharecropping remain in the fields and the communities, and the legacies of a coercive system of labor continue to affect race relations, income disparities, mass incarceration, educational attainment, health outcomes, and a host of other social problems. The end of sharecropping raises some complicated, long-lasting issues about agriculture in the South, the turbulent changes in southern labor, continuity and change in the region's culture, and the US South's relationship to the Global South.

Southern agriculture has always been part of global networks of commodity exchange. Colonists came to the South to develop plantations to raise agricultural products for the European market, hoping to replicate the success of sugar plantations in the Caribbean and South America. In the colonial and early national period, landowners imported slaves as part of the transatlantic slave trade and sold a small number of products, primarily tobacco and rice, to European markets. With the invention of the cotton gin, the plantation system exploded in the southern US, and cotton flooded the global marketplace, propelling the industrialization of Western Europe and supporting the development of the US financial system. For more than a century, the United States was the world's leading producer of cotton, but the profound alienation of southern laborers from the global marketplace led to a perception of the South as insular.[4] This insularity, however, has declined significantly as the tobacco industry in the United States has dwindled, as cotton has mechanized, and as other nations, such as India, China, Uzbekistan, and Mexico, have increased their cotton production, toppling the United States as the world's leading producer.[5] "Globalization is nothing new in the empire of cotton," Sven Beckert writes, "but the ability of capitalists to utilize a number of states and thus remain free of the demands of all of them is new."[6] Neoliberal globalization has accelerated the process of change in many systems of commodity production as corporations use massive systems of transportation and new technologies to expand markets and decrease production costs.[7]

Neoliberal globalization has consolidated capital and marginalized laborers, compounding the alienation and displacement of southern agricultural workers. The process of dispossession that began with mechanization after World War II has accelerated with global flows of capital in the twenty-first century, effectively stripping southern agriculture of its traditional labor pool. Today, machines perform the vast majority of the work involved in cultivating cotton and producing textiles, and international corporations have moved production facilities to places where labor costs are lowest, such as Pakistan or Vietnam. Meanwhile, immigrant laborers from Mexico and Central America have taken many of the menial jobs in agriculture and processing in the South. In addition to a host of other impacts on the region, these processes expose the function of manufactured dependency that landowners used to bind sharecroppers to their crops. The landowners were dependent upon cheap, abundant labor, so they contrived an elaborate system to force laborers to produce crops. This method, however, was not unique, and Beckert states that "the violence of market making—forcing people to labor in certain locations and certain ways—has been a constant throughout the history of the empire of cotton."[8] Without the need for cheap labor, southern agriculture has effectively abandoned the labor force, leaving rural communities to decline and forcing workers to leave for other opportunities or fall into abjection.

The South was the nation's number one economic problem during the Great Depression because sharecropping forced millions of workers into poverty. Today, the residue of sharecropping continues to define the region's social structure, political polarization, and cultural output, but, much like the vague outlines evoking the placement of cabins in cotton fields, the effects are not always readily discernible. Americans have a tendency to forget about sharecropping as the economic paradigm that dominated the South for a century, yoking slavery to freedom and ossifying the region's race and class stratification. Thus, we are less likely to see how the afterlife of sharecropping continues to resonate in the South and less likely to understand how the South progressed from Emancipation to the present. If we focus our attention, however, we can find the ongoing influences of sharecropping on the contemporary South. The region has changed in some radical ways, becoming more urban and cosmopolitan, but those changes have much to do with the end of sharecropping, which has forced populations to move and consolidate in urban areas. The economy has also expanded, at least partially because the end of sharecropping has allowed for greater diversification and innovation in the region. For many parts of the rural South, however, the end of sharecropping has been a story of decline.

### Relics of Sharecropping: Contemporary Cotton Farming in Mississippi

Decline is most evident in the areas that were highly dependent on sharecropping, such as the Mississippi Delta. "Thirty years ago, when I first came to the Delta," Gerard Helferich writes in *High Cotton: Four Seasons in the Mississippi Delta* (2007), "the landscape was still punctuated with the relics of sharecropping—unpainted shacks with their roofs stove in and their flimsy porches buried in kudzu, faded plantation stores with names barely legible above the doors through which so many tenants had passed in anticipation and dread. Though you have to look a little harder to find them now, these memorials remain."[9] Helferich's book documents cotton farming in Mississippi in 2005, the year when Hurricanes Katrina and Rita hit the Gulf coast, and the book blends the history of cotton production, which he claims "determine[d] the history of the Delta and the South, [and] shaped the story of the nation," with a yearlong accounting of a Mississippi cotton farmer growing a crop using modern methods.[10] In a follow-up article published in 2014, "White Gold," he revisits the same farmer to describe the changes that have taken place in cotton farming over the following decade. These nonfiction narratives offer a useful lens through which to observe the afterlife of sharecropping in the Delta, the place James Cobb once labeled "the most southern place on earth."[11]

Helferich focuses on Zack Killebrew, a descendant of Mississippi sharecroppers who has been farming in the Delta since 1975, when some of the labor was still being performed by hand. Over forty years of cotton farming, Killebrew experiences many changes in cotton farming, but the most significant change is the growth of scale. Killebrew runs a medium-sized operation, but Helferich notes that cotton farms are expanding, with most farmers having seven thousand acres in cultivation and some growing up to forty thousand acres. "It hasn't been just greed driving this growth but survival," Helferich notes. "To stay in business, small farmers have to expand."[12] Cotton farmers face several pressures driving the race to expand, including international cotton prices, costs of mechanization, dwindling labor supply, and uncertainty about government subsidies, and all of these pressures are to some degree a result of neoliberal globalization. The result is that capital is consolidating, and many farmers are being forced out. Pointing to a fifty-acre plot that his father once farmed, Killebrew says, "It used to be a man could make a livin' on that much land. Now you got to have thousands of acres to make any money. . . . we've got so much foreign competition. It's discouragin' to know you don't have enough land to be able to make any money. Overhead is so high you can't make nothin.'"[13] Cotton farmers regularly face the prospect of losing money because profit margins are slim owing to international competition, so the industry relies on government price supports and subsidies to remain viable.

Significant international competition in the cotton market is a recent phenomenon. D. Clayton Brown explains in *King Cotton in Modern America* (2011) that US cotton dominated the global marketplace for decades, as most countries that produced cotton used it in their own domestic production rather than selling it abroad, but with the collapse of the Soviet Union and the rise of the Chinese economy, major competitors emerged, and the US share of the global market has shrunk.[14] Global competition has lowered the price for cotton, and "thanks to a worldwide glut, the price of cotton had been flat for decades, even as costs such as land rent, fuel, and fertilizer had climbed."[15] At the same time that global competition has lowered prices, it has led producers to seek cheaper means of production because the producers with the lowest costs are more likely to make money. Depressed labor markets in parts of Asia, for example, produce cotton for lower costs, so international producers are more likely to increase production in those areas. Sven Beckert observes that "the empire of cotton has continued to facilitate a giant race to the bottom, limited only by the spatial constraints of the planet."[16] The Delta remains trapped within a system of entrenched poverty that hampers its ability to generate new industries and to compete with the global labor marketplace. "The area desperately needs jobs," Helferich writes, "but employers are loath to locate here, given the low educational attainment of the workforce. There's tremendous competition for shrinking non-profit and government funds, and Delta communities generally haven't shown the close black-white cooperation needed to make their strongest case to potential donors."[17] He quotes Jo Prichard, director of development for the Mississippi Center for Nonprofits, who says, "With the new global economy, the Delta must compete for jobs with Third World countries like India, and that's an uphill struggle."[18] Globalization has placed pressure on all aspects of the cotton growing system.

The response to these economic pressures on the federal level for the past several decades has been price supports and subsidies. According to Paulette Ann Meikle, "Agriculture in the eleven Delta counties is highly dependent upon subsidies from the federal government. From 1995 to 2010, farm subsidies to the eleven Delta counties totaled more than two billion dollars, supporting about 3,000 farms. On average, individual farmers received more than $80,000 per year."[19] How much a farmer receives in a year depends on several factors, including drought, international competition, and domestic politics. Helferich explains that in a best-case scenario when Killebrew produces a large crop, he can expect to receive a $40,000 direct payment from the government, but if the crop suffers, he can receive up to $350,000 in price supports and countercyclical payments. "It is largely through this government assistance that cotton is still a viable industry in the United States," he writes.[20] These subsidies are politically contentious for a few reasons. First, they disproportionately benefit larger farmers, allowing larger farms to make greater capital investments and to consolidate land and resources. Second, while the government subsidizes several crops, including corn and soybeans, cotton receives the largest aggregate subsidy, and it only benefits a small number of states, so the program comes under intense scrutiny when Congress debates a new farm bill. Third, US subsidies give American farmers a competitive advantage on the international market, undercutting the actual cost of production and flooding the market with underpriced cotton. Beckert notes, "In 2002, Brazil lodged a lawsuit against the United States through the World Trade Organization, alleging that the government's cotton subsidies violated its own previous trade commitments."[21] As a result of the settlement, the United States also supports Brazilian cotton farmers. "For the poorer nations," Helferich comments, "it's an issue of economic justice. For Zack and his neighbors, it's a question of survival. Already struggling even with the subsidies, they can't imagine getting by without them."[22]

The subsidies, a holdover from the Agricultural Adjustment Act payments instituted during the Great Depression, are important because contemporary cotton production is capital-intensive. Sharecropping was a labor-intensive system, but as cotton production has become more mechanized, it involves increasingly expensive, sophisticated machines to replace the need for manual labor. "Technology drives cotton farming," Clayton Brown writes. "It is not unique in this respect, but modern farmers' adaptation of technology and the willingness—almost the rush—to experiment with advances contrast with cotton farmers of a half century earlier, who were known to stick with old habits."[23] Contemporary cotton farmers use planting devices enabled with GPS to plant seeds in densities and depths tailored for specific soil compositions. Sophisticated cotton pickers, such as the John Deere 7760, pick fields and automatically roll the cotton into two-ton bales, and one machine, which retails for nearly $600,000, can pick more than five thousand acres in a three-week span using just three people. When Gerard Helferich studied Zack Killebrew in 2005, he used a pair of John Deere 4960 tractors: "Thanks to chemicals and machines, Zack can work his farm with two full-time employees and two part timers, instead of the dozens of hands it would have taken a hundred years ago."[24] In 2014, Zack's sons, Heath and Keath, use even more expensive machines that "sell for more than $800,000, [but] to Heath and Keath, and to other planters with enough acreage to justify the expense, they're invaluable. The Killebrews have purchased four. If it weren't for the devices, the brothers have told me, they wouldn't grow cotton at all."[25] For them, the cost of expensive equipment is more productive than the cost of labor, and these machines improve efficiency and increase scale and productivity.

Machines are not the only technology involved in contemporary cotton farming, however. Sharecroppers spent the majority of their labor planting cotton, chopping cotton to reduce weeds, applying poison to fight boll weevils and other pests, and picking cotton. Today, machines accomplish the work of planting and picking cotton, and chemicals accomplish the work of weed control and pest control. Nearly all of the cotton planted in the United States today is genetically modified to be resistant to the most commonly used glycophosphate herbicides such as Monsanto's Roundup, so the herbicide can be applied to the entire field, and they also contain a gene from the bacteria *Bacillus thurengiensis,* or "Bt," that makes them resistant to many pests. The seeds that Zack Killebrew uses are also coated with fungicide and insecticide, so the seeds he plants, which are naturally brown, have been "given a bright-blue chemical jacket bearing little resemblance to anything in the plant kingdom."[26] These modified seeds are expensive, costing $7.50 a pound. In addition to the costly seeds, contemporary cotton farming involves expensive fertilizers, herbicides, and pesticides. Describing a typical workday for the farmer, Helferich writes, "Cotton farming is a chemical-dependent business, and Zack will spend much of his time today shuttling between the fields and the seed store, ferrying supplies to his men. Inside the firm's corrugated metal shed, which once housed a cotton gin, dozens of fertilizers, insecticides, and other products wait on pallets, their cases stamped with muscular brand names like Armor and Touchdown."[27] Some of these chemicals will be applied using tractors in the fields, and others, such as the defoliant used to remove leaves from the plants before picking, will be spread by crop dusting aircraft.

Contemporary cotton farming in the United States is a high-technology field that has complicated effects on international trade, the environment, and domestic labor. While Helferich focuses much of his attention on Killebrew's investment in technology, the greatest change in cotton farming over the past few decades is the amount of labor required to produce a crop. Killebrew maintains just two full-time employees, Charlie and Johnny, and "like generations who worked the Delta before them, Charlie and Johnny, are black."[28] Helferich's nod to the generations before them connects these two men to the legacy of slavery and sharecropping and implies that Charlie and Johnny are likely descendants of generations of Black people who have worked on cotton farms in the Delta. "The plantation era left a legacy that has had a significant impact on current conditions in the region," Paulette Ann Meikle notes, "as it created the foundational structure that was in place as globalization began to shape the Delta."[29] In other words, contemporary labor relations bear the marks of decades of racial paternalism and oppression. Helferich writes:

> For some of Zack's workers, children of the Delta's black sharecroppers, what's so striking is not how much has changed over a generation but how little. Like their parents, they may still derive their living from working cotton on white men's land—and no longer even as tenants,

but as wage workers, having reverted to the practice rejected by their predecessors. The early black sharecroppers at least had the hope of one day buying some land of their own. But the current generation is apt to share the later tenants' view that for them, nothing is about to change for the better.[30]

Helferich's tone in this passage reeks of paternalism and pessimism, but he is correct that the end of sharecropping has been complicated for the descendants of sharecroppers, leaving them little opportunity in the land where their ancestors worked for generations.

Considering the lack of opportunity in the area, Helferich writes, "many of those with the ability and means continue to leave the Delta, realizing the escape that their sharecropping forebears yearned for nearly a century ago."[31] The Delta's population declined by almost one third between 1945 and 1970, and the decline has continued since then. According to the 1970 census, the Delta's population was 313,000, and it dwindled to 223,000 in 2010.[32] Technology may be a chief reason for population decline because "mechanization and chemicals drastically reduced the need for workers in the fields," but the population decline is more complicated than a single issue.[33] Sharecropping was a form of exploitation labor through economic coercion, and Helferich claims that "it could be said that technology finally freed the slaves, or at least the end of sharecropping, . . . and now freed from the yoke of cotton, they began to demand their civil rights."[34] He suggests that the end of sharecropping was a benefit because it allowed former sharecroppers, specifically African Americans, greater access to mobility and propelled the civil rights movement, leading to voting rights and economic opportunity. Despite these advances, progress has been uneven, leaving people like Zack's workers mired in poverty. Helferich struggles to explain why this is the case: "Some suggest we still haven't done enough to offset the economic dependence, the disruption to family life, and the lack of education wrought by centuries of slavery and sharecropping."[35] While some may perceive the end of sharecropping as liberating, the lack of other opportunities compounded with the absence of a social safety net and educational development means that millions of people have been effectively forced to leave their homes for the prospect of work elsewhere, which is not guaranteed. Meanwhile, the entrenched poverty that lingers in many of the most productive cotton areas, such as eastern South

Carolina, central Georgia, southern Alabama, and the Mississippi Delta, reveals the long-term consequences of labor exploitation. Declining population in these areas is a symptom of a problem, not a solution.

This shift in population and economic opportunity has led to a pattern of uneven development labeled "two Souths." As Anderson, Schulman, and Wood explain, "Metropolitan areas are expanding as new high technology and service industries connect them to the global economy. Rural regions that initially grew because of their ability to attract manufacturing jobs are declining. In addition, new immigrants are taking the place of African Americans at the bottom of many southern labor markets."[36] This uneven development phenomenon clearly affects the Delta. At Holmes Gin, the local cotton processing plant that Helferich describes in Tchula, Mississippi, all but two of the employees are Mexican. The gin owner tells Helferich "they're better workers than the local people, more reliable with more initiative."[37] Hiring immigrant workers amplifies the economic inequities in the community. "The foreign workers at the gin mean that the overwhelmingly black residents of Tchula don't benefit from those jobs, temporary though they are. But since the introduction of the mechanical picker and weed-killing chemicals, the high jobless rate in the Delta has always fallen most heavily on African Americans," which Helferich identifies as part of a generational pattern of exploitation.[38] "Their ancestors were brought to the Deep South to plant cotton, and for nearly a century after Emancipation, the black sharecroppers remained bound to the same fields. Then when their labor was no longer needed, they were expelled from the land, either to find work in the cities or to languish in the same towns that their forebears helped to build."[39] This pattern of uneven development is one of the clearest indications of the afterlife of sharecropping because global labor migrations have shifted immigrant workers into exploitative rural occupations, such as agriculture and chicken processing, and forced the local population to seek positions in manufacturing or the service industry in expanding urban areas.

Contemporary cotton production continues to be problematic, creating issues in international trade, environmental protection, and domestic labor decades after the end of sharecropping. "For three centuries," Helferich writes, "relations between the races were dictated by cotton's demand for cheap abundant labor. Today that need is gone, but cotton continues to haunt our racial landscape just as it still dominates the flat sultry landscape of the Mississippi Delta."[40] Considering the problems involved with cotton production, one may reasonably wonder why farmers continue to grow it and why politicians continue to subsidize it. When cotton consumption declined in the 1970s, cotton producers banded together to create a glossy corporate entity, Cotton Incorporated, that rebranded cotton textiles, distancing cotton from its difficult history and making emotional appeals to consumers, and the combination of marketing and political lobbying has largely stabilized cotton's market share among American consumers.[41] Competition from international producers, however, is more difficult to address, and cotton production in the U.S. is declining. In his follow-up article, "White Gold," Helferich revisits Zack Killebrew, who has quit cotton farming and switched to peanuts. Beginning in 2007, two years after *High Cotton*, "the crop plummeted, until three years later barely 300,000 acres were planted statewide. For 2013, the National Cotton Council of America projected that figure would be only about 200,000, but when the wet spring delayed planting beyond the window for corn, cotton acreage rose to 320,000—still a drop of 73 percent from the season that I spent with Zack."[42] Global economic currents will dictate cotton's future.

Today, cotton projects an image as a modern agricultural industry. Clayton Brown claims that "cotton only rarely catches the attention of journalists and essayists because the suffering and oppression of tenants are no longer an issue, and novelists can only refer to a time past if they wish to conjure up the drama and pathos of cotton. Though poverty is visible in cotton-growing areas, the pain that went with sharecropping and migrant labor has fortunately gone, but so has the romanticism."[43] He suggests that sharecropping is consigned to the past, but the legacy of sharecropping continues to affect the present. Looking closely at the visible vestiges of poverty in the region, we can find influences of sharecropping on racial and economic inequality across the South that affect the lives of millions of people and that continue to influence social, political, and cultural practices. We can also see that while sharecropping is a feature of historical novels, such as John Grisham's *A Painted House* or Hilary Jordan's *Mudbound*, the legacy and practice of labor exploitation continues to resonate in southern literature and culture.[44]

## "Progress, Maybe": Literature of Postsharecropping Labor

The documentary *LaLee's Kin: The Legacy of Cotton* (2001) focuses on the family of Laura Lee "LaLee" Wallace, a former sharecropper from Tallahatchie County, Mississippi, and it exposes the challenges facing a community after the end of sharecropping. It opens with several members of the community recalling sharecropping and describing their experiences picking cotton and the coercive living conditions they endured, but they commonly lament that, since the emergence of mechanization, there are no jobs available in the community. Lalee lives in a mobile home paid for with government assistance, and she depends on federal disability supplements to live. The home has no running water or telephone, and she cares for several of her grandchildren and great-grandchildren, who attend an underfunded, underperforming school. In one scene, Lalee scrounges together broken pencils and loose-leaf paper to give to her great-grandchildren so that they can go to school, where they are pressured to pass a high-stakes test to get the school system off probation. The school superintendent explains that the system's lag is the result of generations of employment exploitation. During sharecropping, schools were closed during cotton harvest, and many of the people of Lalee's generation are functionally illiterate, which has led to cascading generations of poor education and lack of opportunity. Since the end of sharecropping, the community has been left with enduring social problems, including entrenched poverty, low educational attainment, high rates of unemployment, poor health care, drug use, mass incarceration, and pervasive hopelessness. Although sharecropping ended by the 1970s, its legacy continues to affect the lives of people in former sharecropping areas.

Several novels depict agricultural labor in the South in the generation since the end of sharecropping, and they illustrate that the social structures that supported sharecropping continue to resonate in the region's culture. These novels indicate that rural, agricultural communities struggle with poverty, population decline, scarce employment opportunities, and a host of other long-term social problems that stem from the cultural residue of sharecropping. They also depict agricultural labor in the South as inherently exploitative because it still employs many of the same devices to coerce labor and manufacture dependency that had been used during sharecropping. In these novels, labor exploitation adapts to the conditions of mechanization and globalization efficiently. Bebe Moore Campbell's novel *Your Blues Ain't Like Mine* (1992) offers a longitudinal narrative of a Mississippi Delta community in the forty years after the murder of Armstrong Todd, a teenager from Chicago killed by white men. Inspired by the murder of Emmett Till, the novel explores how the community changes over time even as the murder continues to haunt the families of both the victim and the perpetrators.[45] Cynthia Shearer's novel *The Celestial Jukebox* (2005) depicts a Mississippi Delta community at the beginning of the twenty-first century as casino capitalism, globalized flows of labor exploitation, and plantation tourism reorganize the local economy. In Natalie Baszile's novel *Queen Sugar* (2014), a woman whose parents migrated from Louisiana to Los Angeles returns to the South to run a sugar plantation bequeathed to her by her father, forcing her to take responsibility for owning and managing the same plantation where he had once been a day laborer. James Hannaham offers a grim vision of contemporary agricultural labor in *Delicious Foods* (2015). His book depicts human trafficking and modern slavery on a vegetable farm in Louisiana that uses drugs, debt, and violence to coerce labor. Collectively, these novels demonstrate that the culture of labor exploitation continues after the end of sharecropping.

All of these novels are set on former sharecropping plantations that have adapted to new labor practices. The Pinochet plantation dominates the landscape and the community in *Your Blues Ain't Like Mine*. Stonewall Pinochet is the area's largest planter and leader of the "Honorable Men of Hopewell," a cabal of planters with "blood on their hands," who manipulate the community's power structure to systematically disempower, disfranchise, and demean African Americans.[46] *The Celestial Jukebox* is set in the fictional Mississippi Delta community Madagascar, the site of Israel Abide's plantation, which has been converted into the Lucky Leaf Casino. Even though the plantation no longer exists, it still connects the remaining members of the community. In *Queen Sugar*, Charley Bordelon inherits the former Lejeune Plantation, where her "daddy worked one summer when he was a boy," as a day laborer "making a dollar a day."[47] He was thirteen then, and the plantation owner beat him for drinking from a bucket before the white workers. He leaves the South and raises a family in California, but he eventually purchases the plantation and bequeaths it to his daughter in a symbolic gesture of intergenerational power and control. *Delicious Foods* takes place at Summerton, the plantation of Sextus Fusilier, which Hannaham describes as having "a grandeur that went deep beneath the surface—not a showy type of class, but an elegance so lived-in that it didn't need to prove anything."[48] In each of these works, the plantation signifies power based on economic and social control. These sites continue to be associated with exploitative forms of labor while also evoking complicated cultural nostalgia that connects historical socioeconomic paradigms based on slavery and sharecropping with the present.[49]

Mechanization has changed the systems of labor on these plantations, but the legacy of sharecropping continues to linger in the communities' built geography. Lafayette, the nearest city to Charley Bordelon's plantation in *Queen Sugar,* continues to be segregated, and African Americans live in "'The Quarters'—the side of town where Miss Honey and most of the other black residents lived, a neighborhood that was *literally* over the railroad tracks."[50] The Quarters are a holdover from sugar plantation culture when laborers were clustered into tight communities with proximity to the plantations. In *Your Blues Ain't Like Mine,* Campbell mentions a similar cluster of sharecroppers' homes on the Pinochet Plantation—"the Quarters, a compound of rented two-room tarpaper shacks where the field hands and sharecroppers who worked the nearby plantations lived, surrounded by yards full of Johnson-grass and buttercups and an occasional neat clapboard that some enterprising Negro had managed to erect."[51] A farmer in *The Celestial Jukebox* who farms the land where the Abide plantation once stood "developed the habit of plowing around the Abide house the same way he plowed around the cinderblock church and small cemetery that accompanied it, and around the arpeggio of sharecropper shacks that had once belonged to the big house."[52] In this case, the tractor that replaced the sharecroppers' labor preserves their cabins, leaving the memorial trace of sharecropping on the landscape. The presence of cabins in these novels indicates that the cultural effects of sharecropping continue to play a role in the communities, influencing race and labor relations a generation after sharecropping ended.[53]

While the sharecroppers' quarters are still visible, much of the agricultural labor has been mechanized, which displaces most of the manual labor and requires costly investments in machinery. Campbell frequently references the changes in plantation culture as machines replace workers. The book opens with cotton pickers singing in the fields, but later a character notices "the dull hum of an International Harvester dusting the sprouting cotton with weed killer," and she remarks that "looking out on the fields and seeing only steel machines and occasionally one or two men made her feel empty and lonely."[54] The transition to mechanization changes the socioeconomic structure of agriculture from an emphasis on cheap labor to expensive machines. Financing machines is one of the key challenges that Charley Bordelon faces in *Queen Sugar.* She is shocked to learn that "a new tractor's a hundred thousand. Combine'll set you back two fifty."[55] She and her farm manager look for creative ways to buy machinery and to keep what machines they have running to remain productive. Machines become signifiers for capital in these texts, symbolizing the capacity to raise a crop and maintain a way of life. In *The Celestial Jukebox,* one character notices a collection of cotton-pickers and combines for sale arrayed outside the casino, and "he wondered for a confused moment why the gaming company would be going into the farm implement business, and then the answer rose in his heart and sickened him. This was a cemetery for farmers' dreams."[56] He realizes that farmers have lost these machines gambling in the casino, meaning that they have effectively lost their livelihoods. The machines outside the casino symbolize the inherent gamble of capital-intensive farming in the era of globalization when numerous external pressures challenge profitability.

With the decline in agricultural labor and the contraction of small farms, employment opportunities wane in former sharecropping areas, leading to efforts to diversify the economy, and these novels illustrate some of the new industries that have developed. In Northwest Mississippi, once the nation's densest sharecropping area, casinos have emerged as major industries, specifically in the area of Tunica. In *The Celestial Jukebox,* the Lucky Leaf casino commodifies plantation culture into nostalgic parody, such as "mindless murals of the old moss-draped *trompe l'oeil* plantations on the walls."[57] The casino economy contributes to the growth of tourism in the area, which also markets a parodic version of plantation culture.[58] In one instance, Shearer depicts a "busload of German tourists" who gape at the South and invoke notions of the past, such as "a young female in bib overalls with wet green hair and brass ring through her nose" who breathlessly asks a local resident, "Show us please where you keep the slafe! Where do you keep your slafe?"[59] These industries market the region's historical reputation for labor exploitation, while other industries devise new ways to exploit labor. In *Your Blues Ain't Like Mine,* Campbell describes the development of commercial catfish farming in the Delta. Stonewall Pinochet has the foresight to realize that the cotton industry is declining, so he proposes converting cotton fields into catfish ponds.⁶⁰ His son, however, realizes that "the new industry his father was heralding offered nothing to the legions of poor whites and blacks who had become idle because of mechanization of cotton farming. The profit margin of catfish farming would be maintained by the abundance of cheap labor in the area."⁶¹ Pinochet names the enterprise "New Plantation Catfish Farm and Processing Plant," clearly indicating that the new industry will follow the same labor paradigm as sharecropping.⁶² The farm in *Delicious Foods*, meanwhile, grows fruits and vegetables, such as watermelons and tomatoes, that are too delicate to be harvested by machines, so they require substantial amounts of manual labor. The farm recruits workers from among the most desperate people, including prostitutes, drug addicts, and alcoholics, and forces them into brutal, coercive labor.

These postsharecropping industries use systems of labor exploitation based on sharecropping. As the catfish ponds are constructed in *Your Blues Ain't Like Mine*, people eagerly anticipate opportunities for work. "There hadn't been prospects for employment in Hopewell since the last of the manual laborers had been run off cotton plantations by automatic cotton pickers and chemical weed killers," Campbell writes. "The Quarters was rife with rumors of jobs and prosperity."⁶³ When one person approaches Pinochet's son about a job, however, he dampens her enthusiasm, telling her "You don't understand. It's going to be just as bad as—as sharecropping ever was."⁶⁴ His prediction proves to be accurate, and later one employee complains, "Them same people that own the New Plantation, they worked the niggers to death picking cotton. Now they're trying to pull the same shit."⁶⁵ One of the few incentives for industries to locate in former sharecropping areas historically was the availability of low-wage, exploitable workers. In the era of globalization, however, immigrant workers have migrated to former sharecropping areas to find work, often in inhumane conditions, undercutting the local labor market. In *The Celestial Jukebox*, a farmer contracts Honduran laborers from a human trafficker, and another farmer shames him for not providing them housing. "They got laws now for what you got to give your workers," he says. "Otherwise, these folk come in from these other places and just drag in the same old troubles we got over a long time ago, start up the same old mess all over again."⁶⁶ As Martyn Bone explains, the farmer "is effectively gambling on cheap migrant labor offsetting the fierce competition that he faces from a putatively 'modern' global agricultural economy that, south of the U.S. South, retains the exploitative labor practices of plantation America."[67] One might note that the contemporary South continues to retain exploitative labor practices of the plantation South.

*Delicious Foods* depicts heinously exploitative labor practices that use many of the same mechanisms as sharecropping to coerce laborers into manufactured dependency. After the workers are recruited with promises of comfortable accommodations and easy work, they are driven to a remote farm, dropped into squalid barracks, and forced to sign a contract similar to sharecropping contracts. According to the terms of the contract, they are responsible for the cost of their food, lodging, and other expenses, including drugs.[68] The workers are supposed to pay their debt by working, but the company uses an arbitrary process similar to settlement to determine pay:

> They lined your ass up outside the sleeping area and told you how much you had worked and what pay you got and then hand you the pay right into your palm. Most folks aint get more than ten dollars a day, so for real they hardly give out nothing except more debt. But some days, some folks could make thirty and forty, and everybody striving for that, like the company running some kinda numbers game. Meanwhile, Delicious took out for everything—the meals, the boots, the tubs and sacks they loaned you for the picking, the alcohol, and me especially. They be giving drinks and drugs like it's your birthday party and then laying it all on your credit.[69]

The company uses debt to force the workers into peonage, keeping them in bondage to labor. "Ain't that the definition of slavery?" one worker wonders. "You don't get paid? And if you had signed a fucking contract and agreed to the debt they kept piling on—well, everybody be quietly arguing on the definition of that shit all the time."[70] The premise of *Delicious Foods* recalls sharecropping and also alludes to instances of contemporary human trafficking in agricultural labor, such as the events revealed by the Coalition of Immokalee Workers in Florida, where migrant workers were held in slavery on farms in Florida.[71]

The workers in *Delicious Foods* are kept in debt partly through drug use, which emerges as a new form of exploitation in postsharecropping novels. One of the book's narrators is a character named Scotty, a personification of crack cocaine, who Hannaham uses to illustrate the effects of addiction that keep the other characters connected to the farm.⁷² Drug use also appears in *Your Blues Ain't Like Mine* and *Queen Sugar* as destructive forces that disintegrate family and community bonds. In *Your Blues Ain't Like Mine*, the son of the man who murdered Armstrong Todd develops a heroin addiction that leads to his incarceration. In *Queen Sugar*, Charley Bordelon's brother also uses heroin, and his addiction functions as one of the antagonistic forces putting pressure on the family. Eventually, he steals from the family, nearly causing Charley to lose the sugar plantation, and he shoots a relative before being killed by a police officer in a traffic stop. In both of these examples, the drug users struggle to find employment opportunities, and they turn to drug use in part because of their frustration, but the drug use compounds their inability to find work and puts excessive pressure on their families with adverse social and economic effects on the entire structure, making social mobility difficult.

Systemic exploitation leads workers to stage labor actions in *Your Blues Ain't Like Mine, The Celestial Jukebox*, and *Delicious Foods*, although the effects of these actions are negligible. When a worker cuts her arm in *Your Blues Ain't Like Mine*, she threatens to sue New Plantation, and group of workers hold a mass meeting, promising "there's gon' be some changes made at New Plantation. The Sisters are coming on strong."⁷³ Stonewall Pinochet dies, and his more liberal son, Clayton, assumes ownership of the company, which suggests that labor conditions will improve, but the book does not make that explicit, and the final scene depicts workers picketing the company. In *The Celestial Jukebox*, a representative from the Coalition of Immokalee Workers attempts to start a union among the Honduran field workers, but the human trafficker, Tulia, puts a stop to it. When some of the workers are beaten, Angus Chien, the grocery store owner, warns the farmer, Aubrey, that the workers have rights, but Aubrey responds. "The law always been kinda flexible out here," and he explains that "the whole world would go under if we all paid real wages."⁷⁴ His defense echoes the rationale that has supported systems of agricultural labor exploitation for centuries, revealing that exploitation is persistent rather than expedient. Near the end of *Delicious Foods*, a group of workers escapes from the farm and exposes the operation, which leads to legal charges. However, "them accusations against Delicious ain't had nothing to do with some shit the judge called Certain Irregularities Concerning the Recruitment, Treatment, and Compensation of Laborers."⁷⁵ Instead, the company is charged with polluting the water, evading taxes, and selling drugs, indicating that the rights of workers have little value in the legal system.

The most significant change in agricultural labor since mechanization is the composition of the labor force. As many working-class southerners have migrated away from rural areas, they have left behind a gap for what few labor opportunities exist, and this gap has been largely filled with immigrants from Mexico and Central America.[76] In *The Celestial Jukebox*, a group of Honduran workers, whom Angus Chien assumes are illegal immigrants brought in by the human trafficker to work on Aubrey's farm, visit the store, where they buy food, and Angus plays songs from his jukebox for them "left over from some summer past when there were more Mexican faces in the fields than black ones."[77] The songs, like the Mississippi hot tamale, are traces from an earlier generation of Latino workers in the South when immigrant labor was used to undercut the cost of local workers. Charley employs "black locals and Mexican migrants from Guanajuato" during planting season because, as her farm manager says, "there's no cane planting machine that I know of."[78] She complains that her "labor costs are going to shoot through the roof," and in addition to their payroll, she has to pay for "H-2 visas and the bus tickets from Guanajuato, [and] the expense of fixing up the workers' house behind the shop so they'd have a decent place to sleep."[79] Working with the migrants makes Charley think of the previous generations of laborers—"Native Americans and indentured servants from Ireland and Germany, Chinese, West Indians, and former black slaves—who, through the centuries, had left their families and homelands behind, sometimes voluntarily but sometimes not, to work sugarcane."[80] The contemporary use of immigrant laborers is part of a centuries-long pattern of employing exploitable workers to perform difficult labor. "Under neoliberal capitalism," Martyn Bone explains, "U.S. and especially southern agricultural employers hire immigrants because they lack even rudimentary rights or other forms of protection from the state."[81]

Changes in the labor force reveal the effects of globalization on the US South. Although the South has a reputation for isolationism, its economy has always been part of global patterns of exchange, and periodically groups of immigrants have settled in the region. Angus Chien in *The Celestial Jukebox*, for example, came to Mississippi with his parents as a refugee from China after the Nanjing massacre in 1938. They opened a grocery store in the former Abide plantation commissary because, as James Loewen explains in *The Mississippi Chinese*, "the commissary on the plantation and the plantation store in town practically vanished" after 1940, opening the field to Chinese business owners who could use their racial alterity to serve both white and Black clientele.[82] In the novel, Chien's grocery store continues to serve as the hub of the community, where Black and white customers, in addition to Honduran workers, shop and eat. The novel also features Boubacar, a Mauritanian immigrant who comes to Mississippi to work in the casino, and Shearer uses his character to describe African immigrant communities in Memphis, a cosmopolitan southern city that embodies the neoliberal economy. The global hub of FedEx, "Memphis occupies a unique status as a distribution center in the global economy, but the city continues to struggle with social and economic inequalities as well as its collective identity," Wanda Rushing argues in *Memphis and the Paradox of Place* (2009).[83] For decades, Memphis served as the hub of the southern cotton economy, and its shift into global logistics is an effective synecdoche for changes in the US South since the end of sharecropping.

While immigrants have moved into the rural South to find opportunities, many southerners have left rural areas to settle in cities, often outside the South. *Delicious Foods* opens with Eddie, an escapee from the farm, driving to St. Cloud, Minnesota, to find his aunt, who relocated there when she left the South. He finds work as a handyman and begins to recover from the trauma of his experience on the farm. In *Your Blues Ain't Like Mine*, nearly the entire African American population of Hopewell, Mississippi, moves to Chicago as part of the Great Migration. Some are successful, creating prosperous lives in the urban environment, but they also face challenges, including gang violence and drug use, which leads some people to return to Mississippi. In one case, a mother returns to Mississippi because she believes Hopewell will be a better place for her son to grow up, and her friend responds, "never thought I'd see the day when black folks was leaving Chicago to come back to Mississippi."[84] For some people, despite the generations of exploitation, the South is home, which is also the premise behind *Queen Sugar*. The book opens with Charley driving from Los Angeles to Louisiana, "where the rice and cotton fields yielded to the tropical landscape of sugarcane country."[85] Her father left Louisiana to find opportunities for their family in California, but he uses his life savings to bequeath a sugarcane plantation to his daughter to allow her to take on the role of landowner in the South, signifying a form of intergenerational social mobility that spans the end of sharecropping. Since 1970, more African Americans have moved to the South than left, reversing the Great Migration, but most of them have settled in southern cities.

For the descendants of sharecroppers, returning to the rural South remains problematic. At the end of *Your Blues Ain't Like Mine*, Wydell Todd takes his younger son "down home" to Mississippi.[86] After Wydell's older son, Armstrong, is murdered by white men, Wydell moves to Chicago, where he and his wife run a barber shop and beauty parlor and have another son, W. T. When W. T. is arrested in connection to gang violence, Wydell takes him to Mississippi to show him where the family came from. At the Quarters, Wydell tells him, "This is where me and your mother is from. This is where your brother got killed. I thought you ought to see it one time in your life, just so you'd know. My mama and daddy and your other grandparents, they come from here too."[87] Despite generations of exploitation extending through sharecropping back to slavery, Wydell feels an ancestral connection to this place. Pointing to the New Plantation Catfish Farm, he asks, "You see all that water? Well, it used to be nothing but cotton, and before the machines come, black folks picked that cotton. Me and your mama and your grandparents, your aunties and uncles, we all picked that cotton. We picked that cotton until our fingers bled."[88] He explains to his son that their connection to this place is based primarily on labor exploitation, which explains why the connection to this place is problematic and why so many people would be willing to leave, especially in the absence of other opportunities. From where they stand in the Quarters, they can see picket lines forming at New Plantation as workers demonstrate for better pay and working conditions, and W. T. asks his father what is happening. Wydell answers, "I don't know. Progress, maybe."[89] In former sharecropping areas, however, signs of decline were much more evident than signs of progress.

## Visualizing Hale County

The signs of decline are apparent in Hale County, Alabama. In 1936, sharecropper Frank Tengle and his neighbors, Bud Fields and Floyd Burroughs, went to Greensboro, the seat of Hale County, to apply for federal relief. While waiting outside the courthouse, Tengle met James Agee and Walker Evans, who were on assignment from *Fortune* magazine to write an article

FIGURE 5. Walker Evans, "Frank Tengle, Bud Fields, and Floyd Burroughs, cotton sharecroppers, Hale County, Alabama," Summer 1936. (US Farm Security Administration; Library of Congress)

about the experiences of destitute sharecroppers in the South. They started a conversation, and Evans took some photographs. Believing them to be government agents who might be able to offer relief, Tengle invited them to his home, where Evans and Agee spent weeks taking pictures and documenting the sharecroppers' lives in detail. Evans included pictures of Tengle and his family in his exhibition *American Photographs* at the Museum of Modern Art in 1938 and in *Let Us Now Praise Famous Men* (1941).[90] A few decades later, William Christenberry, a native of Hale County, took photographs of the primitive dogtrot cabin where Tengle lived and painted dynamic abstract images of the house that adumbrated his artistic career, hinting at his fascination with architectural decay.[91] In 1990, writer Dale Maharidge and photographer Michael Williamson included a photograph taken in the home of one of their daughters that shows framed copies of the pictures Walker Evans took of Tengle and his wife in *And Their Children after Them* (1989), placing the pictures within the picture and directly connecting the texts.[92] RaMell Ross uses a long tracking shot of Greensboro in one of the opening scenes of his documentary *Hale County This Morning, This Evening* (2018) that ends at the courthouse were Evans and Agee met

Tengle almost ninety years earlier, creating a cycle of images that spans nearly ninety years in the history of a rural southern county.

Hale County has attracted the attention of some of the greatest documentary photographers and filmmakers in the US who have generated an extensive visual record of social decline in the postsharecropping area over the past century. Once a prosperous agricultural area in the Alabama Black Belt, the county has lost substantial population since 1930, declining from more than 26,000 residents then to less than 15,000 in 2020, according to census data, and more than a quarter of the county's population lives below the poverty line. Hale County has become virtually synonymous with poverty in American visual vernacular, transforming "the faces, landscapes, and architecture of the poor into images that resonated with educated, middle-class audiences."[93] The visual record of Hale County extends back to the beginning of the twentieth century when Martha Strudwick Young and J. W. Otts published a collection of photographs and local color dialect poems titled *Plantation Songs for My Lady's Banjo* (1901).[94] The ongoing fascination with the county, however, began in earnest with Walker Evans's work, which includes some of the most famous photographs in American art. Coincidently, William Christenberry, the most influential visual artist from the South, was born less than a mile from the Tengles' farm just a few weeks after Evans took those pictures. Although he was raised in Tuscaloosa and lived most of his live in Memphis and Washington, DC, he returned to Hale County frequently and took his most famous photographs in the county, creating a documentary record that spans from 1960 to the early 2000s. Maharidge and Williamson went to Hale County about fifty years after Agee and Evans to revisit the sites and families that they documented and record the changes that occurred, and their book, which reveals that the end of sharecropping in the area has only deepened poverty in the county, won a Pulitzer Prize for nonfiction. In 2009, RaMell Ross moved to Hale County to teach GED classes and coach basketball, and he spent years photographing there using a large-format camera, "to be in dialogue with guys like Walker Evans and William Christenberry."[95] He began shooting a film in 2012 that follows two of the young men in his program, Quincy Bryant and Daniel Collins, over a period of five years and juxtaposes scenes of their lives with hypnotic images filmed in the county. His experimental documentary film, *Hale County This Morning, This Evening*, won several major awards and was nominated for an Academy Award.

One might reasonably wonder why this particular county has attracted so much attention. Hale County is not particularly prominent, historic, or picturesque, yet it is indelibly embedded in the nation's visual memory. The record originates in New Deal propaganda because Walker Evans went there while employed by the Farm Security Administration to take pictures documenting the need for federal intervention in rural antipoverty programs.[96] *Fortune* magazine borrowed his services for the intended article on southern sharecroppers, but the photographs belonged to the US government and were intended to promote federal social welfare programs. William Stott notes, however, that Evans "would not want to be associated with the word 'propaganda.'"[97] While he recognized "documentary photography is concerned with influencing people's responses to contemporary social facts," he aspired to produce provocative works that used light, form, and composition to achieve an aesthetic effect.[98] His images, for example, often use cross lighting to highlight linear shadows on structures, and he frequently places the focal point of an image at an angle to the background to heighten the contrast. Yet, despite his emphasis on artistic details, his photographs became signifiers for poverty, and all of the documentarians that have followed his example have amplified the county's association with rural southern poverty. The Hale County documentaries, thus, visually record the effects of labor exploitation and an extractive economy over an extended period, illustrating the collapse of the dominant labor paradigm and the subsequent process of population decline and environmental decay. This visual archive illustrates the impact of the end of sharecropping on the descendants of sharecroppers and on the land where they worked and the communities where they lived.

Other places have been the subject of documentary photographs, of course, but Hale County is significant not only for the caliber of the documentarians who have recorded the area but also for the duration of the documentation. Agee and Evans spent approximately three weeks in the county, long enough for Evans to take dozens of photographs and for Agee to take copious notes on the sharecroppers' lives. Although Evans exhibited some of the pictures he took and compiled a photo documentary companion to Agee's text in *Let Us Now Praise Famous Men*, the images did not gain significant popular recognition until the reissue of the book in 1960 following Agee's death. Christenberry was studying art at the University of Alabama when the book was republished, and using a simple Brownie camera that he received as a Christmas present, and "with *Let Us Now Praise Famous Men* as a guide, he retraced the steps of his predecessors, often making new photographs in the places that Evans and Agee had been."[99] Christenberry moved to New York after finishing school, and he introduced himself to Evans, who admired his photographs and encouraged his work. Although he did not live permanently in Alabama after school, he made regular visits to Hale County over a period of fifty years, and he frequently photographed the same sites, creating a record of their process of change and devolution. Maharidge and Williamson spent a few weeks in Hale County, and they deliberately followed Agee and Evan's steps and took comparison photographs that demonstrate the effects of time on the people and landscape, illustrating that the end of sharecropping has had a deleterious impact on the community. Ross, meanwhile, filmed extensively over a period of five years, capturing intimate details in his subjects' lives, which he compresses into a seventy-six-minute film that intersperses a narrative of their lives with visual montages of the environment. His film reveals that the twenty-first century offers few new opportunities for the people of Hale County. With the exception of a gap between 1936 and 1960, documentarians have consistently recorded images of Hale County for nearly a century, allowing viewers to observe the county's decline in systematic detail and providing context to understand the process of devolution.

The Hale County documentarians share a realist aesthetic that enhances the archival characteristic of the documentary record. Evans, who was praised for his realism, established the essential characteristics of the documentary aesthetic, which include head-on compositions, minimal affect in portraits, structures centered and framed in their environment, and detail shots that juxtapose contrasting images. William Stott asserts that "Evans does not 'expose' the reality he treats, he reveals it—or better, he lets it reveal itself. He does not seek out, he in fact avoids, the spectacular, the odd, the piteous, the unseemly."[100] James Curtis, however, argues that Evans "helped perpetuate popular misconceptions that cameras do not lie and that photographs are true because they are mechanical reproductions of reality. Documentary photography derived its power and authority from artful manipulations of these fictions."[101] In the documentary aesthetic, both of these positions are accurate, and they reflect the relationship between the documentarian and the subject. The documentarian selects the image and places it in context, and the image tells the story that the documentarian wishes to communicate. The Hale County images are especially powerful because of the temporal context that reveals the effects of time on the images. According to Grace Hale, this process of returning to the same image over time is a crucial element of the aesthetic of southern documentary photography. She writes, "return as a practice, a process, a subject, and an aesthetic structures time and, in this way, marks and makes history. How we understand and give form and meaning to change over time becomes as much the subject of this work as what exists on the other side of the lens."[102] This process of returning tells a story of decline and decay in the rural South, so the Hale County images project an aesthetic of declension that reveals the effects of economic exploitation over time.

The faces of people in Hale County portraits reflect the effects of sharecropping. Walker Evan's famous portrait of Allie Mae Burroughs, for example, shows a twenty-seven-year-old woman ravaged with labor and anxiety.[103] The strong cross light on her face reveals wrinkles on her brow, eyes, and mouth that belie her age, and her lips and eyes are set firmly, making her face look like a mask concealing her emotions. The horizontal lines of the siding on the house behind her emphasize the planes of her face and suggest the plowed furrows of the cotton field, coalescing the site of her work with her body into an embodied vision of labor. Maharidge and Williamson include a diptych of Margaret Ricketts, the pseudonym for one of Frank Tengle's daughters, in *And Their Children after Them*.[104] The top image is an Evans photograph of her standing over a large bowl at the kitchen table washing dishes after a family meal. The bottom image mimics the first with her standing at the kitchen table over a dishpan. In both pictures, her body faces the table, but she looks toward the camera, and the two pictures invite comparisons. In Evans's picture, she is a young woman, and her hair plastered with sweat and the rough boards of the kitchen catching light from the open windows indicate labor and poverty. In the Williamson picture, she is an elderly woman, and her wrinkled skin and gnarled feet show the effects of a lifetime of labor, while the meager, disordered kitchen illustrates that she continues to live in poverty. Together, the pictures manifest the effects of time and human decay on a woman born into sharecropping. The scenes in Ross's *Hale County This Morning, This Evening* have a similar effect as they show the experiences of generational poverty and the futility of economic advancement in a community with few opportunities. The children in the film appear destined to follow the paths of their parents, who are locked in

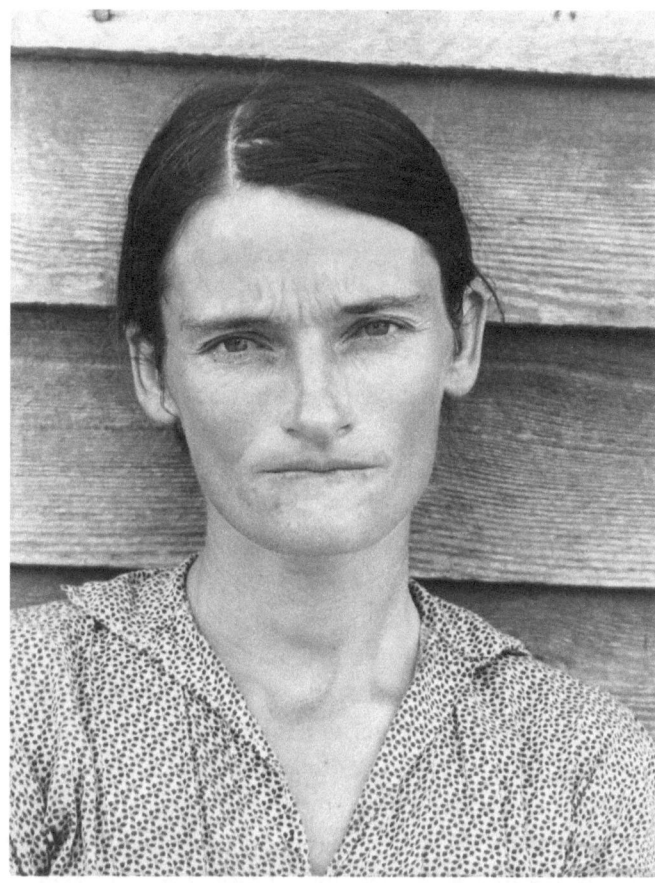

FIGURE 6. Walker Evans, "Allie Mae Burroughs, wife of cotton sharecropper. Hale County, Alabama," Summer 1936. (US Farm Security Administration; Library of Congress)

a cycle of labor exploitation. In one scene, for example, a toddler runs in circles for an extended period, expending an enormous amount of energy but making no progress.

The portraits of people in Hale County tell a complicated story about race. The majority of the people in the county are Black, but all of the people in the pictures Evans includes in *Let Us Now Praise Famous Men* are white, which sets an inaccurate precedent for the visual representation of southern poverty. They imply that the normative experience of labor and poverty in the sharecropping economy is white, which is far from the case. Political appeals to white southern voters influenced many Depression-era photodocumentaries sponsored by the Farm Security Administration, so Evans deliberately sought out white subjects.[105] Christenberry, who rarely photographs people, includes some pictures of Black people among his collection *Kodachromes*, such as "Country Store, Hale County, Alabama, 1976," which shows three young, Black men lounging outside a tiny, dilapidated store covered with rusty tin advertisements, but these images are unusual among his work, and the focus of the picture is the store, not the people.[106] Maharidge and Williamson attempt to recontextualize race by including several photographs of Black people in *And Their Children after Them*, including portraits of a family who lived near the white sharecropping families that Agee and Evans studied, but the lack of referents to the 1930s removes the powerful comparative impact of temporal decline. RaMell Ross upends the racial narrative in both *Hale County This Morning, This Evening* and his photography collections "South County AL (A Hale County) 2018" and "South County AL (A Hale County) 2012."[107] In the same way that Evans omits blackness, Ross omits whiteness by showing images exclusively of Black people, effectively producing a negative of the white image of rural southern poverty. He explains how color affects his images: "My film naturally extends from my large-format photography, which looks at my insider-outsider relationship with the historic South and considers the iconic use of the African-American body. Here, the tropes of skin are suspended in an arch of meaning to provide space to deconstruct our thoughts as they assist the decoding of the images."[108] The key phrase "tropes of skin" highlights the fact that skin color affects the way the viewer perceives the image, so by maintaining focus on the Black subject, Ross normalizes African American experience.

Many of the Hale County images focus on architecture, and the structures indicate the endemic poverty in the area and illustrate the process of economic decline. Most of the scenes in *Hale County This Morning, This Evening* take place in mobile homes and HUD properties, which reflects the entrenched poverty that persists in the county. These structures are the modern equivalent of the shacks where sharecroppers lived. Some of Evans's most eloquent pictures use the trope of architecture to reveal how people live, such as his pictures of the sharecroppers' cabins, outbuildings, kitchens, fireplaces. His picture of the fireplace in the Burroughs's cabin, for example, invites comparisons to an altar as the whitewashed mantel topped with a crudely carved lintel contrasts with the unpainted wood walls.[109] A table covered with a white tablecloth before the unlit firebox holds vases, urns adorn the mantelpiece, and a calendar decorated with an image of a beautiful woman hangs like an icon above the hearth. Christenberry photographed structures obsessively, taking pictures of homes, barns, stores, and other structures, almost always without the presence of people. His images, nonetheless, depict "the most intimate aspects of people's daily human existence" by focusing attention on where and how people live and marking the mutability of their mark on the landscape.[110] One of his earliest pictures replicates an Evans picture of a store and cotton warehouse in Stewart, Alabama. His picture, taken twenty-five years later, shows the same structures abandoned and empty, graphically representing the end of the sharecropping economy.

Christenberry's career as a documentary photographer began as sharecropping came to an end in the Black Belt, and he documented the area's decline over the course of five decades. In several cases, he photographed the same structure repeatedly over time, such as a church in Sprott, Alabama, that he photographed in 1971, 1981, and 1990.[111] In the earlier pictures, the crude, white building has two towers flanking the front entrance that evoke a primitive version of a cathedral, but the later image shows the same building without the distinctive towers, looking conventional and uninteresting. The change indicates that, although inanimate, the building is a dynamic entity constantly in development as long as it is in use. In another example, Christenberry photographed a structure from 1967 to 2004 that began as a dilapidated crossroads store.[112] Over time, the building is given a new facade, it is decorated with amateur murals, a lean-to is added, it becomes a juke joint called The Underground Club, it is painted red, then green, then red again, and finally it is completely rebuilt as a tidy, light blue nightclub called The Underground Railroad. The evolution of this structure reveals its use value. When crossroads stores, once the foundation of the microfinance economy of sharecropping, lost their value, this structure was repurposed to generate income in another way. In some of Christenberry's most evocative photo series, he captures the devolution of an abandoned structure that has lost its use value. One example is "Building with False Brick Siding, Warsaw, Alabama (1974–1994)."[113] The earliest image in this series shows a small building, likely a shotgun house, with the proportions of a Roman temple, that has been covered with asphalt siding printed with a brick pattern. In the pictures taken over the following two decades, the building is covered with vines, and trees grow around it until it eventually disappears into the growth as forest consumes the structure and surrounding field. These pictures vividly depict the effect of the end of sharecropping on the built environment as people left the area to find work in other places, leaving their homes and fields to return to wildness.

Landscape pictures make the relationship to the environment apparent. Agricultural economies harness vast tracts of land crops, and at the height of sharecropping a nearly unbroken field of cotton extended across the Black Belt. Evans includes only one landscape image in *Let Us Now Praise Famous Men*, and it shows a small garden plot enclosed with a sagging fence amid a field of cotton. The image reflects the economic reality of sharecropping, where cotton production occupied the greatest share of space, and food production for the family was allowed only a small area.[114] Postsharecropping landscapes, meanwhile, often show land in distress after decades of use. Christenberry's "Alabama Landscape, near Tuscaloosa, Alabama, 1980," for example, shows eroded cliffs of red clay sparsely dotted with scrub pines in a field that looks infertile and exhausted.[115] In other images, such as "Kudzu in Early Morning Light, Hale County, Alabama, October, 1983," he shows landscapes engulfed in kudzu, the vine intended to impede erosion that covered fields and buildings in strangling vines.[116] Michael Williamson also includes pictures of eroded gullies and kudzu covered hills in *And Their Children after Them*, reinforcing the visual trope of unproductive, exhausted land.[117] RaMell Ross's landscape shots, on the other hand, shift upward to focus on the sky with long shots of a powerful storm, phases of the moon, the sun through black smoke, and embers floating upward from a fire. In addition to being dreamlike, these images signify that the land itself is no longer the primary source of revenue for people in the area.

The documentaries largely omit images of agricultural labor. Evans includes two pictures of cotton picking in *Let Us Now Praise Famous Men*, one of a young woman, Lucille Burroughs, with a sack over her shoulder, bent over picking lint from bolls, and another of Bud Fields, with his hands on his hips, standing between rows of cotton with a sack hanging from his shoulder.[118] These pictures contextualize the families' economic exploitation by making their relationship with cotton production visible. Later pictures, however, demonstrate the absence of cotton and imply the transition in the local economy. In *And Their Children after Them*, Michael

Williamson includes a picture of a farmer who he calls Joe Bridges standing in the same field where Bud Fields once stood. A caption describes Bridges as "a bankrupt farmer who leases the land from Margraves and will be the last to plow it" (258). Margraves is a direct descendant of the landowner the families worked for in Let Us Now Praise Famous Men, so this tenant-landowner relationship suggests some continuity in the economic system, but there are some significant changes. The picture's caption indicates that Bridges is "standing in his field of soybeans on Hobe's Hill, the same ground where Bud Woods [Fields] planted cotton" (259). By this time, cotton production has given way to soybean crops, which are cultivated mechanically, although even this agricultural system is in peril at the time. Thirty years later, RaMell Ross indicates that agricultural labor in the county has continued to change. He includes a long tracking shot of cotton fields in Hale County This Morning This Evening taken from a moving car. There are no workers or machines in the fields, so they appear benign, yet they evoke the legacy of labor exploitation in the county. However, few people in Hale County work in cotton production because, as Ross states in an intertitle, "nearly everyone works in the catfish plant." Catfish aquaculture has replaced agriculture as the largest employer in Hale County as the fields have been repurposed into ponds and as the descendants of sharecroppers are employed in the catfish processing plants.

Viewed in context with each other, these documentaries chart the process of social and economic change in a county over a period of decades, revealing the effects on the people, structures, and environment as sharecropping ends, labor opportunities erode, and population declines. The pictures are powerful and informative, but their persistence and popularity raise a number of questions. Why are documentarians drawn to this place? Why do these images resonate with viewers? What stories do these challenging pictures tell? What affect do these images project? Considering America's prevailing narrative of success and progress, these pictures of poverty and decline seem incongruous, which leads to the answer to some of these questions. These pictures force us to interrogate our perceptions of the region and its population. They make the experience of labor exploitation visible, which aligns them with a tradition of documentary photography that extends to the work of Jacob Riis and Lewis Hine of stark, disturbing pictures that depict the people who make the American narrative of progress and success possible. Documentary photographs humanize the experience of exploitation by focusing the viewer's attention on specific details of the subject's experience. RaMell Ross explains that viewers are often willfully unaware of the experience of Black people, in particular, and people who live in poverty, in general. He says, "We don't often truly consider the embeddedness of black folks in the American imaginary. America would not exist in its current form without the long history of the black experience, of course; and what that means, very viscerally, on the visual level, is almost impossible to consider. You can think hypothetically or romantically about living in another town or going to another school. But consider how the symbolic associations tied to whiteness in America have meaning only because of the symbolic associations tied to blackness; how one set of cultural aesthetics are often created, consciously or not, in opposition to others."[119] The images of Hale County allow the viewer to recognize these oppositions, encounter the visage of the other, and imagine their lived experience. Ross's comment focuses specifically on blackness, which his images highlight, but the extended record of Hale County documentaries exposes the experience of rural poverty for whites as well as Blacks, although even the consistent focus on poverty has often marginalized blackness.

The Hale County documentaries reveal an extended declension narrative. Ironically, the narrative begins with a period of economic crisis during the Great Depression, but those photographs, sponsored by the federal government, indicate popular concern and governmental intervention into rural poverty. Since then, the issues facing the rural poor have faded from the national consciousness. Meanwhile, sharecropping as a system of labor has ended, leading to a massive restructuring of rural labor across the South. Although sharecropping was a socioeconomic problem that endured for nearly a century, the end of sharecropping has not led to improvements in the lives of the rural poor. In some respects, conditions are worse as jobs continue to be scarce, which has led many people to leave rural areas to seek opportunities in more urban areas. Those people who have stayed in rural areas continue to be exploited in new forms of labor and to endure generational poverty, while the land in the rural South bears the scars of generations of misuse. These documentary images illustrate that the collapse of exploitative, extractive economic systems does not lead to progress and prosperity. The persistence of white supremacist politics in the rural South indicates that the utility of oppression exceeds economic controls because maintaining inequality is crucial to maintaining political control.

The culture of rural southern poverty, therefore, endures long after the end of sharecropping.

The penultimate picture in *Let Us Now Praise Famous Men* establishes another recurring trope in Hale County documentaries. The picture shows a weathered grave in a swept cemetery marked with a simple board and a plate.[120] Over the course of his career, Christenberry took several pictures of graves and markings. His picture "Child's Grave with Rosebuds, Hale County, Alabama, 1975" mimics the composition and angle of Evans's picture, showing a small weathered grave marked with boards at each end and a row of artificial roses along the center of the mound.[121] Many of his cemetery pictures depict swept graveyards near country churches, and the graves are often decorated with makeshift items, such as crosses made from egg cartons. "The mourners and their perished kin could clearly afford nothing more," writes Trudy Wilner Stack, "but their loss is no less felt."[122] The final picture that Michael Williamson includes in *And Their Children after Them* shows a cemetery in a rural country churchyard with a recent grave in the foreground marked with bouquets of artificial flowers.[123] One of the most emotional scenes of *Hale County This Morning, This Evening* is the funeral of an infant child that takes place in a rural churchyard cemetery. The repetition of the grave images conveys a powerful message about the lives of the people in the rural community. The grave coalesces the bodies of the laborers with the land they worked, and the crude, weathered graves reflect the poverty they lived in. The decorations represent the family members who survive them and the generational cycle of poverty that will continue after their death.

An intertitle in *Hale County This Morning, This Evening* asks, "what happens when all the cotton is picked?" This enigmatic question invites us to think about the future of Hale County. On a literal level, the county continues to produce cotton, but due to mechanization, the cotton industry, which once maintained a vast exploited labor force, does not employ a significant number of people and is no longer the county's economic linchpin. Because the county has a dearth of employment opportunities, the population has declined, the people who remain live in intractable poverty, and new industries have developed that continue to exploit the available labor force. On a metaphorical level, Ross's question indicates that there are few obvious paths forward for the people of Hale County. One of the subjects of his documentary pursues basketball as a way out of generational poverty. The film shows him practicing doggedly and follows his excitement at being recruited to play at Selma University, which he hopes, against enormous odds, can lead him to professional basketball. When he is cut from the team, he returns to Hale County. With no obvious prospects, his future is uncertain. Perhaps he will work at the catfish plant, perhaps he will leave, perhaps he will scrape together some other opportunity, or perhaps he will be trapped in the system of mass incarceration that disproportionately threatens Black men in the South. His experience crystalizes the poignant message of Ross's film, which visualizes the joy and sorrow of rural Black life in the South, but it also represents the final irony of sharecropping. The end of sharecropping has not led to social progress in the South, and more than a generation after mechanization, sharecropping continues to affect life in the South.

The essays in the influential collection *The Myth of Southern Exceptionalism* (2010) challenge the long-standing idea that the US South is a distinctive region of the United States. There are many good reasons to take this position, at least in part because the exceptional South thesis has allowed generations of scholars to project notions of backwardness and depravity onto the South while asserting that the United States is an otherwise progressive nation. A bit of scrutiny, however, reveals that the entire nation suffers from enduring legacies of exploitation, inhumanity, and intolerance. Yet, to the extent that the South is a distinctive region, sharecropping is its defining characteristic. At the end of the Civil War, the region could—hypothetically speaking—have been reincorporated into the United States. The Reconstruction amendments and the Freedmen's Bureau were efforts at federal intervention to extend national policies to the entire country, but circumstances dictated a different course. The necessity to produce agricultural commodities led the federal government to effectively abstain from protecting human rights in the South. Slavery ended, but new forms of labor exploitation, political control, social manipulation, and cultural hegemony emerged, so the South did, in fact, differ in some substantive ways from the rest of the United States. The entire country, however, is complicit in allowing the history of sharecropping and human rights abuses in the South to transpire.

Understanding the culture of sharecropping helps to explain why segregation was effective and persistent in the South, why millions of people migrated out of the South, and why a movement for civil rights was necessary a century after Emancipation. It also helps to explain why New Deal interventions were politically successful in the South and why the Sun Belt economy rapidly emerged after World War II. And it helps to explain why the South continues to lag behind the rest of the United States in many markers of social progress, including educational attainment, incarceration rates, life expectancy, and per capita income. Millions of southerners labored as sharecroppers, often in family units working in successive generations, and in some areas, landless farmers far exceeded landowning farmers. Sharecropping also involved Black, white, and in some cases, Latino, workers, so it greatly complicates the region's racial history. The impact of sharecropping on the South was immense.

Scholars of southern studies have an obligation to remember sharecropping. Not only is it essential to our understanding the historical development of southern culture, but it is also our duty to the millions of families who endured exploitation to account for their experiences and to find ways to tell their stories. Their experiences are often hidden in plain sight. An enormous amount of scholarship has focused on the legacy of slavery, on race relations, on social class, on agriculture, and on globalization. All of these topics interrelate with sharecropping, and any study of the South since Emancipation should account for the role of sharecropping. When works of literature, such as *Absalom, Absalom!* and *Gone with the Wind*, avoid representing the experience of sharecroppers, scholars have an opportunity to interrogate this erasure. Many works do portray sharecroppers, and developing a dialogue between the works that do represent sharecroppers and those that do not will lead to more nuanced and perceptive readings of these texts.

In a functional sense, sharecropping ended fifty years ago, but it continues to resonate in American culture. A provision in the American Rescue Plan, President Joe Biden's enormous stimulus plan to invigorate the US economy after the Covid-19 pandemic, allocates $5 billion to disadvantaged farmers. This outlay is a small gesture to compensate African American farmers who have been systematically discriminated against by the US Department of Agriculture. According to an article in the *Washington Post*, "Black farmers in America have lost more than 12 million acres of farmland over the past century, mostly since the 1950s, a result of what agricultural experts and advocates for Black farmers say is a combination of systemic racism, biased government policy, and social and business practices that have denied African Americans equitable access to markets."[124] This policy, however, does not account for the millions more of farmers, Black and white, who were denied the opportunity to acquire land, generate income, and pass down assets for generations because they were ensnared in sharecropping. When we think about reparations and addressing historical discrimination, we should recognize the legacy of sharecropping and its effect on inequality and injustice in the United States.

# NOTES

## 1. SHARECROPPING, LABOR EXPLOITATION, AND SOUTHERN LITERATURE

1. Buell, *Dream of the Great American Novel*, 286.
2. Dozens of critics have addressed issues of slavery in Faulkner's work, specifically *Absalom, Absalom!* Two especially perceptive pieces are "Faulkner and Slavery" by Darwin Turner and "Accounting for Slavery: Economic Narratives in Morrison and Faulkner" by Erik Dussere. Tim Ryan explores slavery as a literary paradigm in *Calls and Responses: The American Novel of Slavery since Gone with the Wind*.
3. Faulkner, *Absalom, Absalom!*, 169.
4. Mitchell, *Gone with the Wind*, 827.
5. Mitchell, 36.
6. Godden, *Fictions of Labor*, 119.
7. Woofter, *Landlord and Tenant*, 179.
8. Odum led an influential research group at the University of North Carolina that included Rupert Vance, Guy Johnson, and others. The group published dozens of works about race, regional planning, and folk sociology.
9. A New Deal agency, the Farm Security Administration focused resources on modernizing rural farmers and improving living conditions for marginalized farmers. The administration included a photography unit that generated propaganda for their policy initiatives by documenting the grim living conditions of America's poorest agricultural workers. Some of the nation's leading photographers worked for the unit, including Walker Evans, Dorothea Lange, Marion Post Walcott, and Gordon Parks, and they captured many iconic images of American poverty. For more information, see *Picturing Poverty: Print Culture and FSA Photographs* by Cara A. Finnegan.
10. Guterl, "Plantation," 22–29.

11. Atkinson, "Labor," 48–59.
12. Romine, *Narrative Forms*, 113.
13. Duck, *Nation's Region*, 77.
14. Rubin, *Gallery of Southerners*, xiv.
15. Simpson, *Fable*, 22.
16. Several intellectual historians have analyzed the ideas and beliefs of individuals involved with the Agrarian movement. In *The Idea of The American South*, Michael O'Brien examines several of the key figures in the movement and explores their compulsion to defend the concept of southern tradition. Daniel Joseph Singal contextualizes their thought with other elite white southerners along a broader ideological spectrum in *The War Within*. *The Rebuke of History* by Paul V. Murphy connects the Agrarians to southern conservatism and the ideas of reactionaries such as Richard Weaver and M. E. Bradford.
17. Twelve Southerners, *I'll Take My Stand*, xix.
18. Kreyling, *Inventing Southern Literature*, 6.
19. Ownby, "Three Agrarianisms," 6.
20. In *Slaves for Hire*, John Zaborney establishes that slave renting was a widespread practice in the antebellum South, involving a broad range of people who could not afford to own slaves in slavery.
21. Sharecropping has been common in many places throughout history. England, France, Italy, and Spain each had their own systems of sharecropping that originated in feudalism, and the practice was also used frequently in Africa and Asia. For broader studies of sharecropping, see *Sharecropping and Sharecroppers*, edited by T. J. Byers, and *Agrarian Revolution* by Jeffery Paige.
22. In *The Problem of Freedom*, Thomas Holt offers an interesting comparative study of a postemancipation economic transition. He documents the shift from slavery to free labor in Jamaica from 1838 to 1932, and while the period was tumultuous, many former slaves became landowners in the process.
23. To see the text of President Johnson's Amnesty Proclamation, visit https://www.loc.gov/resource/rbpe.23502500/.
24. Mandle, *Not Slave, Not Free*, 12.
25. Royce, *Origins of Southern Sharecropping*, 2.
26. Litwack, *Been in the Storm*, 447.
27. Jaynes, *Branches without Roots*, 232.
28. In *Roll, Jordan, Roll*, Eugene Genovese argues that paternalism, more than market forces, defined the relationship between masters and slaves, and James Roark examines the effects of Emancipation on slaveholders' ideology and their sense of loss in *Masters without Slaves*.

29. Economic historians have attempted to explain the development and persistence of sharecropping using rationalist arguments based on measurable economic data. Joseph Reid has argued that sharecropping was a rational response under the market conditions. Roger Ransom and Richard Sutch examine institutional constraints that hampered economic growth in the postbellum South, and Edward Royce contends that constricting possibilities led to the emergence of sharecropping. Gerald David Jaynes describes sharecropping as a symbiotic system that initially benefited both planters and laborers but eventually led to racialized market forces. Recently, Debapriya Sen had proposed a theory of sharecropping on the basis of price behavior in agriculture and the imperfectly competitive nature of rural product market. All of these theories offer insight into the economic challenges sharecropping presents, but only Jaynes sufficiently recognizes the ideological forces that often override economic rationality.
30. Many example contracts can be found in the compendium *Freedom: A Documentary History of Emancipation, 1861–1867, Series 3: Volume 2: Land & Labor, 1866–1867*. One elaborate contract issued by the South Carolina Freedmen's Bureau attempted to establish a precedent for labor relations between landowners and laborers. It stipulates standards of behavior, guidelines for dismissal, provisions of equipment and materials, and division of crops (110–11). In some respects, the policies it stated became standard and customary in many sharecropping arrangements, and the standard contract applies the imprimatur of the federal government on the system. The basic contract, however, arrogates most rights to the landowner, only extending explicitly stated privileges and rights to the laborer.
31. Woodman, *New South, New Law*, 5.
32. Pete Daniel describes the extent of peonage in *The Shadow of Slavery*. Although technically illegal, peonage was commonly practiced throughout the South as an extension of sharecropping, forcing many workers into virtual slavery despite the Thirteenth Amendment.
33. Southern states developed systems of convict leasing as a means of generating revenue after the Civil War, using the "except as a punishment for a crime" clause as a means of forcing vast labor forces into involuntary servitude. Convicts were often worked to death in inhumane conditions. For more on convict leasing, see *Slavery by Another Name* by Douglas Blackmon and *Twice the Work of Free Labor* by Alex Lichtenstein.
34. For studies of international cotton markets, see *Empire of Cotton* by Sven Beckert and *Cotton* by Giorgio Riello.
35. Wright, *Old South, New South*, 50.

36. Aiken, *Cotton Plantation South*, 30–31. Sharecropping has been practiced outside the US South, particularly on midwestern wheat farms, but the arrangements were much less pervasive, less deeply entrenched, and more equitable. They also tended to give way quickly to wage labor or farm ownership. See "Social Origins" by Max Pfeffer.
37. Rubin, *Plantation County*, 10.
38. Mandle, *Roots of Back Poverty*, 28
39. Marx discusses the nature of feudalism in *Capital*, chapter 26, and *German Ideology*, chapter 1.
40. Roemer, *General Theory*, 122.
41. Wright, *Classes*, 75.
42. Mayer, *Analytical Marxism*, 59.
43. Woofter, *Landlord and Tenant*, 91.
44. Ideology is a crucial concept in Marxist theory. In the preface to *A Contribution to the Critique of Political Economy*, Marx conceptualizes the theory that the ideological superstructure reinforces the economic base. Raymond Williams defines ideology as "abstract and false thought" in *Keywords* (128), and other theorists, such as Louis Althusser and Antonio Gramsci, have illustrated how ideology can be used to condition, control, and coerce a population.

## 2. SHARECROPPING, RECONSTRUCTION, AND POSTBELLUM LITERATURE

1. Peter Wood has written extensively about Winslow Homer's images of race and slavery; see *Near Andersonville* and *Winslow Homer's Images of Blacks*.
2. Details about Walker's life and his paintings can be found in *William Aiken Walker, Southern Genre Painter* by August P. Trovaioli and Roulhac B. Toledano.
3. Stephen Prince examines postbellum print culture and "the nation's abandonment of egalitarian possibilities of Reconstruction" in *Stories of the South*.
4. Foner, *Reconstruction*, 143.
5. Claude Oubre details the policy reversals that defrauded Black landowners in *Forty Acres and a Mule*.
6. De Forest's essays were collected and published as *A Union Officer in the Reconstruction*.
7. Tourgée, "South as a Field," 402.
8. Tourgée, 403.
9. Tourgée, 406.
10. Cable, "Literature," 45.

11. Tourgée, *A Fool's Errand*, 117.
12. Bill Hardwig discusses Tourgée's complicated racial attitudes in "Who Own the Whip? Chesnutt, Tourgée, and Reconstruction Justice," and Peter Caccavari considers Tourgée and Reconstruction politics in "Reconstructing Reconstruction: Region and Nation in the Work of Albion Tourgée."
13. Tourgée, *Bricks without Straw*, 35.
14. Cable, *John March*, 39.
15. Foner, *Reconstruction*, 129.
16. Roark, *Masters without Slaves*, 158–60.
17. Tourgée, *Fool's Errand*, 121–22.
18. Tourgée, *Bricks without Straw*, 176.
19. Tourgée, 177.
20. Tourgée, 35.
21. A compilation of papers from the Freedmen's Bureau can be found in René Hayden et al., *Freedom: A Documentary History of Emancipation, 1861–1867*.
22. Jennifer Larson examines De Forest's service in the Freedmen's Bureau and his complicated attitudes toward race and the South in "Plotting the Benefit of the Human Race."
23. De Forest, *Union Officer*, 29.
24. De Forest, 29.
25. Freedmen's schools were probably the most significant and lasting intervention of the Bureau. Peter Schmidt examines the representation of education in postbellum literature in *Sitting in Darkness*.
26. While a judge in North Carolina, Tourgée heard an enticement case. At issue was an inequitable contract, and he ruled in favor of the sharecropper and was overturned by a higher court (Olsen, *Carpet Bagger's Crusade*, 181).
27. Tourgée, *Bricks without Straw*, 271.
28. Tourgée represented the plaintiff before the Supreme Court in the case of Plessy v. Ferguson. Mark Elliott traces his racial politics and legal career in *Color-Blind Justice*.
29. Leon Litwack's *Been in the Storm So Long* is an extensive litany of indignities, humiliations, and victimizations that African Americans suffered after Emancipation.
30. Cable, "Freedman's Case," 61.
31. Cable, 61.
32. In *Patriotic Gore*, Edmund Wilson describes the book as "completely synthetic, and it was most unfortunate that Cable, in attempting so serious a book, should have played into the hands of his critics by producing so thorough a bore" (584).

33. Jennifer Greeson argues that White portrays the South as a "domestic Africa for the United States, a site upon which the nation proved its civilizing might to be the equal of Europe's" ("Expropriating," 117). One has to wonder how civilized any of these places proved to be.
34. King, *Great South*, 306.
35. Kennedy-Nolle, *Writing Reconstruction*, 16.
36. Karen Keely gives a more extensive list of reconciliation romances and delineates their plot conventions in "Marriage Plots and National Reunion: The Trope of Romantic Reconciliation in Postbellum Fiction."
37. Silber, *Romance of Reunion*, 116.
38. Silber, 107–8.
39. Beckert, *Empire of Cotton*, 275–78.
40. In addition to the fact that cotton exports were a billion-dollar industry in the 1860s, Gene Dattel documents in *Cotton and Race in the Making of America* that one of the key measures for retiring war debt was a 2.5-cent-per-pound tax on cotton producers (229). Ed Baptist states in *The Half Has Never Been Told* that at the end of the Civil War, "The US economy still needed the overseas earnings generated by the South's power in the world cotton market" (407–8). There were pressing economic realities that made cotton production essential in the postbellum period.
41. Page, *Red Rock*, 45.
42. Page, 46.
43. Powell, *New Masters*, 18.
44. Paul Gaston exposes the use of economic boosterism as a veil for entrenched racism and conservatism in *The New South Creed*, and Ed Ayers catalogs the contradictions, complications, and intractable problems of the postbellum period in *The Promise of the New South*.
45. Page, *Red Rock*, 212.
46. De Forest, *Bloody Chasm*, 145.
47. De Forest, 276.
48. Gregory Jackson argues, "*The Bloody Chasm* is ultimately the proper balance between sovereignty and subordination, consent and coercion, and subjection and subjectivity in both nuptial and civic relationships" (281).
49. Page, *Red Rock*, 581.
50. Joyce Warren discusses women's property rights in *Women, Money, and the Law*, and Jeffory Clymer examines how gendered property issues relating to slavery are represented in *Family Money: Property, Race, and Literature in the Nineteenth Century*.
51. Blight, *Race and Reunion*, 4.

52. Keely, "Marriage Plots and National Reunion."
53. Blight, *Race and Reunion*, 211.
54. In *This Republic of Suffering*, Drew Gilpin Faust describes the ways that death on a vast scale changed American culture in the wake of the war. Although these scars of grief were still visible decades after the war, reconciliation often superseded regional antagonism.
55. Woolson, *Rodman the Keeper*, 195.
56. The Lost Cause has been the subject of a significant amount of scholarship, but some of the most important studies are *Ghosts of the Confederacy* by Gaines Foster, *Dixie's Daughters* by Karen Cox, and *The Myth of the Lost Cause and Civil War History*, edited by Gary Gallagher and Alan Nolan.
57. Charles Reagan Wilson explains how the Lost Cause became a civil religion in *Baptized in Blood: The Religion of the Lost Cause, 1865–1920*.
58. Mixon, *Southern Writers*, 32.
59. Page, *In Ole Virginia*, 10.
60. Page, *Negro*, 32. Page's book is similar to *The Plantation Negro as a Freeman* by Phillip A. Bruce, a paternalistic text about managing Black labor on tobacco plantations in Virginia. He suggests that sharecropping is ineffective for tobacco production because laborers need more supervision to cultivate tobacco than cotton.
61. Page, 82.
62. Page, 93.
63. Page, 163.
64. Page, 173.
65. In *Red Rock*, Mammy Kendra refuses to accept wages from her former owner, preferring to remain in essentially her same station as a slave (66).
66. Page, 286.
67. Harris, *Free Joe*, 8.
68. Harris, 8.
69. James Kinney argues a similar point in "Race in the New South: Joel Chandler Harris's 'Free Joe and the Rest of the World.'"
70. Nilon, "Ending of *Huckleberry Finn*," 66.
71. Wells, *Romances of the White Man's Burden*, 4.
72. Woodward, *Strange Career of Jim Crow*, 22–23.
73. Harper, *Iola Leroy*, 198.
74. C. C. O'Brien offers a fascinating analysis of Harper's complicated political activism in "The White Women All Go for Sex," as does Elizabeth Petrino in "We Are Rising as a People." Both articles suggest that Harper's naïveté was a calculated political position.

75. Harper, *Iola Leroy*, 200.
76. Ida B. Wells is an example of an African American writer who faced serious consequences for criticizing white supremacy. After she published *Southern Horrors*, her newspaper office was burned, and she was effectively exiled from the South. She continued to criticize racism, but she was never safe in the South. For details about her life and work, see Paula Giddings, *Ida: A Sword among Lions*.
77. Mary Kuhn offers an insightful analysis of Chesnutt's representation of naval stores as an extractive industry in eastern North Carolina in "Chesnutt, Turpentine, and the Political Ecology of White Supremacy." She explains that pine tree plantations mediated between the natural environment and agricultural plantations that produced cotton and tobacco.
78. Eric Sundquist offers a brilliant reading of Chesnutt's depiction of the South's "performance—its often disingenuous display of racial harmony and Black progress, or its calculated explanations for the lack of either" in the "Charles Chesnutt's Cakewalk" chapter of *To Wake the Nations* (273). Unfortunately, he does not extend his analysis to *The Colonel's Dream*, a novel that uses many of the same trickster methods as Chesnutt's earlier fiction.
79. Richard Brodhead describes how Chesnutt navigated the northern literary economy in *Cultures of Letters* (193). Francesca Sawaya offers an excellent description of how Chesnutt used patronage to his advantage, a dynamic that invites comparison to his depictions of Julius and Peter, the African American characters who manipulate their white benefactors, in "That Friendship of the Whites."
80. Andrews, *Literary Career of Charles W. Chesnutt*, 224.
81. Chesnutt, *Colonel's Dream*, iii.
82. Chesnutt, 17.
83. Chesnutt, 23.
84. Page, *In Ole Virginia*, 26.
85. Andrews, *Literary Career of Charles W. Chesnutt*, 239.
86. Chesnutt, *Colonel's Dream*, 29.
87. Chesnutt, 29.
88. Chesnutt, 29.
89. Chesnutt, 59.
90. Chesnutt, 66, 69.
91. Chesnutt, 280.
92. Woodward, *Origins of the New South*, 131.
93. Christine Wooley argues that Chesnutt's use of "dreams" is crucial to the text. She writes, "Chesnutt's attention to the fictional—or, in the novel's parlance,

to 'dreams'—exemplifies his ongoing interest in reformulating antebellum, and often sentimental, models of sympathetic encounters between Blacks and whites that fueled the abolitionist movement and which, he believed, could be harnessed to remake the postbellum South." The fact that these are fictions, however, suggests that they would be difficult to implement in reality. See "The Necessary Fictions of Charles Chesnutt's *The Colonel's Dream*."

94. Chesnutt, *Colonel's Dream*, 78.
95. Chesnutt, 105.
96. For details about peonage and the 1903 Coosa and Tallapoosa County trials, see Pete Daniel, *Shadow of Slavery*, and Douglas Blackmon, *Slavery by Another Name*.
97. Chesnutt, "Peonage," 395–96.
98. Chesnutt, *Colonel's Dream*, 281.
99. Chesnutt, 294.
100. Wilson, *Whiteness in the Novels of Charles W. Chesnutt*, 149
101. Fortune, *Black and White*, 28.
102. Fortune, 35.
103. Fortune, 35.
104. Fortune, 94.
105. Fortune, 174–75.
106. Fortune, 241–42.
107. Du Bois, *Black Reconstruction*, 549.
108. Du Bois, 549.
109. Du Bois, 549.
110. Edwards, *Gendered Strife and Confusion*, 78.
111. Thomas, *Literature of Reconstruction*, 14. This book offers a refreshing and insightful analysis of Reconstruction literature emphasizing intertextuality among black and white writers, but it virtually ignores the development of sharecropping.
112. Beckert, *Empire of Cotton*, 306.

### 3. THE NEW SLAVERY

1. For detailed accounts, see Walter White, *Man Called White*, and Ida B. Wells-Barnett, "Arkansas Race Riot."
2. Quoted in Woodruff, *American Congo*, 92.
3. Quoted in Arthur Waskow, *From Race Riot to Sit-In*, 122.
4. Woodruff, *American Congo*, 106.
5. Tannenbaum, *Darker Phases of the South*, 126, 127.

6. For data, see 1920 Census, Census Monograph 4. Farm Tenancy in the United States, 121–29.
7. Giesen, *Boll Weevil Blues*, 48.
8. Stribling, *Store*, 313.
9. In *One Kind of Freedom*, Roger Ransom and Richard Sutch offer an extended economic analysis of the merchant's role in the postbellum economy. Larian Angelo responds to their analysis in "Wage Labour Deferred: The Recreation of Unfree Labour in the US South" to argue that planters were the chief architects of the postbellum economy. Both groups benefited from the exploitation of laborers, and, as the novels illustrate, their roles frequently overlapped.
10. In "Testing the Limits of Tragedy: History and Ideology in John Faulkner's *Dollar Cotton*," Ted Atkinson points out the connections between *Dollar Cotton* and William Faulkner's work, particularly *Absalom, Absalom!* Matthew Lessig describes the Agrarians' displeasure with Stribling's work and their preference for Faulkner in "*The Store*, or T. S. Stribling's Paragraph in the History of Critical Race Studies," and Judith Bryant Wittenberg traces Stribling's influence on Faulkner in "William Faulkner, T. S. Stribling Trilogistic Intertextuality and the Politics of Criticism."
11. For a history of the furnish system, see Thomas D. Clark's essay "The Furnishing and Supply System in Southern Agriculture."
12. Faulkner, *Dollar Cotton*, 44.
13. Faulkner, *Hamlet*, 98.
14. Stribling, *Store*, 108–11.
15. For a thorough account of the laws and court cases that enforced crop lien laws, see Harold Woodman, *New South—New Law*.
16. Stribling, *Store*, 106.
17. Faulkner, *Dollar Cotton*, 133.
18. Percy, *Lanterns on the Levee*, 276.
19. Percy, 278.
20. Percy, 280.
21. Stribling, *Store*, 547–48.
22. Lessig, "*The Store*, or T. S. Stribling's Paragraph," 52.
23. Woodman, *King Cotton and His Retainers*, 294.
24. Faulkner, *Dollar Cotton*, 229.
25. Faulkner, 231.
26. Johnson, Embree, and Alexander, *Collapse of Cotton Tenancy*, 31.
27. Garside, *Cotton Goes to Market*, 41.
28. Patterson, *Slavery and Social Death*, 293.

29. Patterson, 294.
30. Jay Mandle describes the scarcity of federal data in *The Roots of Black Poverty*, 39.
31. Woodson, *Rural Negro*, 26–32.
32. Tolnay, *Bottom Rung*, 4.
33. Litwack, *Trouble in Mind*, 137.
34. Because most school systems in the South refused to make significant investments in educating African American children, social justice philanthropies emerged to construct schools. The most prominent was the Rosenwald program, funded by Julius Rosenwald, president of Sears, Roebuck and Co., which constructed more than five thousand schools across the South. For details on the program, see *You Need a Schoolhouse* by Stephanie Deutsch.
35. Du Bois, *Quest of the Silver Fleece*, 40.
36. In *Sitting in Darkness*, Peter Schmidt describes the imaginary independent school that Du Bois creates as his "alternative vision" to the industrial education model that Booker T. Washington advocated (197).
37. Kelley, *Inchin' Along*, 59.
38. Lee, *River George*, 22.
39. Tolnay, *Bottom Rung*, 12. In *Dark Journey*, Neil McMillen documents that in some exceptional cases Black farmers accumulated large tracts of land, sometimes through thrift and hard work and sometimes through the intercession of a white intermediary (116–18). These instances, however, were outliers.
40. Du Bois, *Quest of the Silver Fleece*, 199.
41. Henderson, *Ollie Miss*, 67.
42. Henderson, 35.
43. Pickens, "Lynching and Debt Slavery," 211.
44. Lee, *River George*, 21–22.
45. Du Bois, *Souls of Black Folk*, 101.
46. Du Bois, 108.
47. Du Bois, 110.
48. Most critics have dismissed Du Bois's novel as at best problematic and at worst failed. Du Bois's reflexive Victorianism complicates his approach to the subject, but his imagination of sharecropping deserves consideration if only for the sociological implications it suggests. For examples of the critical reception of *The Quest of the Silver Fleece*, see Maurice Lee, "Du Bois the Novelist: White Influence, Black Spirit, and *The Quest of the Silver Fleece*." Tomos Hughes's essay "'Can We Imagine This Spectacular Revolution?': Counterfactual Narrative and the 'New World Peasantry' in W. E. B. Du Bois' *Scorn*

and *Black Reconstruction*" offers an interesting reading of the manuscript of Du Bois's first novel, which was not published.
49. McInnis, "Behold the Land," 74.
50. Du Bois, *Quest of the Silver Fleece*, 101.
51. Lee, *River George*, 39.
52. Daniel, *Shadow of Slavery*, 19.
53. In *Slavery by Another Name*, Doug Blackmon discusses the notorious case of J. W. Pace, an Alabama landowner charged with peonage in federal court. He audaciously claimed that the laborers on his land were not peons but slaves because federal law offered no provision for enforcing the Thirteenth Amendment. See 117–54.
54. Griggs, *Hindered Hand*, 123.
55. Du Bois, *Quest of the Silver Fleece*, 70.
56. McMillen, *Dark Journey*, 137–40.
57. Pickens, "Lynching and Debt Slavery," 211. In *A Festival of Violence*, Stewart Tolnay and E. M. Beck analyze the correlation between lynching and the price of cotton, and they find that lynching responds to economic factors. See 119–66.
58. Griggs, *Hindered Hand*, 136.
59. Kelley, *Inchin' Along*, 265.
60. Carter G. Woodson tells an anecdote in *The Rural Negro* of "Negroes so long accustomed to the forced labor [who] have come to regard this as their permanent status." A young woman accompanied a white family to New Jersey where local people contrived to remove her from the white family and help her find an independent living, but "she grieved to get back to her master" (84). The echoes between this story and accounts of slavery are disturbing.
61. Henderson, *Ollie Miss*, 276.
62. Christin Taylor comments, "Henderson's depiction of Ollie's work opens labor as a viable option for single black women, bringing them into the picture of labor concerns" (*Labor Pains*, 41). Her analysis explores how Henderson's novel combines proletarian labor concerns with gender issues.
63. Bontemps, "Summer Tragedy," 135–48.
64. Kroll, *Cabin in the Cotton*, 103.
65. Even though white sharecroppers outnumbered Black sharecroppers, economic histories of sharecropping tend to focus primarily on Black sharecroppers. This may be because the linkage between slavery and sharecropping is apparent, but the fact that whites were incorporated into the system illustrates its perniciousness as a form of exploitation. By the same token, relatively little criticism has been written about the pre-Great

Depression literature of white sharecroppers. One exception is Richard Gray's *Southern Aberrations*, which discusses several obscure southern novels to counter the pervasive denial of southern poverty that stemmed from the Agrarians' prejudice against sociology in literature. See chapter 4.

66. Ransom and Sutch, *One Kind of Freedom*, 104–5.
67. Wright, *Old South, New South*, 108.
68. Kroll, *Cabin in the Cotton*, 20.
69. Green, *This Body the Earth*, 152.
70. Kroll, *Cabin in the Cotton*, 242.
71. Scarborough, *Can't Get a Redbird*, 30.
72. Scarborough, 47.
73. Scarborough, 198.
74. Green, *This Body the Earth*, 15.
75. Bethea, *Cotton*, 10.
76. In *White Trash*, Nancy Isenberg argues that impoverished whites have consistently been socially marginalized in the United States.
77. Bethea, *Cotton*, 96.
78. Bethea, 99, and Paul Green, *This Body the Earth*, 9.
79. Kroll, *The Cabin in the Cotton*, 261. In his autobiography, *I Was a Sharecropper*, Kroll recounts an anecdote in which his mother turned red with anger and forced her children to read aloud and recite multiplication tables to demonstrate that they weren't white trash, 30–32.
80. Kroll, *Cabin in the Cotton*, 270.
81. Green, *This Body the Earth*, 44.
82. Kroll, *Cabin in the Cotton*, 71.
83. Kroll, 249.
84. Scarborough, *Can't Get a Redbird*, 247.
85. Scarborough, 66.
86. Green, *This Body the Earth*, 20.
87. For a thorough discussion of working condition in cotton mills, see *Like a Family: The Making of a Southern Cotton Mill World*, edited by Jacquelyn Hall et al., 44–113.
88. Robertson, *Red Hills and Cotton*, 275.
89. Scarborough, *Can't Get a Redbird*, 362.
90. Bethea, *Cotton*, 315.
91. Scarborough, *Can't Get a Redbird*, 408.
92. Green, *This Body the Earth*, 422.
93. Scholarship on the Great Migration, the diaspora of African Americans out of the South, dwarfs scholarship of southern out-migration as a whole, which

reflects the impact of African American migration on cities outside the South. Three early works expose the early effects of the movement: *A Century of Negro Migration* by Carter G. Woodson, *Negro Migration* by T. J. Woofter, and *The South Goes North* by Robert Coles. Some of the most important later studies include *Land of Hope* by James Grossman, *The Promised Land* by Nicholas Lemann, and *The Warmth of Other Suns* by Isabel Wilkerson.

94. Gregory, *Southern Diaspora*, 19.
95. Gregory, 26, 28.
96. Dozens of works depict the experience of African Americans who moved from the South to the North, such as Jean Toomer's *Cane*, Richard Wright's *Native Son*, and Ralph Ellison's *Invisible Man*. Although books about this experience are common, few books describe the experience of African American sharecroppers leaving the South. *Native Son*, for example, depicts a family that has already relocated from Mississippi to Chicago, omitting the component of departure from the text. Lawrence Rodgers gives a sustained analysis of books depicting the Great Migration in *Canaan Bound*.
97. Battat, *Ain't Got No Home*, 9.
98. Battat, 4.
99. Griffin, *Who Set You Flowin'*, 3.
100. Lawrence Rodgers describes the fugitive migrant plot convention, on which the sharecropper migration plot is based, in *Canaan Bound*, 28–29.
101. Grossman, *Land of Hope*, 47.
102. Attaway, *Blood on the Forge*, 38.
103. Matthew D. Lassiter and Joseph Crespino's collection *The Myth of Southern Exceptionalism* interrogates that persistent maneuver among American historians to project the nation's sins and ills onto the South, leaving the rest of the nation comparatively more moral. The essays in their collection indicate that no part of the nation has a legitimate claim to the moral high ground.
104. Chad Berry explains how white southern migrants assimilated in *Southern Migrants, Northern Exiles*, and Wilkerson describes the lives of Black southerners after migration in *The Warmth of Other Suns*. A generation after migration, most whites had thoroughly assimilated with their local communities, but redlining and de facto segregation kept African Americans marginalized.

## 4. AMERICA'S NUMBER ONE ECONOMIC PROBLEM

1. Cosgrove, "Under a Mississippi Sun."
2. "Biggest Cotton Plantation," 128. Luce began *Fortune* magazine as a luxury publication for America's wealthiest capitalists, but the magazine began its

run just after the Depression began, and its staff included several socialist-leaning intellectuals. As Michael Augspurger explains in *An Economy of Abundant Beauty:* Fortune *Magazine and Depression America*, it included articles about poor workers interspersed with its articles about industrial titans and advertisements for luxury goods for a while before Luce purged the staff of liberals. The profile of Oscar Johnston, who also headed the Agricultural Adjustment Administration finance division, is much more consistent with the magazine's conservative politics. For the record, Johnston's company, D&PL, was the single largest beneficiary of AAA payouts.
3. Mertz, *New Deal Policy and Southern Rural Poverty*, 5.
4. Johnson, Embree, and Alexander, *Collapse of Cotton Tenancy*, 1.
5. Woofter, *Landlord and Tenant*, 72.
6. Rabinowitz, *They Must Be Represented*, 7.
7. Scholars of proletarian literature have largely ignored novels about sharecropping, focusing instead on novels that depict class struggle among urban industrial workers. See, for example, Barbara Foley's *Radical Representations* and Michael Denning's *The Cultural Front*. However, the issues of class consciousness and labor exploitation that typify proletarian novels are equally resonant in Depression-era novels about sharecropping.
8. Carlton and Coclanis, *Confronting Southern Poverty*, 129.
9. Baldwin, *Poverty and Politics*, 4.
10. Carlton and Coclanis, *Confronting Southern Poverty*, 47.
11. Fite, *Cotton Fields No More*, 130.
12. Biles, *South and the New Deal*, 40.
13. Wright, *Old South, New South*, 228. An econometric study by Briggs Depew, Price Fishback, and Paul Rhode, "New Deal or No Deal in the Cotton South: The Effect of the AAA on the Agricultural Labor Structure," suggests "that the AAA played a significant role in the displacement of black and white sharecroppers and black managing tenants even though it was a violation of AAA contracts for landlords to displace these workers," 466.
14. Conrad, *Forgotten Farmers*, 66
15. Myrdal, *American Dilemma*, 258.
16. Paul Mertz explains that the FSA never lived up to its expectations. Although it helped stabilize some farmers in land ownership, "it was always clear that rural rehabilitation never came close to its goal of reaching all low income farmers" (*New Deal Policy*, 207).
17. Although not as well-known as some of his peers, Woofter was an important early sociologist of race. Mark Ellis traces his relationships with several other important social scientists and racial activists in *Race Harmony and Black Progress: Jack Woofter and the Interracial Cooperation Movement*. In

addition to the government studies discussed here, Woofter also cowrote another book based on his analysis, *Seven Lean Years*.
18. The increase in tenants was one of the key points used to make the case for the Bankhead-Jones Act in *Farm Tenancy*, 3–5.
19. Woofter, *Landlord and Tenant*, 85.
20. Holley, Winston, and Woofter, *Plantation South*, 46.
21. Woofter, *Landlord and Tenant*, xviii.
22. Holley, Winston, and Woofter, *Plantation South*, 54.
23. Woofter and Fisher, *Plantation South Today*, 14.
24. Holley, Winston, and Woofter, *Plantation South*, 18. Woofter's analyses typically rely upon numerical data, but in *Seven Lean Years* (written with Ellen Winston) he offers some character sketches that humanize the tenant farmers on relief, 94–102.
25. Woofter, *Landlord and Tenant*, 91.
26. Holley, Winston, and Woofter, *Plantation South*, 28.
27. Woofter, *Landlord and Tenant*, 143.
28. Woofter, 110.
29. Woofter, 153.
30. Woofter, 179.
31. Woofter, 184–90.
32. *Farm Tenancy*, 10.
33. Woofter, *Landlord and Tenant*, 166.
34. Carlton and Coclanis, *Confronting Southern Poverty*, 70.
35. Carlton and Coclanis, 78.
36. Holley, Winston, and Woofter, *Plantation South*, 76.
37. Robert L. Snyder describes the film's reception in *Pare Lorentz*, 63–75.
38. Knepper, "Nation's Bioregion," 101.
39. Kirby, *Mockingbird Song*, 240–41.
40. Faulkner, *Men Working*, 18.
41. John Faulkner's novel invites comparisons to William Faulkner's short story "The Tall Men" (1941). In the story, a government agent goes to the Macallums' farm to arrest Anse and Lucius for failing to register with selective service, and the agent expects them to be the kind of "people who lie about and conceal the ownership of land and property in order to hold relief jobs" (46). He learns that they are, instead, rugged individualists who have refused to grow cotton because the government had "begun to interfere with how a man farmed his own land" (55). They resent government intrusion and bureaucracy, but as their generations of military service prove, they are willing to serve their country. In William Faulkner's story, the independent farmers are noble figures.

42. Faulkner, *Men Working*, 67.
43. Faulkner, 75.
44. Faulkner, 163.
45. Faulkner, 165.
46. Faulkner, 300.
47. Caldwell, "Tenant Farmer," 5.
48. Caldwell, 11.
49. Caldwell, 27.
50. Biles, *South and the New Deal*, 53.
51. Powdermaker, *After Freedom*, xiii.
52. Hortense Powdermaker gives a more complete story of her time in Indianola in her memoir, *Stranger and Friend*. Fifty years after Powdermaker's visit to Indianola, Patricia Alyward Farr revisited to community to find people who remembered Powdermaker, and she discovered that several of her informants did recall her visit, and they had amusing anecdotes about the Yankee woman.
53. Singal, *War Within*, 91.
54. Vance, *Human Factors in Cotton Culture*, 295.
55. Louis Mazzari explains in *Southern Modernist* that Raper wrote the book to explain the waves of outmigration from southern farming communities: "How would a modern, progressive society respond to these refugees from a dying, agrarian past? To Raper, this was the most important question facing modern America. The answer would portend the prospects of democracy in machine-age America and throughout the world," 107.
56. Johnson, *Shadow of the Plantation*, 6.
57. Egerton, *Speak Now Against the Day*, 91.
58. Johnson, Embree, and Alexander, *Collapse of Cotton Tenancy*, 5.
59. Johnson, *Shadow of the Plantation*, 16.
60. Vance, *Human Factors in Cotton Culture*, 210.
61. Rubin, *Plantation County*, 10.
62. Dollard reflected on his time in Indianola in an interview with William Ferris. He lived in a boarding house owned by Craig Claiborne's mother, and he was harassed for breaking racial protocols, such as referring to African Americans with honorific titles.
63. Dollard, *Caste and Class*, 62.
64. Dollard, 63.
65. Davis, Gardner, and Gardner, *Deep South*, 232.
66. Adams and Gorton, "Southern Trauma," 335.
67. Powdermaker, *After Freedom*, 82.
68. Raper, *Preface to Peasantry*, 75.

69. Hagood, *Mothers of the South*, 5.
70. Johnson, *Shadow of the Plantation*, 150.
71. Rubin, *Plantation County*, 27.
72. Johnson, Alexander, and Embree, *Collapse of Cotton Tenancy*, 22.
73. Johnson, *Shadow of the Plantation*, 128.
74. Powdermaker, *After Freedom*, 87.
75. Johnson, *Shadow of the Plantation*, 25.
76. Davis, Gardner, and Gardner, *Deep South*, 223.
77. Powdermaker, *After Freedom*, 88.
78. Raper, *Preface to Peasantry*, 158.
79. Vance, *Human Geography of the South*, 202–3.
80. Rubin, *Plantation County*, 98.
81. Raper, *Preface to Peasantry*, 272.
82. Johnson, Embree, and Alexander, *Collapse of Cotton Tenancy*, 51.
83. Powdermaker, *After Freedom*, 138.
84. Vance, *Human Geography*, 497.
85. Johnson, Embree, and Alexander, *Collapse of Cotton Tenancy*, 44; Dollard, *Class and Caste*, 131.
86. Hagood, *Mothers of the South*, 244.
87. Vance, *Human Factors in Cotton Culture*, 185.
88. Johnson, *Shadow of the Plantation*, 212.
89. Raper, *Preface to Peasantry*, 126.
90. Johnson, Embree, and Alexander, *Collapse of Cotton Tenancy*, 64–69.
91. Quoted in Kidd, "Dissonant Encounters," 40.
92. Kidd, "Dissonant Encounters," 42–43.
93. One of the precursors for Caldwell and Bourke-White's book was an interesting collaboration between Julia Peterkin and Doris Ulmann, *Roll, Jordan, Roll* (1932). It is a photo documentary of sorts that pairs Ulmann's gauzy images of plantation life with Peterkin's minstrel sketches of African Americans in South Carolina. At about the same time that this book was published, Eudora Welty was considering publishing a collection of her own photographs and stories. Harriett Pollack documents that Welty's publisher declined the project because they were too similar to Peterkin and Ulmann's project (*Eudora Welty's Fiction and Photographs*, 72). Welty eventually published a collection of photographs, *One Time, One Place*, in 1971, but stories that would have accompanied the pictures were lost.
94. Stott, *Documentary Expression and Thirties America*, 214.
95. In her memoir, *Portrait of Myself*, Margaret Bourke White explains how the project developed. She was working for *Fortune* magazine and learned

about an author who "wanted to do a book with pictures that would show the authenticity of the people and conditions about which he wrote" (113). Initially, their relationship was turbulent and the project was delayed, but they eventually became lovers and were married for a few years, during which they collaborated on another photo documentary about the rise of fascism in Europe.

96. Two other photo documentaries were published in collaboration with the Farm Security Administration, but they deliberately focus on the entire country rather than rural southerners, although they do include some of the photographs taken in the South. Sherwood Anderson wrote *Home Town* (1940) as a paean to America's small towns, and it extends many of the themes about community life that he develops in *Winesburg, Ohio* (1919). Archibald MacLeish wrote the highly underrated long poem *Land of the Free* (1938) using FSA photographs to illustrate the nation's sense of resolve in the face of uncertainty during the Depression.

97. James Curtis explains that Stryker explicitly did not value aesthetics. He writes: "There was no doubt in Stryker's mind that his photographers had 'produced some great pictures, pictures that will live the way great paintings live, But is it art? Is any photography art? I've always avoided this particular controversy,' Stryker contended. . . . Uncomfortable with art, Stryker did not hesitate to summon other words to define his life's work: sociology, journalism, history, and above all education" (*Mind's Eye, Mind's Truth*, 11).

98. Quoted in Anderson, *Home Town*, 143.

99. Natanson, *Black Image in the New Deal*, 59. Natanson notes that almost 10 percent of the images in the FSA library were African American subjects, but the racial politics of the time made the use of these images complicated and potentially controversial.

100. Stott, *Documentary Expression and Thirties America*, 9.

101. Rabinowitz, *They Must Be Represented*, 35–36.

102. Allred, *American Modernism and Depression Documentary*, 7.

103. Caldwell and Bourke-White, *You Have Seen Their Faces*, i. The book ends with a highly technical note from Margaret Bourke-White about her photography technique that describes the cameras and lighting she used and how she manipulated the subjects for the photographs: "Sometimes I would set up the camera in a corner of the room, sit some distance away from it with a remote control in my hand, and watch our people while Mr. Caldwell talked with them. It might be an hour before their faces or gestures gave us what we were trying to express, but the instant it occurred the scene

was imprisoned on a sheet of film before they knew what was happening" (Caldwell and Bourke-White, *You Have Seen Their Faces*, 51).

104. Caldwell and Bourke-White, *You Have Seen Their Faces*, unnumbered. Margaret Bourke-White describes their process of writing captions as "a real collaboration." They arranged pictures on the floor, and each wrote separate captions for what they imagined the subject of the picture would be thinking, then often combined their ideas to produce the text. "We did not want the matter of whether the pictures 'illustrated' the text, or the words explained the pictures, to have any importance," she explains. "We wanted a result in which the pictures and words truly supplemented one another, merging into a unified whole" (Bourke-White, *Portrait of Myself*, 137).

105. Wright, *Twelve Million Black Voices*, 30. Mehdi Ghasemi reads Wright's use of first-person plural as "documentary fiction" ("Equation of Collectivity," 72), and Jason Puskar analyzes the disconnect between the work of the white photographers who produced the images and Wright's racialized narrative voice ("Black and White and Read," 168).

106. In *The Making of James Agee*, Hugh Davis claims that "both Agee and Walker Evans were heavily influenced by the surrealist movement as it developed in New York during the 1930s, so much that any consideration of [*Let Us Now Praise Famous Men*] that does not take their appropriation of avant-garde ideas and techniques into account is fundamentally lacking" (53).

107. Nixon, *Forty Acres and Steel Mules*, 3.

108. Nixon contributed an essay on the southern economy to the Agrarian collection *I'll Stand My Stand*, but he disavowed his relationship with the Agrarians. In the preface to *Forty Acres and Steel Mules*, he writes, "There is not only kinship but discrepancy between the present study and my chapter in *I'll Take My Stand*, and I wish to anticipate any possible critic in making this point. I participated in the 'agrarian' indictment of the American industrial system of the nineteen-twenties, but I seek a broader program of agricultural reconstruction" (v).

109. Caldwell and Bourke-White, *You Have Seen Their Faces*, 11.

110. Agee and Evans, *Let Us Now Praise Famous Men*, 363.

111. Caldwell and Bourke-White, *You Have Seen Their Faces*, 11.

112. Nixon, *Forty Acres and Steel Mules*, 25.

113. Wright, *Twelve Million Black Voices*, 35.

114. Agee and Evans, *Let Us Now Praise Famous Men*, 319.

115. Lange and Taylor, *American Exodus*, 40.

116. Agee and Evans, *Let Us Now Praise Famous Men*, 115.

117. Agee and Evans, 118.

118. Nixon, *Forty Acres and Steel Mules*, 20.
119. Wright, *Twelve Million Black Voices*, 43.
120. Raper and De Reid, *Sharecroppers All*, 35 and 146. Louis Mazzari argues that Raper's actual focus in *Sharecroppers All* is on American capitalism rather than southern agriculture. He writes, "Raper expanded the rope of feudalism he had explored in *Preface to Peasantry* in stating the theme of the book—that American capitalism, if it continued to restrict citizens from participating in democratic action, would betray the promise of greater equality of opportunity" (*Southern Modernist*, 183).
121. Hullinger, *Plowing Through*, 36.
122. Nixon, *Forty Acres and Steel Mules*, 57.
123. Raper and De Reid, *Sharecroppers All*, 41.
124. Wright, *Twelve Million Black Voices*, 49.
125. Agee and Evans, *Let Us Now Praise Famous Men*, 120.
126. Caldwell and Bourke-White, *You Have Seen Their Faces*, 44.
127. Nixon, *Forty Acres and Steel Mules*, 90; Lange and Taylor, *American Exodus*, 152, 254.
128. Agee and Evans, *Let Us Now Praise Famous Men*, 207.
129. Agee and Evans, 14.
130. Raper, *Sharecroppers All*, vi.
131. Raper, 145.
132. Caldwell and Bourke-White, *You Have Seen Their Faces*, 28.
133. Kester, *Revolt among the Sharecroppers*, ii.
134. Lowell K. Dyson gives a history of agricultural labor movements in *Red Harvest*. He notes that, except for the Sharecroppers Union, almost all of the agricultural unions affiliated with the Communist Party were located in the Midwest and West Coast.
135. In 1929, workers at the Loray cotton mill in Gastonia, North Carolina, went on strike, leading to a violent backlash by strikebreakers. The strike was unsuccessful, but it became a key touchstone for labor organizing in the South. For details on the strike, see John Salmond's *Gastonia 1929: The Story of the Loray Mill Strike*.
136. Conrad, *Forgotten Farmers*, 94.
137. These oral histories contrast substantially with *On Shares: Ed Brown's Story* by Jane Maguire. Brown was a sharecropper from south Georgia who worked passively for a sequence of difficult landowners.
138. Thomas, "Plight of the Sharecropper," 4.
139. Kester, *Revolt among the Sharecroppers*, 37.
140. Mitchell, *Mean Things Happening*, 22.

141. Honey, *Sharecroppers' Troubadour*, 43.
142. Ross, *Rise and Fall*, 82.
143. Simon, *Share-cropper*, 190–91.
144. Kelley, *Hammer and Hoe*, 56.
145. James Giesen interrogates Theodore Rosengarten's collaborative role as recorder, writer, and editor of Cobb's oral history in "Creating 'Nate Shaw': The Making and Remaking of *All God's Dangers*."
146. Rosengarten, *All God's Dangers*, 309.
147. Mitchell, *Mean Things Happening*, 47.
148. Conrad, *Forgotten Farmers*, 84.
149. Kester, *Revolt among the Sharecroppers*, 57.
150. Kester, 72.
151. Kester, 56.
152. Thomas, "Plight of the Share-cropper," 15.
153. Manthorne, "View from the Cotton," 2010.
154. Manthorne, 2010.
155. Simon, *Share-cropper*, 196.
156. Kester, *Revolt among the Sharecroppers*, 18.
157. Ross, *Rise and Fall*, 101.
158. Kester, *Revolt among the Sharecroppers*, 33.
159. Simon, *The Share-cropper*, 168.
160. Mitchell, *Mean Things Happening*, 42.
161. Grubbs, *Cry from the Cotton*, 25.
162. Mitchell, *Mean Things Happening*, 61.
163. Conrad, *Forgotten Farmers*, 178.
164. Honey, *Sharecroppers' Troubadour*, 47–48.
165. Mitchell, *Mean Things Happening*, 82.
166. The text of the newsreel is quoted in H. L. Mitchell, *Mean Things Happening*, 102–3. The newsreel can be found online at https://www.youtube.com/watch?v=Q-I5aX7qZtQ.
167. Mitchell, *Mean Things Happening*, 91.
168. Conrad, *Forgotten Farmers*, 91. One of the most notorious events during the reign of terror was the whipping of Willie Sue Blagden, a middle-class white woman. While the beatings and murders of many sharecroppers were mostly ignored, her story garnered national headlines. Jennifer Ritterhouse explores the incident in "Woman Flogged: Willie Sue Blagden, the Southern Tenant Farmers Union, and How an Impulse for Story Led to a Historiographical Corrective."
169. Honey, *Sharecroppers' Troubadour*, 89.

170. Kester, *Revolt among the Sharecroppers*, 81.
171. Simon, *The Share-cropper*, 213–18.
172. Brown, "Sharecroppers," 182.
173. Grubbs, *Cry from the Cotton*, 81.
174. Kelley, *Hammer and Hoe*, 169, 170.
175. Kester, *Revolt among the Sharecroppers*, 92.
176. Martin, *Howard Kester*, 100.
177. Mitchell describes the survey question and results in *Mean Things Happening*, 125–27.
178. Cantor, *Prologue to the Protest Movement*, 64.
179. Jarod Roll's photo essay, "'Out Yonder on the Road': Working Class Self-Representation and the 1939 Roadside Demonstration in Southeast Missouri," explains how the strike became a visual text in political discourse.
180. In the essay "Sharing Time: C. L. R. James and Southern Agrarian Movements," Walter Taylor offers a provocative analysis of James's agenda, which is based more on Communist infighting between Trotskyites and Stalinists than on the rights of sharecroppers.
181. James, "With the Sharecroppers," 25.
182. James, 31.
183. Ross, *Rise and Fall*, 101.
184. Ross, 5.
185. Simon, *Share-cropper*, 246–47.
186. O'Connor, "Crop," 733.
187. *Tobacco Road* is a highly problematic text. The Jeeters in the novel are not technically sharecroppers. They had been sharecroppers, but the absentee landowner ceases planting because of the diminished price of cotton, so the Jeeters are squatters on the land, and they are unable to get credit from any of the local stores for food, fertilizer, or seed. They are, thus, utterly destitute to the point of starvation as a result of economic forces, although the novel strongly suggests that their depravity is the cause of their abjection. Most readers of the salacious novel focus their attention on the family's sexual promiscuity and their astonishingly poor judgment, missing the impact of the economic dynamics. In fact, the novel implies that the Jeeters would be better off as sharecroppers with a landowner to extend them credit to buy food and seed to plant a crop and to provide paternalistic control to curb the family's outrageous behavior. Caldwell's short story "Kneel to the Rising Sun" offers a comparatively sympathetic portrayal of sharecroppers laboring in the thrall of a sadistic, racist landowner. The fact that Caldwell's works have become synonymous with portrayals of sharecroppers has had

an overall deleterious and demeaning effect on the cultural representation of sharecropping.
188. Foley, *Radical Representations*, 109
189. Peeler, *Hope among Us Yet*, 151.
190. Rylee, *Deep Dark River*, 26.
191. Perry, *Hold Autumn in Your Hand*, 8.
192. Perry, 36. Jean Renoir's film *The Southerner* (1945) was based on *Hold Autumn in Your Hand*. For a discussion of the film and novel, see Hart Wegner's essay "A Chronicle of Soil, Seasons, and Weather: Jean Renoir's *The Southerner*."
193. Davis, *White Scourge*, ix.
194. By the 1930s, east Texas was one of the largest cotton-producing regions in the nation. Neil Foley's book *The White Scourge: Mexicans, Blacks, and Poor Whites in Texas Cotton Culture*, which borrows its title from Davis's book, describes labor conditions in the area.
195. Russell, *Wind is Rising*, 4.
196. Russell, 92.
197. Russell, 93.
198. Munz, *Land without Moses*, 1–2.
199. Munz, 24.
200. Munz, 88.
201. Munz, 88.
202. Munz, 115.
203. Munz, 233.
204. John Steinbeck describes landowners reluctantly turning tenants off their land in *The Grapes of Wrath* because "a bank or finance company owned the land" (41). In his book, the families turned off, including the Joads, begin an extended exodus to California. This book shares many similarities with sharecropper novels, but the plot focuses primarily on the family's journey, while most sharecropper novels depict families restricted to their land by debt and coercion.
205. The postbellum southern penal system was modeled directly on slavery. In *Worse than Slavery*, David Oshinsky describes Parchman State Penitentiary, a state-owned cotton plantation, where inmates spent their sentences working in cotton fields.
206. Rylee, *Deep Dark River*, 284.
207. Daniel, *Shadow of Slavery*, 11.
208. Munz, *Land without Moses*, 203.
209. Wilson, *High John the Conqueror*, 9.
210. Perry, *Hold Autumn in Your Hand*, 224.

211. Munz, *Land without Moses*, 144.
212. Munz, 164.
213. Perry, *Hold Autumn in Your Hand*, 204.
214. Jacquelyn Dowd Hall discusses Grace Lumpkin's involvement with the southern labor movement and the Communist Party in "Women Writers, the 'Southern Front,' and the Dialectical Imagination." This particular essay focuses mostly on Lumpkin's role in textile mill strikes and her novel about Ella Mae Wiggins, *To Make My Bread*. Lumpkin's work organizing sharecroppers and *A Sign for Cain* are less well known.
215. Lumpkin, *Sign for Cain*, 204.
216. Wright was officially a member of the Communist Party, and the story was originally published in a Communist journal, *The Masses*. The story, thus, reflects many of the characteristics of communist ideology.
217. Wright, *Uncle Tom's Children*, 410.
218. Russell, *Wind Is Rising*, 144.
219. Russell, 170.
220. Lanham, *Stricklands*, 15.
221. Lanham, 65.
222. The Southern Tenant Farmers Union was active in Oklahoma where Odis Sweeden, a Native American man, was an organizer among Native American communities. See H. L. Mitchell, *Mean Things Happening*, 77.
223. Munz, *Land without Moses*, 56.
224. Lanham, *Stricklands*, 103.
225. Lanham, 103
226. Perry, *Hold Autumn in Your Hand*, 249.
227. Perry, xii.
228. Munz, *Land without Moses*, 367.
229. Munz, 15.
230. Aiken, *Cotton Plantation South*, 120.

## 5. THE END OF SHARECROPPING

1. Charles Aiken explains that the introduction of agricultural machinery led to new paradigms of agricultural labor and reorganized sharecropping plantations. On many plantations, cabins in the fields were destroyed and replaced with nucleated workers' quarters, and workers labored in gangs under an overseer, much as slaves had worked before the Civil War. He refers to this twentieth-century reversion to nineteenth-century labor as the "neoplantation" (*Cotton Plantation South*, 110–13).
2. Holley, *Second Great Emancipation*, 193.

3. Walker, *Grange Copeland*, 234.
4. Gaines, *Jane Pittman*, 12.
5. Street, *New Revolution*, 63.
6. Walker, *Grange Copeland*, 8.
7. Wright, *Old South, New South*, 241.
8. Walker, *Grange Copeland*, 127.
9. Daniel, *Breaking the Land*, 244.
10. Economic historians have engaged in a long-running debate about whether mechanization pushed out labor or whether other labor opportunities created a need for mechanization. Richard Day argues that machines pushed laborers out of farming, Willis Peterson and Yoav Kislev argue that labor pull exerted a greater force, and Wayne A. Grove and Craig Heinicke argue that acreage reduction and mechanization pushed laborers out of the fields.
11. Maharidge and Williamson, *And Their Children after Them*, 103.
12. Maharidge and Williamson, 103.
13. Maharidge and Williamson, 82. In *Mule South to Tractor South*, George Ellenberg explains that many southern farmers were reluctant to give up on mules because "mules simply appeared to be too useful to be supplanted by machines" (100).
14. Maharidge and Williamson, *And Their Children after Them*, 82.
15. Walker, *Grange Copeland*, 113.
16. Day, "Economics of Technological Change," 429–30.
17. Aiken, *Cotton Plantation South*, 102.
18. Street, *New Revolution*, 170.
19. Peterson and Kislev, "Cotton Harvester in Retrospect," 205.
20. Street, *New Revolution*, 100–106.
21. Street, 133.
22. Maharidge and Williamson, *And Their Children after Them*, 41.
23. Quoted in Brown, *King Cotton*, 129.
24. Maharidge and Williamson, *And Their Children after Them*, 43–44.
25. Grove and Heinicke, "Better Opportunities or Worse?" 738.
26. Maharidge and Williamson, *And Their Children after Them*, 131–32. Charles Aiken explains that displaced sharecropping families often found housing in federally subsidized housing complexes in rural communities in "New Type of Black Ghetto."
27. In *Southern Paternalism and the American Welfare State*, Lee Alston and Joseph Ferrie argue that "mechanization of cotton was the major catalyst for bringing about the rapid expansion of the federal welfare state and the massive outmigration from the rural South" (119).

28. Critics have addressed the representation of racial progress in Gaines's novel. In "'We Ain't Going Back There': The Idea of Progress in *The Autobiography of Miss Jane Pittman*," William L. Andrews describes the novel as a "dialectic between progress and regress" (563), and Robert Patterson argues that "*The Autobiography of Miss Jane Pittman* deploys Black freedom struggles as points of departure to elucidate the shortcomings of exodus politics as a strategy for empowerment" ("Rethinking Definitions," 341).
29. Walker, *Grange Copeland*, 249.
30. Walker, 248.
31. Theodore Mason observes that *The Third Life of Grange Copeland* is "a novel dominated by the idea of cycle and repetition" ("Alice Walker's 'The Third Life,'" 299).
32. Walker, *Grange Copeland*, 230.
33. Maharidge and Williamson, *And Their Children after Them*, 97.
34. Gaines, *Jane Pittman*, 157.
35. Gaines, 168.
36. Mandle, *Roots of Black Poverty*, 90.
37. Walker, *Grange Copeland*, 243.
38. Walker, 246.
39. Daniel, "African American Farmers," 9. In "The Great Land Robbery," Vann R. Newkirk documents that "98 percent of black agricultural landowners in America" have been dispossessed, mostly since the 1950s: "They have lost 12 million acres over the past century."
40. Walker, *Grange Copeland*, 80. Gilbert Fite explains that in the 1950s and 1960s several new agricultural programs emerged in the South, including dairy, cattle, poultry, eggs, peanuts, soybeans, fruit, and timber (*Cotton Fields No More*, 199–206). Ironically, the USDA and various progressive groups had been advocating for diversification as a means to ameliorate labor tension for decades.
41. Walker, *Grange Copeland*, 144.
42. Maharidge and Williamson, *And Their Children after Them*, 212.
43. Street, *New Revolution*, 149.
44. Maharidge and Williamson, *And Their Children after Them*, v.
45. Mandle, *Roots of Black Poverty*, 96.
46. Maharidge and Williamson, *And Their Children after Them*, 250–51.
47. De Jong, *You Can't Eat Freedom*, 4.
48. Killens, *'Sippi*, 278.
49. Gaines, *Of Love and Dust*, 26
50. Gaines, 225.

51. Killens, *'Sippi*, vi.
52. Killens, vii-viii.
53. Fair, *Many Thousand Gone*, 5.
54. Fair, 6.
55. Killens, *'Sippi*, 99.
56. Gaines, *Of Love and Dust*, 248; Fair, *Many Thousand Gone*, 23.
57. Kelley, *Different Drummer*, 132.
58. There are several excellent works that describe the populations flow known as the Great Migration, such as Nicholas Lemann's *The Promised Land: The Great Black Migration and How It Changed America* and Isabel Wilkerson's *The Warmth of Other Suns: The Epic Story of America's Great Migration*.
59. Kelley, *Different Drummer*, 123.
60. Kelley, 183.
61. Kelley, 183.
62. Sundquist, "Promised Lands," 281.
63. Killens, *'Sippi*, xii.
64. Jones, *White Band*, 16.
65. Killens, *'Sippi*, 253.
66. Gilyard, *John Oliver Killens*, 219.
67. In *SNCC's Stories*, Sharon Monteith examines the archives of SNCC print culture, including field reports, pamphlets, newsletters, fiction, essays, poetry, and plays, which describe the experiences of SNCC volunteers and operatives.
68. Walker, *Meridian*, 77.
69. The gender roles that Walker depicts in the civil rights movement have been the subject of several essays, including "Remembering the Dream: Alice Walker, *Meridian* and the Civil Rights Movement" by Roberta Hendrickson; "Presenting Our Bodies, Laying Our Case: The Political Efficacy of Grief and Rage during the Civil Rights Movement in Alice Walker's *Meridian*" by Shermaine M. Jones; and "Alice Walker's *Meridian*, Feminism, and the 'Movement'" by Susan Danielson. In *Local People*, John Dittmer states that "although the movement of the 1960s did not eliminate gender discrimination within its ranks, it came closer to the ideal of an egalitarian community than had any major social movement in this nation's history" (127).
70. In Junius Edwards's 1963 novel *If We Must Die*, Will Harris, an African American Korean War veteran, attempts to register to vote in an unnamed southern city. The novel illustrates both why voting was important to a person who had served in the military and the demeaning methods registrars used to deny voting rights.

71. Walker, *Meridian*, 102.
72. Walker, 102.
73. Killens, *'Sippi*, 209.
74. Killens, 317.
75. Killens, 317.
76. In the same year that *'Sippi* was published, Senator Robert Kennedy visited Mississippi, drawing media attention to the starvation and poverty rampant in the Delta. See *Delta Epiphany* by Ellen B. Meacham.
77. Fair, *Many Thousand Gone*, 64.
78. Fair, 78.
79. Fair, 106.
80. Jones, *White Band*, 61.
81. Killens, *'Sippi*, 311–12.
82. Killens, 254.
83. Killens, 267.
84. Killens, 267.
85. Killens, 270.
86. Killens, 280.
87. Killens, 290.
88. Killens, 293.
89. Killens, 373.
90. McAdam, *Freedom Summer*, 81.
91. Killens, *'Sippi*, 359.
92. Kwame Ture, formerly known as Stokely Carmichael, explains the ideology in *Black Power*, cowritten with Charles V. Hamilton.
93. Killens, *'Sippi*, 385.
94. Killens, 386.
95. Kelley, *Different Drummer*, 178.
96. Fair, *Many Thousand Gone*, 18.
97. Fair, 24.
98. Charles Payne writes, "the collapse of the cotton-based economy removed the most fundamental reasons for controlling Blacks" (*I've Got the Light*, 20). He argues that lynching was a means of controlling labor, and he notes a correlation between the number of lynchings in plantation areas and the price of cotton.
99. Fair, *Many Thousand Gone*, 107.
100. Fair, 111.
101. Fair, 113.
102. Killens, *'Sippi*, 428.

103. Killens, 430.
104. Killens, 431.
105. Walker, *Meridian*, 202.
106. Walker, 203.
107. Walker, 189. Meridian and Lynne have a complicated relationship in the novel, but as Suzanne Jones explains in *Race Mixing*, the volatility of their relationship is based on equality (73).
108. Walker, *Meridian*, 189.
109. Walker, 190.
110. Walker, 190.
111. Flowers, *Throwed Away*, 50.
112. Flowers, 51.
113. Flowers, xi.
114. Berry, *Home Ground*, 7.
115. Andrews, "In Search," 42.
116. Kroll, *I Was a Sharecropper*, 71.
117. Moody, *Coming of Age*, 3.
118. Moody, 10. Angela Pulley Hudson argues that Moody's autobiography associates the spatial experience of Mississippi with pain. Concerning this incident with George Lee, she writes, "The association of pain with freedom is not only interconnected with Anne's racial and socioeconomic position but also with her shifting relationship to her family. This early identification of homeland and family with immobility, imprisonment, and violence marks the beginning of Anne's melancholic attachment to Mississippi" ("Mississippi Lost and Found," 284).
119. King and Riley, *Daddy King*, 30.
120. Zack Vernon observes that "the poverty and violence of Crews's sharecropping and tenant farming community was so extreme that his memoir is pervaded with grotesque rhetoric, imagery, and anecdotes" ("Enfreakment," 196).
121. Crews, *Childhood*, 40.
122. Lewis and D'Orso, *Walking with the Wind*, 6.
123. Lewis and D'Orso, 28.
124. Flowers, *Throwed Away*, 47.
125. Crews, *Childhood*, 32.
126. Flowers, *Throwed Away*, 36.
127. Moody, *Coming of Age*, 87.
128. Moody, 88.
129. Moody, 90.

130. Lewis and D'Orso, *Walking with the Wind*, 10.
131. Lewis and D'Orso, 10.
132. King and Riley, *Daddy King*, 24.
133. King and Riley, 24.
134. Flowers, *Throwed Away*, 64.
135. King and Riley, *Daddy King*, 41.
136. King and Riley, 44.
137. Carter, *An Hour before Daylight*, 50.
138. Carter, 51.
139. Carter, 51.
140. Carter, 66. Carter's defenses of sharecropping echo William Alexander Percy's arguments in *Lanterns on the Levee*. Percy writes, "I happen to believe that profit-sharing is the most moral system under which human beings can work together and I am convinced that if it were accepted in principle by capital and labor, our industrial troubles would largely cease. So on Trail Lake [his family's plantation] I continue to be partners with the sons of ex-slaves and to share fifty-fifty with them" (278). John Hodges, who was the child of Mississippi sharecroppers, exposes the power dynamics of the relationship. He explains, "blacks were important to the structure of the southern aristocracy. While few aristocrats would disagree with this statement, they may not be willing to acknowledge the extent of their indebtedness to the blacks about them. Percy himself has some sense of the worth of blacks to his own identity as a southern aristocrat" ("William Alexander Percy's *Lanterns*," 41). Percy's supposed profit sharing is a veneer on a paternalistic system of racial and economic exploitation. Despite what Percy and Carter claim, there was no equitable system of sharecropping.
141. Carter, *An Hour before Daylight*, 52.
142. McLaurin, *Separate Pasts*, 17.
143. McLaurin, 26.
144. King and Riley, *Daddy King*, 37.
145. Lewis and D'Orso, *Walking with the Wind*, 41.
146. Flowers, *Throwed Away*, 91.
147. Flowers, 6.
148. Flowers, 214.
149. For details on the rise of the Sun Belt, see B. L. Weinstein and R. E. Firestine, *Regional Growth and Decline in the United States: The Rise of the Sunbelt and the Decline of the Northeast*, and David Goldfield, "The Urban South: A Regional Framework."
150. Flowers, *Throwed Away*, 186.

151. Flowers, 186.
152. Flowers, 191.
153. James Gregory documents in *The Southern Diaspora* that more than seven million southerners left the South between 1950 and 1980. At the same time, southern cities grew rapidly, outpacing most cities in the Northeast and Midwest, so the region's population grew even as people left rural areas. According to John F. McDonald, "The population of 18 metropolitan areas [in the South] more than doubled from 1950 to 1970 to 18.24 million as the population of the South increased by 36.9%" ("Urban Areas").
154. Crews, *Childhood*, 128.
155. Lewis and D'Orso, *Walking with the Wind*, 17.
156. King and Riley, *Daddy King*, 98.
157. McLaurin, *Separate Pasts*, 4.
158. Moody, *Coming of Age*, 130.
159. Lewis and D'Orso, *Walking with the Wind*, 47.
160. Moody, *Coming of Age*, 277.
161. McLaurin, *Separate Pasts*, 176.
162. Flowers, *Throwed Away*, 78.
163. Flowers, 209.

### 6. THE AFTERLIFE OF SHARECROPPING

1. "Senator Tim Scott."
2. Bella and Elfrink. "Warnock."
3. Over the past decade, the Mississippi Delta has developed a tourist economy that commodifies aspects of sharecropping in ways that echo plantation tourism. In Clarksdale, Mississippi, for example, tourists can visit Ground Zero Blues Club, a facsimile of a Delta juke joint co-owned by actor Morgan Freeman, and they can spend the night at Shack Up Inn, a hotel composed of air-conditioned sharecropper cabins arranged on the grounds of the Hopson Plantation.
4. Olsson, "South in the World," 68.
5. In the 2000s, in the wake of the North American Free Trade Agreement, the exodus of southern textiles, and the influx of immigrants into the South, southern studies took a global turn as scholars reflected on the South's complicated relationship to not only the United States but also other countries. Some of the key works from this approach are *Grounded Globalism* by James L. Peacock; *The American South in a Global World*, edited by James L. Peacock, Harry L. Watson, and Carrie R. Matthews; and *Globalization and the American South*, edited by James C. Cobb and William Stueck.

6. Beckert, *Empire of Cotton*, 438.
7. In *Memphis and the Paradox of Place*, Wanda Rushing offers a case study of globalization in a southern city. Once the nexus of the Delta cotton economy, the city has evolved into a hub for logistics and transportation with a diverse population. Many of the social processes that she describes that contribute to the city's change are consequences of the end of sharecropping.
8. Beckert, *Empire of Cotton*, 441.
9. Helferich, *High Cotton*, 107.
10. Helferich, xii.
11. In *The Most Southern Place on Earth*, James Cobb argues that the Delta clung to antebellum social and economic practices, specifically the cultivation of cotton, into the late twentieth century, becoming a subculture within the US South.
12. Helferich, *High Cotton*, 17.
13. Helferich, 258–59.
14. Brown, *King Cotton in Modern America*, 362.
15. Helferich, "White Gold," 29.
16. Beckert, *Empire of Cotton*, 440.
17. Helferich, *High Cotton*, 261.
18. Helferich, 261.
19. Meikle, "Globalization and Its Effects," 139.
20. Helferich, *High Cotton*, 239.
21. Beckert, *Empire of Cotton*, 438.
22. Helferich, *High Cotton*, 19.
23. Brown, *King Cotton in Modern America*, 378
24. Helferich, *High Cotton*, 33.
25. Helferich, "White Gold," 32.
26. Helferich, *High Cotton*, 53.
27. Helferich, 57.
28. Helferich, 55.
29. Meikle, "Globalization and Its Effects," 134.
30. Helferich, *High Cotton*, 108.
31. Helferich, 108.
32. Meikle, "Globalization and Its Effects," 135.
33. Helferich, *High Cotton*, 7.
34. Helferich, 204.
35. Helferich, 214.
36. Anderson, Schulman, and Wood, "Globalization and Uncertainty," 483.
37. Helferich, *High Cotton*, 203.
38. Helferich, 203.

39. Helferich, 203–4.
40. Helferich, 216.
41. In *Cotton's Renaissance*, Timothy Curtis Jacobson and George David Smith give a corporate history of Cotton Incorporated.
42. Helferich, "White Gold," 30.
43. Brown, *King Cotton in Modern America*, 374.
44. Both of these novels are set in a historical version of sharecropping, and they project contemporary issues onto the past. Grisham's book, *A Painted House*, is set in 1952, and it portrays the cultural tensions that develop when Mexican migrant workers pick cotton in Arkansas. While migrant workers picked cotton in Texas, Arkansas, Louisiana, and Mississippi throughout the twentieth century, Grisham uses this conceit to explore the issues involving immigration in the South. In *Mudbound* by Hilary Jordan, a Black sharecropper and a white cotton farmer return from World War II, where their wartime trauma interacts with racial segregation and violence.
45. For investigation of the relationship between Campbell's novel and the cultural memory of Till's murder, see Suzanne Jones's essay "Childhood Trauma and Its Reverberations in Bebe Moore Campbell's *Your Blues Ain't Like Mine*" and Koritha Mitchell's essay "Mamie Bradley's Unbearable Burden: Sexual and Aesthetic Politics in Bebe Moore Campbell's *Your Blues Ain't Like Mine*."
46. Campbell, *Your Blues Ain't Like Mine*, 108.
47. Baszile, *Queen Sugar*, 123, 124.
48. Hannaham, *Delicious Foods*, 233.
49. In *Wounds of Returning*, Jessica Adams examines the resonance of the plantation in the contemporary cultural imagination. She disconnects plantations from sharecropping, which skews her analysis, but she explains that plantations often function as tourist sites that commodify imaginative, sanitized versions of slavery while also presenting narratives based on haunting, which suggests that site's problematic past.
50. Baszile, *Queen Sugar*, 40.
51. Campbell, *Your Blues Ain't Like Mine*, 5.
52. Shearer, *Celestial Jukebox*, 14.
53. In *Freedom Farmers: Agricultural Resistance and the Black Freedom Movement*, Monica C. White recounts several instances of African Americans creating independent agricultural enterprises as a means of resisting exploitative labor practices, such as Fannie Lou Hamer's Freedom Farm Cooperative.
54. Campbell, *Your Blues Ain't Like Mine*, 302.
55. Baszile, *Queen Sugar*, 32.

56. Shearer, *Celestial Jukebox*, 186.
57. Shearer, 183.
58. In "Racial Politics of Casino Gaming in the Delta," Sharon Wright Austin and Richard T. Middleton argue that casinos in the Delta are effectively an extension of plantation culture because political figures convinced "landowning elites that they should either sell or lease their land to casino owners or risk losing money because of a declining agricultural industry" (55). They explain that casinos have allowed former plantation owners to maintain political and economic power while former sharecroppers now work in wage labor positions in the casinos.
59. Shearer, *Celestial Jukebox*, 103.
60. *Catfish Dream* by Julian Rankin documents the oral history of Ed Scott, the first nonwhite owner of a catfish plant in Mississippi. It recounts his father's rise from sharecropper to landowner and the racial turbulence Scott encountered when he opened his plant. It reveals that economic development in the Delta is often problematic.
61. Campbell, *Your Blues Ain't Like Mine*, 222.
62. Campbell, 312.
63. Campbell, 326.
64. Campbell, 328.
65. Campbell, 377.
66. Shearer, *Celestial Jukebox*, 208.
67. Bone, *Where the New World Is*, 165.
68. Hannaham, *Delicious Foods*, 102.
69. Hannaham, 134.
70. Hannaham, 173.
71. The Coalition of Immokalee Workers has agitated for the rights of migrant workers with some success, exposing the involuntary servitude that continues to persist in American agriculture. Barry Estabrook gives an exposé of this system in *Tomatoland*, which focuses on the vegetable industry in southern Florida.
72. Hannaham explains his decision to use the drug as a narrator in an interview with NPR. He says, "It came about rather naturally for something that seemed so odd" ("If Drugs Could Talk").
73. Campbell, *Your Blues Ain't Like Mine*, 384.
74. Shearer, *Celestial Jukebox*, 135.
75. Hannaham, *Delicious Foods*, 343.
76. The waves of Latino immigration since the 1990s have had significant effects on the South's political, economic, and social infrastructure. For more

information on these effects, see Arthur D. Murphy, Colleen Blanchard, and Jennifer A. Hill, eds., *Latino Workers in the Contemporary South*; Mary E. Odem and Elaine Lacy, eds., *Latino Immigrants and the Transformation of the U.S. South*; and Helen B. Marrow, *New Destination Dreaming: Immigration, Race, and Legal Status in the Rural American South*.

77. Shearer, *Celestial Jukebox*, 90.
78. Baszile, *Queen Sugar*, 235.
79. Baszile, 235, 236.
80. Baszile, 239.
81. Bone, *Where the New World Is*, 12.
82. Loewen, *Mississippi Chinese*, 53. Neil Segars discusses Shearer's representation of Chinese groceries in "How to Be Chinese in Mississippi: Representation of a Chinese Grocer in Cynthia Shearer's *The Celestial Jukebox*."
83. Rushing, *Memphis*, 9.
84. Campbell, *Your Blues Ain't Like Mine*, 394.
85. Baszile, *Queen Sugar*, 3.
86. Campbell, *Your Blues Ain't Like Mine*, 430.
87. Campbell, 432.
88. Campbell, 432.
89. Campbell, 431.
90. Agee used pseudonyms for the families in *Let Us Now Praise Famous Men*, but Evans marked the photographs with the families' actual names. For the sake of consistency and clarity, I will use the actual names in this section. The spelling of Tengle's name varies from source to source, sometimes appearing as "Tingle." Evans's show at the Museum of Modern Art was the first solo show by a photographer at the museum, and the contents of the show can be found in the collection *Walker Evans: American Photographs*. All of Evans's photographs taken for the Farm Security Administration are cataloged on the Library of Congress website. Since he did not use page numbers or plate numbers for the images in *Let Us Now Praise Famous Men*, I will cite the images using their corresponding URL on the website.
91. Christenberry, "Tingle House, near Akron, Alabama, 1961," in *William Christenberry*, plate 95, and "Tenant House 1, 1960," plate 96. Howard Fox writes that Christenberry "frequently cites his 'Tenant House 1, 1960' as a 'breakthrough painting'" primarily because it focalized on the subject matter of "his memory of the places from his past" (*William Christenberry*, 189). One of Christenberry's rare portraits shows one of the Tengle children, "Elizabeth Tingle, near Akron, Alabama, 1964," in *William Christenberry*, plate 34.
92. Maharidge and Williamson, *And Their Children after Them*, plate 16.

93. Matthews, *Capturing the South*, 195.
94. In addition to this text, Howell Raines wrote an article for *New York Times Magazine* about Hale County that explains the feelings of exploitation some of the families felt about their depiction in *Let Us Now Praise Famous Men*.
95. Gottlieb, "RaMell Ross." Ross wrote an essay, "Extra Familiar Completeness," for the catalog of a show of Christenberry's work.
96. For more on the political agenda of the Farm Security Administration, see William Stott, *Documentary Expression in Thirties America*; Paula Rabinowitz, *They Must Be Represented*; and Jeff Allred, *American Modernism and Depression Documentary*.
97. Stott, *Documentary Expression*, 283.
98. Stott, 283.
99. Southall, *Of Time and Place*, 8
100. Stott, *Documentary Expression*, 268.
101. Curtis, *Mind's Eye, Mind's Truth*, 23.
102. Hale, "Signs of Return," 14.
103. Evans, "Allie Mae Burroughs, wife of cotton sharecropper. Hale County, Alabama," https://lccn.loc.gov/2017762301. Several critics have written eloquently about this portrait. See, for example, Alix Beeston's excellent essay "Icons of Depression."
104. Maharidge and Williamson, *And Their Children after Them*, plate 3.
105. In *The Black Image in the New Deal*, Nicholas Natanson argues that FSA photographers took a significant percentage of photographers of Black subjects. Evans, however, was among the photographers who took the lower percentage of photographs of African Americans. Overall, between 34 percent and 38 percent of FSA photographs showed Black subjects, but only 20 percent of Evans's photographs showed Black subjects (73).
106. Christenberry, *Kodachromes*, unnumbered.
107. These photography collections can be found at ramellross.com.
108. "RaMell Ross," Filmakermagazine.com, https://filmmakermagazine.com/people/RaMell-ross/#.YLPg3ahKg2w.
109. Evans, "Fireplace in bedroom of Floyd Burroughs' cabin. Hale County, Alabama," https://lccn.loc.gov/2017762298.
110. Fox, *William Christenberry*, 192.
111. Christenberry, *William Christenberry*, plates 1, 2, and 4.
112. Christenberry, plate 41.
113. Christenberry, plate 19.
114. Evans, "Bud Fields' Garden, Hale County, Alabama," https://lccn.loc.gov/2017758320.

115. Christenberry, *Southern Photographs*, plate 94.
116. Christenberry, *William Christenberry*, plate 23.
117. Maharidge and Williamson, *And Their Children after Them*, 79.
118. Evans, "Lucille Burroughs Picking Cotton, Hale County, Alabama," https://lccn.loc.gov/2017758388. The picture of Bud Fields does not appear in the Library of Congress archive.
119. Fraser, "Filming the Black Belt."
120. Evans, "Sharecropper's grave. Hale County, Alabama," https://www.loc.gov/pictures/item/2017762334/.
121. Christenberry, *William Christenberry*, plate 15.
122. Stack, "Material Remains," 33.
123. Maharidge and Williamson, *And Their Children after Them*, 80.
124. Reilly, "Relief Bill."

→ BIBLIOGRAPHY ←

Adams, Jane, and D. Gorton. "Southern Trauma: Revisiting Caste and Class in the Mississippi Delta." *American Anthropologist* 106, no. 2 (June 2004): 334–45.
Adams, Jessica. *Wounds of Returning: Race, Memory, and Property on the Postslavery Plantation*. Chapel Hill: University of North Carolina Press, 2012.
Agee, James, and Walker Evans. *Let Us Now Praise Famous Men*. Boston: Houghton Mifflin, 1988.
Aiken, Charles. "A New Type of Black Ghetto in the Plantation South." *Annals of the Association of American Geographers* 80, no. 2 (1990): 223–46.
———. *The Cotton Plantation South since the Civil War*. Baltimore: Johns Hopkins University Press, 1998.
Allred, Jeff. *American Modernism and Depression Documentary*. New York: Oxford University Press, 2010.
Alston, Lee, and Joseph Ferrie. *Southern Paternalism and the American Welfare State: Economics, Politics, and Institutions in the South, 1865–1965*. New York: Cambridge University Press, 1999.
Anderson, Cynthia D., Michael D. Schulman, and Phillip J. Wood, "Globalization and Uncertainty: The Restructuring of Southern Textiles." *Social Problems* 48, no. 4 (2001): 478–98.
Anderson, Sherwood. *Home Town*. New York: Alliance Book Corporation, 1940.
Andrews, William L. "In Search of a Common Identity: The Self and the South in Four Mississippi Autobiographies." In *Bridging Southern Cultures: An Interdisciplinary Approach*, edited by John Lowe, 39–56. Baton Rouge: Louisiana State University Press, 2005.
———. *The Literary Career of Charles W. Chesnutt*. Baton Rouge: Louisiana State University Press, 1980.
———. "'We Ain't Going Back There': The Idea of Progress in *The Autobiography of Miss Jane Pittman*." *African American Review* 50, no. 4 (Winter 2017): 563–66.

Angelo, Larian. "Wage Labour Deferred: The Recreation of Unfree Labour in the US South." *The Journal of Peasant Studies* 22, no. 4 (July 1995): 581–644.
Arnow, Harriette. *The Dollmaker*. New York: Macmillan, 1954.
Atkinson, Ted. "Labor." In *Keywords for Southern Studies*, edited by Jennifer Greeson and Scott Romine, 48–59. Athens: University of Georgia Press, 2016.
———. "Testing the Limits of Tragedy: History and Ideology in John Faulkner's *Dollar Cotton*." *Mississippi Quarterly* 54, no. 4 (Fall 2001): 527–39.
Attaway, William. *Blood on the Forge*. New York: Doubleday & Co., 1941.
Augspurger, Michael. *An Economy of Abundant Beauty: Fortune Magazine and Depression America*. Ithaca: Cornell University Press, 2004.
Austin, Sharon Wright, and Richard T. Middleton. "Racial Politics of Casino Gaming in the Delta." In *Resorting to Casinos: The Mississippi Gambling Industry*, edited by Denise von Herrmann, 42–57. Jackson: University Press of Mississippi, 2006.
Ayers, Ed. *The Promise of the New South: Life after Reconstruction*. New York: Oxford University Press, 1993.
Baldwin, Sidney. *Poverty and Politics: The Rise and Decline of the Farm Security Administration*. Chapel Hill: University of North Carolina Press, 1968.
Baptist, Edward. *The Half Has Never Been Told: Slavery and the Making of American Capitalism*. New York: Basic Books, 2014.
Battat, Erin Royston. *Ain't Got No Home: America's Great Migrations and the Making of an Interracial Left*. Chapel Hill: University of North Carolina Press, 2014.
Baszile, Natalie. *Queen Sugar*. New York: Penguin, 2014.
Beckert, Sven. *Empire of Cotton: A Global History*. New York: Knopf, 2014.
Beeston, Alix. "Icons of Depression." *Arizona Quarterly* 73, no. 2 (Summer 2017): 1–36.
Bella, Timothy, and Tim Elfrink. "Warnock, Georgia's first Black senator, Honors Mother and 'the 82-Year-Old Hands that used to Pick Somebody Else's Cotton.'" *Washington Post*, Jan. 6, 2021. https://www.washingtonpost.com/nation/2021/01/06/raphael-warnock-mother-cotton-georgia-election/.
Berry, J. Bill. *Home Ground: Southern Autobiography*. Columbia: University of Missouri Press, 1991.
Berry, Chad. *Southern Migrants, Northern Exiles*. Urbana: University of Illinois Press, 2000.
Bethea, Jack. *Cotton*. New York: Houghton Mifflin, 1928.
"Biggest Cotton Plantation." *Fortune* 15, no. 3 (March 1937): 125–60.
Biles, Roger. *The South and the New Deal*. Lexington: University Press of Kentucky, 2014.

Blackmon, Douglas. *Slavery by Another Name: The Re-Enslavement of Black Americans from the Civil War to World War I.* New York: Random House, 2008.
Blight, David. *Race and Reunion: The Civil War in American Memory.* Cambridge: Belknap Press, 2001.
Bone, Martyn. *Where the New World Is: Literature about the U.S. South at Global Scales.* Athens: University of Georgia Press, 2018.
Bontemps, Arna. "A Summer Tragedy." In *The Old South: "A Summer Tragedy" and Other Stories of the Thirties*, 135–148. New York: Dodd, Mead & Co, 1973.
Bourke-White, Margaret. *Portrait of Myself.* New York: Simon and Schuster, 1943.
Brodhead, Richard. *Cultures of Letters.* Chicago: University of Chicago Press, 1993.
Brooks, Robert. *The Agrarian Revolution in Georgia, 1865–1912.* New York: AMS Press, 1971.
Brown, D. Clayton. *King Cotton in Modern America: A Cultural, Political, and Economic History since 1945.* Jackson: University Press of Mississippi, 2011.
Brown, Sterling. "Sharecroppers." In *The Collected Poems of Sterling A. Brown*, edited by Michael S. Harper. New York: Harper and Row, 1989.
Bruce, Phillip. *The Plantation Negro as a Freeman.* New York: G. P. Putnam and Sons, 1889.
Buell, Lawrence. *The Dream of the Great American Novel.* Cambridge: The Belknap Press of Harvard University Press, 2014.
Byers, T. J., ed. *Sharecropping and Sharecroppers.* London: Frank Cass, 1983.
Cable, George Washington. "The Freedman's Case in Equity." In *The Negro Question*, edited by Arlin Turner, 49–74. New York: Norton, 1958.
———. *John March, Southerner.* New York: Charles Scribner's Sons, 1894.
———. "Literature in the Southern States." In *The Negro Question*, edited by Arlin Turner, 37–46. New York: Norton, 1958.
Caccavari, Peter. "Reconstructing Reconstruction: Region and Nation in the Work of Albion Tourgée." In *Regionalism Reconsidered: New Approaches to the Field*, edited by David Jordan, 119–138. New York: Garland Publishing, 1994.
Caldwell, Erskine. *Tenant Farmer.* New York: Phalanx Press, 1935.
Caldwell, Erskine, and Margaret Bourke-White. *You Have Seen Their Faces.* New York: Modern Age Books, 1937.
Campbell, Bebe Moore. *Your Blues Ain't Like Mine.* New York: Random House, 1992.
Cantor, Louis. *A Prologue to the Protest Movement: The Missouri Sharecropper Roadside Demonstration of 1939.* Durham: Duke University Press, 1969.
Carlton, David, and Peter Coclanis. *Confronting Southern Poverty in the Great Depression: The Report on Economic Conditions of the South with Related Documents.* New York: Bedford/St. Martin's, 1996.

Carter, Jimmy. *An Hour before Daylight: Memories of a Rural Boyhood.* New York: Simon & Schuster, 2001.
Chesnutt, Charles W. *The Colonel's Dream.* New York: Doubleday, Page, and Company, 1905.
———. *Conjure Tales and Stories of the Color Line.* New York: Penguin, 1992.
———. "Peonage, or the New Slavery." *Voice of the Negro* (Sept. 1904): 394–97.
Christenberry, William. *Kodachromes.* New York: Aperture, 2010.
———. *William Christenberry.* New York: Aperture, 2006.
———. *William Christenberry: Southern Photographs.* New York: Aperture, 1983.
Clark, Thomas D. "The Furnishing and Supply System in Southern Agriculture since 1864." *Journal of Southern History* 12, no. 1 (February 1946): 24–44.
Clymer, Jeffory A. *Family Money: Property, Race, and Literature in the Nineteenth Century.* New York: Oxford University Press, 2013.
Cobb, James C. *The Most Southern Place on Earth: The Mississippi Delta and the Roots of Regional Identity.* New York: Oxford University Press, 1992.
Cobb, James C., and William Stueck, eds. *Globalization and the American South.* Athens: University of Georgia Press, 2005.
Coles, Robert. *The South Goes North.* New York: Little, Brown, 1967.
Conrad, David. *The Forgotten Farmers: The Story of Sharecroppers in the New Deal.* Urbana: University of Illinois Press, 1965.
Cosgrove, Ben. "Under a Mississippi Sun: Portraits of Depression-Era Sharecroppers." *Time,* October 23, 2014. http://time.com/3525476/under-a-mississippi-sun-portraits-of-depression-era-sharecroppers/.
Cox, Karen L. *Dixie's Daughters: The United Daughters of the Confederacy and the Preservation of Confederate Culture.* Gainesville: University Press of Florida, 2003.
Crews, Harry. *A Childhood: The Biography of a Place.* New York: Harper and Row, 1978.
Curtis, James. *Mind's Eye, Mind's Truth: FSA Photography Reconsidered.* Philadelphia: Temple University Press, 1989.
Daniel, Pete. "African American Farmers and Civil Rights." *The Journal of Southern History* 73, no. 1 (February 2002): 3–38.
———. *Breaking the Land: The Transformation of Cotton, Tobacco, and Rice Cultures since 1880.* Urbana: University of Illinois Press, 1985.
———. *Dispossession: Discrimination against African American Farmers in the Age of Civil Rights.* Chapel Hill: University of North Carolina Press, 2013.
———. *The Shadow of Slavery: Peonage in the South, 1901–1969.* Urbana: University of Illinois Press, 1972.
Danielson, Susan. "Alice Walker's *Meridian,* Feminism, and the 'Movement.'" *Women's Studies* 16 (1989): 317–30.

Dattel, Gene. *Cotton and Race in the Making of America: The Human Costs of Economic Power.* Chicago: Ivan R. Dee, 2009.
Davis, Allison, Burleigh Gardner, and Mary Gardner. *Deep South: A Social Anthropological Study of Caste and Class.* Chicago: University of Chicago Press, 1965.
Davis, Edward. *The White Scourge.* San Antonio: The Naylor Co., 1940.
Davis, Hugh. *The Making of James Agee.* Knoxville: University of Tennessee Press, 2008.
Day, Richard. "The Economics of Technological Change and the Demise of the Sharecropper." *American Economic Review* 57, no. 3 (1967): 427–49.
De Forest, John W. *The Bloody Chasm.* Freeport, NY: Books for Libraries, 1972.
———. *A Union Officer in the Reconstruction.* Edited by James H. Croushore and David Potter. Hamden, CT: Archon Books, 1968.
De Jong, Greta. *You Can't Eat Freedom: Southerners and Social Justice after the Civil Rights Movement.* Chapel Hill: University of North Carolina Press, 2016.
Denning, Michael. *The Cultural Front: The Laboring of American Culture in the Twentieth Century.* New York: Verso, 1997.
Depew, Briggs, Price Fishback, and Paul Rhode. "New Deal or No Deal in the Cotton South: The Effect of the AAA on the Agricultural Labor Structure." *Explorations in Economic History* 50 (2013): 466–86.
Deutsch, Stephanie. *You Need a Schoolhouse: Booker T. Washington, Julius Rosenwald, and the Building of Schools for the Segregated South.* Chicago: Northwestern University Press, 2015.
Dickson, Deborah, Susan Froemke, and Albert Maysles, dir. *LaLee's Kin: The Legacy of Cotton.* Maysles Films Inc., 2001.
Dittmer, John. *Local People: The Struggle for Civil Rights in Mississippi.* Urbana: University of Illinois Press, 1995.
Dolinar, Brian. *The Black Cultural Front: Black Writers and Artists of the Depression Generation.* Jackson: University Press of Mississippi, 2012.
Dollard, John. *Class and Caste in a Southern Town.* Garden City, NY: Doubleday & Company, Inc., 1957.
Du Bois, W. E. B. *Black Reconstruction in America.* New York: Oxford University Press, 2007.
———. *The Quest of the Silver Fleece.* New York: Oxford University Press, 2007.
———. *The Souls of Black Folk.* New York: Library of America, 1990.
Duck, Leigh Anne. *The Nation's Region: Southern Modernism, Segregation, and U.S. Nationalism.* Athens: University of Georgia Press, 2009.
Dussere, Erik. "Accounting for Slavery: Economic Narratives in Morrison and Faulkner." *Modern Fiction Studies* 47, no. 2 (Summer 2001): 329–55.

Dyson, Lowell. *Red Harvest: The Communist Party and American Farmers.* Lincoln: University of Nebraska Press. 1982.

Edwards, Junius. *If We Must Die.* 1957. Washington, DC: Howard University Press, 1985.

Edwards, Laura. *Gendered Strife and Confusion: The Political Culture of Reconstruction.* Urbana: University of Illinois Press, 1997.

Egerton, John. *Speak Now Against the Day: The Generation Before the Civil Rights Movement in the South.* New York: Knopf, 1994.

Ellenberg, George. *Mule South to Tractor South: Mules, Machines, and the Transformation of the Cotton South.* Tuscaloosa: University of Alabama Press, 2007.

Elliott, Mark. *Color-Blind Justice: Albion Tourgée and the Quest for Racial Equality.* New York: Oxford University Press, 2006.

Ellis, Mark. *Race Harmony and Black Progress: Jack Woofter and the Interracial Cooperation Movement.* Bloomington: Indiana University Press, 2013.

Estabrook, Barry. *Tomatoland: How Modern Industrial Agriculture Destroyed Our Most Alluring Fruit.* New York: Andrews McNeel, 2012.

Fair, Ronald. *Many Thousand Gone.* New York: Harcourt, Brace, and World, 1965.

*Farm Tenancy: Report of the President's Committee.* Washington, DC: United States Government Printing Office, 1937.

Farr, Patricia Aylward. "Key Informants in Cottonville: Revisiting Powdermaker's Mississippi." *Journal of Anthropological Research* 47, no. 4 (Winter 1991): 389–402.

Faulkner, John. *Dollar Cotton.* New York: Harcourt, Brace, and Co, 1942.

———. *Men Working.* New York: Harcourt, Brace, and Co, 1941.

Faulkner, William. *Absalom, Absalom!* New York: Random House, 1936.

———. *The Hamlet.* New York: Vintage, 1991.

———. "The Tall Men." In *The Collected Stories of William Faulkner,* 45–62. New York: Vintage, 1995.

Faust, Drew Gilpin. *This Republic of Suffering: Death and the American Civil War.* New York: Vintage, 2009.

Ferris, William. "John Dollard: Caste and Class Revisited." *Southern Cultures* 10, no. 2 (Summer 2004): 7–18.

Finnegan, Cara A. *Picturing Poverty: Print Culture and FSA Photographs.* Washington, DC: Smithsonian Books, 2003.

Fite, Gilbert C. *Cotton Fields No More: Southern Agriculture, 1865–1980.* Lexington: University Press of Kentucky, 1984.

Flowers, Linda. *Throwed Away: Failures of Progress in Eastern North Carolina.* Knoxville: University of Tennessee Press, 1990.

Foley, Barbara. *Radical Representations: Politics and form in U.S. Proletarian Fiction, 1929–1941.* Durham: Duke University Press, 1993.

Foley, Neil. *The White Scourge: Mexicans, Blacks, and Poor Whites in Texas Cotton Culture.* Berkeley: University of California Press, 1997.

Foner, Eric. *Reconstruction: America's Unfinished Revolution, 1863–1977.* New York: Harper & Row, 1988.

Fortune, T. Thomas. *Black and White: Land, Labor, and Politics in the South.* New York: Arno Press, 1968.

Foster, Gaines M. *Ghosts of the Confederacy: Defeat, the Lost Cause, and the Emergence of the New South.* New York: Oxford University Press, 1987.

Fox, Howard. *William Christenberry.* New York: Aperture, 2006.

Fraser, Max. "Filming the Black Belt: An Interview with RaMell Ross." *Dissent*, Fall 2019. https://www.dissentmagazine.org/article/filming-the-black-belt-an-interview-with-RaMell-ross.

Gaines, Ernest. *The Autobiography of Miss Jane Pittman.* Columbus, OH: McGraw-Hill, 2000.

———. *Of Love and Dust.* New York: Norton, 1979.

Gallagher, Gary W., and Alan T. Nolan, eds. *The Myth of the Lost Cause and Civil War History.* Bloomington: Indiana University Press, 2000.

Garside, Alston Hill. *Cotton Goes to Market.* New York: Frederick Stokes Company, 1935.

Gaston, Paul. *The New South Creed: A Study in Southern Myth Making.* New York: Knopf, 1970.

Genovese, Eugene. *Roll, Jordan, Roll: The World the Slaves Made.* New York: Vintage, 1976.

Ghasemi, Mehdi. "An Equation of Collectivity: We + You in Richard Wright's *12 Million Black Voices.*" *Mosaic* 51, no. 1 (March 2018): 71–86.

Giddings, Paula. *Ida: A Sword among Lions.* New York: Harper Books, 2009.

Giesen, James. *Boll Weevil Blues: Cotton, Myth, and Power in the American South.* Chicago: University of Chicago Press, 2011.

———. "Creating 'Nate Shaw': The Making and Remaking of *All God's Dangers.*" In *Reading Southern Poverty between the Wars, 1918–1939*, edited by Richard Godden and Martin Crawford, 163–77. Athens: University of Georgia Press, 2006.

Gilyard, Keith. *John Oliver Killens: A Life of Black Literary Activism.* Athens: University of Georgia Press, 2010.

Godden, Richard. *Fictions of Labor: William Faulkner and the South's Long Revolution.* New York: Cambridge University Press, 1997.

Goldfield, David. "The Urban South: A Regional Framework." *The American Historical Review* 86, no. 5 (December 1981): 1009–34.

Gottlieb, Alkiva. "RaMell Ross: Variety's 10 Documentarians to Watch in 2018." *Variety*, April, 20, 2018. https://variety.com/gallery/10-documentarians-to-watch-2018/ramell-ross_photograph-by-maya-krinsky_courtesy-of-cinema-guild/.

Gray, Richard. *Southern Aberrations: Writers of the American South and the Problems of Regionalism*. Baton Rouge: Louisiana State University Press, 2000.

Green, Paul. *This Body the Earth*. New York: Harper and Brothers, 1935.

Greeson, Jennifer. "Expropriating *The Great South* and Exporting 'Local Color.'" In *Transhemispheric American Studies*, edited by Caroline Levander and Robert Levine, 116–39. New Brunswick, NJ: Rutgers University Press, 2008.

———. *Our South: Geographic Fantasy and the Rise of National Literature*. Cambridge: Harvard University Press, 2010.

Gregory, James N. *The Southern Diaspora: How the Great Migration of Black and White Southerners Changed America*. Chapel Hill: University of North Carolina Press, 2005.

Griffin, Farrah Jasmine. *Who Set You Flowin'? The African American Migration Narrative*. New York: Oxford University Press, 1995.

Griggs, Sutton. *The Hindered Hand; or, The Return of the Repressionist*. Miami: Memnosyne Publishing, 1969.

Grisham, John. *A Painted House*. New York: Doubleday, 2001.

Grossman, James R. *Land of Hope: Chicago, Black Southerners, and the Great Migration*. Chicago: University of Chicago Press, 1989.

Grove, Wayne A., and Craig Heinicke, "Better Opportunities or Worse? The Demise of Cotton Harvest Labor, 1949–1964." *The Journal of Economic History* 63, no. 3 (September 2003): 736–67.

Grubbs, Donald. *Cry from the Cotton: The Southern Tenant Farmers Union and the New Deal*. Chapel Hill: University of North Carolina Press, 1971.

Guterl, Matthew Pratt. "Plantation." In *Keywords for Southern Studies*, edited by Jennifer Greeson and Scott Romine, 22–29. Athens: University of Georgia Press, 2016.

Hagood, Margaret Jarman. *Mothers of the South: Portraiture of the White Tenant Farm Woman*. Chapel Hill: University of North Carolina Press, 2011.

Hale, Grace. "Signs of Return: Photography as History in the U.S. South." *Southern Cultures* 25, no. 1 (Spring 2019): 12–41.

Hall, Jacquelyn Dowd. "Women Writers, the 'Southern Front,' and the Dialectical Imagination." *The Journal of Southern History* 69, no. 1 (2003): 3–38.

Hall, Jacquelyn Dowd, James L. Leloudis, Robert Rodgers Korstad, Mary Murphy, Lu Ann Jones, and Christopher B. Daly, eds. *Like a Family: The Making of a Southern Cotton Mill World*. Chapel Hill: University of North Carolina Press, 2000.

Hannaham, James. *Delicious Foods*. New York: Back Bay Books, 2015.

———. "If Drugs Could Talk." *All Things Considered*, National Public Radio, March 13, 2015. https://www.npr.org/2015/03/13/391914914/if-drugs-could-talk-in-delicious-foods-they-do

Hardwig, Bill. "Who Owns the Whip? Chesnutt, Tourgée, and Reconstruction Justice." *African American Review* 36, no. 1 (Spring 2002): 5–20.

Harper, Frances Ellen Watkins. *Iola Leroy; or, Shadows Uplifted*. Mineola, NY: Dover, 2010.

Harris, Joel Chandler. *Free Joe and Other Sketches*. Ridgewood, NJ: Gregg Press, 1967.

Hayden, René, et al. *Freedom: A Documentary History of Emancipation, 1861–1867. Series 3: Volume 2, Land and Labor, 1866–1867*. Chapel Hill: University of North Carolina Press, 2013.

Helferich, Gerard. *High Cotton: Four Seasons in the Mississippi Delta*. Berkeley: Counterpoint, 2007.

———. "White Gold: Can Cotton Make a Comeback in the Land Where It Was Once King?" *Virginia Quarterly Review* 90, no. 2 (Spring 2014): 26–39.

Henderson, George Wylie. *Ollie Miss*. Tuscaloosa: University of Alabama Press, 1988.

Hendrickson, Roberta. "Remembering the Dream: Alice Walker, *Meridian* and the Civil Rights Movement." *MELUS* 24, no. 3 (Fall 1999): 111–28.

Hobson, Fred. *But Now I See: The White Southern Racial Conversion Narrative*. Baton Rouge: Louisiana State University Press, 1999.

———. *Tell About the South: The Southern Rage to Explain*. Baton Rouge: Louisiana State University Press, 1983.

Hodges, John O. "William Alexander Percy's *Lanterns*: A Reply from a Mississippi Sharecropper's Son." *Southern Quarterly* 43, no. 1 (Fall 2005): 29–48.

Holley, Donald. *The Second Great Emancipation: The Mechanical Cotton Picker, Black Migration, and How They Shaped the Modern South*. Fayetteville: University of Arkansas Press, 2000.

Holley, William, Ellen Winston, and Thomas J. Woofter. *The Plantation South, 1934–1937*. New York: Da Capo Press, 1971.

Holt, Thomas. *The Problem of Freedom: Race, Labor, and Politics in Jamaica and Britain, 1832–1938*. Baltimore: Johns Hopkins University Press, 1992.

Honey, Michael. *Sharecroppers' Troubadour: John L. Handcox, the Southern Tenant Farmers Union, and the African American Song Tradition*. New York: Palgrave, 2013.

Hudson, Angela Pulley. "Mississippi Lost and Found: Anne Moody's Autobiograph(ies) and Racial Melancholia." *a/b: Auto/Biography Studies* 20, no. 2 (2005): 282–96.

Hughes, Langston. "Share-Croppers." *The Collected Poems of Langston Hughes*. Edited by Arnold Rampersad and David Roessel. New York: Vintage, 1995. 185.

Hughes, Tomos. "'Can We Imagine This Spectacular Revolution?': Counterfactual Narrative and the 'New World Peasantry' in W. E. B. Du Bois' *Scorn* and *Black Reconstruction*." *ELH* 87, no. 1 (Spring 2020): 179–210.

Hullinger, Edwin Ware. *Plowing Through: The Story of the Negro in Agriculture*. New York: William Morrow, 1940.

Isenberg, Nancy. *White Trash: The 400-Year Untold Story of Class in America*. New York: Penguin, 2017.

Jacobson, Timothy Curtis, and George David Smith. *Cotton's Renaissance: A Study in Market Innovation*. New York: Cambridge University Press, 2001.

James, C. L. R. "With the Sharecroppers." In *C. L. R. James on the "Negro Question,"* edited by Scott McLemmee, 22–34. Jackson: University Press of Mississippi, 1996.

Jarrett, Gene Andrew. *Representing the Race: A New Political History of African American Literature*. New York: New York University Press, 2011.

Jaynes, Gerald David. *Branches without Roots: Genesis of the Black Working Class in the American South, 1862–1882*. New York: Oxford University Press, 1986.

Jewison, Norman, dir. *In the Heat of the Night*. United Artists, 1967.

Johnson, Charles S. *Shadow of the Plantation*. Chicago: University of Chicago Press, 1934.

Johnson, Charles S., Edwin Embree, and W. W. Alexander. *The Collapse of Cotton Tenancy*. Chapel Hill: University of North Carolina Press, 1935.

Jones, Carter Brooke. *The White Band*. New York: Funk & Wagnalls, 1959.

Jones, Shermaine. "Presenting Our Bodies, Laying Our Case: The Political Efficacy of Grief and Rage during the Civil Rights Movement in Alice Walker's *Meridian*." *Southern Quarterly* 52, no. 1 (Fall 2014): 179–95.

Jones, Suzanne. "Childhood Trauma and Its Reverberations in Bebe Moore Campbell's *Your Blues Ain't Like Mine*." In *Emmett Till in Literary Memory and Imagination*, edited by Harriet Pollack and Christopher Metress, 161–77. Baton Rouge: Louisiana State University Press, 2008.

———. *Race Mixing: Southern Fiction since the Sixties*. Baltimore: Johns Hopkins University Press, 2002.

Jordan, Hilary. *Mudbound*. New York: HarperCollins, 2008.

Keely, Karen A. "Marriage Plots and National Reunion: The Trope of Romantic Reconciliation in Postbellum Literature." *Mississippi Quarterly* 51, no. 4 (Fall 1998): 621–48.

Kelley, Robin D. G. *Hammer and Hoe: Alabama Communists during the Great Depression*. Chapel Hill: University of North Carolina Press, 2015.

Kelley, Welbourne. *Inchin' Along*. New York: William Morrow and Co, 1932.
Kelley, William Melvin. *A Different Drummer*. New York: Anchor Books, 2019.
Kennedy-Nolle, Sharon D. *Writing Reconstruction: Race, Gender, and Citizenship in the Postwar South*. Chapel Hill: University of North Carolina Press, 2015.
Kester, Howard. *Revolt among the Sharecroppers*. New York: Arno Press, 1969.
Kidd, Stuart. "Dissonant Encounters: FSA Photographers and the Southern Underclass, 1935–1943." In *Reading Southern Poverty between the Wars, 1918–1939*, edited by Richard Godden and Martin Crawford, 25–47. Athens: University of Georgia Press, 2006.
Killens, John Oliver. *'Sippi*. New York: Trident Press, 1967.
King, Edward. *The Great South*. Baton Rouge: Louisiana State University Press, 1972.
King, Martin Luther, Sr., and Clayton Riley. *Daddy King: An Autobiography*. New York: William Morrow and Company, 1980.
Kinney, James. "Race in the New South: Joel Chandler Harris's 'Free Joe and the Rest of the World.'" *American Literary Realism* 33, no. 3 (Spring 2001): 235–51.
Kirby, Jack Temple. *Mockingbird Song: Ecological Landscapes of the South*. Chapel Hill: University of North Carolina Press, 2006.
Knepper, Steven. "The Nation's Bioregion: The South in Pare Lorentz's *The River*." *The Southern Quarterly* 55, no. 1 (Fall 2017): 88–103.
Kreyling, Michael. *Inventing Southern Literature*. Jackson: University Press of Mississippi, 1998.
Kroll, Harry Harrison. *The Cabin in the Cotton*. New York: Ray Long & Richard R. Smith, 1931.
———. *I Was a Sharecropper*. New York: Bobbs Merrill, 1937.
Kuhn, Mary. "Chesnutt, Turpentine, and the Political Ecology of White Supremacy." *PMLA* 136, no. 1 (2021): 39–54.
Lange, Dorothea, and Paul Taylor. *An American Exodus: A Record of Human Erosion*. New York: Reynal and Hitchcock, 1939.
Lanham, Edwin. *The Stricklands*. New York: Little, Brown and Co., 1939.
Larson, Jennifer. "'Plotting the Benefit of the Human Race': The Freedmen's Bureau in John W. De Forest's *Miss Ravenel's Conversion* and *A Union Officer in the Reconstruction*." *South Carolina Review* 40, no.2 (Spring 2008): 117–29.
Lassiter, Matthew D., and Joseph Crespino. *The Myth of Southern Exceptionalism*. New York: Oxford University Press, 2010.
Lee, George W. *River George*. New York: The Macaulay Company, 1937.
Lee, Maurice. "Du Bois the Novelist: White Influence, Black Spirit, and *The Quest of the Silver Fleece*." *African American Review* 33, no. 3 (Fall 1999): 389–400.
Lemann, Nicholas. *The Promised Land: The Great Black Migration and How it Changed America*. New York: Knopf, 1991.

Lessig, Matthew. "*The Store*, or T. S. Stribling's Paragraph in the History of Critical Race Studies." *Southern Quarterly* 41, no. 3 (Spring 2003): 137–55.
Lewis, John, and Michael D'Orso. *Walking with the Wind: A Memoir of the Movement.* New York: Simon & Schuster, 1998.
Lichtenstein, Alex. *Twice the Work of Free Labor: The Political Economy of Convict Labor in the New South.* New York: Verso Press, 1996.
Link, William. *The Paradox of Southern Progressivism, 1880–1930.* Chapel Hill: University of North Carolina Press, 1992.
Litwack, Leon. *Been in the Storm So Long: The Aftermath of Slavery.* New York: Vintage, 1979.
———. *Trouble in Mind: Black Southerners in the Age of Jim Crow.* New York: Knopf, 1998.
Loewen, James. *The Mississippi Chinese: Between Black and White.* Cambridge: Harvard University Press, 1971.
Lorentz, Pare, dir. *The River.* Washington, DC: Farm Security Administration, 1938.
Lumpkin, Grace. *A Sign for Cain.* New York: Lee Furman, Inc, 1935.
Maguire, Jane. *On Shares: Ed Brown's Story.* New York: Norton, 1975.
Maharidge, Dale, and Michael Williamson. *And Their Children after Them: The Legacy of* Let Us Now Praise Famous Men: *James Agee, Walker Evans, and the Rise and Fall of Cotton in the South.* New York: Seven Stories Press, 1989.
Mandle, Jay. *Not Slave, Not Free: The African American Economic Experience since the Civil War.* Durham: Duke University Press, 1992.
———. *The Roots of Black Poverty: The Southern Plantation Economy after the Civil War.* Durham: Duke University Press, 1978.
Manthorne, Jason. "The View from the Cotton: Reconsidering the Southern Tenant Farmers' Union." *Agricultural History* 84, no. 1 (Winter 2010): 20–45.
Marrow, Helen B. *New Destination Dreaming: Immigration, Race, and Legal Status in the Rural American South.* Palo Alto: Stanford University Press, 2011.
Martin, Robert. *Howard Kester and the Struggle for Social Justice in the South, 1904–1977.* Charlottesville: University Press of Virginia, 1991.
Marx, Karl. *Capital: A Critique of Political Economy.* New York: Vintage Books, 1976.
———. *A Contribution to the Critique of Political Economy.* Chicago: C. H. Kerr, 1904.
———. *The German Ideology.* New York: International Publishers, 1947.
Mason, Theodore O., Jr. "Alice Walker's *The Third Life of Grange Copeland*: The Dynamics of Enclosure." *Callaloo* 12, no. 2 (1989): 297–309.
Matthews, Scott L. *Capturing the South: Imagining America's Most Documented Region.* Chapel Hill: University of North Carolina Press, 2018.
Mayer, Tom. *Analytical Marxism.* Thousand Oaks, CA: Sage, 1994.

Mazzari, Louis. *Southern Modernist: Arthur Raper from the New Deal to the Cold War.* Baton Rouge: Louisiana State University Press, 2006.

McAdam, Doug. *Freedom Summer.* New York: Oxford University Press, 1988.

McDonald, John F., "Urban Areas in the Transformation of the South: A Review of Modern History." *Urban Studies Research* (2013). https://doi.org/10.1155/2013/376529.

McInnis, Jarvis. "'Behold the Land': W. E. B. Du Bois, Cotton Futures, and the Afterlife of the Plantation in the US South." *The Global South* 10, no. 2 (2016): 71–98.

McLaurin, Melton. *Separate Pasts: Growing Up White in the Segregated South.* Athens: University of Georgia Press, 1987.

McMillen, Neil. *The Dark Journey: Black Mississippians in the Age of Jim Crow.* Urbana: University of Illinois Press, 1989.

Meacham, Ellen B. *Delta Epiphany: Robert F. Kennedy in Mississippi.* Jackson: University Press of Mississippi, 2018.

Meikle, Paulette Anne. "Globalization and Its Effects on Agriculture and Agribusiness in the Mississippi Delta: A Historical Overview and Prospects for the Future." *Journal of Rural Social Sciences* 31, no. 2 (2016): 130–54.

Mertz, Paul. *New Deal Policy and Southern Rural Poverty.* Baton Rouge: Louisiana State University Press, 1978.

Mitchell, H. L. *Mean Things Happening in This Land: The Life and Times of H. L. Mitchell, Co-Founder of the Southern Tenant Farmers Union.* Montclair, NJ: Allanheld, Osmun & Co., 1979.

Mitchell, Koritha. "Mamie Bradley's Unbearable Burden: Sexual and Aesthetic Politics in Bebe Moore Campbell's *Your Blues Ain't Like Mine.*" *Callaloo* 31, no. 4 (2008): 1048–67.

Mitchell, Margaret. *Gone with the Wind.* New York: Macmillan, 1936.

Mixon, Wayne. *Southern Writers and the New South Movement, 1865–1913.* Chapel Hill: University of North Carolina Press, 1980.

Monteith, Sharon. *SNCC's Stories: The African American Freedom Movement in the Civil Rights South.* Athens: University of Georgia Press, 2020.

Moody, Anne. *Coming of Age in Mississippi.* New York: Doubleday, 1968.

Munz, Charles Curtis. *Land without Moses.* New York: Harper & Brothers, 1938.

Murphy, Arthur D., Colleen Blanchard, and Jennifer A. Hill, eds. *Latino Workers in the Contemporary South.* Athens: University of Georgia Press, 2001.

Murphy, Paul V. *The Rebuke of History: The Southern Agrarians and American Conservative Thought.* Chapel Hill: University of North Carolina Press, 2001.

Myrdal, Gunnar. *An American Dilemma: The Negro Problem and Modern Democracy.* New York: Harper & Bros., 1944.

Natanson, Nicholas. *The Black Image in the New Deal: The Politics of FSA Photography*. Knoxville: University of Tennessee Press, 1992.
Newkirk, Vann R. "The Great Land Robbery." *The Atlantic*, September 2019. https://www.theatlantic.com/magazine/archive/2019/09/this-land-was-our-land/594742/.
Nilon, Charles H. "The Ending of *Huckleberry Finn*: 'Freeing the Free Negro.'" In *Satire or Evasion? Black Perspectives on Huckleberry Finn*, edited by James S. Leonard, Thomas A. Tenney, and Thadious Davis. Durham, NC: Duke University Press, 1992. 62–76.
Nixon, Herman C. *Forty Acres and Steel Mules*. Chapel Hill: University of North Carolina Press, 1938.
O'Brien, C. C. "'The White Women All Go for Sex': Frances Harper on Suffrage, Citizenship, and the Reconstruction South." *African American Review* 43, no. 4 (Winter 2009): 605–20.
O'Brien, Michael. *The Idea of the American South, 1920–1941*. Baltimore: Johns Hopkins University Press, 1979.
O'Connor, Flannery. "The Crop." In *O'Connor: Collected Works*, 732–40. New York: Library of America, 1988.
Odem, Mary E., and Elaine Lacy, eds. *Latino Immigrants and the Transformation of the U.S. South*. Athens: University of Georgia Press, 2009.
Odum, Howard. *Southern Regions of the United States*. Chapel Hill: University of North Carolina Press, 1936.
Offord, Carl. *The White Face*. New York: Robert M. McBride & Co., 1943.
Olsen, Otto. *Carpet Bagger's Crusade: The Life of Albion Winegar Tourgée*. Baltimore: Johns Hopkins University Press, 1965.
Olsson, Tore C. "The South in the World Since 1865: A Review Essay." *Journal of Southern History* 87, no. 1 (February 2021): 67–108.
Oshinsky, David. *Worse Than Slavery: Parchman Farm and the Ordeal of Jim Crow Justice*. New York: Free Press, 1997.
Oubre, Claude. *Forty Acres and a Mule: The Freedmen's Bureau and Black Land Ownership*. Baton Rouge: Louisiana State University Press, 1978.
Ownby, Ted. "Three Agrarianisms and the Idea of a South without Poverty." In *Reading Southern Poverty between the Wars, 1918–1939*, edited by Richard Godden and Martin Crawford, 1–24. Athens: University of Georgia Press, 2006.
Page, Thomas Nelson. *In Ole Virginia*. 1887. Chapel Hill: University of North Carolina Press, 1969.
——. *The Negro: The Southerner's Problem*. New York: Charles Scribner's Sons, 1904.
——. *Red Rock*. Albany, NY: NCUP, Inc, 1991.

Paige, Jeffery. *Agrarian Revolution*. New York: Free Press, 1978.
Patterson, Orlando. *Slavery and Social Death: A Comparative Study*. Cambridge: Harvard University Press, 1982.
Patterson Robert J. "Rethinking Definitions and Expectations: Civil Rights and Civil Rights Leadership in Ernest Gaines's *The Autobiography of Miss Jane Pittman*." *The South Atlantic Quarterly* 112, no. 2 (Spring 2013): 339–63.
Payne, Charles M. *I've Got the Light of Freedom: The Organizing Tradition and the Mississippi Freedom Struggle*. Berkeley: University of California Press, 2007.
Peacock, James L. *Grounded Globalism: How the U.S. South Embraces the World*. Athens: University of Georgia Press, 2010.
Peacock, James L., Harry L. Watson, and Carrie R. Matthews, eds., *The American South in a Global World*. Chapel Hill: University of North Carolina Press, 2005.
Peeler, David. *Hope among Us Yet: Social Criticism and the Social Solace in Depression America*. Athens: University of Georgia Press, 1987.
Percy, William Alexander. *Lanterns on the Levee*. Baton Rouge: Louisiana State University Press, 1995.
Perry, George Sessions. *Hold Autumn in Your Hand*. Albuquerque: University of New Mexico Press, 1975.
Peterson, Willis, and Yoav Kislev. "The Cotton Harvester in Retrospect: Labor Displacement or Replacement?" *The Journal of Economic History* 46, no. 1 (March 1986): 199–216.
Peterkin, Julia, and Doris Ulmann. *Roll, Jordan, Roll*. New York: Robert O. Ballou, 1933.
Petrino, Elizabeth. "'We are Rising as a People': Frances Harper's Radical Views on Class and Racial Equality in 'Sketches of Southern Life.'" *American Transcendental Quarterly* 19, no. 2 (June 2005): 133–53.
Pfeffer, Max. "Social Origins of Three Systems of Farm Production in the United States." *Rural Sociology* 48, no. 4 (1983): 540–62.
Pickens, William. "Lynching and Debt Slavery." In *Witnessing Lynching: American Writers Respond*, edited by Anne P. Rice, 209–15. New Brunswick, NJ: Rutgers University Press, 2003.
Pollack, Harriett. *Eudora Welty's Fiction and Photography: The Body of the Other Woman*. Athens: University of Georgia Press, 2016.
Powdermaker, Hortense. *After Freedom: A Cultural Study of the Deep South*. New York: Russell and Russell, 1966.
———. *Stranger and Friend: The Way of an Anthropologist*. New York: Norton, 1966.
Powell, Lawrence. *New Masters: Northern Planters During the Civil War and Reconstruction*. New Haven: Yale University Press, 1980.

Prince, Stephen. *Stories of the South: Race and the Reconstruction of Southern Identity, 1865–1915*. Chapel Hill: University of North Carolina Press, 2014.

Puskar, Jason. "Black and White and Read All Over: Photography and the Voices of Richard Wright." *Mosaic* 49, no. 2 (June 2016): 167–83.

Rabinowitz, Paula. *They Must Be Represented: The Politics of Documentary*. New York: Verso, 1994.

Raines, Howell. "Let Us Now Revisit Famous Folk." *New York Times Magazine*, May 25, 1980. 31–46.

Rankin, Julian. *Catfish Dream: Ed Scott's Fight for His Family Farm and Racial Justice in the Mississippi Delta*. Athens: University of Georgia Press, 2018.

Ransom, Roger, and Richard Sutch. *One Kind of Freedom: The Economic Consequences of Emancipation*. New York: Cambridge University Press, 2001.

Raper, Arthur. *Preface to Peasantry: A Tale of Two Black Belt Counties*. Chapel Hill: University of North Carolina Press, 1936.

———. *Tenants of the Almighty*. New York: Macmillan, 1943.

Raper, Arthur, and Ira De Reid. *Sharecroppers All*. New York: Russell and Russell, 1941.

Reid, Joseph D., Jr. "Sharecropping as an Understandable Market Response: The Post-Bellum South." *The Journal of Economic History* 33, no. 1 (March 1973): 106–30.

Reilly, Laura. "Relief Bill Is Most Significant Legislation for Black Farmers since Civil Rights Act, Experts Say." *Washington Post*, March 8, 2021. https://www.washingtonpost.com/business/2021/03/08/reparations-black-farmers-stimulus/.

Riello, Giorgio. *Cotton: The Fabric That Made the Modern World*. New York: Cambridge University Press, 2013.

Ritterhouse, Jennifer. "Woman Flogged: Willie Sue Blagden, the Southern Tenant Farmers Union, and How an Impulse for Story Led to a Historiographical Corrective." *Rethinking History* 18, no. 1 (2014): 97–121.

Roark, James. *Masters without Slaves: Southern Planters in the Civil War and Reconstruction*. New York: Norton, 1978.

Rodgers, Lawrence R. *Canaan Bound: The African American Great Migration Novel*. Urbana: University of Illinois Press, 1992.

Roemer, John. *A General Theory of Exploitation and Class*. Cambridge: Harvard University Press, 1982.

Roll, Jarod. "'Out Yonder on the Road': Working Class Self-Representation and the 1939 Roadside Demonstration in Southeast Missouri." *Southern Spaces*, March 2010. https://southernspaces.org/2010/out-yonder-road-working-class-self-representation-and-1939-roadside-demonstration-southeast-missouri/.

Romine, Scott. *Narrative Forms of Southern Community*. Baton Rouge: Louisiana State University Press, 1999.

Rosengarten, Theodore. *All God's Dangers: The Life of Nate Shaw*. Chicago: University of Chicago Press, 1974.

Ross, James. *The Rise and Fall of the Southern Tenant Farmers Union in Arkansas*. Knoxville: University of Tennessee Press, 2018.

Ross, RaMell. "Extra Familiar Completeness." *Memory Is a Strange Bell: The Art of William Christenberry*. New Orleans: Ogden Museum of Art, 2020.

——, dir. *Hale County This Morning, This Evening*. Distributed by The Cinema Guild, 2018.

Royce, Edward. *The Origins of Southern Sharecropping*. Philadelphia: Temple University Press, 1993.

Rubin, Louis. *A Gallery of Southerners*. Baton Rouge: Louisiana State University Press, 1982.

Rubin, Morton. *Plantation County*. Chapel Hill: University of North Carolina Press, 1951.

Rushing, Wanda. *Memphis and the Paradox of Place: Globalization in the American South*. Chapel Hill: University of North Carolina Press, 2009.

Russell, William. *A Wind Is Rising*. New York: Charles Scribner's Son, 1950.

Ryan, Tim. *Calls and Responses: The American Novel of Slavery since Gone with the Wind*. Baton Rouge: Louisiana State University Press, 2008.

Rylee, Robert. *Deep Dark River*. New York: Farrar and Rinehart, 1935.

Salmond, John A. *Gastonia 1929: The Story of the Loray Mill Strike*. Chapel Hill: University of North Carolina Press, 1995.

Sawaya, Francesca. "'That Friendship of the Whites': Patronage, Philanthropy, and Charles Chesnutt's *The Colonel's Dream*." *American Literature* 83, no. 4 (December 2011): 775–801.

Scarborough, Dorothy. *Can't Get a Redbird*. New York: Harper and Brothers, 1929.

——. *In the Land of Cotton*. New York: MacMillan, 1923.

Schmidt, Peter. *Sitting in Darkness: New South Fiction, Education, and the Rise of Jim Crow Colonialism, 1865–1920*. Jackson: University Press of Mississippi, 2008.

Segars, Neil. "How to Be Chinese in Mississippi: Representation of a Chinese Grocer in Cynthia Shearer's *The Celestial Jukebox*." *The Global South* 3, no. 2 (Fall 2009): 50–63.

Sen, Debapriya. "A Theory of Sharecropping: The Role of Price Behavior and Imperfect Competition." *Journal of Economic Behavior & Organization* 80, no. 1 (September 2011): 181–99.

"Senator Tim Scott says in RNC speech: Family 'went from cotton to Congress in one lifetime.'" *CBS News*, August 25, 2016. https://www.cbsnews.com/video

/senator-tim-scott-says-in-rnc-speech-that-his-family-went-from-cotton-to-congress-in-one-lifetime/.

Shearer, Cynthia. *The Celestial Jukebox*. Athens: University of Georgia Press, 2005.

Silber, Nina. *The Romance of Reunion: Northerners and the South, 1865–1900*. Chapel Hill: University of North Carolina Press, 1993.

Simon, Charlie May. *The Share-cropper*. New York: E. P. Dutton & Co, 1937.

Simpson, Lewis. *The Fable of the Southern Writer*. Baton Rouge: Louisiana State University Press, 1994.

Singal, Daniel Joseph. *The War Within: From Victorian to Modernist Thought in the South, 1919–1945*. Chapel Hill: University of North Carolina Press, 1982.

Snyder, Robert. *Pare Lorentz and the Documentary Film*. Reno: University of Nevada Press, 1993.

Southall, Thomas W. *Of Time and Place: Walker Evans and William Christenberry*. Fort Worth, TX: Amon Carter Museum, 1990.

Spivak, John L. *Hard Times on a Southern Chain Gang*. Columbia: University of South Carolina Press, 2012.

Stack, Trudy Wilner. "Material Remains." In *Christenberry Reconstruction: The Art of William Christenberry*, by Trudy Wilner Stack, William Christenberry, and Allen Tullos, 30–42. Jackson: University Press of Mississippi, 1996.

Steinbeck, John. *The Grapes of Wrath*. New York: Viking, 1976.

Stott, William. *Documentary Expression and Thirties America*. New York: Oxford University Press, 1973.

Street, James H. *The New Revolution in the Cotton Economy: Mechanization and Its Consequences*. Chapel Hill: University of North Carolina Press, 1957.

Stribling, T. S. *The Store*. Tuscaloosa: University of Alabama Press, 1985.

Sundquist, Eric. "Promised Lands: A Different Drummer." *Triquarterly* 107 (Winter 2000): 268–84.

———. *To Wake the Nations: Race in the Making of American Literature*. Cambridge, MA: Belknap Press, 1993.

Tannenbaum, Frank. *Darker Phases of the South*. New York: G. P. Putnam's and Co, 1924.

Taylor, Christin Marie. *Labor Pains: New Deal Fictions of Race, Work, and Sex in the South*. Jackson: University Press of Mississippi, 2019.

Taylor, Walter. "Sharing Time: C. L. R. James and Southern Agrarian Movements." *Social Text* 30, no. 2 (Summer 2012): 75–98.

Thomas, Brook. *The Literature of Reconstruction Not in Plain Black and White*. Baltimore: John Hopkins University Press, 2017.

Thomas, Norman. *The Plight of the Share-cropper*. New York: The League for Industrial Democracy, 1934.

Tolnay, Stewart. *The Bottom Rung: African American Family Life on Southern Farms*. Urbana: University of Illinois Press, 1999.

Tolnay, Stewart, and E. M. Beck. *A Festival of Violence: An Analysis of Southern Lynchings, 1882–1930*. Urbana: University of Illinois Press, 1995.

Tourgée, Albion. *Bricks without Straw*. New York: Fords, Howard, & Hulbert, 1880.

———. *A Fool's Errand*. New York: Fords, Howard & Hulbert, 1879.

———. "The South as a Field for Fiction." Reprinted in "Albion W. Tourgee on the Fictional Use of the Post-Civil War South." *Southern Studies* 17 (1978): 399–409.

Trovaioli, August P., and Roulhac B. Toledano. *William Aiken Walker, Southern Genre Painter*. Baton Rouge: Louisiana State University Press, 1972.

Ture, Kwame, and Charles V. Hamilton. *Black Power: The Politics of Liberation*. New York: Vintage, 1992.

Turner, Darwin. "Faulkner and Slavery." In *The South and Faulkner's Yoknapatawpha: The Actual and the Apocryphal*, edited by Evans Harrington and Ann J. Abadie, 62–85. Jackson: University Press of Mississippi, 1977.

Twain, Mark. *Adventures of Huckleberry Finn*. New York: Penguin, 2014.

Twelve Southerners. *I'll Take My Stand*. New York: Harper & Bros, 1930.

"25 New Faces of Independent Film: RaMell Ross." *Filmmaker*, 2015. https://filmmakermagazine.com/people/ramell-ross/#.YLmLJ_lKg2x.

US Census Bureau. 1920 Census, Census Monograph 4. Farm Tenancy in the United States. https://www.census.gov/library/publications/1924/dec/monograph-4.html.

Vance, Rupert. *Human Factors in Cotton Culture: A Study in the Social Geography of the American South*. Chapel Hill: University of North Carolina Press, 1929.

———. *Human Geography of the South: A Study in Regional Resources and Human Adequacy*. Chapel Hill: University of North Carolina Press, 1935.

Vernon, Zackary. "The Enfreakment of Southern Memoir in Harry Crews's *A Childhood*." *Mississippi Quarterly* 67, no. 2 (Spring 2014): 193–211.

Walker, Alice. *Meridian*. New York: Harcourt, 1976.

———. *The Third Life of Grange Copeland*. New York: Washington Square Press, 1988.

*Walker Evans: American Photographs*. New York: The Museum of Modern Art, 2012.

Warren, Joyce. *Women, Money, and the Law: Nineteenth-Century Fiction, Gender, and the Courts*. Iowa City: University of Iowa Press, 2005.

Waskow, Arthur. *From Race Riot to Sit-In: A Study in the Connections between Conflict and Violence*. New York: Doubleday, 1966.

Wegner, Hart. "A Chronicle of Soil, Seasons, and Weather: Jean Renoir's *The Southerner*." *Southern Quarterly* 19, no. 4 (1981): 58–69.

Weinstein, B. L., and R. E. Firestine. *Regional Growth and Decline in the United States: The Rise of the Sunbelt and the Decline of the Northeast*. New York: Praeger, 1978.
Wells, Jeremy. *Romances of the White Man's Burden: Race, Empire, and the Plantation in American Literature, 1880–1936*. Nashville: Vanderbilt University Press, 2011.
Wells-Barnett, Ida B. "The Arkansas Race Riot." Chicago, 1919.
Welty, Eudora. *One Time, One Place: Mississippi in the Depression*. New York: Random House, 1971.
White, Monica M. *Freedom Farmers: Agricultural Resistance and the Black Freedom Movement*. Chapel Hill: University of North Carolina Press, 2018.
White, Walter. *A Man Called White*. Bloomington: Indiana University Press, 1948.
Wilkerson, Isabel. *The Warmth of Other Suns: The Epic Story of America's Great Migration*. New York: Random House, 2010.
Williams, Heather A. *Help Me to Find My People: The African American Search for Family Lost in Slavery*. Chapel Hill: University of North Carolina Press, 2012.
Williams, Raymond. *Keywords: A Vocabulary of Culture and Society*. New York: Oxford University Press, 1976.
Wilson, Charles Reagan. *Baptized in Blood: The Religion of the Lost Cause, 1865–1920*. Athens: University of Georgia Press, 1980.
Wilson, Edmund. *Patriotic Gore: Studies in the Literature of the Civil War*. Boston: Northeastern University Press, 1984.
Wilson, John. *High John the Conqueror*. Fort Worth: Texas Christian University Press, 1998.
Wilson, Matthew. *Whiteness in the Novels of Charles W. Chesnutt*. Jackson: University Press of Mississippi, 2004.
Wittenberg, Judith Bryant. "William Faulkner, T. S. Stribling, Trilogistic Intertextuality and the Politics of Criticism." *Faulkner Journal* 13, nos. 1–2 (Fall-Spring 1997–1998): 149–62.
Wood, Peter. *Near Andersonville: Winslow Homer's Civil War*. Cambridge: Harvard University Press, 2010.
Wood, Peter, and Karen C. C. Dalton. *Winslow Homer's Images of Blacks: The Civil War and Reconstruction Years*. Austin: University of Texas Press, 1988.
Woodman, Harold. *King Cotton and His Retainers: Financing and Marketing the Cotton Crop of the South, 1800–1925*. Lexington: University of Kentucky Press, 1968.
———. *New South—New Law: The Legal Foundations of Credit and Labor Relations in the Postbellum Agricultural South*. Baton Rouge: Louisiana State University Press, 1995.

Woodruff, Nan. *American Congo: The African American Freedom Struggle in the Delta.* Cambridge: Harvard University Press, 2003.
Woodson, Carter G. *A Century of Negro Migration.* Washington, DC: AMS Press, 1970.
———. *The Rural Negro.* Washington, DC: The Association for the Study of Negro Life and History, 1930.
Woodward, C. Vann. *Origins of the New South, 1877–1913.* Baton Rouge: Louisiana State University Press, 1981.
———. *The Strange Career of Jim Crow: Third Edition.* New York: Oxford University Press, 1974.
Woofter, Thomas Jackson. *Landlord and Tenant on the Cotton Plantation.* New York: Da Capo Press, 1971.
———. *Negro Migration.* New York: W. D. Gray, 1920.
Woofter, Thomas J., and A. E. Fisher. *The Plantation South Today.* Washington, DC: United States Government Printing Office, 1940.
Woofter, Thomas Jackson, and Ellen Winston. *Seven Lean Years.* Chapel Hill: University of North Carolina Press, 1939.
Wooley, Christine. "The Necessary Fictions of Charles Chesnutt's *The Colonel's Dream.*" *Mississippi Quarterly* 65, no. 2 (Spring 2012): 173–98.
Woolson, Constance F. *Rodman the Keeper: Southern Sketches.* New York: Garrett, 1969.
Wright, Erik Olin. *Classes.* New York: Verso, 1975.
Wright, Gavin. *Old South, New South: Revolutions in the Southern Economy since the Civil War.* Baton Rouge: Louisiana State University Press, 1997.
Wright, Richard. *Twelve Million Black Voices.* New York: Arno Press, 1969.
———. *Uncle Tom's Children. Richard Wright: Early Works.* New York: Library of America, 1991.
Young, Martha. *Plantation Songs for My Lady's Banjo.* New York: R. H. Russell, 1901.
Zaborney, John. *Slaves for Hire: Renting Enslaved Laborers in Antebellum Virginia.* Baton Rouge: Louisiana State University Press, 2012.

## INDEX

academic achievement gap, 4, 52
Agee, James: 23, 180, 233, 235, 268n106; see also *Let Us Now Praise Famous Men* (Agee & Evans)
Agrarian movement, 8–9, 10, 250n16, 258n10, 268n108, 271n180
Agricultural Adjustment Act (AAA), 102, 103, 104, 106, 108, 111, 114, 116, 123, 137, 141, 142, 143–45, 148–49, 159, 160, 165, 219, 262–63n2, 263n13
agricultural primitivism, 181
Aiken, Charles, 9, 16, 165, 173, 252n36, 273n1, 274n26
Albany Movement, 184
Alexander, Will W., 104, 115, 116
Allen, T. A., 145
Allred, Jeff, 127
American Farmers Union, 147
Anderson, Cynthia D., 222
Andrews, William L., 53, 54, 198, 275n28
Arnow, Harriette, 22, 92
Atkinson, Ted, 7, 258n10
Attaway, William, 22, 92

Baldwin, Sidney, 102
Bankhead Cotton Control Act, 102, 159
Bankhead-Jones Farm Tenant Act (1937), 103, 104, 109, 116, 264n18
Baszile, Natalie: *Queen Sugar*, 225, 226, 227, 230
Battat, Erin R., 92

Beckert, Sven, 10, 40, 214–15, 217, 218
Berry, Arnold, 130
Berry, J. Bill, 198
Bethea, Jack, 22, 84
Biden, Joe, 247
Biles, Roger, 114
Black Belt, 78, 235, 241, 242
black codes, 10, 15, 21, 36, 48, 50, 51, 52, 55, 61
Black farmers, 74, 76, 77, 79, 200, 205, 247–48
Black landowners, 123, 252n5, 259n39, 275n39
blackness, 195, 240, 244
Black Power, 193
Black separatism, 193
Black sharecroppers: 22, 61, 63, 65, 69, 74–75, 81–83, 88–89, 96–97, 99–100, 130–31, 170, 183, 205, 221, 260–61n65, 263n13; see also Hullinger, Edwin Ware
Blight, David, 44
Boles, Chester, 179
Bone, Martyn, 228–29, 231
Bontemps, Arna, 82
boosterism, 110, 254n44
Bourke-White, Margaret: *You Have Seen Their Faces*, 124–26, 128, 130, 166, 266n93, 266–67n95, 267–68n103, 268n104
Brooke, Carter: *White Band, The*, 183, 187, 191, 194

Brooks, Robert, 3
Brown, D. Clayton, 217, 219, 223
Brown, Sterling, 146
*Brown v. Board of Education* (1954), 183, 187, 190, 208
Bryant, Quincy, 187, 235
Burroughs, Allie Mae, 238, *239*
Burroughs, Floyd, 233–34, *234*
Burroughs, Lucille, 242

Cable, George Washington: 32, 53; *John March, Southerner*, 31, 37–38, 253n32; Reconstruction portrayal, 21, 31, 32, 33, 37
Caldwell, Erskine: "Tenant Farmer," 113; *Tobacco Road*, 112, 126, 150, 271–72n187; *You Have Seen Their Faces*, 124–26, 128, 130, 133, 134–35, 166, 266n93, 266–67n95, 267–68n103, 268n104
Camp, Lawrence, 101
Campbell, Bebe Moore: *Your Blues Ain't Like Mine*, 225, 226–28, 230, 233
Cantor, Louis, 148
capitalism, 17–18, 134, 148, 149, 166, 225, 231, 269n120
Carmichael, Stokely, 193, 277n92
Carpenter, C. T., 145, 146
Carter, Jimmy: *Hour Before Daylight, A*, 198, 203–4, 210, 279n140
Chalmers, Thomas Hardie, 109
Chaney, James, 188, 192
Chesnutt, Charles: 44, 53, 57, 59, 256n77, 256n79; *Colonel's Dream, The*, 21, 53–55, 58, 256n78, 256–57n93; concept of freedom, 54–55, 60
Christenberry, William, 25, 234, 235, 236–37, 240, 241, 242, 245, 284n91
Christianity, 160
Civilian Conservation Corps (CCC), 110
civil rights movement: 1, 7, 11, 169, 180, 182–95, 208–10, 211; Black voters/voting, 188, 189, 192–93, 208, 276n70; white resistance, 190, 191–92; *see also* Albany Movement; *Brown v. Board of Education*; Carmichael, Stokely; Chaney, James; Congress on Racial Equality; Council of Federated Organizations; Freedom Schools; Freedom Summer; Goodman, Andrew; Jim Crowism; King, Martin Luther, Jr.; Lowndes County Freedom Organization; March on Washington for Freedom and Jobs; Mississippi Democratic Freedom Party; Nashville Student Movement; racial violence; racism; Schwerner, Michael; segregation; Selma to Montgomery Freedom Marches; Student Nonviolent Coordinating Committee; Till, Emmett; Voting Rights Act (1965)
Coalition of Immokalee Workers (Florida), 229, 230, 283n71
Cobb, James C., 138, 216, 281n11
Cobb, Ned, 137, 138, 140
Collins, Daniel, 187, 235
Commission on Interracial Cooperation, 104, 115, 116
Committee on Farm Tenancy, 104
Communism: 59, 102, 136, 139, 146, 147, 149, 151, 158, 160–62, 164, 188, 269n134, 271n180; *see also* Lumpkin, Grace; Wright, Richard
Congress of Industrial Organizations, 149
Congress on Racial Equality (CORE), 188
Conrad, David, 103, 136, 145, 270n168
consumerism, 100
convict leasing, 58, 251n33
Cotton Incorporated, 223
cotton industry: 10, 21, 28, 40–42, 44, 61, 68, 105, 116, 117, 120, 132, 154, 172, 177–79, 215–17, 220, 222–23, 233, 242–43, 254n40, 255n60, 272n194, 272n205, 277n98, 281n7, 281n11; export of, 29–30, 39, 69, 97, 100, 102; and government subsidies, 102, 112, 160, 218; and mills/processing plants, 56, 57, 58, 100, 159, 222, 269n135; picking of, 6, 98, 106, 122,

148, 168–71, 173–75, 184, 202, 213, 224, 226, 227, 282n44; and plantation system, 98, 101, 109–10, 123, 228; and price instability, 15–16, 64, 70–73, 99–100, 102, 106, 138, 149, 153, 156, 260n57, 271n187; and sharecroppers/sharecropping, 4, 16–17, 27–28, 41, 63–66, 69–70, 83–90, 99, 103, 106, 134, 139, 142, 145, 154–55, 181, 200–201, 219, 221, 224, 234, 239; and slavery, 3, 61–62, 72, 78–79; and tenant farming, 122, 131, 177, 180–81; and white supremacy, 29, 123; *see also* Agricultural Adjustment Act (AAA); Bankhead Cotton Control Act; mechanization: and cotton production

Council of Federated Organizations (COFO), 188

Crews, Harry: *Biography of a Place, The*, 198, 199–200, 201–2, 207, 210, 278n120

Curtis, James, 237, 267n97

Dabbs, James McBride, 209
Daniel, Pete, 9, 80, 158, 172, 178, 187, 251n32
Davis, Allison, 117, 118
Davis, Edward: *White Scourge, The*, 154, 272n194
Davis, Elizabeth, 117, 118
Day, Richard, 173, 274n10
De Forest, John W.: *Bloody Chasm, The*, 21, 39, 42, 44, 254n48; Freedmen's Bureau, 31, 35–36, 253n22
de Jong, Greta, 183
Delano, Jack, 126
Delta and Pine Land Company (D&PL), 98
Delta Cooperative Farm, 147
Denning, Michael, 151, 263n7
De Reid, Ira, 126, 131, 132, 269n120
documentaries/documentary photography: 124–35, 171, 234–43, 267n96, 267n99; *see also* Agee, James; Bourke-White, Margaret; Caldwell, Erskine; Christenberry, William; Delano, Jack; Evans, Walker; Hine, Lewis; Lange, Dorothea; Nixon, Herman Clarence; Otts, J. W.: *Plantation Songs for My Lady's Banjo*; Parks, Gordon; Riis, Jacob; Ross, RaMell: *Hale County This Morning*; Rosskam, Edwin: *Twelve Million Black Voices*; Stryker, Roy; Taylor, Paul Schuster; Wright, Richard: *Twelve Million Black Voices*; *You Have Seen Their Faces*; Young, Martha Strudwick: *Plantation Songs for My Lady's Banjo*

Dolinar, Brian, 151
Dollard, Elizabeth, 117
Dollard, John, 23, 117–18, 123, 265n62
domestic imperialism, 7
drug addiction, 229–30
Du Bois, W. E. B.: 60, 259n36; *Quest of the Silver Fleece, The*, 75, 76, 78–79, 81, 259–60n48; and sharecroppers, 22, 60, 77; *Souls of Black Folks, The*, 47, 78
Duck, Leigh Anne, 7

East, Clay, 135, 146
educational disparity, 224
education inequality, 169, 205–6
Edwards, Laura, 61
Eisenstaedt, Alfred, 98
Elaine massacre, 64, 65, 66, 141
Elliott, Maud Howe, 39
Ellison, Ralph: *Invisible Man*, 93, 262n96
Emancipation, 176
Embree, Edwin R., 104, 106, 116
Evans, Walker: 233, 235, 249n9, 268n106; *see also Let Us Now Praise Famous Men* (Agee & Evans)
Extension Service, 110

Fair, Lonnie, 98
Fair, Ronald: *Many Thousand Gone*, 183, 185, 190, 194
farm ownership: 103, 252n36; *see also* Black landowners

Farm Security Administration (FSA), 103, 104, 107, 108, 110, 114, 124, 126–27, 132, 236, 240, 249n9, 263n16, 285n105
farm subsidies, 114, 176, 217–19, 223
fascism, 8, 266–67n95
Faulkner, John: 113; *Dollar Cotton*, 68, 70–71, 258n10, 264n41; *Men Working*, 23, 111, 112–13, 264n41
Faulkner, William: 67, 112, 184, 264n41; *Absalom, Absalom!*, 1–2, 166, 249n2, 258n10; sharecropping portrayal, 1, 3–4, 5, 22, 68
Federal Emergency Relief Administration (FERA), 103, 107, 108, 113, 114
federal housing projects, 4, 107, 176
feudalism, 15, 18, 132, 250n21, 269n120
Fields, Bud, 233–34, *234*, 242, 243
Fisher, A. E., 105
Fite, Gilbert, 9, 275n40
Flowers, Linda: *Throwed Away*, 196–97, 198, 201, 203, 205, 206, 210
Foley, Barbara, 151, 263n7
Foner, Eric, 30, 33
Foreman, Clark, 104
Fortune, T. Thomas, 59, 60
Freedmen's Bureau, 12, 14–15, 21, 30, 35, 36, 52, 61, 108, 246, 251n30, 253n25, 282n53
Freedom Rides, 208
Freedom Schools, 188
Freedom Summer, 182, 184, 188, 189, 208

Gaines, Ernest: *Autobiography of Miss Jane Pittman, The*, 24, 170, 176, 177, 179, 211, 275n28; *Of Love and Dust*, 183, 184, 185, 193, 194
Gardner, Burleigh, 117, 118
Gardner, Mary, 117, 118
generational poverty, 246
George, Walter, 101
Giesen, James, 66, 270n145
Gilyard, Keith, 188
globalization, 214–15, 217–18, 280n5, 281n7

Godden, Richard, 4
Goodman, Andrew, 188, 192
gradualism, 50
Gray, Richard, 139
Gray, Tommy, 139
Great Depression: 11, 98, 134, 171; and Black Americans, 99, 120, 182; fascism/collectivism anxieties, 8, 262–63n2; and government intervention, 114, 121–22, 219; and labor activism, 135, 136, 162; and sharecroppers/sharecropping, 5, 16, 20, 22–23, 98–99, 100–101, 115–18, 121–22, 124, 138–39, 154–55, 165, 203, 215
Great Depression sharecropper fiction: 22–23, 92, 97, 150–66, 263n7; *see also* Lanham, Edwin: *Stricklands, The*; Lumpkin, Grace: *Sign for Cain, A*; Munz, Charles: *Land Without Moses*; Perry, George Sessions: *Hold Autumn in Your Hand*; Russell, William: *Wind is Rising, A*; Rylee, Robert: *Deep Dark River*; Spivak, John L.: *Hard Times on a Southern Chain Gang*; White, Edward: *White Scourge, The*; Wilson, John W.: *High John the Conqueror*; Wright, Richard: *Uncle Tom's Children*
Great Migration, 232, 233, 261–62n93, 262n96, 262n104, 280n153
Green, Paul: *This Body the Earth*, 22, 84, 88
Greeson, Jennifer Rae, 7, 254n33
Gregory, James N., 91, 254n48, 280n153
Griffin, Farrah Jasmine, 93
Griggs, Sutton: *Hindered Hand, The*, 80
Grisham, John: *Painted House, A*, 223, 282n44
Grossman, James, 94, 261–62n93
Grubbs, Donald, 143
Gudger, Floyd, 173
Guterl, Matthew Pratt, 7

Hagood, Margaret Jarman, 116, 119, 123
Hale County, Alabama, 233–45, 285n94
Hale, Grace, 238
Handcox, John, 137, 138, 143, 145–46

Hannaham, James: *Delicious Foods*, 225–26, 229–30, 283n72
Harper, Frances Ellen Watkins: *Iola Leroy*, 51, 255n74
Harris, Joel Chandler: 39; "Free Joe and the Rest of the World," 21, 49
Helferich, Gerard, 24, 216–23
Henderson, Donald, 149
Henderson, George Wylie, 22, 75, 260n62
Hentz, Caroline Lee: *Planter's Northern Bride, The*, 39
Himes, Chester, 151
Hine, Lewis, 243
Hobson, Fred, 197, 209
Holley, Donald, 169
Homer, Winslow, 26, 27, 29, 252n1
Honey, Michael, 137
Hughes, Langston, 151
Hullinger, Edwin Ware, 126, 132
human trafficking, 231
hurricanes, 216

illiteracy/literacy, 66, 101, 192, 197
immigrant labor/immigrants: 222, 228, 229, 231–32, 283–84n76; *see also* Coalition of Immokalee Workers (Florida)
imperialism, 20
individualism, 17, 147
industrialization: 28, 54, 168, 173; *see also* sharecroppers/sharecropping: mechanization of
Institute for Human Relations (Yale), 115
Institute for Research in Social Science (UNC), 104
International Harvester, 175
*In the Heat of the Night*, 168
isolationism, 231

James, C. L. R., 148, 271n180
Jarrett, Gene, 51
Jaynes, Gerald David, 14, 52, 251n29
Jim Crowism, 11, 19, 22, 50, 52, 83, 97, 162, 176
John Deere tractors, 219

Johnson, Andrew, 12, 29, 30
Johnson, Charles S., 23, 114, 116–17, 119, 120, 122, 123
Johnston, Oscar, 98, 262–63n2
Jones, Carter Brooke: *White Band, The*, 183, 191
Jordan, Hilary: *Mudbound*, 223, 282n44
Julius Rosenwald Fund, 104, 116

Keely, Karen A., 44, 254n36
Kelley, Melvin: *Different Drummer, A*, 182–83, 185–86
Kelley, Robin D. G.: *Hammer and Hoe*, 139–40
Kelley, Welbourne, 22; *Inchin' Along*, 75
Kelley, William Melvin: *Different Drummer, A*, 182–83, 185–86, 193–94
Kennedy-Nolle, Sharon D., 38
Kester, Howard, 135, 137–38, 140–41, 142, 146, 147
Killbrew, Heath, 219
Killbrew, Keath, 219
Killbrew, Zack, 216–17, 218, 219, 220–21, 223
Killens, John Oliver: *'Sippi*, 24, 183, 184, 185, 187–88, 189, 191, 194–96, 211
King, Charles: *War Time Wooing, A*, 39
King, Edward: *Great South, The*, 38, 208
King, Martin Luther, Jr., 193, 195–96, 208
King, Martin Luther, Sr.: *Daddy King*, 198, 199, 202–3, 205, 207–8, 210
King, Seabury, 154, 155
Kirby, Jack Temple, 110
Knepper, Steven, 110
Kreyling, Michael, 9
Kroll, Harry Harrison: *Cabin in the Cotton, The*, 87, 261n79; *I Was a Sharecropper*, 198, 199, 210, 261n79; *This Body the Earth*, 22, 84–85

labor activism: 7, 23, 41, 65, 85, 135–37, 138–41, 143–50, 161–62, 166, 269n134, 269n135, 271n179; *see also* Communism; Congress of Industrial Organizations; Elaine massacre; Progressive

314　INDEX

labor activism (*continued*)
　Farmers and Household Union of America; socialism; Sharecroppers Union; Southern Tenant Farmers Union (STFU); United Cannery, Agricultural, Packing Allied Workers of America (UCAPAWA); United Textile Workers
*LaLee's Kin: The Legacy of Cotton*: 224
Lange, Dorothea, 7, 126, 127, 249n9
Lanham, Edwin: *Stricklands, The*, 152, 162–63
Lee, George Washington: 22, 199, 278n118; *River George*, 75, 80
*Let Us Now Praise Famous Men* (Agee & Evans), 126, 128, 129, 130–33, 170–71, 234–37, 284n90
Lewis, John: *Walking with the Wind*, 194, 198, 199, 200–201, 202–3, 205, 207, 208
Link, William, 66
Litwack, Leon, 13, 75, 253n29
Loewen, James, 231
Logan, Virgil, 140
Lorentz, Pare: *Plow That Broke the Plains, The*, 109; *River, The*, 23, 109, 110
Lost Cause, 44, 45–47, 255n56, 255n57
Louise, Maggie, 180
Lowndes County Freedom Organization, 184
Luce, Henry, 98, 262–63n2
Lumpkin, Grace: Communist activism, 161, 164, 273n214; *Sign for Cain, A*, 152, 157, 161
Lumpkin, Katharine Du Pre, 209
lynching, 3, 19, 48, 50, 52, 58, 63, 77, 81, 88, 89, 95, 115, 139, 145, 194–95, 199, 260n57, 277n98

MacLeish, Archibald, 124
Maharidge, Dale: *And Their Children After Them*, 24, 170–71, 172–73, 175, 176, 177, 179–80, 181, 235, 237, 238, 240, 274n26

Malcolm X, 194
Mandle, Jay, 10, 17, 178, 181, 259n30
Manthorne, Jason, 141
March on Washington for Freedom and Jobs, 208
Martin, Robert, 147
Marxism, 18, 19, 59, 148, 150, 252n39, 252n44
Mayer, Tom, 18
McAdam, Doug, 192
McInnis, Jarvis, 78
McLaurin, Melton: *Separate Pasts: Growing Up White in the Segregated South*, 198, 204–5, 208, 209, 210
mechanization: 177–78, 186–87, 211, 215, 231; and Black Americans, 24, 178, 179–80, 187, 228; and civil rights movement, 6, 24, 207; and cost-effectiveness, 20, 171, 172, 227; and cotton production, 23, 24, 122, 169, 171, 174, 177, 214, 217, 219, 228, 245, 274n10; and government intervention, 176, 274n27; and the labor force, 16, 167, 171, 181, 183, 215, 231, 274n10; long process of, 171, 173–74; and sharecroppers/sharecropping, 6, 123, 126, 168–71, 179–80, 181, 183, 184, 186, 197, 205, 211–12, 221, 224, 226, 246
Meikle, Paulette Ann, 218, 220
merchants, 2, 10, 15, 22, 67–69, 72, 73, 78, 82, 89, 96, 97, 111–12, 258n9
Mertz, Paul, 99, 263n16
migrant labor, 4, 6, 215, 223, 228, 231, 282n44
minstrelsy/minstrel ventriloquism, 128, 129
Mississippi Democratic Freedom Party, 188
Mitchell, H. L., 135, 137, 138, 140, 143–45, 147
Mitchell, Margaret: *Gone With the Wind*, 1, 2, 5, 6, 7, 25, 166, 247; sharecropping portrayal, 1, 3, 4, 5
modernism, 17, 127

INDEX    315

Moody, Adline, 199
Moody, Anne: 208, 210, 278n118; *Coming of Age in Mississippi*, 198, 199, 202, 278n118
Morris, Willie, 209
Munz, Charles: *Land Without Moses*, 23, 153, 155–56, 157, 158, 159, 160, 163
Myers, Mary Connor, 143
Myrdal, Gunnar, 103

Nashville Student Movement, 208
National Association for the Advancement of Colored People (NAACP), 162, 208
National Cotton Council of America, 223
nationalism, 32
naturalism, 152
New Deal, 247
New Deal, 8, 11, 99, 101–2, 103, 110–11, 114–16, 119, 121–22, 124, 126, 130, 132, 140, 159, 176, 236, 247, 249n9, 263n16, 267n99, 285n105
Nilon, Charles H., 50
Nixon, Herman Clarence: *Forty Acres and Steel Mules*, 126, 130, 132, 133, 268n108
nonviolence philosophy, 194, 195
Norcross, Hiram, 140

O'Connor, Flannery, 150
Odum, Howard, 5, 23, 104, 115–16, 249n8
Offord, Carl, 22, 92
Otts, J. W.: *Plantation Songs for My Lady's Banjo*, 235
Ownby, Ted, 9

Page, Thomas Nelson: "Marse Chan," 21, 46, 47; *Negro: The Southerner's Problem, The*, 47, 48, 255n60; racism, 48, 49; *Red Rock*, 21, 39, 42–44, 47, 255n65; slavery apologism, 46, 47, 48, 54
Parks, Gordon, 127, 249n9

paternalism, 7, 14, 29, 44–51, 54, 61, 70, 87, 102, 131, 168, 203, 211, 220–21, 250n28, 274n27
Patterson, Orlando, 17, 74
Peeler, David, 151
pellagra, 113, 122
penal systems, 2, 52, 158, 272n205
peonage, 15, 52, 57–58, 60, 80–81, 97, 120, 145, 158, 163, 229, 251n32, 260n53
Percy, William Alexander: 115; *Lanterns on the Levee*, 7, 70; sharecropping defense, 70, 279n140
Perry, George Sessions: *Hold Autumn in Your Hand*, 23, 152, 153–54, 159–60, 164, 272n192
pest control, 219
Pickens, William, 77, 81
plantation tourism, 225, 227, 280n3
postsharecropping literature: 224–33; *see also* Baszile, Natalie: *Queen Sugar*; Campbell, Bebe Moore: *Your Blues Ain't Like Mine*; Hannaham, James: *Delicious Foods*; Shearer, Cynthia: *Celestial Jukebox, The*
postsharecropping memoirs, 196–211, 212; *see also* Carter, Jimmy: *Hour Before Daylight, A*; Crews, Harry: *Biography of a Place, The*; Flowers, Linda: *Throwed Away*; King, Martin Luther, Sr.: *Daddy King*; Kroll, Harry Harrison: *I Was a Sharecropper*; Lewis, John: *Walking with the Wind*; McLaurin, Melton: *Separate Pasts: Growing Up White in the Segregated South*; Moody, Anne: *Coming of Age in Mississippi*
Powdermaker, Hortense, 23, 114, 115, 117, 119, 120, 121, 265n52
Powell, Lawrence, 42
Prichard, Jo, 218
Progressive Era, 11, 20, 49, 66, 99, 136
Progressive Farmers and Household Union of America, 63

Rabinowitz, Paula, 100, 127
racial violence: 36, 96, 183, 184, 194; *see also* lynching
racism: 35, 49, 83, 96, 118, 202, 206, 207–8, 209, 213, 256n76; critiques of, 256n76; and economic control, 207; entrenchment of, 20, 33, 75, 123, 209; institutionalization of, 169, 187; systemic, 30, 65, 123, 247
Ransom, John Crowe, 8
Ransom, Roger, 10, 83, 251n29, 258n9
Raper, Arthur, 115, 116, 119, 121, 123, 126, 129, 131, 132, 134–35, 265n55, 269n120
realism, 152, 237
Reconstruction, 176, 246
Reconstruction literature, 61, 257n111
Reed, Gladys, 124, *125*, 134
regionalism, 4, 45
religious fundamentalism, 3
Resettlement Administration, 103, 109, 147
rickets, 122
Ricketts, Margaret (pseudonym), 238
Riefenstahl, Leni, 109
Riis, Jacob, 124
Rodgers, Lawrence, 93, 262n96, 262n100
Roemer, John, 18
romanticism, 223
Romine, Scott, 7
Roosevelt, Franklin D., 101, 102, 104, 109, 153, 163
Rosengarten, Theodore, 137, 138, 140
Rosenwald schools, 75, 259n34
Ross, James, 139, 149
Ross, RaMell, 25, 234, 235, 237, 285n95; *Hale County This Morning, This Evening*, 238, 240, 242, 243–44, 245–46
Rosskam, Edwin, *Twelve Million Black Voices*, 126, 127
Rothstein, Arthur, 124, 148
Roundup (Monsanto), 219
Royce, Edward, 10, 13, 251n29
Rubin, Louis, 8
Rubin, Morton, 16, 117, 119

Rushing, Wanda, 232, 281n7
Russell, William: *Wind is Rising, A*, 152, 154–55, 162
Rust, John, 175
Rust, Mack, 175
Rylee, Robert: *Deep Dark River*, 152, 153, 159, 164

Scarborough, Dorothy, 84, 89
Schulman, Michael D., 222
Schwerner, Michael, 188, 192
Scott, Tim, 213
segregation, 3, 4, 5, 7, 19, 49–50, 96, 117–18, 182, 183, 187, 190–91, 196, 207, 209, 211, 226, 246–47, 262n104, 282n44
Selma to Montgomery Freedom Marches, 184, 208
sharecropping/sharecroppers: 15, 25, 65, 74, 247–48, 250n21, 251n29, 251n30, 252n36, 270n168, 282n49; and agrarianism, 9; and agricultural diversification, 169, 179, 214; and civil rights, 51; and class divisions, 18, 86–87; contractual nature of, 13, 15, 38, 52, 64, 86, 120, 137; culture of, 17, 20–21; defenses of, 70; as economic crisis, 5, 8, 10–11, 14, 20, 22–23, 101, 199, 200; effects on poverty, 4, 9, 10, 13, 20, 66, 77–80, 88, 98–102, 104–6, 109, 138–39; effects on race, 4, 11, 13, 88, 118–19, 124, 200, 226; emergence/development of, 1, 3–4, 7, 10–11, 13–14, 16, 20–21; ending of, 170–71, 175, 179–81, 207, 210, 211, 214; evictions/displacement, 177, 178–81, 182, 184; and exploitative landowners, 103, 119–20, 121, 137, 154, 165, 178; federal government intervention, 105–6, 107, 111, 112–13, 114, 122, 126, 165, 176, 236; ideology of, 4, 8, 11, 17, 19, 21, 75; and migration, 22, 90–96, 101, 169, 185–86, 197, 207, 231, 232, 262n103; and nomadism, 198; and paternalism, 7, 21, 70; power dynamics of, 2, 4, 5,

14, 17, 59, 200, 203; predatory credit practices, 99–100, 101, 106, 111–12, 140, 158, 229; representations of, 100–101, 124; and social mobility, 76, 78, 85, 90, 120, 205, 213, 232; vis-à-vis slavery, 4, 7, 8, 10, 13, 17, 32, 34, 41, 48, 59, 62, 71–72, 75, 78, 184–85, 200, 203, 226, 229, 233, 250n22, 260–61n65; and white supremacy, 60, 61, 62, 65; women, 116, 119, 238–39; *see also* Black sharecroppers; cotton industry: and sharecroppers/sharecropping; Du Bois, W. E. B.: and sharecroppers; feudalism; Great Depression: and sharecroppers/sharecropping; immigrant labor/immigration; labor activism; Marxism; mechanization: and sharecroppers/sharecropping; white sharecroppers

Sharecroppers Union (Alabama), 139, 140, 146, 269n134

sharecropping unionization narratives, 135, 136–38; *see also* Kelley, Robin D. G.: *Hammer and Hoe*; Kester, Howard: *Revolt Among the Sharecroppers*; Thomas, Norman: *Plight of the Sharecropper, The*

Shaw, Ned. *see* Cobb, Ned

Shearer, Cynthia: *Celestial Jukebox, The*, 225, 227, 228, 230, 231–32

Silber, Nina, 39, 40

Simon, Charlie May: *Sharecropper, The*, 137, 138, 139, 141–43, 146, 149–50

Simpson, Lewis, 8

single-party politics, 3, 197

Smith, Lillian, 209

social Darwinism, 154

Socialism, 8, 102, 136, 138, 146–47, 152

southern exceptionalism, 96, 246, 246–48, 262n103

Southern Tenant Farmers Museum, 135

Southern Tenant Farmers Union (STFU), 135, 136, 137, 140–42, 143–44, 146–47, 148–49, 162–63, 175, 182, 273n222

Spivak, John L.: *Hard Times on a Southern Chain Gang*, 151, 152, 156, 158

Stack, Trudy Wilner, 245

Steinbeck, John, 22, 92, 160, 272n204

Steinway & Sons, 98

Stott, William, 125, 127, 236, 237

Street, James H., 171, 180

Stribling, T. S., 22

Stryker, Roy, 126–27, 267n97

Student Nonviolent Coordinating Committee (SNCC), 188, 208, 276n67

sugar, 15, 77, 214, 225, 226, 230, 231, 232

Sun Belt, 191, 206, 211, 247

Sundquist, Eric, 187, 256n78

Sutch, Richard, 10, 83, 251n29, 258n9

Talmadge, Eugene, 113

Tannenbaum, Frank, 65

Tart, Clarence Lee, 204

Taylor, Paul Schuster: *American Exodus*, 126, 131, 133

tenant farmers/farming: 102, 103, 104–5, 108, 124, 196–97, 204, 206

Tengle, Frank, 233–34, 234, 238

Tennessee Valley Authority (TVA), 110

Thirteenth Amendment, 157

Thomas, Brook, 61, 257n111

Thomas, Norman: *Plight of the Sharecropper, The*, 137, 138, 141

Till, Emmett, 190, 199, 208, 225

tobacco, 15, 201, 207, 214, 255n60, 256n77

Tolnay, Stewart, 76, 260n57

Tourgeé, Albion, 21, 31, 32, 33, 34, 36, 253n26, 253n28

traditionalism, 20

Trumpauer, Joan, 208

Twain, Mark, 49

unemployment, 5, 22, 55, 113, 143, 151, 175, 224

United Cannery, Agricultural, Packing Allied Workers of America (UCAPAWA), 149

United Textile Workers, 136
U.S. Commission on Civil Rights, 178

Vance, Rupert, 115–16, 117, 121, 122, 123, 249n8
Voting Rights Act (1965), 192

wage labor, 3, 6, 12–13, 17, 18, 21, 33, 41, 52, 76, 111, 114, 138–39, 172, 252n36, 283n58
Walker, Alice: 171; *Meridian*, 188–89, 195, 196, 276n69, 278n107; *Third Life of Grange Copeland, The*, 24, 172, 173, 176, 178, 179, 275n31, 275n40
Walker, William Aiken, 26, 28, 28
Wallace, Laura Lee "LaLee," 224
Warner, Lloyd, 117
Warnock, Raphael, 213
Warnock, Verlene, 213
Warren, Robert Penn, 8
Washington, Booker T., 59, 259n36
weed control, 219, 222
Wells, Jeremy, 50
Wells-Barnett, Ida B., 63, 256n76
Wells-Barnett, Ida B., 63, 256n76
White Citizens' Councils, 183, 190, 191
White, Edward, 152, 272n194
White, Erik Olin, 18
White, Gavin, 10, 16, 83, 172
white ruralism, 9
white sharecroppers: 22, 69, 83–85, 87–90, 94, 97, 99–100, 141, 162, 182, 190, 197, 208, 240, 244, 256n76, 260–61n65, 263n13
white trash, 86, 261n76, 261n77

White, Walter, 63, 254n33
Whitfield, Owen, 148
Williams, Heather, 35
Williamson, Michael: *And Their Children After Them*, 24, 170–71, 181, 235, 237, 238, 240, 242–43, 245, 274n13, 274n26
Wilson, Ben, 84, 85, 89, 90
Wilson, John W.: *High John the Conqueror*, 152, 158, 159
Wilson, Matthew, 58
women's property rights, 43, 254n50
Wood, Peter, 26, 252n1
Wood, Philip J., 222
Woodruff, Nan, 64
Woods, Bud, 243
Woodson, Carter G., 74, 260n60
Woodward, C. Vann, 50, 56
Woofter, Thomas J., 5, 19, 23, 104–6, 107, 108, 263–64n17, 264n24
Woolston, Constance F., 39, 45
Works Progress Administration (WPA), 111, 112, 114
World War II, 11, 23, 92, 114, 172, 176, 282n44
Wright, Gavin, 172
Wright, Richard, 23, 126, 268n105; Communism, 161, 164–65, 273n216; *Native Son*, 93, 262n96; *Twelve Million Voices*, 129, 130–31, 132, 268n105; *Uncle Tom's Children*, 152, 156–57, 161, 163–64

Young, Martha Strudwick, 235
Young, Martha Strudwick: *Plantation Songs for My Lady's Banjo*, 235

THE AMERICAN SOUTH SERIES

*The Princess of Albemarle: Amélie Rives, Author and Celebrity at the Fin de Siècle*
Jane Turner Censer

*In the* True Blue's *Wake: Slavery and Freedom among the Families of Smithfield Plantation*
Daniel B. Thorp

*Against the Hounds of Hell: A Life of Howard Thurman*
Peter Eisenstadt

*Facing Freedom: An African American Community in Virginia from Reconstruction to Jim Crow*
Daniel B. Thorp

*Capital and Convict: Race, Region, and Punishment in Post–Civil War America*
Henry Kamerling

*The Uplift Generation: Cooperation across the Color Line in Early Twentieth-Century Virginia*
Clayton McClure Brooks

*The Risen Phoenix: Black Politics in the Post–Civil War South*
Luis-Alejandro Dinnella-Borrego

*Designing Dixie: Tourism, Memory, and Urban Space in the New South*
Reiko Hillyer

*A Deed So Accursed: Lynching in Mississippi and South Carolina, 1881–1940*
Terence Finnegan

*Radical Reform: Interracial Politics in Post-Emancipation North Carolina*
Deborah Beckel

*Religion and the Making of Nat Turner's Virginia: Baptist Community and Conflict, 1740–1840*
Randolph Ferguson Scully

*From Yeoman to Redneck in the South Carolina Upcountry, 1850–1915*
Stephen A. West

*What Reconstruction Meant: Historical Memory in the American South*
Bruce E. Baker

*Black, White, and Olive Drab: Racial Integration at Fort Jackson, South Carolina, and the Civil Rights Movement*
Andrew H. Myers

*Murder, Honor, and Law: Four Virginia Homicides from Reconstruction to the Great Depression*
Richard F. Hamm

*South by Southwest: Planter Emigration and Identity in the Slave South*
James David Miller

*A Way out of No Way: Claiming Family and Freedom in the New South*
Dianne Swann-Wright

*The Lynching of Emmett Till: A Documentary Narrative*
Christopher Metress, editor

*Ladies and Gentlemen on Display: Planter Society at the Virginia Springs, 1790–1860*
Charlene M. Boyer Lewis

*Forgotten Time: The Yazoo-Mississippi Delta after the Civil War*
John C. Willis

*Bloody Promenade: Reflections on a Civil War Battle*
Stephen Cushman

*Slave in a Box: The Strange Career of Aunt Jemima*
M. M. Manring

*Haunted Bodies: Gender and Southern Texts*
Anne Goodwyn Jones and Susan V. Donaldson, editors

www.ingramcontent.com/pod-product-compliance
Lightning Source LLC
Chambersburg PA
CBHW031435230426
43668CB00007B/537